ELITE STUDENT EDITION

5 STEPS TO A 5

AP Physics 1:
Algebra-Based

2024

ELITE STUDENT EDITION

5 STEPS TO A 5™

AP Physics 1: Algebra-Based

2024

Greg Jacobs

McGraw Hill

New York   Chicago   San Francisco   Athens   London   Madrid
Mexico City   Milan   New Delhi   Singapore   Sydney   Toronto

1 2 3 4 5 6 7 8 9   LHS   28 27 26 25 24 23
1 2 3 4 5 6 7 8 9   LHS   28 27 26 25 24 23 (Elite Student Edition)

ISBN   978-1-265-32297-7
MHID   1-265-32297-X

e-ISBN   978-1-265-32341-7
e-MHID   1-265-32341-0

ISBN   978-1-265-32444-5 (Elite Student Edition)
MHID   1-265-32444-1

e-ISBN   978-1-265-33153-5 (Elite Student Edition)
e-MHID   1-265-33153-7

McGraw Hill, the McGraw Hill logo, 5 Steps to a 5, and related trade dress are trademarks or registered trademarks of McGraw Hill and/or its affiliates in the United States and other countries and may not be used without written permission. All other trademarks are the property of their respective owners. McGraw Hill is not associated with any product or vendor mentioned in this book.

AP, Advanced Placement Program, and College Board are registered trademarks of the College Board, which was not involved in the production of, and does not endorse, this product.

The series editor was Grace Freedson, and the project editor was Del Franz. Series design by Jane Tenenbaum.

McGraw Hill products are available at special quantity discounts to use as premiums and sales promotions or for use in corporate training programs. To contact a representative, please visit the Contact Us pages at www.mhprofessional.com.

McGraw Hill is committed to making our products accessible to all learners. To learn more about the available support and accommodations we offer, please contact us at accessibility@mheducation.com. We also participate in the Access Text Network (www.accesstext.org), and ATN members may submit requests through ATN.

CONTENTS

STEP 4   # Review the Knowledge You Need to Score High

STEP 5

Build Your Test-Taking Confidence

ELITE
STUDENT
EDITION

5 Minutes to a 5

PREFACE

How is this book different from all other AP Physics prep books?

The quality of the prep book starts with the author. Greg Jacobs has taught all versions of AP (and non-AP) physics since 1996. His hundreds of students over the years have a greater than 99 percent pass rate; more than 70 percent earn 5s. Greg has graded the exams, he has written questions that have appeared on exams, and he has taught teachers how to teach to the exams. The leading blog about physics teaching is his—"Jacobs Physics." (Take a look at it.) Greg knows what he's talking about, and the proof is in the results and feedback from his students.

AP Physics 1 emphasizes conceptual understanding over algebraic manipulation, and so does this book. So many people presume that physics is about finding the right numbers to plug into the right equation. That couldn't be further from the truth. Successful physics students can explain why they chose a specific equation. They can explain what values for each variable are reasonable, and why. They can explain the *physical* meaning of any mathematical manipulation—how would this problem look in the laboratory? What equipment would be used to measure these values? The AP Physics 1 Exam mostly asks questions that are not about number crunching. Greg has been teaching "beyond the numbers" for years, and he brings his expertise in explaining complex concepts in simple language.

Your textbook is impenetrable, even to senior physics majors. This prep book is readable. Be honest—when you read your textbook, you really just try the problems at the end of the chapter, then look back for a template of how to do those problems. Well, this book's content review is structured around this very method. Greg poses example questions and talks you through them. On the way, he shows you the relevant facts and equations, as well as *how you are supposed to know they are relevant*. He explains not just the answer, but the thought process behind the answer. You do not have to be already good at physics to understand the text.

This book's practice tests and practice questions are authentic. One of the primary tenets of Greg's physics teaching is that in-class tests should look exactly like the real AP exams. The College Board has published a curriculum guide that provides express guidance as to the style and content of the exam questions. Greg's practice tests are derived directly from what the curriculum guide says. He has vast experience phrasing questions in the style seen on College Board exams.

Every practice question includes not just an answer, but also a thorough explanation of how to get that answer. The back of your textbook may provide answers like "2 m/s" or "increase." Huh? Skim through and look at the solutions to the practice exam, and to the end-of-chapter questions. They're complete. This book's solutions explain everything, even sometimes the common mistakes that you might have made by accident. Exam readers expect thoroughness on the free-response problems—you should expect the same from your prep book.

It is not possible to prepare well for AP Physics merely by using recycled material from previous AP or honors physics courses. Even after eight years of AP Physics 1, the majority of teachers—and every AP prep book bar this one—keep using the same problems and presentations, just tweaking the covered topics to match the new exam.

And students in those classes, students who use those prep books, have a comeuppance on exam day. The AP Physics 1 Exam asks for explanations, not calculations; it does not give pity points for writing relevant equations. And in eight years there have been only two—TWO—problems requiring numerical answers in the free-response section. AP Physics 1 demands a revolutionarily different approach to learning physics. Your parents' generation might kvetch about cell phones and the Internet, but if they're still doing business by landline and U.S. mail, well, they're lucky to be doing business at all. Ditto for your teacher who moans about the good old days when physics was taught with calculation after calculation.

ACKNOWLEDGMENTS

The original idea for this book came many moons ago, when my AP students in 1999 couldn't stand the other review books on the market. "We can write a better book than that," they said. And we did. Justin Kreindel, Zack Menegakis, Adam Ohren (who still owes me four sandwiches from Mississippi Sweets for poking Jason during class), Jason Sheikh, and Joe Thistle were the cast members for that particular opera.

Josh Schulman, also a member of that 1999 class, was the one who buckled down and put pen to paper, or rather fingers to computer keys. His first draft of a book forced me to revise and finish and publish.

Del Franz has been a fabulous editor for this and other projects. I appreciate his toils.

The faculty and administration at Woodberry Forest School, in particular former science department chairman **Jim Reid**, deserve mention. They have been extraordinarily supportive of me professionally.

Two amazing physics teachers have vetted this new book for the new exam. They have done tremendous work in exchange for nothing but a free cup of coffee. Thank you, **Jeff Steele** (who gave feedback on the practice tests) and **Matt Sckalor** (who read every content chapter). I owe you both.

Thank you to those who sent in errata from the first edition. I'm particularly indebted to Glenn Mangold and Drew Austen, who sent in three pages' worth of edits, along with careful and thorough justifications for each—wow. Joseph Rao, Patrick Diehl, Mike Pozuc, Shannon Copeland, Frank Noschese, Hugh Ross, Ron Qian, and I'm sure others I've missed have also sent in corrections or thoughts that I've used. And to all of the *Jacobs Physics* blog readers, know that I deeply appreciate the comments, e-mails, and conversations you send my way.

Most important, thank you to Shari and Milo for putting up with me during all of my writing projects.

—Greg Jacobs

ABOUT THE AUTHORS

Greg Jacobs is chair of the science department at Woodberry Forest School. Over the years, Greg has taught all flavors of AP physics. He is a reader and consultant for the College Board, which means he grades AP physics exams, and he runs professional development seminars for other AP teachers. Greg is president of the USAYPT, a nonprofit organization promoting physics research at the high school level. Greg was recently honored as an AP Teacher of the Year by the Siemens Foundation. Outside the classroom, Greg has coached football, baseball, and debate. Greg broadcasts football, baseball, soccer, and basketball games via Internet audio. He writes the physics teaching blog "Jacobs Physics," available at https://jacobsphysics.blogspot.com. Greg runs conceptual physics institutes for teachers each summer online from his classroom.

Greg would like to thank Jeff Steele for writing the third practice test. Jeff teaches in central Virginia, grades AP exams, and judges the U.S. Invitational Young Physicists Tournaments with Greg. Jeff is also a coauthor of the *5 Minutes to a 5* section of the Elite Student's version of this book.

INTRODUCTION: THE FIVE-STEP PROGRAM

Welcome!

I know that preparing for the Advanced Placement (AP) Physics 1, Algebra-Based Exam can seem like a daunting task. There's a lot of material to learn and some of it can be challenging. But I also know that preparing for the AP exam is much easier—and a lot more enjoyable—if you do it with a friendly, helpful guide. So order the pizza (see "Pantheon of Pizza" in the Appendix) and let's get started.

First, you should know that physics does not lend itself well to cramming. Success on the AP exam is most likely the result of actually learning and *understanding* physics in your AP Physics 1 course. If you are opening this book in the first semester or early in the second semester, be sure to read Chapter 6, which contains strategies to get the most out of your physics class in terms of preparation for the AP exam.

Of course, this book can also be instrumental in helping you score high. *5 Steps to 5: AP Physics 1, Algebra-Based* is composed of practical, score-raising items you won't necessarily get in your AP course, including in-depth information about the test, proven strategies to attack each type of question on the exam, an easy-to-follow review of content, and two very realistic practice tests.

Organization of the Book: The Five-Step Program

You will be taking a lengthy, comprehensive exam in May. You want to be well prepared so that the exam takes on the feel of a command performance, not a trial by fire. Following the Five-Step program is the best way to structure your preparation.

Step 1: Get to Know the Exam and Set Up Your Study Program

You need to get to know the exam—what's on it and how it's structured—so there are no surprises on test day. Understanding the test is the first step in preparing for it. And you need a plan. Step 1 gives you the background and structure you will need before you start exam preparation.

Step 2: Determine Your Test Readiness

Your study program should *not* include cramming absolutely everything about physics into your head in the weeks before the test; that can't be done. Instead, you'll need to assess your strengths and weaknesses and prioritize what you need to review. The physics fundamentals self-assessment in Chapter 4 will help you do just that. Note that the questions in this self-assessment are not written in the style of the actual questions on the AP Physics 1 Exam. They are designed to quickly determine your strengths and weaknesses, not to mimic actual test questions.

Then, in Chapter 5 you'll be introduced to the different types of questions found on the actual AP Physics 1 Exam. The self-assessment in this chapter allows you to see how you do on each of the different types of questions and to identify the question types with which you need the most practice. The results from both self-assessments—the fundamentals self-assessment in Chapter 4 and the question-type assessment in Chapter 5—should help you develop your study plan and determine which chapters in this book you'll spend the most time on.

Step 3: Develop Strategies for Success

Read this if it's the first semester or the beginning of the second semester of your course.

The focus of the remaining chapters in Step 3 is developing effective strategies to approach each of the question types found on the AP Physics 1 Exam. Sure, I know you've been listening to general test-taking advice and have been taking multiple-choice standardized tests practically your whole life. But the chapters in this section contain *physics*-specific advice. And the AP Physics 1, Algebra-Based Exam has questions—even in the multiple-choice section—that are probably unlike any you've encountered previously in your standardized test taking. Chapter 7 focuses on strategies for question types found on both the multiple-choice and free-response sections of the test. Chapter 8 looks at strategies for types of questions found only on the free-response section, and finally, Chapter 9 suggests strategies for question types that appear only in the multiple-choice section of the test.

Step 4: Review the Knowledge You Need to Score High

Step 4 contains a comprehensive review of the topics on the AP exam. Now, you've probably been in an AP Physics class all year and you've likely read (or at least tried to read!) your textbook. Our review is not meant to be another textbook. It's only a review—an easy-to-follow, step-by-step review focused exclusively on the things likely to appear on the AP exam. The review is not as detailed as your textbook, but it's more germane to what's actually on the AP Physics 1 Exam. Chapters 10 through 15 provide a review of different aspects of mechanics, Chapter 16 focuses on electricity, and Chapter 17 focuses on waves.

These review chapters are appropriate both for quick skimming (to remind yourself of salient points) and for in-depth study, with plenty of sample problems you can work through. Each review chapter contains several questions in the format of the free-response questions actually found on the test. Use these questions both to test your knowledge and to practice with the types of questions you'll encounter on the test.

Finally, in Chapter 18, you'll find extra drills on some of the most common physics situations tested on the AP exam. The old saying is true: practice makes perfect.

Step 5: Build Your Test-Taking Confidence

This is probably the most important part of this book: full-length practice tests that closely reflect what you'll encounter in the actual test. Unlike other practice tests you may take, these come with thorough explanations. One of the most important elements in learning physics is making, and then learning from, mistakes. This book doesn't just tell you what you got wrong; we explain why your answer is wrong and how to do the problem correctly. It's okay to make a mistake here because, if you do, you probably won't make the same mistake again on that day in mid-May. In fact, it's a good idea to read not only the solutions to the problems you got wrong, but also the solutions for the problems you weren't sure of or simply happened to guess correctly.

The Graphics Used in This Book

To emphasize particular skills and strategies, we use icons throughout this book. An icon in the margin will alert you that you should pay particular attention to the accompanying text. We use these three icons:

1. This icon points out a very important concept or fact that you should not pass over.

2. This icon calls your attention to a problem-solving strategy that you may want to try.

3. This icon indicates a tip that you might find useful.

ELITE STUDENT EDITION

5 STEPS TO A 5

AP Physics 1: Algebra-Based

2024

STEP 1

Get to Know the Exam and Set Up Your Study Program

CHAPTER 1

Frequently Asked Questions About the AP Physics 1 Exam

IN THIS CHAPTER

Summary: This chapter provides the basic information you need to know about the AP Physics 1, Algebra-Based Exam. Learn how the test is structured, what topics are tested, how the test is scored, as well as basic test-taking information.

Key Ideas

✪ It's not possible to "game" this test. In order to get a good score, *you must know your physics.*

✪ Half of the test consists of multiple-choice questions and the other half of free-response questions. Each section accounts for half of your score.

✪ A score of 3 or above makes you qualified for credit from most colleges and universities.

✪ Topics on the exam include the following:

   I. Force and Motion
     - How things move
     - Rotation
     - Gravitation
   II. Conservation Laws
     - Collisions: impulse and momentum
     - Work and energy
     - Rotation

> ✪ The focus of the test is not numbers and equations. You may use a calculator and an equation sheet, but these will not be very helpful because far more explanations and verbal responses are required than calculations and numerical answers.

FAQs: The AP Physics Program

Chapter 2 contains the answers to some of the most frequently asked questions about the AP Physics 1, Algebra-Based course and exam. If you have additional questions, check out the College Board's "AP Central" web pages (http://apcentral.collegeboard.com). Another helpful resource for the test is the author's physics teaching blog at https://jacobsphysics .blogspot.com.

What Is AP Physics 1, Algebra-Based, and How Is It Different from a Typical Advanced Physics Course?

AP Physics 1 is a first-time, no-calculus physics course covering mechanics.[1] The AP Physics 1 Exam involves fewer topics than typical high school or college introductory courses, but it requires far more explanations and verbal responses than calculations and numerical answers.

Even though most advanced physics courses require loads of numerical answers and mathematical manipulation, AP Physics 1 requires you to be able to do only two things mathematically: (1) solve straightforward algebraic equations, and (2) use the basic definitions of the trigonometric functions sine, cosine, and tangent. There's no completing the square, no trigonometric identities—just the basic stuff you learned in your algebra and geometry courses.

The next chapter contains more information about how the AP Physics 1, Algebra-Based curriculum differs from the old AP Physics B course and other traditional advanced physics courses.

Who Should Take the AP Physics 1, Algebra-Based Course?

The AP Physics 1 course is ideal for *all* college-bound high school students. For those who intend to major in math or the heavy-duty sciences, Physics 1 serves as a perfect introduction to college-level work. For those who want nothing to do with physics after high school, Physics 1 is a terrific terminal course—you get exposure to many facets of physics at a rigorous yet understandable level.

Most important, for those who aren't sure in which direction their college career may head,[2] the Physics 1 course can help you decide: "Do I like this stuff enough to keep studying it, or not?"

What Are the Other AP Physics Courses?

In addition to AP Physics 1, the College Board now offers three other AP Physics courses.

---

[1] The first AP Physics 1 Exam was given in May 2015. For the previous four decades, AP Physics B was the College Board's algebra-based introductory physics exam.

[2] That may be most of you reading this book.

AP Physics 2 is designed as an algebra-based follow-up to AP Physics 1. In the same style of requiring depth of understanding and verbal explanation, AP Physics 2 covers electricity, magnetism, fluids, thermal physics, and atomic and nuclear physics.

The AP Physics C courses are *only* for those who have already taken a solid introductory physics course and are considering a career in the physical sciences or math. Physics C consists of two separate, calculus-based courses: (1) Newtonian Mechanics, and (2) Electricity and Magnetism. Of course, the Physics 1 and Physics 2 courses cover these topics as well. However, the C courses go into greater mathematical depth and detail. The problems are more involved, and they demand a higher level of mathematical ability, including differential and integral calculus, and some differential equations. You can take either or both 90-minute Physics C exams. The AP Physics C exams have not changed in many years. If you decide to attempt the Physics C Exam, try *5 Steps to a 5: AP Physics C.*

Is One Exam Better than the Other? Should I Take More than One?

We strongly recommend taking only one exam—and make sure it's the one your high school AP course prepared you for! Physics C is not considered "better" than Physics 1 or 2 in the eyes of colleges and scholarship committees. They are different courses with different intended audiences. It is far better to do well on the one exam you prepared for than to attempt something else and do poorly.

Why Should I Take an AP Physics Exam?

Many of you take an AP Physics exam because you are seeking college credit. A score of 3 or above makes you qualified for credit from most colleges and universities. This means you are one or two courses closer to graduation before you even start college!

Therefore, one compelling reason to take an AP exam is economic. How much does a college course cost, even at a relatively inexpensive school? You're talking several thousands of dollars. If you can save those thousands of dollars by paying less than a hundred dollars now, why not do so? Even if you do not score high enough to earn college credit, the fact that you elected to enroll in an AP course tells admissions committees that you are a high achiever and are serious about your education.

You'll hear a whole lot of misinformation about AP credit policies. Don't believe anything a friend (or even a teacher) tells you; instead, find out for yourself. One way to learn about the AP credit policy of the school you're interested in is to look it up on the College Board's official website, at http://collegesearch.collegeboard.com/apcreditpolicy/index.jsp. Even better, contact the registrar's office or the physics department chair at the college directly.

FAQs: The AP Physics 1 Exam

"I've heard that no one does well on AP Physics 1. Is that true?" That's a rather melodramatic and, um, *false* statement. For example, in 2019, 73,000 students passed (i.e. earned 3 or better on) the AP Physics 1 exam. That's 15,000 more students than the number who even took the AP Physics C Mechanics exam!

Now, it's certainly true that Physics 1 is a difficult exam. There's no way to guess, to game the test, to pass without a true understanding of physics. But college professors and admissions committees now understand just how well Physics 1 prepares students to continue their study of physics. Physics C scores have skyrocketed over the past eight years, as has performance in college-level calculus-based physics classes. Why? Because so many students have such an improved grounding in the conceptual underpinnings of physics . . . which they gained through taking AP Physics 1.

The good news is, colleges know well how this exam has changed. Those students who pass AP Physics 1 are showing a significantly higher level of accomplishment than those who pass AP English or AP US History. Good scores—not just 5s, but 4s and 3s, too—are being rewarded in college admissions and credit.

I Heard the AP Physics 1 Exam Is Changing. Is that True?

The College Board has released a draft course and exam description for a slightly different test in the future. Eventually, the AP Physics 1 exam will include the study of fluids, as well as a few other minor additions. But that "future" is not May 2024. This year's exam will be exactly the same as in the past few years.

What Is the Format of the AP Physics 1 Exam?

The following table summarizes the format of the AP Physics 1 Exam.

Table 1.1   AP Physics 1 Exam Structure

	AP PHYSICS 1		
SECTION	NUMBER OF QUESTIONS	TIME LIMIT	PERCENT OF SCORE
I. Multiple Choice	50	1 hour and 30 minutes	50%
II. Free Response	5	1 hour and 30 minutes	50%

What Types of Questions Are Asked on the Exam?

The multiple-choice questions all have four choices. Most are traditional multiple-choice questions, the kind you are already familiar with. But a five-question subsection of the multiple-choice portion is designated as "multiple correct" questions: you will be asked to choose *two* of the answers as correct. On these questions, you must mark both of the correct choices in order to earn credit.

The free-response section includes two short problems similar in style to end-of-chapter textbook problems; they include open-ended problem solving, as well as "justify-your-answer," verbal-response items. Another short problem requires a written response in paragraph form. One of the longer free-response questions is posed in a laboratory setting, asking for descriptions of experiments and analyses of results. The other long question is called the "qualitative-quantitative translation," which asks you to solve a problem numerically or symbolically and then explain in words how you got to your solution and what the solution means.

More details about these kinds of questions and how to deal with them can be found in Chapter 7 ("Strategies to Approach the Questions on the Exam") of this book.

Who Writes the AP Physics Exam?

Development of each AP exam is a multiyear effort that involves many folks. At the heart of the effort is the AP Physics Development Committee, a group of college and high school physics teachers who are typically asked to serve for three years. The committee and other physics teachers create a large pool of multiple-choice questions. With the help of the testing experts at Educational Testing Service (ETS), these questions are then pretested with college students for accuracy, appropriateness, clarity, and assurance that there is no ambiguity in the choices. The results of this pretesting allow each question to be categorized by degree of difficulty. After several more months of development and refinement, Section I of the exam is ready to be administered.

The free-response questions that make up Section II go through a similar process of creation, modification, pretesting, and final refinement so that the questions cover the necessary areas of material and are at appropriate levels of difficulty and clarity. The committee includes the chief reader of the exams, who ensures that the proposed free-response problems can be graded consistently, fairly, and rapidly. An ETS specialist works with the committee to ensure that topic coverage and the scope of the exam are appropriate; the specialist makes sure that the exam tests what it's supposed to test.

At the conclusion of each AP reading and scoring of exams, the exam itself and the results are thoroughly evaluated by the committee and by ETS. In this way, the College Board can use the results to make suggestions for course development in high schools and to plan future exams.

What Topics Appear on the Exam?

The *Curriculum Framework* says nothing about the units or topics typically taught in an introductory physics class. Instead, the *Framework* is organized around six "Big Ideas" of physics that are each exemplified in numerous topics. So it's not possible to say exactly what topics are covered and to what extent. However, a careful reading of the *Curriculum Framework* can give a hint.

To get your head around these big ideas, think of the exam as broken up into halves:

I. *Force and Motion*
II. *Conservation Laws*

Now, your physics class probably was structured around specific content units, not around these big ideas. So I've broken up the chapters in this book into content areas. Note that rotation and gravitation, in particular, overlap two big ideas:

I. *Force and Motion*
    How things move (ch. 10)
    Forces and Newton's laws (ch. 11)
    Rotation (ch. 14)
    Gravitation (ch. 15)
    Simple harmonic motion (ch. 16)

II. *Conservation Laws*
    Collisions: impulse and momentum (ch. 12)
    Work and energy (ch. 13)
    Rotation (ch. 14)
    Gravitation (ch. 15)

Do I Get to Use a Calculator? An Equation Sheet?

Well, yes. But please don't expect these things to help you much. The course is not about numbers and equations. If you come into the exam thinking you'll find the right equation on the equation sheet and then solve that equation with a calculator, you're going to be blown out of the water. In fact, I wish the College Board had decided *not* to allow calculators and equation sheets. They give a false sense of what kinds of questions will be asked on the exam and of how to prepare for them. (See Chapter 7 for more information about the types of questions you will encounter.)

Suffice it to say that you don't need the equation sheet because by test day, you will already know and understand the important relationships between quantities that underlie the physics questions that will be asked. And if you don't know the correct relationship, I don't advise picking through the dense and incomprehensible equation sheet; you're more likely to waste time than to find something useful there.

Regarding the calculator, you probably shouldn't use it more than a few times on the entire exam. Most problems won't involve calculation at all, but rather reasoning with equations and facts. Many of the problems that at first glance look like calculations can be solved more quickly and easily with semiquantitative reasoning.[3] The few problems that do require calculation will usually involve straightforward arithmetic (e.g., the mass of the cart will be 1 kg or 0.5 kg, not 0.448 kg).

How Is My Multiple-Choice Section Scored?

The multiple-choice section of the AP Physics 1 Exam is worth half of the final score. Your answer sheet is run through a computer, which adds up your correct responses. The number of correct responses is your raw score on the multiple-choice section. No partial credit is awarded, even for the "multiple correct" items—either you choose both of the right answers, or you don't.

If I Don't Know the Answer, Should I Guess?

Yes. There is no penalty for guessing.

Who Grades My Free-Response Questions?

Every June, a group of physics teachers gathers for a week to assign grades to test takers' hard work. Each of these readers spends a day or so getting trained on only one question. Because each reader becomes an expert on that question, and because each exam book is anonymous, this process provides for consistent and unbiased scoring of that question.

During a typical day of grading, a random sample of each reader's scores is selected and cross-checked by experienced "table leaders" to ensure that consistency is maintained throughout the day and the week. Each reader's scores on a given question are also statistically analyzed to make sure scores are not given that are significantly higher or lower than the mean scores given by other readers of that question.

---

[3]By *semiquantitative reasoning* I mean something like, "If I double the net force with the same mass, I also double acceleration by $F_{net} = ma$. So the new acceleration is twice the old acceleration of 1.2 m/s per second, so the answer is 2.4 m/s per second."

Will My Exam Remain Anonymous?

You can be absolutely sure that your exam will remain anonymous. Even if your high school teacher happens to randomly read your booklet, there is virtually no way he or she will know that exam is yours.[4] To the reader, each student is a number, and to the computer, each student is a bar code.

What about that permission box on the back? The College Board uses some exams to help train high school teachers so that they can help the next generation of physics students to avoid common mistakes. If you check this box, you simply give permission to use your exam in this way. Even if you give permission, your anonymity is maintained.

How Is My Exam Score Determined, and What Does It Mean?

Each section counts for 50 percent of the exam. The total composite score is thus a weighted sum of the multiple-choice and free-response sections. In the end, when all of the numbers have been crunched, the chief faculty consultant converts the range of composite scores to the five-point scale of the AP grades.

This conversion is not a true curve; it's not that there's some target percentage of 5s to give out. This means you're not competing against other test takers. Rather, the five-point scale is adjusted each year to reflect the same standards as in previous years. The goal is that students who earn 5s this year are just as strong as those who earned 5s in 2016 and 2017.

In the exam's first year, it took about 70% of the available points to earn a 5; it took about 55% of the points to earn a 4; and about 40% of the points to earn a 3. I've used similar percentages in the tables at the end of the practice exams in this book to give you a rough example of a conversion. When you complete the practice exams, you can use this to give yourself a hypothetical grade.

Point is, you are NOT expected to get classroom-style scores of 90% for an A. The exam is intended to differentiate between levels of students, and the exam tests far more than pure recall, so 70% is a very strong score, not a weak score.

You should receive your AP grade in early July.

How Do I Register and How Much Does It Cost?

Registration for AP exams must be completed by mid-November.[5] You do not have to be enrolled in an officially titled AP Physics course to register for the exam. In many schools, an honors or college prep class, plus this book and some out-of-class practice, will prepare you just fine for the exam.

In 2023, the fee for taking the exam is $95. Students who demonstrate financial need may receive a reduction—you can find out more from your school's AP coordinator or the College Board website.

What if I'm Not Sure in November Whether I Want to Take the Exam?

Sign up anyway.

If you're in an official AP class, the College Board has provided all sorts of excellent resources that your teacher can share with you—including an outstanding workbook of activities, including personal progress checks that can be used throughout the year,

---

[4]Well, unless you write something like, "Hi, please kick Mr. Kirby in the butt for me. Thank you! Sincerely, George."
[5]*For those who are taking a second-semester-only class, the registration deadline is in March.*

including a bank of extra questions written by the development committee. Between these resources and this book, you will not encounter any surprises on the exam.

The College Board has done considerable research at pilot schools to determine whether requiring registration in November has an effect on student performance. They found out that it does—a dramatic effect. Students who committed in November to taking the exam outperformed those who didn't commit until March by an enormous margin.

I'm sure some wiseacres will say, "but I just know I'm gonna fail." That's called defeatism, and you shouldn't tolerate that from yourself. If you were to tell your softball coach, "Hey, I'm going to strike out at the plate, let grounders go through my legs, and drop all the fly balls hit to me," would the coach let you play? More likely, he or she would kick you off the team! When you pretend that you can't do anything in physics, you do yourself a tremendous disservice.

When in doubt regarding registration procedures, the best source of information is the College Board's website collegeboard.org.

What If My School Doesn't Offer AP Physics at All?
How Can I Take the Exam?

Any high school student is allowed to register for the exam, not just those who are taking an officially designated AP Physics course.

If your school doesn't offer any of the four AP Physics courses, then you should look at the content outlines and talk to your teacher. Chances are, you will want to take the AP Physics 1, Algebra-Based Exam, and chances are that you will have to do a good bit of independent work to delve deeper than your class discussed and practice the verbal responses necessary on this new exam. If you are a diligent student in a rigorous course, you will probably be able to do fine.

Your counseling office will be able to give you information about how to sign up for and where to take the test.

What Should I Bring to the Exam?

On exam day, I suggest bringing the following items:

- Several pencils and an eraser that doesn't leave smudges
- Black or blue pens for the free-response section[6]
- A ruler or straightedge
- A watch so that you can monitor your time (You never know if the exam room will have a clock on the wall.)
- Your school code
- Your photo identification and social security number
- Tissues
- Okay, fine, a calculator, if it makes you happy (Don't you dare use it more than a few times.)
- Your quiet confidence that you are prepared (Please don't study the morning before the exam—that won't do you any good. Stop the studying the night before, and relax. Good luck.)

---

[6]Yes, I said *pens*. Your rule of thumb should be to do graphs in pencil and everything else in pen. If you screw up, cross out your work and start over. Then if you change your mind about what you crossed out, just circle it and say, "Hey, reader, please grade this! I didn't mean to cross it out!"

CHAPTER 2

Understanding the Exam:
The AP Physics 1 Revolution

IN THIS CHAPTER

Summary: The AP Physics 1, Algebra-Based Exam requires less calculation and more written explanations of physics than any previous standardized physics exam. This chapter provides a deeper analysis of the AP Physics 1, Algebra-Based Exam, explaining what the test is like and how it is different from traditional physics tests.

Key Ideas

✪ The AP Physics 1, Algebra-Based Exam is less focused on getting the "right" numerical answer to a problem and more focused on explaining and applying the concepts of physics.

✪ The AP Physics 1, Algebra-Based Exam is no walk in the park. Although it covers fewer topics, has fewer questions, and contains less math than the old AP Physics B Exam, it requires a deeper understanding of physics. The AP Physics 1 Exam is more difficult than a typical high school honors physics exam.

What Happened to the AP Physics Test?

The AP Physics 1, Algebra-Based Exam is not like anything your parents, or even possibly your older cousins, took. The AP Physics 1, Algebra-Based curriculum has undergone a radical transformation that has eliminated the advanced mathematics but added a profound understanding of the science of physics.

A Little History

In the 1970s and 1980s, a typical physics professor gave lectures heavily focused on mathematics to first-year students and then administered exams that demanded clever algebraic manipulation. The AP Physics B exams of that era reflected the mathematical nature of college physics.

In the 1990s, a new generation of physics professors promoted a different kind of physics teaching that was just as rigorous but that demanded more explanation and less algebraic skill. The meaning of the math became more important than the math itself. AP exams began to include more questions asking for descriptions of experimental techniques, for justification of numerical answers, and for explanations in words.

When the College Board received a grant to redesign their science courses in the early 2000s, the curriculum design committee decided to move even further away from calculation and more toward verbal explanation. They minimized the number of topics on the newest AP physics exams, and they decreased the number of questions on the exams. That way, they reasoned, the exam could demand more writing and more detailed explanations in the responses.

Goal of the AP Physics 1 Revolution: The *Best* College Physics Course, Not Just the "Typical" College Physics Course

The fundamental purpose of the College Board's AP program has always been to give advanced high school students access to college-level coursework. Historically, the goal was to create exams that mimic the content and level of the typical, average courses at an American university.

However, in redesigning their science courses, the development committees aimed higher—the stated goal now is for the AP exams to reflect best practices as well as the content and difficulty level of only the best college courses. In general, the "best" college classes include lots of demonstrations, laboratory work, and descriptive as well as calculational physics.

What Is AP Physics 1? Eleven Things You Should Know About the Course and Exam

You'll do better on a test if you understand the test and what's being tested. In this section you'll learn key facts about the AP Physics 1 Exam—facts that will help you know what to expect and, as a result, better prepare for the test.

1. AP Physics 1 Is Not a Broad Course

Whereas the old AP Physics B course included between five and eight major topic areas, AP Physics 1 is limited to just mechanics:

- Force and motion
- Conservation laws

As of 2021, mechanics has been the *only* major topic area of physics. Subtopics of mechanics primarily include motion, force, momentum, energy, harmonic motion, and rotation. AP Physics 1 is designed to replicate the first semester of an algebra-based first-year college course. (AP Physics 2 covers the second-semester material.)

2. AP Physics 1 Is Designed to Be a First-Time Introduction to Physics

The current AP Physics C exams, were developed with the understanding that students would already have taken a high-school-level introduction to physics. But many high school students want to, and are ready to, dive right into algebra-based physics at the college level. AP Physics 1 has been written to set up these students for success. Thus, there is a reduction in the amount of material covered. Even if you've never seen physics before, you will have the time in AP Physics 1 to develop both your content knowledge and your physics reasoning skills enough to perform well on the exam.

3. AP Physics 1 Is Not a Math Course

There are only three middle- and high-school mathematical skills you need in order to understand AP Physics 1 material:

- You must be able to solve algebraic equations in a single variable.
- You must be able to calculate, and to understand the meaning of, the slope and area of a graph.[1]
- You must be able to use the definitions of the basic trig functions sine, cosine, and tangent.[2]

That's it. You studied these things in your middle school, Algebra 1, and geometry courses. You don't need matrices, factoring of polynomials, the quadratic formula, trigonometric identities, conic sections, or whatever else you are studying in Algebra II or precalculus.

4. AP Physics 1 Is Not About Numbers

Yes, you must use numbers occasionally. Yet you must understand that the number you get in answer to a question is always subordinate to what that number represents.

Many misconceptions about physics start in math class. There, your teacher shows you how to do a type of problem, and then you do several variations of that same problem for homework. The answer to one of these problems might be 30,000,000, and another 16.5. It doesn't matter . . . in fact, the book (or your teacher) probably made up random numbers to go into the problem to begin with. The "problem" consists of manipulating these random numbers a certain way to get a certain answer.

In physics, though, *every number has meaning*. Your answer will not be 30,000,000; the answer may be 30,000,000 joules, or 30,000,000 seconds, but not just 30,000,000. If you don't see the difference, you're missing the fundamental point of physics.

We use numbers to represent *real* goings-on in nature. The amount 30,000,000 joules (or 30 megajoules) is an energy; it could be the kinetic energy of an antitank weapon or the gravitational energy of an aircraft carrier raised up a foot or so.[3] Thirty million seconds is a time, not a few hours or a few centuries, but about one year. These two "30,000,000" responses mean entirely different things. If you simply give a number as an answer, you're

---

[1] Note that the calculus extensions of these concepts as "derivatives" and "integrals" are utterly irrelevant to and useless in AP Physics 1.

[2] This knowledge is often expressed as "SOHCAHTOA": In a right triangle, the **S**ine is **O**pposite over **H**ypotenuse. …

[3] Interestingly, when you use this much electrical energy in your house, it would cost you in the neighborhood of $1.

doing a math problem. It is only when you can explain the meaning of a result that you may truly claim to understand physics.

5. AP Physics 1 Requires Quantitative and Semiquantitative Reasoning

You'll only occasionally be asked to make numerical calculations. But you'll often be required to use mathematical *reasoning*.

"Quantitative" reasoning means not only performing direct calculations, but also explaining why those calculations come out the way they do. You'll be asked to explain whether quantities increase or decrease just by looking at the relevant equation, and without necessarily performing the calculations. You'll need to recognize that a problem is solvable when one equation with a single variable can be written, or when two equations with two variables can be written, or even when three equations with three variables can be written. You'll not be asked to solve even mildly complicated multivariable problems, but you must recognize when and explain why they are or aren't solvable.

"Semiquantitative" reasoning involves anticipating how the structure of an equation will affect the result of a calculation, even when no values in the equation are known. Increasing a variable in the numerator of an equation increases the quantity being calculated; increasing a variable in the denominator decreases the quantity being calculated. Doubling a term in the numerator also doubles the entire quantity, except if that term is squared (in which case the quantity is quadrupled) or square-rooted (in which case the quantity is multiplied by 1.4).

For example, the question "Calculate the acceleration of the 250-g cart" will be legitimate on the AP Physics 1 Exam. But more often the question will be rephrased to get at the heart of your ability to reason about physics, not just at your math skills. For example:

- Rank the accelerations of these carts from greatest to least; justify your ranking.
- Can the acceleration of the 250-g cart be calculated from the given information? If not, what other information is required?
- Explain how you would use a graph to determine the acceleration of the 250-g cart.
- How would the acceleration of a 500-g cart compare to the acceleration of the 250-g cart?
- Is the acceleration of the cart greater than, less than, or equal to g?

6. AP Physics 1 Requires Familiarity with Lab Work

Every physics problem that asks for calculation, quantitative reasoning, or semiquantitative reasoning is, in truth, asking for an experimental prediction.

When doing calculations, what differentiates physics from math class? In physics, every calculation can, in principle, be verified by an experimental measurement. Merely using an equation to calculate that a cart's acceleration is 2.8 m/s per second is a math problem, one that you might see in an Algebra 1 class. It's only a physics problem because you can, in fact, go to a cabinet and pull out a 250-g cart and a motion detector that will measure the cart's acceleration. If you set up the situation that was described in the problem, you'd better get an acceleration of 2.8 m/s per second; otherwise, either the calculational approach was incorrect (e.g., the equation you used might not apply to this situation), or the experiment was set up inappropriately (e.g., the problem assumed a level surface, but your track was slanted).

What's particularly nice about AP Physics 1 is that almost every problem posed in this course can be set up for experimental measurement within the realm of most students' experience. Carts can be set up to collide in your classroom. It's straightforward to take smartphone video of cars on a freeway or of a roller coaster. Computerized data collection—generally using equipment from PASCO or Vernier—should be part of your classroom experience, so that you're familiar with using force probes, motion detectors, photogates, and so on.[4]

Any physical situation can spawn a laboratory-based experimental question. Be prepared to describe experiments and to analyze data produced by experiments:

- Describe an experiment that uses commonly available laboratory equipment to measure the acceleration of the 250-g cart.
- In the laboratory, this table of the cart's speed as a function of time was produced. Use the data to determine the car's acceleration.
- The acceleration of the cart is calculated to be 2.8 m/s per second, but in the laboratory, a student measures the cart to have an acceleration of 4.1 m/s per second. Which of the following might explain the discrepancy between theory and experiment?

7. AP Physics 1 Does Not Require That You Perform a Specific Set of Programmed Laboratory Exercises

In AP Biology, students are expected to be familiar with, and to have actually done, a set of experiments. Biology exam questions will refer to these common experiments, expecting prior knowledge to carry students. This approach is completely different from that in AP Physics.

AP Physics certainly requires experimental skills, as described above. Teachers are required by the Course Audit to spend at least 25 percent of class time doing live, hands-on laboratory exercises.[5] Yet, the actual nature of those exercises is left to the teacher. Since virtually every possible AP Physics 1 question can be set up as an experiment, there are limitless possibilities for lab work. Creativity in lab work is prized on the AP Physics exams.

It's critical that you don't think of the "lab" as a place where you follow the steps in a procedure to produce a canned result that matches your teacher's expectation. Rather, think of the lab as a place to play, a place to re-create the calculational problems you've been solving in class. Lab is a place where you test the equations and concepts to see if they work.

> That's silly. Of course these equations and concepts work. Do you really expect me, a high school student, to disprove the conservation of momentum in a collision? Really!

Yeah, no one expects you to win a Nobel Prize in your AP Physics 1 laboratory. What is expected is that you go beyond stating "facts" of physics as gospel. A physicist always asks, "What's the evidence?" "How do we know that?" The AP exam expects you to be able to use conservation of momentum to calculate the speed of a cart after collision, sure; but it also expects you to explain why conservation of momentum is valid in this situation and, this is important, to explain *what evidence exists that conservation of momentum is a valid principle in the first place.*

The "evidence" for each physics fact comes from an experiment. You should be able to articulate how an experiment could be designed to test the validity of any fact; you should

---

[4]If your classroom does *not* have at least one set of PASCO or Vernier probes, your school probably doesn't meet the requirements of the AP Course Audit. Access to some of the same type of laboratory equipment that is available in most colleges is a prerequisite for the College Board allowing a school to label its course as "AP." See the "AP Central" portion of the College Board's official website for details about the Course Audit.

[5]In the pandemic times, everyone understands that teachers did their best to use online simulations, video demonstrations, and other substitutes for experimental work. But that was an exception in extraordinary circumstances. Unless a global plague is affecting school attendance, all AP physics courses—including online courses!—are required to spend at least a quarter of their time with student hands-on equipment doing experimental work.

be able to use equipment creatively to make a measurement of any quantity that might show up in a calculational problem.

8. AP Physics 1 Requires Writing

The free-response questions on the AP Physics 1 Exam will be more similar to those on the AP Biology or AP Economics exams than to those on AP Calculus or AP Physics C exams. Do not expect to answer exclusively in mathematical symbols and numbers. Whereas a typical honors physics question asks primarily for a numerical result, the AP Physics 1 exam will ask for short answers, descriptions, and explanations "without equations or calculations."

This doesn't mean you need to develop your storytelling skills. The writing required is always straightforward and to the point. A perfect response on the AP Physics 1 Exam might draw all sorts of complaints from your English teacher. While you need to use (reasonably) grammatically correct sentences, your language and vocabulary should be simple, not flowery. Your sentence structure doesn't need to be varied and interesting. You don't need to grab your reader's attention or to segue appropriately between paragraphs and ideas.

Just write, without worrying about how your writing sounds to a professional. Imagine that the person reading your writing is a student at the same level of physics as you. Don't explain your answers the way you think a college professor would; explain your answers the way you wish your teacher would explain them—simply and clearly, but completely. Practice this sort of writing on your problem sets.

9. AP Physics 1 Requires "Multiple Representations" of Physics Concepts

This means you should be comfortable explaining physics with words, equations, diagrams, and numbers. When you solve problems in your physics class, practice using these elements in every solution—even if your teacher doesn't explicitly require them. In my own class, if a student doesn't use at least three of these four elements in response to a homework question, the student usually is asked to come in to do the problem again.

Don't be shy about drawing diagrams. Try doing your homework on graph paper or unlined paper, rather than on standard notebook paper. Think of the paper as a blank canvas that needs to be filled in with your understanding of the solution to a problem. Lined notebook paper is far too restricting. It implies that you should be writing rows of words, with maybe an equation. Words can be written on a diagram, possibly with arrows to point out the important parts. Graphs and pictures can be drawn anywhere. Equations don't have to be placed one after the other in columns. A series of equations, however you present them, should always include some words describing the purpose of the equations in the problem's solution.

Then on the exam, you'll be well practiced in interpreting every possible representation of a physics explanation. Don't worry: you'll be asked for such interpretations on the multiple-choice section, and you'll be asked to use multiple representations of concepts on the free-response questions.

10. The AP Physics 1 Exam Is Designed to Give You the Time You Need to Answer the Questions Posed

As the new exams were in the development process, it became clear that the heightened demands for writing, for experimental interpretation and description, and for multiple representations of physics concepts would require a lot of time and thought. The committees in charge of creating AP Physics 1 were in agreement that students must be given the time necessary to respond in a complete way.

Even students with strong physics abilities are often pressed for time on the AP Physics C exams. The rule of thumb there was to spend about one minute per point: one minute on a multiple-choice question, 15 minutes on a 15-point free-response question, and so on. Therefore, students were advised to work quickly, eschewing in-depth thought for quick solution methods.

But AP Physics is designed differently. The rule of thumb is to spend in the neighborhood of *two* minutes per point. You'll get 50 multiple-choice questions to be completed in 90 minutes. Knock a few off quickly, and you can really think carefully about some while easily maintaining a just-under-two-minute-per-problem pace. The free-response section will have two long 12-point questions and three short 7-point questions and also will be 90 minutes in length. Yeah, you'll need to work steadily without dawdling; otherwise, you might run out of time even on this exam. But you'll have time to think before you write; then you'll have time to write everything you need to communicate your answer.

Practice this sort of time management on your homework for physics class. Instead of doing a zillion homework problems as quickly as you can, try picking one or two for a full-on, long-form treatment. Answer using multiple representations. Explain the answer, how you got it, how it would change if the problem inputs changed, and why you used the fundamental approach you used. Make the solution so complete that it could serve as the basis for a set of PowerPoint slides that could present your solution to a classmate. And do it all in less than 30 minutes. When you can do that, you're ready for the AP Physics 1 Exam.

11. AP Physics 1 Is a Difficult, High-Level College Course

Some may get the impression that because calculation is minimized and so few topics are covered, this course will be a "piece of cake." Wrong. My own impression, and the impression of countless AP teachers, is that AP Physics 1 is substantially more difficult than any calculational physics course - *including AP Physics C mechanics.*

People have the false impression that "lots of writing" means "easy to get some credit, because I can use lots of big words full of sound and fury." You will find that the AP readers are as adept at recognizing baloney as they are at recognizing good physics. You will be less likely to find points awarded for attempting to use a correct equation. While partial credit on the free response will still be copiously available, that credit will generally require a good, if incomplete, understanding of physics, and will not be attainable via guesswork.

Expect wailing and gnashing of teeth again when scores come out after the exam, because too many teachers and students are still thinking of physics as plugging numbers into equations. But you won't wail, of course, because you've read this book; you know what to expect; and you know that a true understanding of physics requires that you be able to solve problems, explain how you solved them, explain what concepts you used to solve them, explain why those concepts apply, and explain how you could experimentally demonstrate your solution. Meanwhile, those with gnashed teeth remain stuck with the idea that just producing an answer is enough.

CHAPTER 3

How to Use Your Time

IN THIS CHAPTER

Summary: You'll need to set up a study plan that's personalized to fit your needs and the amount of time you have to prep for the test. This chapter provides information and advice to get you started and outlines what you can do if you have a full year, a semester, or only a few weeks left until test day.

KEY IDEA

Key Ideas

✪ It's not possible to "game" the test—you have to really know your physics. Last-minute cramming won't work since the exam tests your skills and understandings, not your ability to remember facts and formulas.

✪ The most important part of your test prep plan is your AP Physics 1, Algebra-Based course.

✪ Personalize your study plan. Focus your test prep on the topics and types of questions that you find the most troublesome.

✪ Essential elements of any test prep plan are (1) familiarizing yourself with the test, (2) learning the best strategies to use in approaching each of the question types, and (3) taking practice tests.

Personalizing Your Study Plan

First, it's important for you to know that the AP Exam is an authentic physics test. What this means is that it's not possible to "game" this test—in order to do well, *you must know your physics*. It's not possible to slack off and then cram for the test and expect to do well.

The most important part of your study plan is your AP Physics 1 class, which is in fact designed to teach the knowledge and skills required on the exam. Diligent attention to all your lectures, demonstrations, and assignments will save you preparation time in the long run. (See Chapter 6 for strategies to get the most out of your class.)

Your study plan should be personalized based on your needs. Use the diagnostic tools in Step 2 to identify your weaknesses and then build a plan that focuses on these. If you're comfortable with kinematics and projectile problems, why would you spend any time on these? On the other hand, if you're worried about, say, collisions, then spend a couple of evenings reviewing and practicing how to deal with them. Focusing on weaknesses, rather than starting at the beginning and trying to review everything, will allow you to use the time you have to produce the maximum benefit.

Every reader of this book will have a different study plan. You can't follow some one-size-fits-all timetable, and you shouldn't start at the beginning of your course and try to review absolutely everything—you won't be able to do it. Your study plan depends not only on the topics you most need to review, but also on the types of exam questions you find most difficult, and the amount of time you have to study. Develop a realistic plan, and stick to it.

Regardless of when you start to prepare or how much content you want to review, your study plan should include these essential elements:

- Familiarize yourself with the test (Chapters 1 and 2).
- Learn the best strategies to approach each type of test question (Chapters 7 through 9).
- Take complete practice tests (Step 5).

Plan A: You Have a Full School Year to Prepare

If you're opening this book at the beginning of the school year, you're off to a good start. Here's what you can do:

First Semester
- Read Chapter 5 on how to get the most out of your AP Physics 1 class.
- Begin to familiarize yourself with the test (Chapters 1 and 2).
- Start practicing the strategies to approach the different types of questions found on the test (Chapters 7 through 9).
- You can work through the review chapters in this book (Chapters 10 to 18) as you study the same topics in your AP course. This will help you by providing a different perspective on the key content and ensuring you really understand the physics you need to know. Practice using the strategies presented in Chapters 7 through 9 to approach the test-like free-response questions at the end of each review chapter.

Second Semester
- Keep working through the review chapters as you progress through the physics course.
- About three months before the AP exam, use the diagnostic tools in Chapters 4 and 5 to assess your weaknesses. Try to identify both the content areas and types of questions you have the most difficulty with. Then focus your test prep review on the weaknesses you identify.

Six Weeks Before the Test
- Continue to focus on the areas of weakness that you identified based on the self-tests in Chapters 4 and 5.

- Review the strategies in Chapters 7 through 9 to make sure you approach the questions in ways that will help you get your best score.
- Be sure to take the practice tests (Step 5) a couple of weeks before the real test. These tests closely resemble the actual AP Physics 1 Exam. They will help you learn to pace yourself and allow you to experience what the test is really like. Then focus any final content review on the areas that proved troublesome on the practice tests. Also allocate some time to practice answering the question types that gave you the biggest problems.
- Be confident. You've worked all year, and you're really set to do your best.

Plan B: You Have One Semester to Prepare

Most students begin a test prep plan in the second semester. You should still have time to use this book to familiarize yourself with the test, learn the best strategies to approach each type of question, review the topics you find most troublesome, and take practice tests. Here's what you can do:

Second Semester
- Read Chapter 5 on how to get the most out of your AP Physics 1 class.
- Familiarize yourself with the test (Chapters 1 and 2).
- Practice the strategies to approach the different types of questions found on the test (Chapters 7 to 9).
- Two or three months before the AP exam, use the diagnostic tools in Chapters 4 and 5 to assess your weaknesses. Try to identify both the content areas and types of questions you have the most difficulty with. Then focus your test prep review on the topics you identify.

Six Weeks Before the Test
- Continue to focus on the areas of weakness that you identified based on the self-tests in Chapters 4 and 5.
- Review the strategies in Chapters 7 through 9 to make sure you approach the questions in ways that will help you get your best score.
- Be sure to take the practice tests (Step 5) a couple of weeks before the real test. They will help you learn to pace yourself and allow you to experience what the test is really like. Then focus any final content review on the areas in which you didn't do as well. Also practice the question types that proved problematic.
- Be confident. You know the test and the best strategies for the different question types. In addition, you've reviewed the areas in which you felt weakest, and you've taken a practice test. You're set to get a good score.

Plan C: You Have Six Weeks to Prepare

Six weeks should be plenty of time to prepare for the AP exam. You've been working diligently in your class all year, learning the topics as they've been presented. These last weeks should be spent putting it all together. Focus on the topics you feel you most need to review and on problems that cover multiple concepts in one question. Use your test prep time not to try to cram for the test (it won't work), but to familiarize yourself with the exam and learn the best strategies to use to approach the different question types. Most important, take the practice tests in Step 5 of this book. Here's what you can do:

Six Weeks Before the Test
- Familiarize yourself with the test (Chapters 1 and 2).
- Practice the strategies to approach the different types of questions found on the test (Chapters 7 to 9).
- Use the diagnostic tools in Chapters 4 and 5 to assess your weaknesses. Try to identify both the content areas and types of questions you have the most difficulty with. Then pick only a few areas on which to focus your test prep review and learn them well. Don't try to cover everything.
- Be sure to take the practice tests (Step 5) at least a week before the real test. They will help you learn to pace yourself and give you a trial run so you can experience what the test is really like. Then focus any final content review on the areas on which you didn't do as well. Also focus on the question types that gave you the biggest problems.
- Be confident. You know the test and the best strategies for the different question types. In addition, you've reviewed the areas in which you felt weakest and you've taken a practice test. If you've also used your AP course to really learn physics, you're set to get a good score.

STEP 2

Determine Your Test Readiness

CHAPTER 4

Facts to Know for the AP Physics 1 Exam

IN THIS CHAPTER

Summary: Just as a top-class musician can play scales without thought or effort, a top-class AP Physics student knows the fundamental facts underlying the subject.

Key Ideas

✪ I warn you: the exam will not ask you merely to spit back these facts and problem-solving techniques. You must know them, though, in order to attempt the complicated reasoning that is demanded on every question.

✪ I suggest that you use this chapter as a guide all year. Learn the statements not merely through rote memorization, but through use. Use one of the facts or techniques listed in this chapter as the starting point for *every* problem you solve, in this book and in your physics class.

✪ I print these facts out for my class in a small booklet. They find it helpful to carry around for reference whenever they are doing physics.

I. Forces and Motion

Kinematic Definitions

Displacement indicates how far an object ends up from its initial position, regardless of its total distance traveled.

Average velocity is displacement divided by the time interval over which that displacement occurred.

Instantaneous velocity is how fast an object is moving at a specific moment in time.

Position-Time Graphs

To determine how far from the detector an object is located, look at the vertical axis of the position-time graph.

To determine instantaneous speed from a curved position-time graph, take the slope of a tangent line.

To determine which way the object is moving, look at which way the position-time graph is sloped.

A position-time slope like a front slash / means the object is moving away from the detector.

A position-time slope like a back slash \ means the object is moving toward the detector.

Velocity-Time Graphs

To determine how fast an object is moving, look at the vertical axis of the velocity-time graph.

To determine which way the object is moving, look at whether the velocity-time graph is above or below the horizontal axis.

An object is moving away from the detector if the velocity-time graph is above the horizontal axis.

An object is moving toward the detector if the velocity-time graph is below the horizontal axis.

To determine how far an object travels, determine the area between the velocity-time graph and the horizontal axis.

On a velocity-time graph it is not possible to determine how far from the detector the object is located.

The slope of a velocity-time graph is acceleration.

Acceleration

Acceleration tells how much an object's speed changes in one second.

When an object speeds up, its acceleration is in the direction of motion.

When an object slows down, its acceleration is opposite the direction of motion.

Objects in free fall gain or lose 10 m/s of speed every second.

The units of acceleration are m/s per s.

Special Equations for Displacement

When an object is moving at a steady speed v, its displacement is given by $\Delta x = vt$.

When an object starts at rest and speeds up, or when an object slows to a stop, its displacement is given by either $\Delta x = \frac{1}{2}at^2$ or $\Delta x = \frac{v^2}{2a}$.

Algebraic Kinematics

You must follow these steps to solve an algebraic kinematics calculation.

1. Define a positive direction, that is the direction "away from the detector." Label that direction.
2. Indicate in words what portion of motion you are considering, for example, "motion from launch to peak of flight."
3. Fill out a chart, *including signs and units*, of the five kinematics variables:
   v_o initial velocity
   v_f final velocity
   Δx displacement
   a acceleration
   t time for the motion to happen
4. If three of the five variables are known, the problem is solvable; use the kinematics equations to solve.

   $v_f = v_o + at$
   $\Delta x = v_o t + \frac{1}{2}at^2$
   $v_f^2 = v_o^2 + 2a\Delta x$

   A fourth equation may occasionally be useful:

   $\Delta x = \frac{1}{2}t\,(v_o + v_f)$

Projectile Motion

When an object is in free fall,

- Its *vertical* acceleration is always 10 m/s per second.
- Its *horizontal* acceleration is always zero.

Velocities in perpendicular directions add with the Pythagorean theorem, just like perpendicular forces.

The magnitude of an object's velocity is known as its speed.

To approach a projectile problem, make two kinematics charts: one vertical, one horizontal.

Definition of Equilibrium

An object is in equilibrium if it is moving in a straight line at constant speed. This includes an object remaining at rest.

When an object is in equilibrium, forces on that object are balanced.

Newton's Second Law

For all forces other than the force of Earth, objects must be in contact in order to experience a force.

An object's acceleration is in the direction in which forces are unbalanced.

The net force is in the direction in which the forces are unbalanced.

The net force is in the direction of acceleration $a = \dfrac{F_{net}}{m}$.

Solving Problems with Forces

The two-step problem solving process:

1. Draw a free-body diagram.
1a. Break angled forces into components, if necessary.
2. Write two equations, one for Newton's second law in each direction:
     (up forces) − (down forces) = ma
     (left forces) − (right forces) = ma

Note that you should never get a "negative" force, so start the equations in the direction of acceleration. If acceleration is downward, write (down forces) − (up forces) = ma instead.

Mass and Weight

Mass tells how much material is contained in an object.

The units of mass are kilograms.

Weight is the force of a planet acting on an object.

On Earth's surface, the gravitational field is 10 N/kg. This means that on Earth, 1 kg of mass weighs 10 N.

Normal Force

A normal force is the force of a surface on an object in contact with that surface.

A normal force acts perpendicular to a surface.

A platform scale reads the normal force.

Adding Perpendicular Forces

To determine the resultant force, draw the forces to scale. Create a rectangle, and then measure the diagonal of the rectangle and its angle.

The "magnitude" of a force means the amount of the resultant force.

Using x- and y-Components

Any diagonal force can be written in terms of two perpendicular force components, called the x- and y-components.

To determine the amount of each component, draw the diagonal force to scale. Draw dotted lines from the tip of the force arrow directly to the x- and y-axes. Measure each component.

When the angle θ of the diagonal force is measured from the horizontal,

- The horizontal component of the force is the magnitude of the force times cos θ.
- The vertical component of the force is the magnitude of the force times sin θ.

A Free-Body Diagram

1. A labeled arrow representing each force. Each arrow begins on the object and points in the direction in which the force acts.
2. A list of the forces, indicating the object applying the force and the object experiencing the force.

Inclined Planes

When an object is on an inclined plane, break the object's weight into components parallel to and perpendicular to the incline. Do not use x- and y-axes.

- The component of the object's weight parallel to the incline is $mg \sin \theta$.
- The component of the object's weight perpendicular to the incline is $mg \cos \theta$.

Friction Force

The force of friction is the force of a surface on an object acting along the surface.

The force of friction acts in the opposite direction of an object's motion.

The coefficient of friction μ is not a force.

The coefficient of friction is a number that tells how sticky two surfaces are.

The force of friction is equal to the coefficient of friction times the normal force $F_f = \mu F_n$.

The coefficient of kinetic friction is used when an object is moving; the coefficient of static friction is used when an object is not moving. Both types of coefficients of friction obey the same equation.

The coefficient of static friction can take on any value up to a maximum, which depends on the properties of the materials in contact.

For two specific surfaces in contact, the maximum coefficient of static friction is greater than the coefficient of kinetic friction.

Newton's Third Law

Newton's third law says that the force *of* object A *on* object B is **equal** to the force *of* object B *on* object A.

A "third law force pair" is a pair of forces that obeys Newton's third law.

Two forces in a third law force pair can never act on the same object.

Circular Motion

An object moving at constant speed v in a circle of radius r has an acceleration of magnitude v^2/r, directed toward the center of the circle.

Two-Body Problems

In a two-body problem, usually:

- Draw one free-body diagram per object
- Write *netF* = *ma* for each object separately.
- Acceleration is the same for each object.
- One rope = one tension

Gravitation

All massive objects attract each other with a gravitational force.

The **gravitational force** F_G of one object on another is given by $F_G = G\dfrac{M_1 M_2}{d^2}$:

- M is the mass of an object.
- d is the distance between the centers of the two objects.
- G is the universal gravitation constant, 6.7×10^{-11} N·m²/kg².

The **gravitational field** g near an object of mass M is given by $g = G\dfrac{M}{d^2}$, where d represents the distance from the object's center to anywhere you're considering.

The **weight** of an object near a planet is given by mg, where g is the gravitational field due to the planet at the object's location.

The gravitational field near a planet is always equal to the free-fall acceleration.

Two Types of Mass

Gravitational mass is measured by measuring an object's weight using *weight = mg*.

Inertial mass is measured by measuring the net force on an object, measuring the object's acceleration, and using $F_{net} = ma$.

In all experiments ever performed, gravitational mass is equal to inertial mass.

Gravitational Potential Energy

Near the surface of a planet, the potential energy of a planet-object system is *mgh*, with $h = 0$ at the lowest point of the motion.

Away from the surface, the potential energy of a planet-object system is treated differently:

- PE is larger the farther from the planet's center.
- PE has a negative value (except when the object is way far away from the planet, in which case PE is zero).
- The equation for potential energy is $PE = -\dfrac{GMm}{d}$. *Don't use this equation unless you must derive an expression. The negative sign is confusing.*

Orbits

In a circular orbit of a satellite around a planet, consider the planet-satellite system:

- Kinetic energy is constant (same speed)
- Gravitational potential energy is constant (same orbital radius)
- Angular momentum *mvr* is constant (no external torques)
- Total mechanical energy is constant (no external work, and no internal energy)

To find the speed of a circular orbit, set gravitational force $G\dfrac{Mm}{r^2}$ equal to *ma*, with $a = \dfrac{v^2}{r}$.

In an elliptical orbit of a satellite around a planet, consider the planet-satellite system:

- Kinetic energy is *not* constant (speed changes).
- Gravitational potential energy is *not* constant (orbital radius changes).
- Angular momentum *mvr* is constant (no external torques).
- Total mechanical energy is constant (no external work, and no internal energy).

Force of a Spring

The force of a spring is equal to kx, where k is the spring constant, and x is the distance the spring is stretched of compressed.

The spring constant is a property of a spring.

The units of a spring constant are N/m.

Rotational Kinematics—Definitions

Angular displacement θ indicates the angle through which an object has rotated. It is measured in radians.

Average angular velocity ω is angular displacement divided by the time interval over which that angular displacement occurred. It is measured in rad/s.

Instantaneous angular velocity is how fast an object is rotating at a specific moment in time.

Angular acceleration α tells how much an object's angular speed changes in one second. It is measured in rad/s per second.

Angular acceleration and centripetal acceleration are independent. Angular acceleration changes an object's rotational speed, while centripetal acceleration changes an object's direction of motion.

The constant-acceleration kinematics equations for rotation are essentially identical to those for linear motion:

$$\omega_f = \omega_0 + \alpha_t$$

$$\Delta\theta = \omega_0 t + \tfrac{1}{2}\alpha t^2$$

$$\omega_f^2 = \omega_0^2 + 2\alpha(\Delta\theta)$$

Relationship Between Angular and Linear Motion

The linear displacement of a rotating object is given by $r\theta$, where r is the distance from the rotational axis.

The linear speed of a rotating object is given by $v = r\omega$.

The linear acceleration of a rotating object is given by $a = r\alpha$.

Torque

The torque provided by a force is given by $\tau = Fd_\perp$, where $d_\perp$ refers to the "lever arm." (See p. 131 for a more detailed summary of the lever arm.)

Rotational Inertia

Rotational inertia I represents an object's resistance to angular acceleration.

For a point particle, rotational inertia is MR^2, where M is the particle's mass, and R is the distance from the axis of rotation.

For a complicated object, its rotational inertia may be given by an equation relating its mass and radius. These equations will be given as needed.

Rotational inertia of multiple objects add together algebraically.

Newton's Second Law for Rotation

An angular acceleration is caused by a net torque: $\alpha = \dfrac{\tau_{net}}{I}$.

II. Conservation Laws

What Is Conserved?

Mechanical energy is conserved when there is no net work done by external forces (and when there's no internal energy conversion).

Angular momentum is conserved when no net external torque acts.

Momentum in a direction is conserved when no net external force acts in that direction.

Momentum

Momentum is equal to mass times velocity: $p = mv$.

The standard units of momentum are newton·seconds, abbreviated N·s.

The direction of an object's momentum is always the same as its direction of motion.

Impulse

Impulse J can be calculated in either of two ways:

1. Impulse is equal to the change in an object's momentum.
2. Impulse is equal to the force experienced multiplied by the time interval of collision, $J = Ft$.

Impulse has the same units as momentum, N·s.

Impulse is the area under a force vs. time graph.

Conservation of Momentum in Collisions

When no external forces act on a system of objects, the system's momentum cannot change.

The total momentum of two objects before a collision is equal to the objects' total momentum after the collision.

Momentum is a vector: that is, total momentum of two objects moving in the same direction adds together; total momentum of two objects moving in opposite directions subtracts.

A system's center of mass obeys Newton's second law: that is, the velocity of the center of mass changes only when an external net force acts on the system.

Equations for Different Forms of Energy

All forms of energy have units of joules, abbreviated J.

- **Kinetic energy:** $KE = \frac{1}{2}mv^2$. Here, m is the mass of the object, and v is its speed.
- **Gravitational potential energy:** $PE = mgh$. Here, m is the mass of the object, g is the gravitational field, and h is the vertical height of the object above its lowest position.
- The term ***mechanical energy*** refers to the sum of a system's kinetic and potential energy.

- **Spring potential energy:** $PE = \frac{1}{2}kx^2$. Here, k is the spring constant, and x is the distance the spring is stretched or compressed from its equilibrium position. (See the later section about springs.)
- **Rotational kinetic energy:** $KE_r = \frac{1}{2}I\omega^2$. Here, I is the rotational inertia of the object, and ω is the angular speed of the object.
- **Internal energy** is heat energy that causes an increase in the temperature of the system.

Work-Energy Theorem

Problem-solving process:

- Define the object or system being described.
- Define the two positions you're considering.
- Draw an annotated energy bar chart.
- Write an equation based on the energy bar chart, with one term per bar:

  Bars + bars = bars: sum of all energy forms in position 1 + work done by external forces = sum of all energy in position 2

Definition of Work

Positive work is done by a force parallel to an object's displacement.

Negative work is done by a force antiparallel to an object's displacement.

No work is done by a force acting perpendicular to an object's displacement.

Work is a scalar quantity—it can be positive or negative, but does not have a direction.

The area under a force vs. displacement graph is work.

Power

Power is defined as the amount of work done in one second, or energy used in one second:

power = work / time

The units of power are joules per second, which are also written as watts.

An alternative way of calculating power when a constant force acts is *power = force · velocity*.

Energy in a Collision

In an *elastic* collision, mechanical energy of the system is conserved.

Collisions for which objects stick together cannot be elastic.

Collisions for which objects bounce off each other may or may not be elastic.

Angular Momentum

Before calculating angular momentum, it is necessary to define a rotational axis.

The angular momentum L of an object is given by:

- $I\omega$ for an extended object
- mvr for a point object, where r is the "distance of closest approach"

Conservation of Angular Momentum

When no torques act external to a system, angular momentum of the system cannot change.

Angular momentum is a vector—angular momentums in the same sense add; angular momentums in opposite senses subtract.

Angular momentum is conserved *separately* from linear momentum. Do not combine them in a single equation.

Angular Impulse

The impulse-momentum theorem can be written for angular momentum, too.

$$\tau \Delta t = \Delta L$$

A change in angular momentum equals the net torque multiplied by the time the torque is applied.

Force of a Spring

A spring pulls with more force the farther the string is stretched or compressed.

The force of a spring is given by the equation $F = kx$. Here, k is the spring constant of the spring, and x is the distance the spring is stretched or compressed.

The spring constant is a property of a spring and is always the same for the same spring.

The standard units of the spring constant are N/m.

Vertical Springs

When dealing with an object hanging vertically from a spring, it's easiest to consider the spring-Earth-object system.

The potential energy of the spring-Earth-object system is $PE = \frac{1}{2}kx^2$, where x is measured from the position where the object would hang in equilibrium.

Simple Harmonic Motion

Many objects that vibrate back and forth exhibit simple harmonic motion. The pendulum and the mass on a spring are the most common examples of simple harmonic motion.

An object in simple harmonic motion makes a position-time graph in the shape of a sine function.

An object in simple harmonic motion experiences a net force whose

- magnitude increases a linear function of distance from the equilibrium position
- direction always points toward the equilibrium position

Definitions involving simple harmonic motion:

- Amplitude (A): the maximum distance from the equilibrium position reached by an object in simple harmonic motion
- Period (T): the time for an object to complete one entire vibration
- Frequency (f): how many entire vibrations an object makes each second

The period of a mass on a spring is given by the equation $T = 2\pi \dfrac{\sqrt{m}}{\sqrt{k}}$. The mass attached to the spring is m; the spring constant of the spring is k.

The period of a pendulum is given by the equation $T = 2\pi \dfrac{\sqrt{L}}{\sqrt{g}}$. The length of the pendulum is L; the gravitational field is g.

The Five Types of Graphs to Know

When the arrows in the equation point in opposite direction (whether something is squared or not):

When the arrows in the equation point in the same direction and nothing is squared:

- In a straight-line graph, the steepness of the graph depends on the quantity that is held constant.

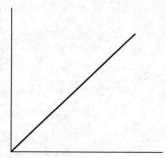

When the arrows in the equation point in the same direction but one of the variables is squared:

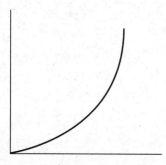

When the arrows in the equation point in the same direction, but one of the variables is under a square root:

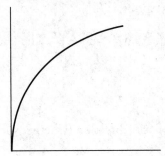

When the vertical-axis variable doesn't change at all:

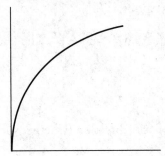

CHAPTER 5

Types of Questions on the AP Physics 1 Exam

IN THIS CHAPTER

Summary: In the previous chapter you learned physics fundamentals. In this chapter you will test yourself on the types of questions found in the AP Physics 1, Algebra-Based Exam. This preview of question types will provide insight into which types of questions will be the most problematic for you. Complete explanations for all the questions in this diagnostic test are included at the end of this chapter.

Key Ideas

✪ In addition to reviewing AP Physics 1, Algebra-Based content and skills, you will need to become familiar with the question types on the exam and assess which types of questions will be most difficult for you.

✪ This self-assessment, should be used to help you develop a personalized test-prep plan based on your needs (see Chapter 3).

Question Types

To do well on the AP Physics exam, you must know physics. There's no way to game the test, to find the trick that works to get the right answers. (Unless you consider physics skills "tricks.")

Nevertheless, you should be familiar with the different ways in which your skills will be assessed. Sure, you've taken multiple-choice and essay tests before, but on the AP Physics 1 Exam, you'll find some multiple-choice and free-response questions unlike anything you've probably seen before. Your test score will improve if you not only review physics subject areas but also become familiar with the types of questions you will encounter and practice responding to these. In Chapters 7 through 9 you'll find proven strategies for attacking each of the question types on the AP Physics 1 Exam. Be sure to familiarize yourself with these, especially for those types of questions that proved difficult for you.

Descriptive Problems (Like Those You've Probably Seen Before)

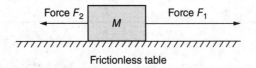

Frictionless table

1. In the preceding diagram, forces F_1 and F_2 are acting on box M which is on a frictionless table. F_1 has a greater magnitude than F_2. Of the following statements about the motion of box M, which is correct?

   (A) Box M is moving to the left.
   (B) Box M is moving to the right.
   (C) Box M is at rest.
   (D) It cannot be determined what direction Box M is moving.

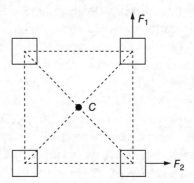

2. Four objects with mass m are rigidly connected and free to rotate in the plane of the page about the center point C. The objects experience two forces, F_1 and F_2, as shown in the preceding diagram. Which of the following statements correctly analyzes how F_1 and F_2 will affect the angular velocity of the objects?

   (A) Both forces apply torque in the same sense, so the angular velocity must increase.
   (B) If the forces F_1 and F_2 are equal in magnitude, the angular velocity will not change.
   (C) The angular velocity would decrease if the objects were initially rotating clockwise.
   (D) F_2 does not apply any torque to the objects, so only F_1 can cause a change in angular velocity.

Calculation Problems (Like Those You've Probably Seen Before)

3. A 2.0-kg ball is dropped such that its speed upon hitting the ground is 3.0 m/s. It rebounds, such that its speed immediately after collision is 2.0 m/s. What is the magnitude of the ball's change in momentum?

   (A) 10 N·s
   (B) 5 N·s
   (C) 2 N·s
   (D) 1 N·s

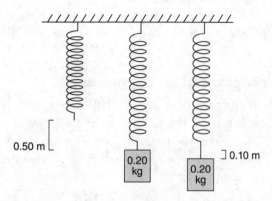

4. When a 0.20 kg block hangs at rest vertically from a spring of force constant 4 N/m, the spring stretches 0.50 m from its unstretched position, as shown in the figure. Subsequently, the block is stretched an additional 0.10 m and released such that it undergoes simple harmonic motion. What is the maximum kinetic energy of the block in its harmonic motion?

   (A) 0.50 J
   (B) 0.02 J
   (C) 0.72 J
   (D) 0.20 J

Ranking Task

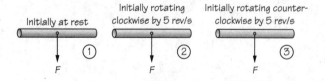

5. Three identical rods experience a single, identical force *F*, as shown in the diagrams. Each rod is initially rotating differently about its left edge, as described. Which of the following correctly ranks the magnitude of each rod's change in angular speed during the first 0.5 s that the force is applied?

   (A) 2 = 3 > 1
   (B) 1 = 2 = 3
   (C) 1 > 2 > 3
   (D) 3 > 2 > 1

Semiquantitative Reasoning

6. A diver leaps upward and forward off of a diving board. As the diver is in the air, he twists his body such that his rotational speed when he hits the water is four times his rotational speed when he left the diving board. When he hits the water, what is the diver's angular momentum about his center of mass?

    (A) Greater than his angular momentum when he left the diving board by a factor of four
    (B) Greater than his angular momentum when he left the diving board, but not by a factor of four
    (C) Less than his angular momentum when he left the diving board
    (D) Equal to his angular momentum when he left the diving board

Description of an Experiment

7. A sprinter running the 100-meter dash is known to accelerate for the first few seconds of the race and then to run at constant speed the rest of the way. It is desired to design an experimental investigation to determine the sprinter's maximum speed v. Which of the following procedures could correctly make that determination?

    (A) Place poles 90 m and 100 m from the race's start. Measure with a stopwatch the time t for the sprinter to travel between the poles. To find v, divide 10 m by t.
    (B) Estimate that the sprinter accelerates for the first 2.5 s. Mark on the track the location of the sprinter after 2.5 s. Use a measuring tape to find the distance d the sprinter traveled in this time. Divide d by 2.5 s to get v.
    (C) Measure with a stopwatch the time t for the sprinter to run the 100 m. To find v, divide 100 m by t.
    (D) Measure with a stopwatch the time t for the sprinter to run the 100 m. Divide 100 m by t^2 to get the average acceleration a. Then since the sprinter starts from rest, v is given by $\sqrt{2(a)(100 \text{ m})}$.

Pulley

Video camera

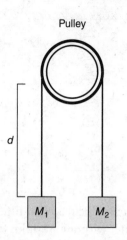

d

M_1 M_2

8. Two blocks of known masses M_1 and M_2, with $M_1 > M_2$, are connected by string over a freely rotating light pulley, as shown in the preceding diagram. A video camera records the motion of the blocks and pulley after the blocks are released from rest in the position shown. It is desired to use the video to measure the angular velocity of the pulley when block m_1 has fallen a known distance d. Which of the following approaches will best make this experimental determination?

(A) Treat the system as a single mass. The net force is the difference between the blocks' weights, $m_1g - m_2g$; Newton's second law gives an acceleration of $a = \left(\dfrac{m_1 - m_2}{m_1 + m_2}\right)g$. Use the kinematic equation $v_f^2 = v_0^2 + 2ad$ with $v_0 = 0$ to determine the final speed of the block; then the angular velocity is this speed divided by the radius of the pulley.

(B) Mark a spot on the edge of the pulley. Run the video until the blocks have gone the distance d. In that time, count the total revolutions that spot makes, including any partial revolutions measured using a protractor. Divide the total revolutions by the time the video ran to get the angular velocity.

(C) Pause the video when mass m_2 has just reached the distance d; note the location of a position on the rim of the pulley. Advance the video one frame. Use a protractor to measure the angle through which the noted location on the pulley moved in that one frame. Divide that angle by the camera's time between frames to get the angular velocity of the pulley.

(D) Make a graph of the position of mass m_1 as a function of time, determining the block's position by pausing the video after every frame. The slope of this graph is the pulley's angular velocity.

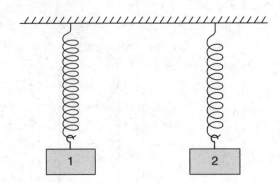

9. Two hanging blocks, each attached to a different spring, undergo oscillatory motion. It is desired to determine, without stopping the motion, which block experiences the greater maximum acceleration. Which of the following procedures would accomplish that determination?

(A) Place a motion detector underneath each block. On the velocity-time graphs output by the detector, look at the maximum vertical axis value, indicating the highest speed that block attained. Whichever block attains the higher speed has the larger acceleration.

(B) Place a motion detector underneath each block. On the velocity-time graphs output by the detector, look at the steepest portion of the graph. Whichever block makes the steeper maximum slope on the velocity-time graph has the greater maximum acceleration.

(C) Place a motion detector underneath each block. On the position-time graphs output by the detector, look at the maximum vertical axis value, indicating the amplitude of the motion. Whichever block oscillates with the larger amplitude has the larger acceleration.

(D) Place a motion detector underneath each block. On the position-time graphs output by the detector, look at the steepest portion of the graph. Whichever block makes the steeper maximum slope on the position-time graph has the greater maximum acceleration.

Analysis of an Experiment

10. In the laboratory, measured net torques τ are applied to an initially stationary pivoted bar. The resulting change in the bar's angular speed after 1 s is measured and recorded as $\Delta\omega$. Which of the following graphs will produce a slope equal to the bar's rotational inertia about the pivot point?

(A) τ versus $\Delta\omega$

(B) τ versus $\dfrac{1}{\Delta\omega}$

(C) τ versus $(\Delta\omega)^2$

(D) τ versus $\sqrt{\Delta\omega}$

Set of Questions Referring to the Same Stem

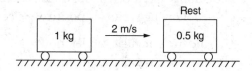

<u>Questions 11 and 12:</u> A 1-kg cart moves to the right at 2 m/s. This cart collides with a 0.5-kg cart that is initially at rest; the carts stick together after the collision. Friction on the surface is negligible.

11. What is the kinetic energy of the two-cart system after the collision?

   (A) 1.3 J
   (B) 0 J
   (C) 0.7 J
   (D) 2 J

12. If instead the carts collide elastically, which of the following is correct about the linear momentum and kinetic energy of the two-cart system after the collision compared to the collision in which the carts stuck together?

   (A) The linear momentum and the kinetic energy will both be greater.
   (B) The linear momentum will be greater, but the kinetic energy will be the same.
   (C) The kinetic energy will be greater, but the linear momentum will be the same.
   (D) The linear momentum and the kinetic energy will both be the same.

Multiple Correct Questions

Questions 13 through 15 are multiple correct: Mark the *two* correct answers.

13. (multiple correct) Cart A initially moves to the left on a smooth track, on which cart B sits at rest. The carts collide elastically. Which of the following quantities is the same before and after the collision? Select two answers.

   (A) the momentum of cart A
   (B) the kinetic energy of cart A
   (C) the total kinetic energy of the two-cart system
   (D) the total momentum of the two-cart system

14. (multiple correct) A car tire initially rotates clockwise with a rotational speed of 20 rad/s. The rotation gradually slows, such that 2 s later the tire rotates clockwise with a rotational speed of 10 rad/s. Considering clockwise as the positive direction, which of the following vectors is positive? Select two answers.

(A) the tire's angular acceleration
(B) the tire's angular momentum
(C) the net torque on the tire
(D) the tire's angular velocity

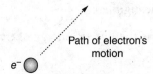

15. (multiple correct) An electron in a vacuum chamber is moving at constant velocity in the direction shown in the preceding diagram. Which of the following force vectors F applied to the electron would increase the electron's kinetic energy? Select two answers.

(A)

(B)

(C)

(D)

Qualitative-Quantitative Translation

Note: The following question is part of a free-response question.

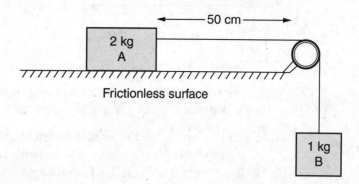

Frictionless surface

16. Two blocks are connected over a light, frictionless pulley, as shown. Block A of mass 2 kg is on a frictionless surface; block B of mass 1 kg hangs freely. The blocks are released from rest, with block A 50 cm from the end of the table.

(a) Calculate the speed of block A when it reaches the end of the table.
(b) The mass of block A is now increased. Explain in words but with specific reference to your calculation in (a) how, if at all, block A's speed at the edge of the table will change.

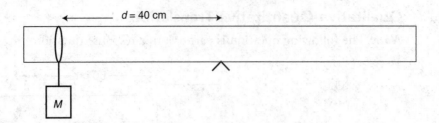

17. A meterstick is pivoted at its center, as shown above. An object of unknown mass m is hung a distance $d = 40$ cm left of the pivot.

   (a) Describe a procedure that would determine, using commonly available laboratory equipment, the torque exerted by the hanging object about the pivot.
   (b) A downward force F is applied at varying distances x to the right of the pivot point. The force F is adjusted at each position such that the meterstick balances.
   (i) On the axes below, sketch what a graph of F vs. x would look like.

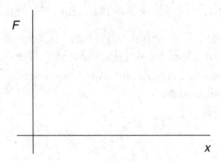

   (ii) Justify why you sketched the shape you did.
   (c) It is desired to use the slope of the best-fit line to an experimental graph to determine the mass m.
   (i) What quantities, when graphed together, would produce a straight line whose slope could be used to determine m?
   (ii) Explain how m would be determined from the slope of the best-fit line.

Solutions for the AP Physics 1 Question Types Assessment

1. (D) The force F_1 is bigger than the force F_2, meaning the net force is in the direction of F_1. Newton's second law says that the direction of acceleration must be the same as the direction of net force. Okay, so the acceleration is to the right. But that doesn't give the direction of motion! If the object is speeding up, it moves right. But if the object is slowing down, it moves left.

2. (C) Both F_1 and F_2 apply a counterclockwise torque. So these torques add together to give a net counterclockwise torque. That means the angular speed must change, but not necessarily increase. If the objects were rotating clockwise to start with, then a counterclockwise net torque would slow the angular speed.

3. (A) The ball has a momentum of 6 N·s downward before the collision. In the collision, the ball has to stop, losing all 6 N·s; then the ball has to gain 4 N·s to go in the other direction. That's a total change of 10 N·s. If you'd prefer to call the downward direction the negative direction, then the change in momentum is the final minus initial momentum: that's $(+4 \text{ N·s}) - (-6 \text{ N·s}) = +10$ N·s.

4. (B) You can look at this two ways. The hard way is to consider the spring energy gained and the gravitational energy lost in stretching the spring the additional 0.10 m separately. The block-earth system loses $mgh = (0.20 \text{ kg})(10 \text{ N/kg})(0.10 \text{ m}) = 0.20$ J of gravitational energy; but the block-spring system gains $\frac{1}{2}kx_2^2 - \frac{1}{2}kx_1^2 = \{\frac{1}{2}(4 \text{ N/m})(0.60 \text{ m})^2 - \frac{1}{2}(4 \text{ N/m})(0.50 \text{ m})^2\} = 0.22$ J of spring energy. Thus, the net work done on the block in pulling it the additional 0.10 m is 0.02 J. That's what is converted into the block's maximum kinetic energy.

You can also look at it the easy way. With a vertical spring, consider the block-earth-spring system as a whole. Define the hanging equilibrium as the zero of the whole system's potential energy; then the potential energy of the whole system can be written as $\frac{1}{2}kx^2$, where x is the distance from this hanging equilibrium position. That's $\frac{1}{2}(4 \text{ N/m})(0.10 \text{ m})^2 = 0.02$ J.

5. (B) The torque provided by F is identical for the three rods, because the force and distance from the fulcrum are the same for all. The rods are identical, so their rotational inertias are the same. By Newton's second law for rotation, $\tau_{net} = I\alpha$, because both τ_{net} and I are the same, the angular acceleration α must also be the same for all rods. Then angular acceleration is change in angular speed per second, and all change speeds by the same amount in the same amount of time.

6. (D) Since the only torques acting on the diver are due to the forces applied by his own muscles, no torques external to the diver act. Thus, angular momentum is conserved.

7. (A) By the last 10 m, the sprinter will be moving at a steady speed, so just dividing distance by time is valid. Choice (B) also divides distance by time, but during the part of the race in which the sprinter is speeding up—invalid. Choice (C) assumes a constant speed for the whole race, which is incorrect according to the problem statement. Choice (D) not only assumes acceleration for the entire race, but uses a horrendously bogus method for finding acceleration. (There's no equation in the world that says acceleration equals distance divided by time squared.)

8. (C) Choice (A) is wrong because it describes a calculational prediction, not an experimental measurement. Choice (D) determines linear velocity, not angular velocity. Choices (B) and (C) both discuss angular velocity experimentally, but Choice (B) gives the *average* angular velocity, while Choice (C) explicitly describes an instantaneous angular velocity because it is finding the angular displacement over a very short time period when the block is essentially at the position d.

9. (B) Acceleration is the slope of a velocity-time graph. Choices (A) and (D) give speed rather than acceleration. Choice (C) is a distance, not an acceleration.

10. (A) The relevant equation relates change in angular speed per second—that is, angular acceleration—to net torque. That's $\tau_{net} = I\alpha$. The rotational inertia is I, and plotting τ_{net} versus α will give the slope equal to I. Which choice is that? Since the angular speed change was measured over 1 s, $\Delta\omega$ *is* the angular acceleration in this case.

11. (A) The initial kinetic energy is possessed only by the 1-kg cart and is equal to $\frac{1}{2}mv^2 = 2$ J. We don't know the speed of the carts after the collision, so we have to calculate that via momentum conservation. (Kinetic energy is *not* conserved because the carts stick together—this is an inelastic collision.) The total momentum before collision is the sum of *mv* for each cart $= 2$ N·s $+ 0 = 2$ N·s. The total momentum after collision must also be 2 N·s by momentum conservation. (Momentum is *always* conserved in a collision.) The carts' combined mass is 1.5 kg, so the speed must be 1.3 m/s in order to multiply to the 2 N·s total. Kinetic energy of the combined masses is now $\frac{1}{2}(1.5 \text{ kg})(1.3 \text{ m/s})^2 = 1.3$ J.

12. (C) Linear momentum is conserved in all collisions, regardless of the elasticity of the collision. The value of the total momentum will be 2 N·s either way. Kinetic energy was lost in the first collision, because kinetic energy is conserved only in an elastic collision. In the second collision, though, no kinetic energy was lost. Therefore, kinetic energy is bigger after the second collision, but smaller after the first collision.

13. (C) and (D) In all collisions, total momentum is conserved; in an elastic collision, which the problem states this is, total kinetic energy is conserved. Conservation of momentum or energy in a collision always means the *total* amount for the system is the same before and after, not that the momentum or kinetic energy of a single object remains the same. Credit is only awarded for getting both choices correct; no partial credit is available on multiple-correct items.

14. (B) and (D) The tire is rotating in the positive direction. Angular velocity and angular momentum are always in the direction of rotation. Since the tire is slowing its rotation, though, angular acceleration must be *opposite* the direction of angular velocity. And by Newton's second law for rotation, net torque is in the same direction as angular acceleration.

15. (A) and (C) Any force that does positive work on the electron will increase the electron's kinetic energy. Positive work means that a component of the force is in the same direction as the electron's motion. Choice (D) is perpendicular to the electron's motion, so that force does no work; choices (A) and (C) all have a component up and to the right, so those forces do work to increase the electron's kinetic energy. Choice (B) has a component in the direction opposite the electron's motion, so choice (B) does work to *decrease* the electron's kinetic energy.

16. (a) Treating the two blocks as a single system, the net force is the 10-N hanging weight. The mass of this two-block system is 3 kg, so by $F_{net} = ma$, the system's acceleration is 10 N/3 kg = 3.3 m/s per second.

    Now, block A starts from rest, travels 0.50 m, and accelerates at 3.3 m/s per second. Using the kinematics equation $v_f^2 = v_o^2 + 2a\Delta x$, we get $v_f = \sqrt{(0) + 2(3.3 \text{ m/s/s})(0.50 \text{ m})} = 1.8$ m/s.

    (b) The net force on the system does not change, because the 10-N weight is still the same. However, the mass of the system increases. The solution in (a) for the acceleration of the system includes the system's mass in the denominator, so the acceleration of the system will decrease.

    Then, since block A still travels the same distance to the edge of the table from rest, the same kinematics equation as in (a) works, but this time with a smaller acceleration. With that acceleration in the numerator of the final speed equation, the final speed will also decrease.

17. (a) [Many possible approaches are valid!] Push down on the meterstick with a force probe, 40 cm to the right of the pivot. Because the meterstick is now in equilibrium, the torque provided by the hanging object is equal to the torque provided by the force probe. That torque is the force probe reading multiplied by 40 cm.

(b)

(i)

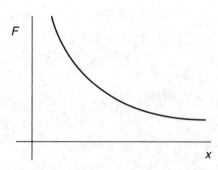

(ii) The relevant equation here comes from balanced torques, $mgd = Fx$. The relationship between F and x is an inverse relationship—when one variable increases, the other decreases to multiply to the same value. An inverse relationship always looks like the graph above.

(c) Solving for F, the relationship in (b) ii becomes $F = mgd\,(1/x)$. Let's put F on the vertical axis, and identify each variable in the straight-line equation $y = mx + b$:

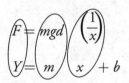

(i) So, the force probe reading F is graphed on the y-axis, $(1/x)$ is graphed on the x-axis.

(ii) The slope is associated with mgd. So to find the mass m, solve algebraically: m is the graph's slope divided by gd.

STEP 3

Develop Strategies for Success

CHAPTER 6

Strategies to Get the Most Out of Your AP Physics Course

IN THIS CHAPTER

Summary: The best way to prepare for the AP Physics 1, Algebra-Based Exam is to make sure you really understand the physics presented in your AP course. This chapter provides strategies you can use to get the most out of your AP Physics 1 class and improve the likelihood that you'll score a 4 or 5 on the test.

Key Ideas

✪ Focus on increasing your knowledge of physics, not on getting a good grade.

✪ Don't spend more than 10 minutes at one time without getting somewhere.

✪ Work with other students.

✪ Ask questions when you don't understand something.

✪ Keep an even temper, and don't cram.

Seven Simple Strategies to Get the Most Out of Your AP Physics Course

Almost everyone who takes the AP exam has just completed an AP Physics course. *Recognize that your physics course is the place to start your exam preparation!* Whether or not you are satisfied with the quality of your course or your teacher, the best way to start preparing for the exam is by doing careful, attentive work in class all year long.

Okay, for many readers, we're preaching to the choir. You don't want to hear about your physics class. In fact, maybe you're reading this chapter only a few weeks before the exam, and it's too late to do much about your physics class. If that's the case, go ahead to the next chapter, and get started on strategies for the test, not the class.

But if you are reading this a couple of months or more before the exam, we think that you can get even more out of your physics class than you think you can. Read these pieces of time-tested advice, follow them, and we promise you'll feel more comfortable about your class *and* about the AP exam.

1. Ignore Your Grade

This must be the most ridiculous statement you've ever read, right? But it may also be the most important of these suggestions. Never ask yourself or your teacher, "Can I have more points on this assignment?" or "Is this going to be on the test?" You'll worry so much about giving the teacher what he or she wants that you won't learn physics in the way that's best for you. Whether your grade on a class assignment is perfect or near zero, ask, "Did I really understand all aspects of these problems?"

Remember, the AP exam tests your physics knowledge. If you understand physics thoroughly, you will have no trouble at all on the AP test. But, while you may be able to argue yourself a better grade in your physics class even if your comprehension is poor, the AP readers are not so easily moved.

If you take this advice—if you really, truly ignore your grade and focus on physics—your grade will come out in the wash. You'll find that you got a very good grade after all, because you understood the subject so well. But you *won't care,* because you're not worried about your grade!

2. Don't Bang Your Head Against a Brick Wall

Our meaning here is figurative (although there are literal benefits as well). Never spend more than 10 minutes or so staring at a problem without getting somewhere. If you honestly have no idea what to do at some stage of a problem, *stop.* Put the problem away. Physics has a way of becoming clearer after you take a break.

On the same note, if you're stuck on some piddly algebra, don't spend forever trying to find what you know is a trivial mistake, say a missing negative sign or some such thing. Put the problem away, come back in an hour, and start from scratch. This will save you time in the long run.

And finally, if you've put forth a real effort, you've come back to the problem many times, and you still can't get it: relax. Ask the teacher for the solution, and allow yourself to be enlightened. You will not get a perfect score on every problem. But you don't care about your grade, remember?

3. Work with Other People

When you put a difficult problem aside for a while, it always helps to discuss the problem with others. Form study groups. Have a buddy in class with whom you are consistently comparing solutions.

Although you may be able to do all your work in every other class without help, I have never met a student who is capable of solving every physics problem on his or her own. It is not shameful to ask for help. It is not dishonest to seek assistance—as long as you're not copying or allowing a friend to carry you through the course. Group study is permitted and encouraged in virtually every physics class around the globe.

4. Ask Questions When Appropriate

We know your physics teacher may *seem* mean or unapproachable, but in reality, physics teachers do want to help you understand their subject. If you don't understand something, don't be afraid to ask. Chances are that the rest of the class has the same question. If your question is too basic or requires too much class time to answer, the teacher will tell you so.

Sometimes the teacher will not answer you directly but will give you a hint, something to think about so that you might guide yourself to your own answer. Don't interpret this as a refusal to answer your question. You must learn to think for yourself, and your teacher is helping you develop the analytical skills you need for success in physics.

5. Keep an Even Temper

A football team should not give up because they allow an early field goal. Similarly, you should not get upset at poor performance on a test or problem set. No one expects you to be perfect. Learn from your mistakes, and move on—it's too long a school year to let a single physics assignment affect your emotional state.

On the same note, however, a football team should not celebrate victory because it scores a first-quarter touchdown. You might have done well on a test, but there's the rest of the nine-month course to go. Congratulate yourself, and then concentrate on the next assignment.

6. Don't Cram

Yes, we know that you got an "A" on your history final because, after you slept through class all semester, you studied for 15 straight hours the day before the test and learned everything. And, yes, we know you are willing to do the same thing this year for physics. We warn you, both from our and from others' experience: *it won't work.* Physics is not about memorization and regurgitation. Sure, there are some equations you need to memorize, but problem-solving skills cannot be learned overnight.

Furthermore, physics is cumulative. The topics you discuss in December rely on the principles you learned in September. If you don't understand the basic relationships between motion and acceleration, how are you supposed to understand the connection between acceleration and net force, or angular acceleration and net torque?

The answer is to keep up with the course. Spend some time on physics every night, even if that time is only a couple of minutes, even if you have no assignment due the next day. Spread your "cram time" over the entire semester.

> **Exam Tip from an AP Physics Veteran**
> We had a rule in our class: no studying the night before the exam. There was no way to learn something new in the few remaining hours. The goal was to be relaxed and confident about what we did know. In fact, the class all got together for a pool party rather than a study session. And every one of us passed, with three-fourths of us getting 5s.

7. Never Forget, Physics is "Phun"

The purpose of all of these problems, experiments, and exams is to gain knowledge about physics—a deeper understanding of how the natural world works. Don't be so caught up in the grind of your coursework that you fail to say "Wow!" occasionally. Some of the things you're learning are truly amazing. Physics gives insight into some of humankind's most critical discoveries, our most powerful inventions, and our most fundamental technologies. Enjoy yourself. You have an opportunity to emerge from your physics course with wonderful and useful knowledge, and unparalleled intellectual insight. Do it.

CHAPTER 7

Strategies to Approach the Questions on the Exam

IN THIS CHAPTER

Summary: This chapter contains tips and strategies that apply to both the free-response and the multiple-choice sections of the AP Physics 1, Algebra-Based Exam. First you'll find information about the tools (calculator, equation sheet, and table of information) you can use on the exam and strategies to make the best use of these tools. Then you'll find strategies for dealing with two common types of AP Physics 1 questions: ranking questions and questions about graphs. Both of these types of questions can be found in the multiple-choice section and in the free-response section of the exam.

Key Ideas

✪ Although you can use a calculator on the exam, you should use it only when it's actually required to do a calculation. It won't help you answer the vast majority of the questions on the AP Physics 1, Algebra-Based Exam.

✪ Questions involving a ranking task often require analysis more than calculation. Ranking questions can be multiple choice or free response. For free-response questions, be sure to indicate clearly the order of your ranking, and if two of the items to be ranked are equal, be sure to indicate that, too.

✪ Graph questions are straightforward, because there are only three things you can do with a graph—take the slope, compute the area under the graph, and read one of the axes directly. Pick the right one, and you're golden.

Tools You Can Use and Strategies for Using Them

Like all AP exams, the AP Physics 1, Algebra-Based Exam consists of both multiple-choice questions (Section I) and free-response items (Section II). The three tools discussed below can be used on both sections of the exam.[1] Keep in mind that just because you *can* use these tools, it doesn't necessarily mean you *should*.

Calculator

The rules of acceptable calculators are the same as those on the SAT or the AP math exams—pretty much any available calculator is okay, including scientific and graphing calculators. Just don't use one with a QWERTY keyboard, or one that prints the answers onto paper.[2] You're not allowed to share a calculator with anyone during the exam.

Wait! Don't Touch That Calculator!

Will a calculator actually help you? Not that much. Exam authors are required to write to the specific learning objectives in the "curriculum framework."[3] Of the 140 learning objectives in the AP Physics 1 curriculum, *only 21 allow for calculation*! For 119 of 140 learning objectives, something else entirely—qualitative prediction, semiquantitative reasoning, analysis and evaluation of evidence, description of experiment, explanation, etc.—is required. You will need to calculate, but not often.

And even then, the "calculation" on the AP exam usually does not require a calculator. For example, you'll answer in symbols rather than numbers; you'll be asked to do an "order of magnitude estimate" in which only the power of 10 matters[4]; the numbers involved will be simple, like 4×2; or the choices will be so far separated that only one answer will make sense, whether or not you actually carry out the calculation.

> But seemingly every problem we did for class required solving an equation and plugging values into that equation. My teacher assigned us a bunch of problems on the computer, with programs like WebAssign. I could never have done those problems without a calculator!

That's very likely true. Being able to perform calculations is, in fact, a first step toward more difficult physics reasoning. Nevertheless, the fact remains—the AP exam will only sometimes require a calculation. And when it does, a calculator will only sometimes be necessary. So wean yourself off of the calculator. Practice approaching every problem with diagrams, facts, equations, symbols, and graphs. Only use the calculator as a last step in a homework problem. Then you'll be well prepared for the kinds of things you'll see on the AP exam.

The Table of Information

There's no need to memorize the value of constants of nature, such as the mass of an electron or the universal gravitation constant. These values will be available to you on the table of information you'll be given.

---

[1]This represents a change from previous AP Physics exams; you used to have access to a calculator only on the free response.

[2]Does anyone actually use printing calculators anymore?

[3]You can refer to the curriculum framework via the AP Physics 1 portion of the College Board's website, https://www.collegeboard.org.

[4]See Chapter 15 (Gravitation) for specific examples of order-of-magnitude estimates.

The Equation Sheet

A one-page list of many relevant equations will be available to you on both sections of the exam.[5] You will be able to see the official equation sheet ahead of time at the AP Physics 1 portion of the College Board's website (https://www.collegeboard.org). Our version of the AP equation sheet is on page 299.

Wait! Don't Touch That Equation Sheet!

Will the equation sheet actually help you? It won't help you that much. Too often, students interpret the equation sheet as an invitation to stop thinking—"Hey, they tell me everything I need to know, so I can just plug-and-chug through the exam." Nothing could be further from the truth.

First, the equation sheet will likely present most equations in a different form than you're used to, or use different notation than your textbook or your class. So what—you've already memorized the equations on the sheet. It might be reassuring to look up an equation during the exam, just to make sure you've remembered it correctly, which is really the point of the equation sheet. But beware. Use your memory as the first source of equations.

If you must use the equation sheet, *don't go fishing*! If a question asks about a velocity, don't just rush to the equation sheet and search for every equation with a V in it. You'll end up using $\rho = \frac{M}{V}$, where the V means volume, not velocity. You'd be surprised how often misguided students do this. Don't be that person.

> So you're saying I'll be given a calculator and an equation sheet, but neither will be much use. Why would I be given useless items?

Suffice it to say that many years ago, calculation was indeed the most important aspect of an AP Physics exam, so the calculator was indispensable. Back then, students were expected to memorize equations. As calculators became more sophisticated, students began to game the test by programming equations into their calculators, effectively gaining an unfair advantage. So the equation sheet was provided to everyone, negating that advantage. Now that calculation is a far less significant part of AP Physics, the calculator will only rarely be useful. But since you might need it a few times in an exam, it's still allowed.

Strategies for Questions That Involve a Ranking Task

You already know there won't be a lot of straight "calculate this" type of questions. So what kinds of questions will there be? One very different sort of question from the standard textbook end-of-chapter homework problem is the ranking question. It can be found among the multiple-choice questions of Section I or in Section II as a free-response question. Here's an example:

> Cart A takes 5 s to come to rest over a distance of 20 m. Cart B speeds up from rest, covering 10 m in 10 s. And Cart C moves at a steady speed, taking 1 s to cover 50 m. All carts have uniform acceleration. Rank the carts by the magnitude of their acceleration. If more than one cart has the same magnitude of acceleration, indicate so in your ranking.

---

[5]Once again, this is a change for AP Physics 1; the equation sheet used to be for free response only.

Notice that you are emphatically *not* asked to calculate the acceleration of each cart. Usually, a ranking task can be solved more simply with conceptual or semiquantitative reasoning than with direct calculation.

In this example, the conceptual approach is probably best. Acceleration is defined as how quickly an object changes its speed. "Magnitude" of acceleration means ignore the direction of acceleration.[6] Cart C doesn't change its speed at all, so it has the smallest acceleration. Cart A goes farther than Cart B and takes less time to do so. Since both change their speeds from or to rest, Cart A must change its speed more quickly than Cart B.

The multiple-choice ranking tasks will have answer choices formatted as inequalities: A > B > C. If two were equal, then you'd see something like A = B > C, which would mean A and B are equal, but are both greater than C.

In the free-response section, you can format your answer to a ranking task any way that is clear. For example, you could list: "(Greatest) A, B, C (least)." Don't forget to make some notation if two of the choices were equal; circle those two and write "these are equal" or something that is crystal clear.

Exam Tip from an AP Physics Veteran

For some people, semiquantitative and qualitative reasoning is much more difficult than just making calculations. You have every right to start a ranking task with several calculations! Then just rank your answers numerically. Sure, some questions will require you to explain your ranking without reference to numbers, but still, feel free to answer with numbers first, and *then* refer to the equations.

In the example above, you could make the calculation for each cart. Use the kinematics equations detailed in Chapter 10. You can calculate that Cart A has an acceleration of 1.6 m/s per second. Cart B has an acceleration of 0.2 m/s per second. And Cart C has an acceleration of zero.

How could you follow your calculation with a nonnumerical explanation, then? Look at how the equations simplified. For Carts A and B, the initial or final speed of zero meant that when you solved in variables for *a*, you got $a = \dfrac{2\Delta x}{t^2}$. Cart A has *both* a bigger distance to travel *and* a smaller time of travel. Cart A's numerator is bigger, denominator smaller, and acceleration bigger than Cart B's.

Strategies for Questions That Involve Graphs

Analyzing data in graphical form will be a skill tested regularly on the AP exam. Good graph questions are straightforward, because there are only *three things you can do with a graph*. Pick the right one, and you're golden.

When you see a graph, the first step must be to *recognize the relevant equation*. In this situation, which equation from the equation sheet relates the *y*- and *x*-variables? I truly mean the equation, not just the units of the axes. Then, the equation will lead you to one of the following three approaches.

---

[6]This can't be determined here anyway, because although Cart A has acceleration opposite its motion, and Cart B has acceleration in the same direction as its motion, we don't know which ways these two carts are moving. But who cares, for this particular question.

What are the three things we can do with this graph?

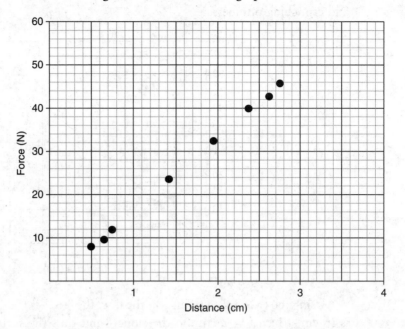

A box sits on a smooth, level surface. The box is attached to a spring. A person pushes the box across the surface, compressing the spring. For each distance the spring compresses, the force applied by the person on the box is measured.

1. Take the Slope of the Graph

You certainly understand that the slope represents the change in the y-variable divided by the change in the x-variable. But to really understand what the slope of a graph means, you can't just say, "It's the change in force divided by the change in distance." Slopes of graphs generally have a physical meaning that you must be able to recognize.

Always start with the relevant equation. If you suspect you're looking for a slope, solve the relevant equation for the y-axis variable; then compare the equation to the standard equation for a line: $y = mx + b$. Here, we're talking about the force of a spring and the distance the spring is stretched—that's covered by the equation $F = kx$. F and x are the vertical and horizontal axes, respectively.

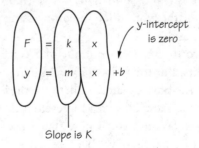

This process of circling the y-variable, circling the x-variable, and then circling the slope will work with any equation.[7] Here, the slope represents k, the spring constant for the spring. So what is the numerical value of the spring constant? You can calculate the

---

[7]And if there's a leftover term with a plus or minus sign, you'll recognize that as the b-value, the y-intercept of the graph.

slope by drawing a best-fit line, choosing two points on the line that are not data points, and crunching numbers.

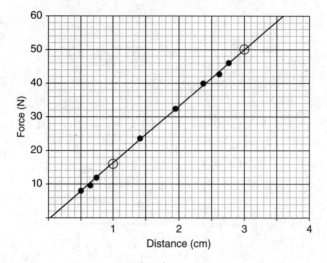

Using the two circled points on the line, the "rise" is (50 N – 16 N) = 34 N. The "run" is (3 cm – 1 cm) = 2 cm. So the slope—and thus the spring constant of the spring—is

$$\frac{34\text{N}}{2\text{cm}} = 17\,\text{N/cm.}$$

2. Calculate the Area Under the Graph

Always start with the relevant equation. The meaning of the area under the graph is generally found by looking at an equation that *multiplies* the vertical and horizontal axes. Here, that would be force times distance. Sure nough, the equation for work is at work here: $W = F \cdot \Delta x_{\parallel}$. The force applied by the person is parallel to the box's displacement, so the work done by the person is the multiplication of the vertical and horizontal axes. That means that to find the work done, take the area under the graph.

How much work did the person do in compressing the spring 3 cm? Usually, when you're taking an area under a graph on the AP exam, just estimate by breaking the graph into rectangles and triangles. In this case the graph is an obvious triangle. The area of a triangle is (½)(base)(height) = (½)(0.03 m)(50 N) = **0.75 J.** If instead the question had asked for the work done in compressing the spring 2 cm, I'd do the same calculation with 0.02 m and 34 N.

Two things to note about that calculation: First, an area under a graph, like a slope, has units. But the units are *not* "square units" or "square meters." The "area" under a graph isn't a true physical area; rather, it represents whatever physical quantity is found by multiplying the axes. This area represents the work done by the person, so it should have units of joules. Second, you'll note that I used 0.03 m rather than 3 cm in calculating the area under this graph. Why? Because without that conversion, the units of the area would have been newton centimeters (N·cm). I wanted to get the work done in the standard units of joules, equivalent to newton meters (N·m). So, I had to convert from centimeters to meters.

3. Read One of the Axes Directly

Often a question will ask for interpolation or extrapolation from a graph. For example, even though the person never used 60 N of force, how far would the spring compress if he or she *had* used 60 N? Just extend the best-fit line, as I already did, and read the horizontal axis: 3.6 cm.

Exam Tip from an AP Physics Veteran
When you draw a best-fit line, just lay your ruler down and truly draw the fit as best as you can. Never connect data point-to-point; never force the best-fit line through (0,0); never just connect the first and last data points. In fact, it's best if you extend the line of best fit as far as you can on the graph, so that you can answer extrapolation questions quickly and easily.

Finally, note that many graphs on the AP Physics 1 Exam will include real data, not just idealized lines. Be prepared to sketch lines and curves that seem to fit the general trend of the data.

CHAPTER 8

Strategies to Approach the Questions: Free-Response Section

IN THIS CHAPTER

Summary: The AP Physics 1, Algebra-Based Exam contains question types you probably have not encountered before. This chapter describes types of questions that appear only in the free-response section of the test and the most effective strategies to attack them. Included in this chapter are strategies and advice on how to approach the laboratory question, the qualitative-quantitative translation question, and the free-response questions in general.

Key Ideas

✪ The free-response section contains five questions to be answered in 90 minutes. Included will be a 12-point lab question, a 12-point qualitative-quantitative translation (QQT), and three 7-point short-answer questions. One of these 7-point problems will require a response in paragraph form.

✪ There are six simple strategies and tips you can use when answering the lab question to make sure you get all the points you deserve (see list in this chapter).

✪ If you're stuck on a QQT, you might consider skipping the part that requires description. If you solve the calculational part first, you may be better able to explain the solution in words.

✪ Remember, you're only expected to get about 70 percent of the available points to earn a top score. Don't skip any part of a free-response question—go for partial credit instead. See the list of tips for what to do and what *not* to do to get the most partial credit possible.

✪ The free-response section of the exam is read and graded by humans. At the end of this chapter is a list of tips to best communicate to the reader your understanding of the concepts being tested.

Structure of the Free-Response Section

The free-response section contains five questions to be answered in 90 minutes.[1] The five questions will *not* be all similar in length and style. Instead, the structure will be as follows, but not necessarily in this order:

- One 12-point question posed in a laboratory setting
- One 12-point qualitative-quantitative translation
- Three 7-point short-answer questions, one of which will require a response in paragraph form

The rule of thumb is to spend about two minutes per point answering each question. Start the exam by picking the problem that you can answer the most quickly—that'll probably be one of the shorter, multipart questions. You probably can do that in *less* than two minutes per point. That leaves extra time for a problem that might require more of your efforts.

Included in this chapter are separate discussions of the strategies to use in approaching qualitative-quantitative translation questions and laboratory questions. Other than understanding the appropriate pace and the strategies with which to approach these new question styles, no real extra preparation is necessary. The best thing about the free-response section of the AP exam is that you've been preparing for it all year long.

Really? I don't recall spending much time in class on test preparation.

But think about all the homework problems you've done. Every week, you probably answer a set of questions, each of which takes a few steps to solve. I'll bet your teacher is always reminding you to show your work carefully and to explain your approach in words.[2] That sounds like what's required on the AP free-response section to me.

How to Approach the Laboratory Question

It is all well and good to be able to solve problems and make predictions using the principles and equations you've learned. However, the true test of any physics theory is whether or not it *works*.

The AP Physics 1, Algebra-Based exam committee is sending a message to students and teachers that laboratory work is an indispensable part of physics. Someone who truly understands the subject must be able to design and analyze experiments. Not just one, but *two* of the seven "science practices" listed in the curriculum guide refer explicitly to experimental physics. One of the five free-response questions is guaranteed to be posed in a laboratory setting, in addition to some multiple-choice questions that have experimental elements. The point is, you cannot ignore lab-based questions.

Your ability to answer questions on experiments starts with laboratory work in your own class. It doesn't matter what experiments you do, only that you get used to working with equipment. You should know what equipment is commonly available to measure

---

[1] This has been and will be the standard form of the exam since 2015. You may hear about the different format in 2020: because of the pandemic, for *that year only* the free response contained only two questions, one QQT and one paragraph response, and thus no laboratory-specific question. In 2020 only, the exam didn't include diagrams or derivations because students had to be able to input their answers via keyboard. In 2021 and beyond, the exam has been back to the standard format described here! Digital exams may be different, but the on-paper exam has been and will be exactly as described.

[2] If your teacher *doesn't* expect you to show work clearly and explain your answer in words, do it anyway—that's good AP exam preparation, see?

various physical quantities, and how that equipment works. You should be comfortable describing in words and diagrams how you would make measurements to verify any calculation or prediction you could possibly make in answering a problem.

Now, "laboratory work" doesn't necessarily mean a 10-page, publishable report. Describing an experiment should be a three-sentence, not a three-page, process; analyzing data generally means reading a graph, as discussed in the section above. Here is an example of part of a free-response question that asks for a description of an experimental process.

Sample Laboratory Question

In the laboratory, you are given a metal block, about the size of a brick. You are also given a 2.0-m-long wooden plank with a pulley attached to one end. Your goal is to determine experimentally the coefficient of kinetic friction, μ_k, between the metal block and the wooden plank.

(a) From the list below, select the additional equipment you will need to do your experiment by checking the line to the left of each item. Indicate if you intend to use more than one of an item.

_____ 200-g mass	_____ 10-g mass	_____ spring scale
_____ motion detector	_____ balance	_____ meterstick
_____ a toy bulldozer that moves at constant speed		
_____ string		

(b) Draw a labeled diagram showing how the plank, the metal block, and the additional equipment you selected will be used to measure μ_k.

(c) Briefly outline the procedure you will use, being explicit about what measurements you need to make and how these measurements will be used to determine μ_k.

Six Simple Strategies and Tips for Answering Descriptive Laboratory Questions

Here are the most effective strategies to use to approach a free-response question that asks for a description of an experimental process like the sample question above.

1. **Follow the directions.** Sounds simple, doesn't it? When the test says, "Draw a diagram," it means you need to draw a diagram. And when it says, "Label your diagram," it means you need to label your diagram. You will likely earn some points just for these simple steps.

> **Exam Tip from an AP Physics Veteran**
> On the 1999 AP test, I forgot to label point B on a diagram, even though I obviously knew where point B was. This little mistake cost me several points.

2. **Use as few words as possible.** Answer the question, and then stop. You can lose credit for an incorrect statement, even if everything else in your answer is perfect. The best idea is to keep it simple.

3. **There is no single correct answer.** Most of the lab questions are open-ended. There might be four or more different correct approaches. Don't try to "give them the answer they're looking for." Just do something that seems to make sense—you're likely to be right.

4. **Don't assume you have to use all the stuff they give you.** It might sound fun to use a light sensor when determining the net torque on a meterstick, but really? A light sensor?

5. **Don't overthink the question.** You're not supposed to win a Nobel Prize for your work. Free-response problems should never take more than 25 minutes to complete, and usually take much less time. Don't expect to design a subatomic particle accelerator; expect to design a quick measurement that can be done in your classroom.

6. **Write for an audience at the same level of physics as you.** That means, don't state the obvious. You may assume that basic lab protocols will be followed. There's no need to tell the reader that you recorded your data carefully, and you do not need to remind the reader to wear safety goggles.

Answering Lab Questions

Now it's time to pull it all together. Here are two possible answers to the preceding sample question. Look how explicit I am about what quantities are measured, how each quantity is measured, and how μ_k is determined. But, like many physicists, I would have flunked out of art school. Your diagrams don't have to look beautiful because AP readers believe in substance over style. All that matters is that all the necessary components are there in the right places.

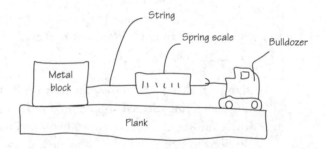

Answer #1

In the laboratory, you are given a metal block, about the size of a brick. You are also given a 2.0-m-long wooden plank with a pulley attached to one end. Your goal is to determine experimentally the coefficient of kinetic friction, μ_k, between the metal block and the wooden plank.

(a) From the list below, select the additional equipment you will need to do your experiment by checking the line to the left of each item. Indicate if you intend to use more than one of an item.

_____ 200-g mass	_____ 10-g mass	✔ spring scale
_____ motion detector	✔ balance	_____ meterstick
✔ a toy bulldozer that moves at constant speed		
✔ string		

(b) Draw a labeled diagram showing how the plank, the metal block, and the additional equipment you selected will be used to measure μ_k.

(c) Briefly outline the procedure you will use, being explicit about what measurements you need to make and how these measurements will be used to determine μ_k.

Use the balance to determine the mass, m, of the metal block. The weight of the block is mg. Attach the spring scale to the bulldozer; attach the other end of the spring scale to the metal block with string. Allow the bulldozer to pull the block at constant speed.

The block is in equilibrium. So, the reading of the spring scale while the block is moving is the friction force on the block; the normal force on the block is equal to its weight. The coefficient of kinetic friction is equal to the spring scale reading divided by the block's weight.

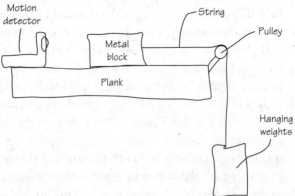

Answer #2

In the laboratory, you are given a metal block, about the size of a brick. You are also given a 2.0-m-long wooden plank with a pulley attached to one end. Your goal is to determine experimentally the coefficient of kinetic friction, μ_k, between the metal block and the wooden plank.

(a) From the list below, select the additional equipment you will need to do your experiment by checking the line to the left of each item. Indicate if you intend to use more than one of an item.

    ✔ 200-g mass   ✔ 10-g mass   _____ spring scale
(several)   (several)

    ✔ motion detector   ✔ balance   _____ meterstick

    _____ a toy bulldozer that moves at constant speed

    ✔ string

(b) Draw a labeled diagram showing how the plank, the metal block, and the additional equipment you selected will be used to measure μ_k.

(c) Briefly outline the procedure you will use, being explicit about what measurements you need to make and how these measurements will be used to determine μ_k.

Determine the mass, m, of the block with the balance. The weight of the block is mg. Attach a string to the block, and pass the string over the pulley. Hang masses from the other end of the string, changing the amount of mass until the block can move across the plank at constant speed. Use the motion detector to verify that the speed of the block is as close to constant as possible.

The block is in equilibrium. So, the weight of the hanging masses is equal to the friction force on the block; the normal force on the block is equal to its weight. The coefficient of kinetic friction is thus equal to the weight of the hanging masses divided by the block's weight.

The Qualitative-Quantitative Translation (QQT)

While physics is *not* about numbers (see Chapter 2), physicists routinely plug values into relevant equations to produce numerical predictions such as "the reading on the scale will be 550 N." In AP language, that's *quantitative* reasoning.

Just as routinely, though, physicists use equations as the basis for a less-specific conceptual prediction. Without using any numbers, it's usually possible to look at the features of an equation—what variables are in the numerator or denominator, what's squared or square rooted, what is added or subtracted—and determine something like "the reading on the scale will increase." In AP language, that's *qualitative* reasoning.

One of the five free-response items on the AP Physics 1 Exam is called a "qualitative-quantitative translation question," abbreviated as QQT. It will generally ask you first for qualitative reasoning, next for quantitative reasoning, and *then* it will expect you to explain in words how the different aspects of your solutions relate to each other. If you think of algebra as the language of physics, the QQT will ask you to translate from algebra to English.

An Important Strategy for Solving QQTs

The fact is, by the time they're through a full year of physics, most first-time physics students are far more comfortable with numerical calculation than they are with verbal description of physics concepts. Partly that's because most physics classes emphasize calculation more than writing; partly it's because people are taught to calculate in elementary school but are rarely asked to write in words how and why a calculation worked.

Play to your strengths. If the first part requires description, skip it and go to the part of the problem that asks for the calculation. Do the calculation. Write out every step carefully, annotating your solution with words explaining the point of each step. Then go back to the parts that require qualitative reasoning. Now, since you've approached the situation the "easier" way, you should have a good clue as to why you did the mathematical steps you did.

The actual qualitative-quantitative translation question will be one of the longer questions on the exam, a 12-point question. Usually only part of the question will directly ask about translating calculation into words, and vice versa. Here's an example of the actual translation portion of such a question.

Sample QQT

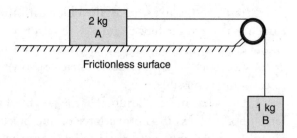

Two blocks are connected over a light, frictionless pulley, as shown. Block A of mass 2 kg is on a frictionless surface; Block B of mass 1 kg hangs freely. The blocks are released from rest. (a) After the blocks are released, is the tension in the rope greater than, less than, or equal to the weight of Block B? Justify your answer in words, without equations or calculations. (b) Calculate the tension in the rope after the blocks are released.

Answering the QQT

Understand that you might see several other parts, say, asking for a free-body diagram of each block, or asking about the behavior of the blocks after Block B hits the ground, or whatever. For now, though, let's just focus on the true translation in Parts (a) and (b).

Even though Part (a) specifically forbids equations and calculations, try approaching it like a calculation problem, anyway. Part (b) asks for the actual value of the tension in the rope. Take care of that first.

Treating the two blocks as a single system, the net force is the 10-N hanging weight. The mass of this two-block system is 3 kg, so by $F_{net} = ma$, the system's acceleration is 10 N/3 kg = 3.3 m/s per second.

Next, consider a system as *just* Block A. The only force acting on Block A is the tension in the rope, so that's the net force. The tension then is the mass of Block A times its acceleration, (2 kg)(3.3 m/s per second) = **6.6 N.**

There's the answer to Part (b), with a nicely explained calculation. What about Part (a)? Well, we at least know the answer from our calculations—the tension is *less than* the 10-N weight of Block B. But now we need to justify the answer without doing the calculation. How do we do that? Describe why the calculation came out as it did, without doing the actual calculation. Be specific about what values are bigger, smaller, or the same throughout the calculation.

Correct Answer #1: "Block A has the same acceleration as the two-block system but less mass than the whole system. Block A experiences a smaller net force than the whole system. The tension is the net force on Block A; the weight of Block B is the net force on the whole system. The tension is less than Block B's weight."

To take a different approach, we know that force problems are best approached with free-body diagrams before plugging in any numbers to equations. An alternative explanation might be to look at a free-body diagram of just Block B.

Correct Answer #2: "The tension pulls up on Block B, and the weight pulls down. Since Block B has a downward acceleration—it speeds up and moves down—the downward forces must be bigger than the upward forces. So the tension is less than the weight."

In either case, you're using words to describe the way you would solve the problem if you were doing a calculation. That's translating from quantitative reasoning to qualitative reasoning—the very definition of a QQT.

What Do the Exam Readers Look For?

The key to doing well on the free-response section is to realize that, first and foremost, these problems test your understanding of physics; next, they test your ability to communicate that understanding. The purpose of the free-response questions is not to see how good your algebra skills are, or how many fancy-sounding technical terms you know, or how many obscure ideas you can regurgitate. You already know from Chapter 1 that the free-response section of the AP Physics 1 Exam is graded by human readers, not a computer. All I'm going to do in this section is give you some important suggestions about how you can best communicate to the reader that you understand the concepts being tested.

All free-response questions are graded by physics teachers who must carefully follow a "rubric" for each question. A rubric is a grading guide—it specifies how points are awarded, including the elements of an answer necessary for both full and partial credit.

You Cannot "Game" the Rubric

It's tempting to try to find that "One Weird Trick" that will guarantee you an extra point or two on the exam. You and your teacher might look at previous years' rubrics[1] and think you see a pattern. But I warn you: Tricks don't work to solve AP Physics 1 problems.

Each rubric is unique. It's created originally by the author of the test question, revised by the exam development committee, adjusted by table leaders based on actual student responses and feedback from colleagues, and finalized mere hours before the reading begins. The College Board does not have hard and fast rules about how a rubric should be written. Each table leader has wide latitude to adjust the rubric so that it awards credit for good physics, and so it does *not* award credit for bad physics.

Rubrics Provide Ample Opportunity for Partial Credit

Recall that you're only expected to get about 70 percent of the available points to earn a top score. You're not supposed to answer every problem perfectly; you're expected to communicate as much physics understanding as possible. Rubrics are designed to award partial credit for answers that are correct but incomplete or that are essentially correct with only minor mistakes.

Thus, your strategy should always be to make a reasonable attempt at each part of every problem. Don't fret that you don't know how to do everything perfectly; just give the best answer you can, and expect to earn credit in proportion to how well you're explaining what you *do* know.

Here are some hints regarding partial credit:

- If you can't solve Part (a) of a multipart problem, don't skip parts (b) through (e)! Sometimes you'll get everything else perfect if you just move along.
- If the answer to Part (b) depends on the answer to Part (a), it's okay to say "I didn't get Part (a), but pretend the answer was 25 m/s." As long as your answer isn't absolutely silly,[2] you will get full or close to full credit. Rubrics are generally designed not to penalize the same wrong answer twice.
- You're not likely to get credit for a bare answer, or an answer you figured out but didn't explain. Virtually every AP Physics 1 problem requires verbal or (occasionally) mathematical justification.

> **Exam Tip from an AP Physics Veteran**
> When I first started physics class, I became frustrated that I didn't get full credit on questions where I thought I understood the right answer. I tried to argue with my teacher after a test: "Here, let me tell you what I was trying to say, so you can give me these points that I deserve." My teacher told me, "So, are you allowed to go to Kansas City where the AP exam is graded, and go along with your test from reader to reader to tell them what you really meant?" From then on, I started being more careful to explain my answers thoroughly on homework problems and on tests. I got an easy 5 on the AP exam.

---

[2] You can find rubrics to old AP Physics exams on the College Board's AP Central website. Be a bit careful with rubrics from old AP Physics B questions, those from 2014 and before; and be careful with rubrics from the 2020 pandemic year. Although the principles of grading to a rubric have not changed with the switch to AP Physics 1, the design of the rubrics *has* changed somewhat.

[3] Like saying that a person not named "Clark Kent" was running 25 m/s.

You should also be aware of some things that will *not* get you partial credit:

- You *cannot* earn partial credit if you write multiple answers to a single question. If AP readers see that you've written two different answers, they are instructed to grade the one that is incorrect, even if the other is correct. If you're not sure of the answer, you can't hedge your bets.

- You *cannot* earn "extra" credit. Readers are not allowed to say, "Wow, that's the most complete answer I've ever heard. Here's +1." Don't include unnecessary information. It won't help, and if you make a misstatement, you will actually lose points. Answer the question fully, and then stop.

Final Advice About the Free-Response Questions

Here are some final tips and advice regarding the free-response section of the test:

- Annotate any calculations with words. Explain why you're using the equation you're using, and show the values you're plugging in.
- If you don't know exactly how to solve part of a problem, it's okay to explain your thinking process as best you can. For example, "I know the centripetal force points toward the center of the satellite's orbit, and I know it's a gravitational force. But the centripetal acceleration cannot be calculated because I don't know the value of this centripetal force." Such an answer might earn partial credit, even if you were supposed to do a calculation.
- Don't write a book. Even a question that asks for a paragraph response should be answered in a few sentences, not a few pages. Get straight to the point.
- If you make a mistake, cross it out. If your work is messy, circle your key points or your final answer so that it's easy to find. Basically, make sure the readers know what you want them to grade and what you want them to ignore.
- If you're stuck on a free-response question, try another one. Question 5 might well be easier for you than Question 1. Get the easy points first, and only after that, try to get the harder points with your remaining time.
- Put units on every numerical answer.
- Don't be afraid to draw—diagrams, graphs, or whatever—in response to a question. These may be useful elements of an explanation, especially on the occasions when you're forbidden from using numbers or equations. Be sure to label diagrams and graphs.
- If your approach is so complicated that it's not doable in 15 to 20 minutes with minimal calculator use, you're doing it wrong. Look for a new way to solve the problem, or just skip it and move on.

CHAPTER 9

Strategies to Approach the Questions: Multiple-Choice Section

IN THIS CHAPTER

Summary: Even the multiple-choice section of the AP Physics 1, Algebra-Based Exam contains types of questions you probably have not encountered before. This chapter contains strategies and tips to attack the multiple-choice questions, including the new "multiple-correct" questions.

Key Ideas

✪ The multiple-choice section contains 50 questions, which require the same sorts of in-depth reasoning as the free-response questions.

✪ There's no guessing penalty, so be sure you mark an answer to every item.

✪ Some questions will be identified as "multiple-correct" questions. For these, you need to choose exactly two answers. There's no partial credit—you have to mark *both* of the correct answers, and *neither* of the wrong answers, to earn your point.

✪ To prepare for the test, practice pacing yourself using multiple-choice problems, and for the ones you miss, write explanations or justifications for the correct answers. This will truly allow you to learn from your mistakes.

✪ The point is, in preparing for the exam it is way too easy to fool yourself into thinking you understand a problem if you look at the solutions too soon.

Multiple-Choice Questions

The multiple-choice section comes first. You have 90 minutes to answer 50 questions. Each question will include four choices (not five, as on the AP Physics C exam). There's no guessing penalty, so be sure you mark an answer to every item.

Before even thinking about strategies, understand that multiple-choice questions require the same sort of in-depth reasoning as do the free-response questions. The only difference is that you're not expected to write out justification for your answers. You will see graphs, calculations, lab questions, ranking tasks, and explanations—everything that you're used to from your physics class and everything that you could see on the free-response section. Don't try to breeze through or to "game" the test. Just answer carefully, justifying each answer in your mind with a fact, equation, or calculation.

You have nearly two minutes per multiple-choice question. Some answers will be obvious; knock these out quickly, so that you leave more time to look at the more complicated questions.

Multiple-Correct: A New Question Type

Probably every multiple-choice test you've ever taken has asked you to pick the *best* answer from four or five choices for each problem. Well, that's gonna change.

A subsection of five questions on the multiple-choice section will include "multiple-correct" questions. For these, you will be asked to choose exactly two answers. There's no partial credit here—you have to mark *both* of the correct answers, and *neither* of the wrong answers, to earn your point.

These multiple-correct items replace the old-style questions with roman numerals I, II, and III. Also note that AP Physics 1, multiple-choice questions will never ask something like, "Which of the following is *not* correct?" The College Board decided that multiple-correct questions were far easier to read and understand than the more confusing styles of past questions. This is supposed to be a physics test, after all, not a set of Hobbit-style riddles.

You will always know which questions are "multiple correct" as opposed to "single answer." The only change to your approach on multiple-correct questions should be that you can't eliminate the three wrong answers to find the one right answer—you have to consider each of the four choices on its own merits.

> **Example:** A cart on a track is moving to the right and has been moving to the
> right for the last 2 s. Choose the correct statements about physical quantities
> related to the cart. Select two answers.
> (A) The cart's displacement vector for the 2 s of motion is directed to the right.
> (B) The cart's instantaneous velocity vector is directed to the right.
> (C) The net force acting instantaneously on the cart is directed to the right.
> (D) The cart's average acceleration over the 2 s of motion is directed to the right.

This question requires just a bit more mental discipline than a standard multiple-choice item. Start by looking at choice (A). Displacement means, where does the cart end up in relation to its starting point? The cart ended up to the right of where it started, so the displacement is to the right. Mark choice (A).

In standard multiple-choice questions, you'd be done, dusted, and reading the next question by now. Not here, though. Keep reading. (B) The direction of instantaneous velocity is simply the direction that the cart is moving in right now. That's also to the right. Also mark choice (B).

Then look at (C) and (D). The direction of acceleration cannot be determined unless we know whether the cart is speeding up or slowing down. Net force is always in the direction of acceleration; because the acceleration direction is unknown, so is the net force direction. Don't mark choices (C) or (D).

Preparing for the Multiple-Choice Section of the Test

Pacing Yourself

Your physics teacher has access to all sorts of multiple-choice questions that are at least somewhat similar to what you'll see on the AP Physics 1 Exam. Several nearly full practice AP Physics 1 exams are available to teachers via their Course Audit account on Collegeboard.com. But you and your teacher shouldn't limit yourselves just to authentic AP Physics 1 questions. Items from released AP Physics B exams since the mid 2000s are usually close to the style of AP Physics 1. You likely have or will see questions from these sources on your in-class tests, your semester exam, or in practice packets. Use your in-class multiple-choice questions as preparation for the real AP Physics 1 Exam.

Whatever you do, *don't* look at a big set of multiple-choice questions at your leisure, trying them and looking up the answers. Instead, take a set of multiple-choice questions as an authentic test. The real exam gives 50 questions in 90 minutes; so you should attempt 25 questions in 45 minutes, for example, or 16 questions in 30 minutes.

Do enough of these practice tests, and you'll learn the correct pace. Are you getting to all the questions? If not, you're going to need to decide your strengths and weaknesses. You'll figure out before the real exam which types of problems you want to attempt first. You'll learn through practice when you're lingering too long on a single problem.

Test Corrections—The Best Way to Prepare for the Test

When you're done with a practice test, *don't* look up the solutions yet. Have someone else check your answers. For each problem you got wrong, talk to a friend about the problem. Either alone or with your friend's help, write out a justification for the correct answer as if this were the free-response exam. Take about half a page for each justification. Have someone else, like your teacher, check your work again, marking the justifications that still are incomplete or incorrect. Do these *again*, even if you need a lot of help.

The point is, in preparing for the exam it is way too easy to fool yourself into thinking you understand a problem if you look at the solutions too soon. That's why your physics class gives tests—not just to put a grade on the report card, but to give you authentic feedback on what you know, and what you need to work on. If you are thorough and careful in correcting your in-class and practice tests, you will find your multiple-choice scores improving rapidly. (But if you show up on exam day without ever taking a practice exam and doing corrections, you will be doing *a lot* of guessing.)

Final Strategies for the Multiple-Choice Section

Here are some final strategies and advice that will help you score higher on the multiple-choice section of the AP Physics 1 Exam:
- Never try to "game" the test. Don't approach a question thinking, "What do they[1] want me to say?" There is no trick, no ulterior motive in the question. Just show your physics knowledge, or take your best guess.

---

[1]Who do you mean by "they" anyway? The test is written by some of the country's best physics teachers. Their job is to test whether you know physics, not to show how clever they are, not to embarrass you, and not to play "gotcha!"

- The multiple-choice questions will not necessarily start easy and get harder (unlike those on the SAT, which start easy and get hard). If you suspect from your practice that you may be pressed for time, know that the problems on your strong topics may be scattered throughout the exam. Problem 50 may be easier for you than problem 5, so pace yourself so that you can get through the whole test and at least get all the easy answers right.
- If you don't see a direct approach to answering a question, look at the choices. They might give you a hint. For example, one of the choices might be way too fast for a car to be moving, or one of the explanations of a concept might contain an obvious error. Then, great, you can eliminate the obvious "stupidicism," guess from the other choices, and move on. Don't dwell on a single question.
- There are no trick questions on this exam. An answer choice cannot "deny the stem." This means, if a problem asks "Which of the following pieces of evidence shows that momentum is conserved in this situation?" one answer choice will not be "Momentum wasn't even conserved."
- Often a good guess is evidence of good physics instincts. Don't be afraid to make a guess based on your intuition. If you've been practicing physics problems appropriately and you've been correcting your practice tests, then your instincts will be finely honed by exam time. What you call a "guess" may well be much better than a shot in the dark.

STEP 4

Review the Knowledge You Need to Score High

CHAPTER 10

How Things Move[1]

IN THIS CHAPTER

Summary: The entire goal of motion analysis is to describe, calculate, and predict where an object is, how fast it's moving, and how much its speed is changing. In this chapter you'll review two separate approaches to make these predictions and descriptions: graphs and algebra.

Definitions

- ✪ The cart's **position** (x) tells where the cart is on the track.
- ✪ The cart's **speed** (v) tells how fast the cart is moving.[2]
- ✪ **Acceleration** (a) tells how much the object's speed changes in one second. When an object speeds up, its acceleration is in the direction of its motion; when an object slows down, its acceleration is opposite the direction of its motion.
- ✪ **Displacement** (Δx) tells how far the object ends up away from its starting point, regardless of any motion in between starting and ending positions.
- ✪ The graphical analysis of motion includes **position-time graphs** and **velocity-time graphs**. On a position-time graph, the slope is the object's speed, and the object's position is read from the vertical axis. For velocity-time graphs, the speed is read from the vertical axis, and the slope is the object's acceleration.

---

[1]We're discussing motion with constant acceleration; that covers pretty much all motion in AP Physics 1 except things attached to springs.

[2]Strictly speaking, speed is the magnitude—the amount—of the velocity vector. Velocity tells how fast something moves, as well as in which direction it moves. I tend to use "speed" and "velocity" interchangeably, especially in this unit; the distinction between the two is not important here.

- ✪ The **five principal motion variables** are:
  v_0 initial velocity
  v_f final velocity
  Δx displacement
  a acceleration
  t time
- ✪ In any case of accelerated motion, when three of the five principal motion variables are known, the remaining variables can be solved for using the kinematic equations.
- ✪ **Free fall** means no forces other than the object's weight are acting on the object.
- ✪ A **projectile** is an object in free fall, but it isn't falling in a straight vertical line. To approach a projectile problem, make *two* motion charts: one for vertical motion and one for horizontal motion.

Introduction to Motion in a Straight Line

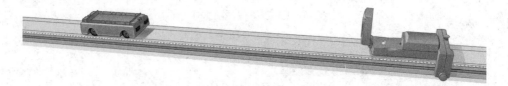

Pretty much all motion problems can be demonstrated with a cart on a track, like in the diagram above. The motion detector can read the location of the cart up to 50 times each second. This detector can make graphs of position or velocity versus time.

The entire goal of motion analysis is to describe, calculate, and predict where the cart is; how fast it's moving; and how much its speed is changing. You'll use two separate approaches to make these predictions and descriptions: graphs and algebra.

Graphical Analysis of Motion

Before you start any analysis, tell yourself which kind of graph you're looking at. The most common mistake in studying motion graphs is to interpret a velocity-time graph as a position-time graph, or vice versa.

Position-Time Graphs

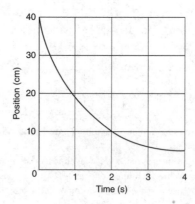

Example 1: The preceding position-time graph represents the cart on the track. The motion detector is located at position $x = 0$; the positive direction is to the left.

An AP exam question could ask all sorts of questions about this cart. How should they be approached? Use these facts, and reason from them.

FACT: In a position-time graph, the object's position is read from the vertical axis.

Look at the vertical axis in Example 1. At the beginning of the motion, the cart is located 40 cm to the left of the detector.[3] After 2 s, the cart is located 10 cm left of the detector. Therefore, in the first 2 s of its motion, the cart moved 30 cm to the right.

FACT: In a position-time graph, the object's speed is the slope of the graph. The steeper the slope, the faster the object moves. If the slope is a front slash (/), the movement is in the positive direction; if the slope is a backslash (\), the movement is in the negative direction.

Wait a second, how can I tell the slope of a curved graph? Just look at how the graph is sloped at one specific place on the graph. If I want to know how fast the object is moving after 2 seconds of motion, I take the slope drawn in the following figure.

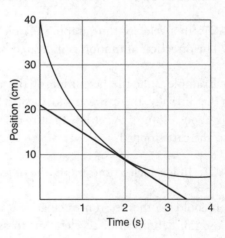

Mathematically, this means you divide (change in y-value)/(change in x-value) to get a speed that's a bit more than 6 cm/s. The exact calculation is not something to obsess over. It's more important to think in terms of comparisons.

You're not often going to be asked "Calculate the speed of the cart at $t = 2$ s." Instead, you'll be asked to describe the motion of the cart in words and to justify your answer. When you describe motion, use normal language that your grandparents would understand. Avoid technical terms like "acceleration" and "negative." Instead, say "slowing down" or "moving to the right." Justify your answer with direct reference to the facts in chapter 4.

Referring back to Example 1, because the slope was steeper at earlier times and shallower at later times, the cart must be slowing down. The car is moving to the right the whole time, because the slope is always a backslash.

---

[3]Why not 40 cm to the right of the detector? Because the position value is +40 cm and the positive direction is left.

Velocity-Time Graphs

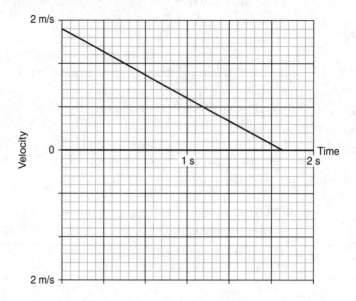

Example 2: The preceding velocity-time graph represents a different cart on the track. The positive direction is to the left.

FACT: In a velocity-time graph, the object's speed is read from the vertical axis. The direction of motion is indicated by the sign on the vertical axis.

In Example 2, at the beginning of the motion, the vertical axis reads 1.8 m/s. This means that initially, the cart was moving 1.8 m/s to the left. After one second, the cart was moving about 0.8 m/s. A bit less than two seconds into the motion, the vertical axis reads zero, so the cart stopped.

FACT: In a velocity-time graph, the object's acceleration is the slope of the graph.

You could do the rise/run calculation to find the amount of the acceleration, or you could use the definition of acceleration to see that the object lost 1 m/s of speed in one second, making the acceleration 1 m/s per second.[4] The cart in Example 2 was slowing down and moving to the left. When an object slows down, its acceleration is opposite the direction of its motion; this cart has an acceleration to the right.

The Mistake

Acceleration is **_not_** the same thing as speed or velocity. Speed says how fast something moves; acceleration says how quickly speed changes. Acceleration doesn't say anything about which way something is moving, unless you know whether the thing is speeding up or is slowing down.

---

[4]Textbooks and problems on the AP exam will write this as 1 m/s². Well, that's silly—what the heck is a "second squared," anyway? When you see that notation, read it as "meters per second per second." I suggest you always write the units of acceleration as "m/s per second." Then you'll be far less likely to make "The Mistake."

Someone who says, "This car has an acceleration of 4 m/s per second, so it is moving at about a jogging pace," has made "The Mistake." The car is speeding up or slowing down by 4 m/s every second; the car could well be an Indy 500 racecar traveling 94 m/s right now, but only 90 m/s a second later.

Someone who says "The cart in Figure 2 has a negative acceleration, so it is moving to the right" has made "The Mistake." An acceleration to the right means either speeding up and moving right, or slowing down and moving left. While the cart's acceleration is negative—after all, the slope of the line is a backslash—the car was slowing down, making the velocity's direction opposite the acceleration's direction. The acceleration is right, and the velocity is left.

It takes a lot of practice to avoid "The Mistake." Just continually remind yourself of the meaning of acceleration (how much an object's speed changes in one second), and you'll get there.

FACT: The object's displacement is given by the area between the graph and the horizontal axis. The location of the object can't be determined from a velocity-time graph; only how far the object ended up from its starting point can be determined.

To find how far the cart in Example 2 moved, take the area of the triangle in the graph,[5] giving about 1.6 m. Since the cart's velocity as read from the vertical axis was positive that whole time, and the positive direction is left, the cart ended up 1.6 m left of where it started. But exactly where it started, no one knows.

Algebraic Analysis of Motion

Example 3: A model rocket is launched straight upward with an initial speed of 50 m/s. It speeds up with a constant upward acceleration of 2.0 m/s per second until its engines stop at an altitude of 150 m.

Sometimes you'll be asked to analyze motion from a description and not a graph. Start your analysis by defining a positive direction and clearly stating the start and the end of the motion you're considering. For example, take the upward direction as positive,[6] and consider from the launch to when the engines stop.

Next, *make a chart* giving the values of the five principal motion variables. Include a plus or minus sign on every one (except time—a negative time value means you're in a Star Trek–style movie). If a variable isn't given in the problem, leave that variable blank.

The Five Principal Motion Variables for Your Chart

v_0 initial velocity
v_f final velocity
Δx displacement
a acceleration
t time

---

[5] The area of a triangle is (1/2) base × height.

[6] Could I have called the downward direction positive? Sure. Then signs of displacement, velocity, and acceleration would all be switched.

For Example 3, the chart looks like this:

v_0	+50 m/s
v_f	
Δx	+150 m
a	+2.0 m/s per second
t	

The acceleration is positive because the rocket was speeding up; therefore, acceleration is in the same direction as the motion, which was upward. Upward was defined as the positive direction here.

FACT: In any case of accelerated motion when three of the five principal motion variables are known, the remaining variables can be solved for using the kinematic equations.

In Example 3, we know three of the five motion variables; therefore, we can find the others, and the physics is *done*.

Whoa there. Um, how is the physics "done"? Don't we have to plug the numbers into the kinematic equations, which incidentally you haven't mentioned yet?

Well, remember the AP Physics 1 revolution: While you will occasionally be asked, say, to calculate how much time the engines run for, you'll just as often be asked something that doesn't involve calculation. For example, "Is it possible to determine the running time of the engines?" Or, "When the engines have run for half of their total run time, is the rocket at a height greater than, less than, or equal to 75 m?"[7]

More to the point, actually doing the math here is, well, a *math* skill, not a physics skill. As long as your answers are reasonable—a model rocket will likely burn for a few seconds, not a few thousand seconds—the exam is likely to award close to full, or sometimes even full, credit for a correct chart and for recognizing the correct equation to use.

FACT: To calculate the missing values in a motion chart, use the three kinematic equations listed as follows. Choose whichever equation works mathematically. Never solve a quadratic equation. If the math becomes overly complicated, try solving for a different missing variable first.

Kinematic Equations

1. $v_f = v_0 + at$

2. $\Delta x = v_0 t + \dfrac{1}{2} at^2$

3. $v_f^2 = v_0^2 + 2a\Delta x$

---

[7] The answer is *less than* 75 m. The rocket is speeding up throughout the time when the engines burn. In the second half of the burn time, the rocket is (on average) moving faster, and so it covers more distance.

Continuing with Example 3, we can use equation (3) to solve for the final velocity of the rocket[8]; this is about 56 m/s.[9] Then we can use equation (1) to get the time before the engines shut off, which is 3 seconds. If you had tried to use equation (2) to solve for time, you would have gotten a quadratic; that's why I said to use equation (3) and then (1).

Objects in Free Fall

FACT: When an object is in free fall, its acceleration is 10 m/s per second[10] toward the ground. "Free fall" means no forces other than the object's weight are acting on the object.

Let's do more with the rocket in Example 3. When the engines stop, the rocket is moving upward at 56 m/s. The rocket doesn't just stop on a dime. It keeps moving upward, but it slows down, losing 10 m/s of speed every second.

Try making a chart for the motion from when the engines stop to when the rocket reaches the peak of its flight. We'll keep the positive direction as upward.

v_0 $+56$ m/s

v_f 0 (The peak of flight is when the object stops to turn around.)

Δx

a -10 m/s per second (There is negative acceleration because free-fall acceleration is always *down*.)

t

Three of the five variables are known so the physics is *done*.

Now, be careful that you keep grounded in what's physically happening, not in the algebra. For example, you might be asked for the maximum height that the rocket in Example 3 reaches.

Good job recognizing that you need equation (3) to solve for Δx. Dropping the units during the calculation, that gives $0^2 = 56^2 + 2(-10)(\Delta x)$. Solving with a calculator you get about 160 m for Δx.

Wait a second! Think what the 160 m answer means—that's the distance the rocket goes between when the engines stop and when the rocket reaches its highest height. That's not the height above the ground, just the additional height after the engines stop! The actual maximum height is this 160 m, plus the 150 m that the rocket gained with its engines on, for a total of 310 m.

If you were blindly plugging numbers into equations, you would have totally missed the meaning behind these different distances. The AP Physics 1 Exam will repeatedly ask targeted questions that check to see whether you understand physical meaning. Calculation? Pah. In comparison, it's not so important.

Projectile Motion

A *projectile* is defined as an object in free fall. But this object doesn't have to be moving in a straight line. What if the object were launched at an angle? Then you treat the horizontal and vertical components of its motion separately.

---

[8]This calculation requires a calculator, of course: $v_f^2 = (50\ \text{m/s})^2 + 2(2\ \text{m/s per second})(150\ \text{m})$. See, here's another reason you're probably not going to have to actually carry out this math—you're not likely to need a calculator more than a few times on the entire exam.

[9]Not 55.67764363 m/s. Don't make me ask your chemistry teacher to talk to you about significant figures again. Just use two or three figures on all values, and we'll all be happy.

[10]No, stop it with the 9.8 m/s per second. The College Board is very clear that you can and should use a free-fall acceleration of 10 m/s per second. Really. Limited calculator use, remember?

Example 4: A ball is shot out of a cannon pointed at an angle of 30° above the horizontal. The ball's initial speed is 25 m/s. The ball lands on ground that is level with the cannon.

FACT: A projectile has no horizontal acceleration and so moves at constant speed horizontally. A projectile is in free fall, so its vertical acceleration is 10 m/s per second downward.

To approach a projectile problem, make *two* motion charts: one for vertical motion and one for horizontal motion.

FACT: To find the vertical component of a velocity at an angle, multiply the speed by the sine of the angle. To find the horizontal component of a velocity at an angle, multiply the speed by the cosine of the angle. This always works, as long as the angle is measured from the horizontal.

Here are the two charts for the ball's motion in Example 4. Consider up and right to be the positive directions. Let's consider the motion while the ball is in free fall—that means, starting right after the ball was shot, and ending right before the ball hits the ground. Note that the initial vertical velocity is (25 m/s)(sin 30°) = 13 m/s. The initial horizontal velocity is (25 m/s)(cos 30°) = 22 m/s. You needed to use your calculator to get these values.

Vertical	**Horizontal**
$v_0 + 22$ m/s	$v_0 + 13$ m/s
v_f	v_f
Δx^0	Δx
a −10 m/s per second	a 0
t	t

Two entries here are tricky. Remember that displacement only means the distance traveled start to end, regardless of what happens in between. Well, this ball landed on "level ground." That means that the ball ends up at the same vertical height from which it was shot; it didn't end up any higher or lower than it started. Thus, vertical displacement is zero.

Second, the final vertical velocity is unknown, not zero. Sure, once the ball hits the ground it stops; but then it's not in free fall anymore. The "final" velocity here is the velocity in the instant before the ball hits the ground.

FACT: The horizontal and vertical motion charts for a projectile must use the same value for time.

The vertical chart is completely solvable, because three of the five variables are identified. Once the time of flight is calculated from the vertical chart, that time can be plugged into the horizontal chart, and *voila*, we have three of five horizontal variables identified; the chart can be completed.

› Practice Problems

Note: Extra drills on describing motion based on graphs can be found in Chapter 18.

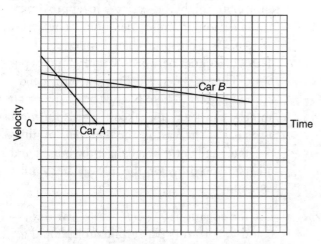

1. The preceding velocity-time graphs represent the motion of two cars, Car A and Car B. Justify all answers thoroughly.

   (a) Which car is moving faster at the start of the motion?

   (b) Which car ends up farther from its starting point?

   (c) Which car experiences a greater magnitude of acceleration?

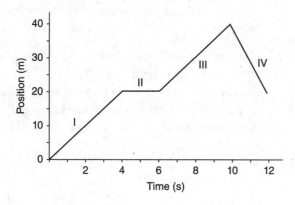

2. The following questions refer to the preceding position-time graph, which is the readout of an eastward-pointing motion detector. Justify all answers thoroughly.

   (a) Rank the speed of the object in each of the four labeled regions of the graph, from fastest to slowest. If the object has the same speed in two or more regions, indicate so in your ranking.

   (b) What total distance did the object travel in the 12 s, including all parts of the motion?

   (c) How far from the object's starting point did the object end up after the 12 s?

   (d) Which of the following objects could reasonably perform this motion?
   (A) A baby crawling
   (B) A sprinter
   (C) A car on the freeway
   (D) A jet airplane during takeoff
   (E) An amoeba in a petri dish

3. A ball is dropped from rest near Earth. Neglect air resistance.[11] Justify all answers thoroughly.

   (a) About how far will the ball fall in 3 s?

   (b) The same ball is dropped from rest by an astronaut on the moon, where the free-fall acceleration is one-sixth that on Earth. In 3 s, will the ball on the moon fall:
   (A) One-sixth as far as the ball on Earth
   (B) One-36th as far as the ball on Earth
   (C) The same distance as the ball on Earth
   (D) Six times as far as the ball on Earth
   (E) Thirty-six times as far as the ball on Earth

Projectile	Initial Horizontal Speed (m/s)	Initial Vertical Speed (m/s)	Time of Flight (s)
A	40.0	29.4	6.00
B	60.0	19.6	4.00
C	50.0	24.5	5.00
D	80.0	19.6	4.00

Data Table

4. Four projectiles, A, B, C, and D, were launched from and returned to level ground. The preceding data table shows the initial horizontal speed, initial vertical speed, and time of flight for each projectile. Justify all answers thoroughly.

   (a) Rank the projectiles by the horizontal distance traveled while in the air.

   (b) Rank the projectiles by the maximum vertical height reached.

   (c) Rank the projectiles by the magnitude of their acceleration while in the air.

---

[11]*Always* neglect air resistance, unless it is extremely, abundantly, and unambiguously clear from the problem's context that air resistance is important (i.e., talking about "terminal velocity").

> Solutions to Practice Problems

1. (a) On a velocity-time graph, speed is read off of the vertical axis. At time = 0, Car A has a higher vertical axis reading than Car B, so Car A is moving faster.

   (b) Displacement is determined by the area under a velocity-time graph. Car A's graph is a small triangle; Car B's graph is a trapezoid of obviously larger area. Both cars' graphs are always above the horizontal axis, so both cars move in the same direction the whole time; Car B moves farther away from its starting point.

   (c) Acceleration is the slope of the velocity-time graph. Car A's graph is steeper, so its acceleration is larger. (Sure, the slope of Car A's graph is negative, but that just means acceleration is in the negative direction, whatever that is; the question asks for the "magnitude" of the acceleration, meaning the amount, regardless of direction.)

2. (a) IV > I = III > II. Speed is the steepness on a position-time graph, without reference to direction (i.e., whether the slope is positive or negative). Segment IV is steepest. Segments I and III seem to be the same steepness. Segment II has 0 slope, so it represents an object that doesn't move.

   (b) It's a position-time graph, so read the vertical axis to figure out where the object is at any time. The object travels from its original position at $x = 0$ m to $x = 40$ m, then backtracks another 20 m. The total distance traveled is 60 m.

   (c) It's a position-time graph, so read the vertical axis to figure out where the object is at the beginning and after 12 s. At the beginning the object was at $x = 0$ m; after 12 s, the object was at position $x = 20$ m. The object traveled 20 m. (If your justification didn't explicitly mention that the object started at $x = 0$ m, or that you must find the *difference* between the final and initial positions, then it's incomplete.)

   (d) At its top speed in segment IV, the object travels 20 m in about 2 s. That's a speed of 10 m/s. If you're familiar with track and field, you'll know that the best sprinters run the 100-m dash in somewhere in the neighborhood of 10 s, so the sprinter is an obvious choice. It might be easier[12] to approximate a conversion to miles per hour. The result of 1 m/s is a bit more than 2 miles per hour. This object goes between 20 and 25 miles per hour. This is the speed of a car on a neighborhood street. There is no way a baby or an amoeba can keep up; takeoff speeds for most airplanes are at least in the high tens of miles per hour; and you'd be a danger to yourself and others if you drove on the freeway at 25 miles per hour.

3. (a) Use the equation $\Delta x = v_0 t + \frac{1}{2} a t^2$ with $v_0 = 0$ and $a = 10$ m/s per second. You should get about 45 m.

   (b) In the equation we use in (a), the time of 3 s is still the same, as is v_0. The only difference is the acceleration a, which is in the numerator and is neither squared nor square rooted. Therefore, reducing a by one-sixth also reduces the distance fallen by one-sixth. That's choice A. (By the way, if your answer is A but your justification included "setting up a proportion" or anything without specific reference to this equation, your answer is incorrect.)

4. (a) Horizontal speed remains constant throughout a projectile's flight. Use $\Delta x = v_0 t + \frac{1}{2} a t^2$ horizontally with the acceleration term equal to zero. That means you're multiplying the horizontal speed by the time of flight. This gives D > C > A = B.

   (b) Regardless of the time of flight, the vertical speed is directly related to the maximum height reached. Why? Use $v_f^2 = v_0^2 + 2a\Delta x$ vertically with $v_f = 0$ and $a = 10$ m/s per second. The bigger the v_0, the bigger the Δx. So A > C > B = D.

   (c) Easy—all objects in free fall have a downward acceleration of 10 m/s per second. A = B = C = D.

---

[12]For an American, who doesn't usually know from meters per second (m/s), anyway. If you'd prefer km/hr, multiply speeds in m/s by about 4 to get km/hr.

〉 Rapid Review

- In a position-time graph, the object's position is read from the vertical axis.

- In a position-time graph, the object's speed is the slope of the graph. The steeper the slope, the faster the object moves. If the slope is a front slash (/), the movement is in the positive direction; if the slope is a backslash (\), the movement is in the negative direction.

- In a velocity-time graph, the object's speed is read from the vertical axis. The direction of motion is indicated by the sign on the vertical axis.

- In a velocity-time graph, the object's acceleration is the slope of the graph.

- In a velocity-time graph, the object's displacement is given by the area between the graph and the horizontal axis. The location of the object can't be determined from a velocity-time graph; only how far it ended up from its starting point can be determined.

- In any case of accelerated motion when three of the five principal motion variables are known, the remaining variables can be solved for using the kinematic equations.

- To calculate the missing values in a motion chart, use the three kinematic equations listed below. Choose whichever equation works mathematically.

    (1) $v_f = v_0 + at$

    (2) $\Delta x = v_0 t + \dfrac{1}{2} at^2$

    (3) $v_f^2 = v_0^2 + 2a\Delta x$

- When an object is in free fall, its acceleration is 10 m/s per second[10] toward the ground. "Free fall" means no forces other than the object's weight are acting on the object.

- A projectile has no horizontal acceleration, and so it moves at constant speed horizontally. A projectile is in free fall, so its vertical acceleration is 10 m/s per second downward.

- To find the vertical component of a velocity at an angle, multiply the speed by the sine of the angle. To find the horizontal component of a velocity at an angle, multiply the speed by the cosine of the angle. This always works, as long as the angle is measured from the horizontal.

- The horizontal and vertical motion charts for a projectile must use the same value for time.

CHAPTER 11

Forces and Newton's Laws

IN THIS CHAPTER

Summary: A force is a push or a pull applied by one object on another object. This chapter describes the construction and use of free-body diagrams, which are key to approaching problems involving forces.

Definitions

- ✪ A **force** is a push or a pull applied by one object and experienced by another object.
- ✪ The **net force** on an object is the single force that could replace all the individual forces acting on an object and produce the same effect. Forces acting in the same direction add together to determine the net force; forces acting in opposite directions subtract to determine the net force.
- ✪ **Weight** is the force of a planet on an object near that planet.
- ✪ The **force of friction** is the force of a surface on an object. The friction force acts parallel to the surface. **Kinetic friction** is the friction force when something is moving along the surface and acts opposite the direction of motion. **Static friction** is the friction force between two surfaces that aren't moving relative to one another.
- ✪ The **normal force** is also the force of a surface on an object. The normal force acts perpendicular to the surface.
- ✪ The **coefficient of friction** is a number that tells how sticky two surfaces are.
- ✪ **Newton's third law** says that the force of Object A on Object B is equal in amount and opposite in direction to the force of Object B on Object A.
- ✪ **Newton's second law** states that an object's acceleration is the net force it experiences divided by its mass, and is in the direction of the net force.

Describing Forces: Free-Body Diagrams

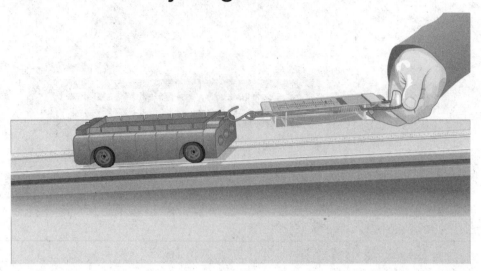

A force is a push or a pull applied by one object and experienced by another object. A force in the laboratory is often measured by a spring scale, as in the preceding picture. In AP Physics 1 we have to understand two aspects of forces. First, we have to describe the application of the force: What are the objects involved, and how much force is applied and in which direction? Next, we have to connect the net force acting on an object to that object's change in velocity.

Start with correct language: an object can "experience" a force, but an object cannot "have" a force. Don't let yourself say, "Ball A has a bigger force than Ball B"—that means nothing. "The net force on Ball A is bigger than on Ball B" is fine, as is "The Earth pulls harder on Ball A than on Ball B."

The canonical method of describing forces acting on an object is to draw a free-body diagram. A free-body diagram should include two elements:

(1) A labeled arrow representing each force, with each arrow beginning on the object and pointing in the direction in which the force acts
(2) A list of all the forces acting on the object, indicating the object applying the force and the object experiencing the force

On the AP exam you'll be asked something like, "Draw and label the forces (not components) that act on the car as it slows down." This means "Draw a free-body diagram."

FACT: Only gravitational and electrical forces can act on an object without contact.[1]

Example 1: A car moving to the right on the freeway applies the brakes and skids to a stop.

Pretty much always start with the force of the Earth on the object, which is commonly known as its weight. Don't call this force "gravity"—that's an ambiguous term. Weight acts downward and doesn't require any contact with the Earth in order to exist.[2] Draw a downward arrow on the dot, label it "weight," and in the list write "Weight: force of Earth on the car."[3]

---

[1]In AP Physics 1, anyway.

[2]Chapter 15, on gravitation, explains more about how to find the weight of an object in a gravitational field.

[3]Why not call it "force of gravity on the car?" Well, because all forces must be exerted by an *object* on another object. Since when is "gravity" an object? ☺

Any other forces must be a result of contact with the car. What's the car touching? It's touching just the ground. Since the car is touching the ground, the ground exerts a normal force perpendicular to the surface. Draw an upward arrow on the dot, label it something like "F_n," and in the list write "F_n: The force of the ground on the car."[4]

Since the car is sliding along the ground, the ground exerts a force of (kinetic) friction. By definition, kinetic friction must always act in the opposite direction of motion—the car skids right along the ground; the friction force acts to the left. Draw a leftward arrow on the dot, label it "F_f," and in the list write "F_f: The force of the ground on the car."[5]

The car is not in contact with anything else, so we're done.

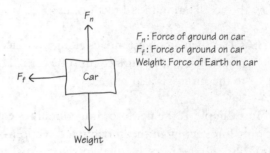

F_n: Force of ground on car
F_f: Force of ground on car
Weight: Force of Earth on car

Whoa there! The car is moving to the right, so what about the force of its motion?

There's no such thing as the "force of motion." All forces must be exerted by an identifiable object; and all nongravitational and nonelectrical forces must be a result of contact. The car is not in contact with anything that pushes the car forward.

Then how is the car moving to the right?

It just is. It is critically important to focus *only* on the problem as stated. Questions about what happened before the problem started are irrelevant. Perhaps at first the car was pushed by the engine, or pulled by a team of donkeys, to start it moving; perhaps it had been in motion since the beginning of time. It doesn't matter. All that matters is that when we tune in to the action, the car is moving right and slowing down.

If the car had been pulled by a team of donkeys to start it moving, wouldn't we put the force of the donkeys on the car on the free-body diagram?

No, because the free-body diagram includes only forces that act *now*, not forces that acted earlier, or forces that will act in the future. If donkeys pulled the car, the force of the donkeys would appear on the free-body while the donkeys were actually pulling. After they let go and the car is slowing down, the donkeys might as well have never existed.

While it's important to learn how to draw a free-body diagram, it's just as important to learn how to *stop* drawing a free-body diagram. Don't make up forces. Unless you can clearly identify the source of the force, don't include the force.

---

[4]It makes no difference what you label the arrow, as long as you define the label in a list. You want to call it N instead of F_n? Be my guest.

[5]Yes, both the friction force and the normal force are properly listed as the force of the ground on the car.

Exam Tip from an AP Physics Veteran
If you see a problem involving forces, try drawing a free-body diagram for each object in the problem, or for a system including multiple objects. A free-body diagram will always be useful, even if you're not explicitly asked to make one.

Determining the Net Force

To determine the net force on an object, treat each direction separately. Add forces that point in the same direction; subtract forces that point in opposite directions. Or, if you know the acceleration in a direction, use $F_{net} = ma$.

FACT: When an object moves along a surface, the acceleration in a direction perpendicular to that surface must be zero. Therefore, the net force perpendicular to the surface is also zero.

In Example 1, the net force horizontally is equal to the force of friction, because that's the only force acting in the horizontal direction—there's no other force to add or subtract. Vertically, the net force is equal to the normal force minus the weight. But since the car is moving along the surface, the vertical acceleration and the vertical net force on the car are zero.

We can conclude, then, that the normal force on the car is equal to the car's weight. This isn't a general fact, though—a normal force is *not* always equal to an object's weight. If more vertical forces are acting, or if the surface is changing speed vertically (as in an elevator), the normal force can be different from the weight.

FACT: The kinetic friction force is equal to the coefficient of kinetic friction times the normal force.

$$F_f = \mu_k F_n$$

A good AP question might describe a second car, identical in mass and initial speed to the car in Example 1, but on a wet freeway. The question might ask you to explain why this second car skids to a stop over a longer distance.

The coefficient of friction is a property of the surfaces in contact. Here, since a wet road is less "sticky" than a dry road, the coefficient of friction has decreased. But since the second car is identical to the first, its weight and thus the normal force of the surface on the car is the same as before. Therefore, by the equation $F_f = \mu F_n$, the new car experiences a smaller force of friction.

With a smaller net force on the second car, its acceleration is also smaller by $F_{net} = ma$. Then the distance traveled during the skid depends on the car's acceleration by the kinematics equation (3), $v_f^2 = v_0^2 + 2a\Delta x$. Take the final speed v_f to zero and solve for Δx to see that acceleration a is in the denominator of the equation. Thus, a smaller acceleration means a larger distance to stop.

Static and Kinetic Friction

You may have learned that the coefficient of friction takes two forms: **static** and **kinetic** friction. Use the coefficient of static friction if something is stationary, and the coefficient of kinetic friction if the object is moving. The equation for the force of friction is essentially the same in either case: $F_f = \mu F_N$.

The only strange part about static friction is that the coefficient of static friction is a *maximum* value. Think about this for a moment—if a book just sits on a table, it doesn't need any friction to stay in place. But that book won't slide if you apply a very small horizontal pushing force to it, so static friction can act on the book. To find the maximum coefficient of static friction, find out how much horizontal pushing force will just barely cause the book to move; then use $F_f = \mu F_N$.

Newton's Third Law

FACT: The force of Object A on Object B is equal in amount and opposite in direction to the force of Object B on Object A. These two forces, which act on different objects, are called Newton's third law companion forces.[6]

In Example 1, then, what's the Newton's third law companion force to the normal force? It's tempting to say, "Oh, the weight." After all, the weight is equal to the normal force and is opposite in direction to the normal force. But that's wrong.

To find the companion force, look at the description of the force in the free-body diagram, and reverse the objects applying and experiencing the force. The normal force is the force of the ground on the car, and that acts upward. Therefore, the third law companion force is the force of the car on the ground, acting downward.

Forces at Angles

FACT: If the net force has both a vertical and a horizontal component, use the Pythagorean theorem to determine the magnitude of the net force, and use the tangent function to determine the direction of the net force.

In most AP problems, though, the net force will be zero in one or both directions. In Example 1, the magnitude of the net force is equal to only the magnitude of the friction force, because the vertical forces must subtract to zero.

If this were an AP problem, chances are it would ask about the connection between the net force and the change in the object's speed. We'll revisit this example later.

A force at an angle is drawn on a free-body diagram just like any other force. But when you're ready to do any analysis on the free-body diagram, start by breaking the angled force into components.

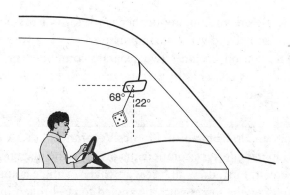

---

[6]Or, sometimes, this is called a Newton's third law force pair.

Example 2: A pair of fuzzy dice is hanging by a string from your rearview mirror, as shown in the preceding figure. You speed up from a stoplight. During the acceleration, the dice do not move vertically; the string makes an angle of $\theta = 22°$ with the vertical. The dice have mass 0.10 kg.

No matter what this problem ends up asking, you'll want to draw a free-body diagram. What forces act on the dice? Certainly the weight of the dice (the force of the Earth on the dice) acts downward. No electrical forces exist, so all other forces must be contact forces. The only object actually in contact with the dice is the string. The string pulls up on the dice at an angle, as shown in the picture. I labeled the force of the string on the dice "T," which stands for "tension"—which means the force of a string.

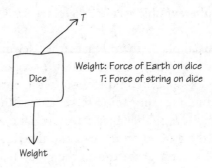

What about the force of the car on the dice?

What about it? The car is not in contact with the dice; the string is. It's the string, not the car, applying the force to the dice.

Determining the Net Force

It's likely that you'd be asked to determine the net force on these dice. But the tension acts both up *and* to the right. How do you deal with the vertical and horizontal forces, then?

FACT: When a force acts at an angle θ measured from the horizontal:

- The vertical component of that force is equal to the amount of the force itself times $\sin \theta$.
- The horizontal component of that force is equal to the amount of the force itself times $\cos \theta$.

Before you do any further work to find the net force, break all individual forces into horizontal and vertical components as best as you can. Here, the weight is already vertical. The tension becomes two separate components: $T\sin 68°$ goes in the vertical direction, and $T\cos 68°$ goes in the horizontal direction. Now you're ready to answer any possible problem.

Exam Tip from an AP Physics Veteran
Do *not* put force components on the same diagram as the force itself. You won't earn full credit. First, draw all forces at whatever angle is appropriate. Then, on a *separate diagram*, redraw the forces with the angled forces broken into components.

FACT: The acceleration of an object is F_{net}/m. This is the same thing as saying

$$F_{net} = ma$$

Whoa. I get that the net force is the horizontal $T\cos 68°$, and that I can write that $T\cos 68° = (0.1 \text{ kg})(a)$. But the problem didn't give me an acceleration, it didn't give the tension—I'm stuck to solve for anything. The College Board screwed this problem up, right?

It's vanishingly unlikely that the problem is unsolvable as posed. You obviously can't ask questions of the College Board during the AP exam. So if you're absolutely sure the exam is screwed up, you can just state where you think the problem is unclear, make up the information you need, and do your best. Chances are, though, that you need to find a creative alternative way to solve the problem.

Look at the problem statement: It said that the dice have a mass of 0.10 kg. This means that the weight of the dice is 1.0 N.[7] Since the dice are moving only in a horizontal direction, vertical acceleration (and the vertical net force on the dice) must be zero. Forces in opposite directions subtract to determine the net force. Here, that means that the up force must equal the down force of 1.0 N. The up force is $T\sin 68°$, which equals 1.0 N. Plug in from your calculator that the sine of 68 degrees is 0.93, and then solve to find the tension is 1.1 N.

Now deal with the horizontal direction. The horizontal net force is $T\cos 68°$, which is $(1.1 \text{ N})(0.37) = 0.41$ N. Since there's no vertical net force, 0.41 N to the right is the entire net force. And then $a = F_{net}/m$, so acceleration is 0.41 N/0.10 kg = 4.1 m/s per second. That's pretty much everything there is to calculate.

The Mistake

It's tempting to use this equation in all sorts of circumstances. For example, I'm sitting in a chair. Since I'm near the Earth, the force of the Earth on me is equal to my weight of 930 N. I know my mass is 93 kg. Use $a = F_{net}/m$. My acceleration must be 930 N/93 kg, or 10 m/s per second.

Um, no. I'm sitting in a chair. My speed isn't changing, so my acceleration is zero. The value of 10 m/s per second of acceleration means I'm in free fall. What went wrong?

I experience more forces than just the force of the Earth, of course. The chair is pushing up on me. Since I know that my acceleration is zero, the chair pushes up on me with 930 N of force. Now the up force and the down force on me subtract to zero. Phew.

Only the *net* force equals mass times acceleration. Never set a force equal to *ma* unless it's the net force.

What Else Could You Be Asked?

The AP exam doesn't like to ask for calculations. So what else could be asked relating to Example 2?

---

[7]On the Earth, 1 kg of mass weighs 10 N. This fact is discussed in more detail in Chapter 15, Gravitation.

Here's one thought: If the dice were to instead hang from a bigger angle than 22° from the vertical, would the tension go up, go down, or stay the same?

The best way to answer this type of question is to make the calculation, and then explain what part of the calculation leads to the correct answer. That's the whole method behind answering questions that involve qualitative-quantitative translation, as discussed in Chapter 8.

Make up a bigger angle: call it 60° from the vertical. (Or choose any number; just make a significant difference in the new situation. Don't choose 23°.) Start back from the beginning: The dice still have a 0.10-kg mass, and the weight of the dice is still 1.0 N. The vertical acceleration is still zero, which means we can set the up force equal to the down force. But now the up force has changed, from $T \sin 68°$ to $T \sin 30°$.[8] Now we set $T \sin 30°$ equal to 1.0 N, giving a tension of 2.0 N.

The answer, then, is that the tension increases. The weight remains the same and the vertical component of tension must stay the same, but since to calculate tension we end up dividing the 1.0-N weight by the sine of the angle from the horizontal, a smaller angle from the horizontal gives a bigger tension.

Exam Tip from an AP Physics Veteran

If you are asked whether something increases, decreases, or stays the same, you might want to start by making a calculation to see numerically what happens to the answer. Be sure to explain *why* the calculation came out the way it did.

Inclined Planes

Treat objects on inclines the same as any other objects. Draw a free-body diagram, break angled forces into components, and use $a = F_{net}/m$ in each direction. The only major difference is that you don't use horizontal and vertical components for the forces. Instead, you look separately at the forces parallel to the incline and at the forces perpendicular to the incline.

Any normal force will be perpendicular to the incline, and so won't have to be broken into components as long as the object is moving up or down the incline. Any friction force will be parallel to the incline and so won't have to be broken into components. It's the weight—the force of the Earth—that will be broken into components.

FACT: On an incline of angle θ (measured from the horizontal), break the weight into components:

- The component of the weight that is parallel to the incline is equal to the weight times $\sin \theta$.
- The component of the weight that is perpendicular to the incline is equal to the weight times $\cos \theta$.

Example problems and extra drills on this frequently tested topic are available in Chapter 18.

---

[8]Remember, we had to measure from the horizontal according to the fact on the previous page.

Multiple Objects

When two masses are connected over a pulley, it's often easiest to start by considering both objects as a single system. Draw the free-body diagram for the entire system, and use $a = F_{net}/m$ to find the acceleration of the system. Then, if you need to find the tension in the connecting rope, or if you need to talk about just one of the two connected objects, draw a new free-body diagram just for that object.

FACT: One rope has just one tension.[9]

An alternative approach is to start by drawing two separate free-body diagrams, one for each object. Write $F_{net} = ma$ for each object separately. Then, recognizing that the tension is the same in each equation, solve algebraically for the acceleration and tension.

› Practice Problems

Note: Extra drills on problems including ropes and inclined planes can be found in Chapter 18.

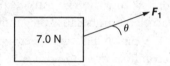

1. A 7.0-N block sits on a rough surface. It is being pulled by a force F_1 at an angle $\theta = 30°$ above the horizontal, as shown above. The block is initially moving to the right with speed 5 m/s. The coefficient of friction between the block and the surface is $\mu = 0.20$. Justify all answers.

    (a) Is it possible for the block to be slowing down? If so, give a possible value of the magnitude of F_1 that would allow the block to slow down. If not, explain why not with reference to Newton's second law.

    (b) In order to double the block's initial speed to 10 m/s, how must the magnitude of the force F_1 change?
    (A) It must double.
    (B) It must quadruple.
    (C) It does not have to change.

2. A drag-racing car speeds up from rest to 22 m/s in 2 s. The car has mass 800 kg; the driver has mass 80 kg.

    (a) Calculate the acceleration of the drag racer.
    (b) Calculate the net force on the drag racer.

    (c) Which experiences a greater net force?
    (A) The driver.
    (B) The car.
    (C) Both the driver and the car experience the same net force.

3. A car slides up a frictionless inclined plane. How does the normal force of the incline on the car compare with the weight of the car?

    (A) The normal force must be equal to the car's weight.
    (B) The normal force must be less than the car's weight.
    (C) The normal force must be greater than the car's weight.
    (D) The normal force must be zero.

4. Bert, Ernie, and Oscar are discussing the gas mileage of cars. Specifically, they are wondering whether a car gets better mileage on a city street or on a freeway. All agree (correctly) that the gas mileage of a car depends on the force that is produced by the car's engine—the car gets fewer miles per gallon if the engine must produce more force. Whose explanation is completely correct?

    Bert says: Gas mileage is better on the freeway. In town the car is always speeding up and slowing down because of the traffic lights, so because $F_{net} = ma$ and acceleration is large, the engine must produce a lot of force. However, on the freeway,

---

[9]This is true unless the rope is tied to or connected over a mass. For example, if the pulley itself had mass, then the rope can have different tensions on each side of the pulley. But that's a rare happening, and that certainly shouldn't require any calculation.

the car moves with constant velocity, and acceleration is zero. So the engine produces no force, allowing for better gas mileage.

Ernie says: Gas mileage is better in town. In town, the speed of the car is slower than the speed on the freeway. Acceleration is velocity divided by time, so the acceleration in town is smaller. Because $F_{net} = ma$, then, the force of the engine is smaller in town, giving better gas mileage.

Oscar says: Gas mileage is better on the freeway. The force of the engine only has to be enough to equal the force of air resistance—the engine doesn't have to accelerate the car because the car maintains a constant speed. Whereas in town, the force of the engine must often be greater than the force of friction and air resistance in order to let the car speed up.

› Solutions to Practice Problems

1. (a) When an object slows down, its acceleration (and therefore the net force it experiences) is opposite the direction of its motion. Here, the motion is to the right, so if the net force is left, it will slow down. To make the net force to the left, choose a value of F_1 such that the rightward component $F_1\cos(30°)$ is less than the friction force acting left.

   Choosing a value is a bit tricky: the value of the friction force itself depends on F_1, because the normal force on the block is 7 N minus the vertical component of F_1. Try choosing an F_1 much smaller than the block's weight, like 1 N. Then the normal force on the block is (7 N) − (1 N)sin 30° = 6.5 N. The friction force becomes $\mu F_n = 1.3$ N. The component of F_1 pulling right is 0.9 N, so the net force will be to the left as required.

   (Any value of F_1 that's less than a bit over 1.4 N will work here. Try it.)

   (b) While the net force is related to acceleration, the net force has no effect on an object's speed. Beyond that, no one has said anything about what happens before the problem, about how that initial speed came about. The forces can all be as indicated, and the object can have any initial speed.

2. (a) The car's speed changes by 22 m/s in 2 s. So the car changes its speed by 11 m/s in 1 s, which is what is meant by an acceleration of 11 m/s per second.

   (b) Newton's second law says that the net force on the racer is the drag racer's mass of 800 kg times the 11 m/s per second acceleration. That gives a net force of 8,800 N.

   (c) The driver and the car must experience the same acceleration because they move together; when the car changes its speed by 11 m/s in one second, so does the driver.[10] To calculate the net force on the driver, the driver's 80-kg mass must be used in Newton's second law, $F_{net} = ma$. With the same a and a smaller mass, the driver experiences a smaller net force (and the car experiences a greater net force).

3. (B) The normal force exerted on an object on an inclined plane equals $mg(\cos\theta)$, where θ is the angle of the incline. If θ is greater than 0, then $\cos\theta$ is less than 1, so the normal force is less than the object's weight.

4. Although Bert is right that acceleration is zero on the freeway, this means that the *net* force is zero; the engine still must produce a force to counteract air resistance. This is what Oscar says, so his answer is correct. Ernie's answer is way off—acceleration is not velocity/time, acceleration is a *change* in velocity over time.

---

[10]Otherwise, the driver would fall out of the car.

〉 Rapid Review

- Only gravitational and electrical forces can act on an object without contact (in AP Physics 1).

- When an object moves along a surface, the acceleration in a direction perpendicular to that surface must be zero. Therefore, the net force perpendicular to the surface is also zero.

- The friction force is equal to the coefficient of friction times the normal force, $F_f = \mu F_n$.

- The force of Object A on Object B is equal in amount and opposite in direction to the force of Object B on Object A. These two forces, which act on different objects, are called Newton's third law companion forces.

- If the net force has both a vertical and a horizontal component, use the Pythagorean theorem to determine the magnitude of the net force, and use the tangent function to determine the direction of the net force.

- When a force acts at an angle θ measured from the horizontal:

  - The vertical component of that force is equal to the amount of the force itself times $\sin\theta$.

  - The horizontal component of that force is equal to the amount of the force itself times $\cos\theta$.

- The acceleration of an object is F_{net}/m (which is the same thing as saying $F_{net} = ma$).

- On an incline of angle θ (measured from the horizontal), break the weight into components:

  - The component of the weight that is parallel to the incline is equal to the weight times $\sin\theta$.

  - The component of the weight that is perpendicular to the incline is equal to the weight times $\cos\theta$.

- One rope has just one tension.

CHAPTER 12

Collisions: Impulse and Momentum

IN THIS CHAPTER

Summary: Whenever you see a collision, the techniques of impulse and momentum are likely to be useful in describing or predicting the result of the collision. In particular, momentum is conserved in all collisions—this means that the total momentum of all objects is the same before and after the collision. When an object (or a system of objects) experiences a net force, the impulse momentum theorem $\Delta p = F \cdot \Delta t$ can be used for predictions and calculations.

Definitions

- ✪ A moving object's **momentum** is its mass times its velocity. Momentum is in the direction of motion.
- ✪ **Impulse** is defined as a force multiplied by the time during which that force acts. The net impulse on an object is equal to the change in that object's momentum.
- ✪ A **system** is made up of several objects that can be treated as a single thing. It's important to define the system you are considering before you treat a set of objects as a system.
- ✪ While total momentum is conserved in all collisions, kinetic energy is conserved only in an **elastic collision**.

Momentum is a useful quantity to calculate because it is often **conserved**; that is, the total amount of momentum available in most situations cannot change. Whenever you see a collision, the techniques of impulse and momentum are most likely to be useful. Try impulse and momentum first, before trying to use force or energy approaches.

The Impulse-Momentum Theorem

Here is the impulse-momentum theorem:

$$\Delta p = F \cdot \Delta t$$

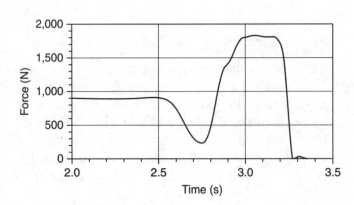

Example 1: A teacher whose weight is 900 N jumps vertically from rest while standing on a platform scale. The scale reading as a function of time is shown in the preceding figure.

A force versus time graph is essentially an invitation to calculate impulse. Since impulse is defined as $F \cdot \Delta t$, from a force versus time graph, impulse is the area under the graph.

Strategy: When you need to take the area of an experimental graph, approximate as best you can with rectangles and triangles.

This graph for Example 1 is tricky—impulse calculations should use the *net* force on an object. The scale reading on the vertical axis of the graph is not the net force; the net force is the scale reading in excess of the person's 900-N weight.

To estimate the impulse given to the jumper in this example, draw a horizontal line at the 900-N mark as a zero point for calculating the net force:

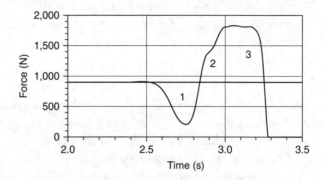

Regions 1 and 2 have somewhat close to the same area, one above and one above the zero net force line; so these areas cancel out. Region 3 looks somewhat like a rectangle, with base something like 0.25 s and height (1,800 N − 900 N) = 900 N. The impulse is then 900 N times 0.25 s, or something like 220 N·s.

> **Exam Tip from an AP Physics Veteran**
> You must be comfortable with this kind of rough approximation. Sure, the impulse could well be more like 228 N·s, or 210 N·s. Who cares? On a free-response item it will be the reasoning behind your calculation that earns credit, much more so than the answer itself. On a multiple-choice item, the choices might be far separated, like (A) 200 N·s; (B) 2,000 N·s; (C) 20,000 N·s; (D) 200,000 N·s. Isn't the choice obvious?

Impulse by itself doesn't say much. The more interesting question about this jumping teacher in Example 1 is the speed with which he leaves the scale. Since impulse is the change in an object's momentum, you know the teacher changed his momentum by 220 N·s. Since he started from rest, his momentum right after leaving the scale is also 220 N·s. Finally, momentum is mass times speed. The teacher's mass is 90 kg,[1] so plug in to the equation $p = mv$: (220 N·s) = (90 kg)v. His speed is 2.4 m/s, or thereabouts.

Conservation of Momentum

Example 2: Cart A, of mass 0.5 kg, moves to the right at a speed of 60 cm/s. Cart B, of mass 1.0 kg, is at rest. The carts collide.

FACT: In any system in which the only forces acting are between objects in that system, momentum is conserved. This effectively means that momentum is conserved in *all* collisions.

---

[1]This is because his weight is 900 N, and on Earth 1 kg weighs 10 N.

Define the system for momentum conservation in Example 2—just the two carts. They apply a force to each other in the collision, but that's it, so momentum is conserved.[2]

A common task in a problem with a collision involves calculating the speed of one or both objects after the collision. Even when a collision-between-two-objects question is qualitative or conceptual in nature, it's often a good idea to try calculating speeds after a collision.

To do this, define a positive direction and then make a chart indicating the mass m and speed v of each cart before and after the collision. I use a "prime" mark (′) to indicate when we're dealing with values after a collision rather than before. Indicate the direction of motion with a plus or minus sign on the velocities.

(Note that it's okay to use centimeters per second [cm/s] rather than meters per second [m/s], as long as you are consistent throughout.)

$$m_A = 0.5 \text{ kg}$$
$$m_B = 1.0 \text{ kg}$$
$$v_A = +60 \text{ cm/s}$$
$$v_B = 0$$
$$v_A' = ?$$
$$v_B' = ?$$

Then write the equation for conservation of momentum.

Uh, where do you get such an equation? I know it's not on the equation sheet on the old or new AP physics exams.

The relevant equation comes from the definition of "conservation," meaning an unchanging quantity. The total change in momentum for the system of the two carts must be zero. Any momentum lost by Cart A is gained by Cart B. Set zero equal to Cart A's change in momentum plus Cart B's change in momentum:

$$0 = (p_A' - p_A) + (p_B' - p_B)$$

Then, knowing that $p = mv$, plug in what you know. I'm going to leave off the units to make the mathematics clearer; since the table above has values and units, it's clear what units are intended.

$$0 = [(0.5) \, v_A' - (0.5)(60)] + [(1.0)v_B' - 0]$$

Is this solvable? Not yet, because it's only one equation with two variables. The information about this collision is incomplete. The collision in Example 2 could thus have all sorts of results.

One possibility is that the carts stick together. In that case, the carts share the same speed: in the notation above, $v_A' = v_B'$. That makes the calculation solvable; replace the vs with a single variable to get $v = 20$ cm/s.

Perhaps the problem statement continues to tell us the speed of one of the carts after the collision. Then the problem is solvable: plug in the value given, and solve for the other v.

---

[2]If friction between the track and the carts were significant, then sure, momentum wouldn't be conserved—the track wasn't considered part of the system, and it's applying a force to the carts. But *even with friction*, if you consider the moments just before and just after the collision, momentum will be essentially conserved. See the following discussion for a time when the momentum of a system is *not* conserved.

The only tricky part here would be, say, if Cart A rebounded after the collision. Then v_A' would take a negative value. But the solution would be approached the same way.

When Is the Momentum of a System *Not* Conserved?

The simple answer goes back to the definition of momentum conservation: The momentum of a system is *not* conserved when a force is exerted by an object that's not in the system.

> **Example 3:** Two identical balls are dropped from the same height above the ground, such that they are traveling 50 cm/s just before they hit the ground. Ball A rebounds with speed 50 cm/s; Ball B rebounds with a speed of 10 cm/s. Each is in contact with the ground for the same amount of time.

Define the system here. If the system is just Ball A, say, then is the momentum of Ball A conserved? Of course not! The problem says that Ball A rebounds, which means it changed its direction and thus its momentum.

Mistake: It's tempting to say that since Ball A didn't change its mass, and since its speed was 50 cm/s before *and* after the collision, that Ball A didn't change its momentum. This is not correct; momentum has direction. An object that changes direction loses all its momentum and then gains some more. If Ball A had mass 2 kg, then it lost 1 N·s of momentum in stopping, and then gained another 1 N·s of momentum in order to rebound—for a total change in momentum of 2 N·s.

> *Wait.* You said in the preceding *Fact* that momentum is conserved in all collisions. What happened?

Well, yes, momentum *is* conserved in all collisions, if you define the system to include the two (or three) objects that are colliding. In Example 3, Ball A is effectively colliding with the entire Earth. If we consider the system of the Earth and Ball A, then momentum is, in fact, conserved. The change in Ball A's momentum is equal to the change in the Earth's momentum. Since the Earth is so mind-bogglingly massive, its speed won't change in any measureable amount.

Mistake: The total momentum for a system of objects is always the same. So in a single collision, the total momentum cannot change. In a problem like Example 3, though, Balls A and B are involved in two separate collisions. Therefore, they can't be part of the same system! Don't use "conservation of momentum" as a reason for anything about Balls A and B to be equal, when Balls A and B are involved in separate collisions.

The point is that momentum conservation is not an effective approach to consider when a ball collides with the entire Earth.[3] Instead, use the impulse-momentum theorem to find out what you can.

The easy question is as follows: Which ball changes its momentum by a greater amount? That'd be Ball A. Both balls lost the same amount of momentum in coming to a brief rest, then rebounded; since Ball A rebounded faster, and since the balls have the same mass, Ball A changed its momentum by a greater amount.[4]

---

[3]Or equivalently, this is not an effective approach to consider when a car collides with a concrete pillar, or a bird collides with the window of a building, etc.

[4]If you need to make up a mass of 2 kg for each ball and plug in numbers (including a plus and minus sign for the direction of velocity) to calculate the total momentum change for each ball, feel free. That's not a bad approach if the words are confusing you.

The harder question is this: Which ball exerted a larger force on the ground during its collision? We know that momentum change equals force times time.[5] With the same time of collision, the bigger force is exerted by the ball with the greater momentum change—that's Ball A.

Similar reasoning can explain why airbags make a car safer. You[6] lose all your momentum in a crash regardless of how you come to rest. Airbags extend the time of the collision between you and the car. In the equation $\Delta p = F \cdot \Delta t$ with the same Δp, a bigger Δt gives a smaller F, so the force you experience is less in an airbag collision.

Elastic/Inelastic Collisions

In elastic collisions, the total kinetic energy of both objects combined is the same before and after the collision. A typical AP problem might pose a standard collision problem and then ask, "Is the collision elastic?" To figure that out, add up the kinetic energies ($\frac{1}{2}mv^2$) of both objects before the collision, add up the kinetic energies of both objects after the collision, and compare. If these kinetic energies are essentially the same, the collision is elastic. If the final kinetic energy is less than the initial kinetic energy, the collision was *not* elastic—kinetic energy was converted, generally to work done by nonconservative forces exerted by one colliding object on the other.[7]

> **Example 4:** Two carts of equal mass move toward each other with identical speeds of 30 cm/s. After colliding, the carts bounce off each other, each regaining 30 cm/s of speed, but now moving in the opposite direction.

Mistake: Never start a collision problem writing anything about kinetic energy. Always start with conservation of momentum. Only move on to kinetic energy conservation if you have to; that is, if you don't have enough information to solve with just momentum conservation, *and* if the problem is explicit in saying that the collision is elastic.

Is momentum conserved in this collision? Yes, and you don't have to do any calculations to show it. In a collision, momentum is always conserved because the only forces acting on the carts are exerted by the carts themselves.

Is kinetic energy conserved in this collision? You've got to do the calculation to check.

> But the carts bounced off each other. Doesn't that automatically mean the collision is elastic?

No. When carts stick together, the collision cannot be elastic. But when carts bounce off each other, the collision might be elastic, or might not be.

Start with the kinetic energy before the collision. In this case, make up a mass for each cart: they're identical, so call them 1 kg each. Each cart has speed 0.30 m/s, so the kinetic energy of each cart before the collision is $\frac{1}{2}(1 \text{ kg})(0.30 \text{ m/s})^2 = 0.045$ J. The combined kinetic energy before collision is thus 0.090 J.

---

[5]**Mistake:** The relevant time in the impulse-momentum theorem is always the time of the collision, *not* the time it takes for a ball to fall through the air.

[6]Hopefully not *you*, personally.

[7]If the final kinetic energy is *greater* than the initial kinetic energy, something weird happened; like a coiled spring was released during the collision, or a firecracker exploded. You'll most often see this sort of "superelastic" collision when the objects are initially at rest and then they are blown apart.

Whoa there—One cart was moving right, the other left; that means the kinetic energies subtract, giving zero total kinetic energy. Right?

Wrong. Kinetic energy is a scalar, which means it has no direction. Kinetic energy can never take on a negative value. Always add the kinetic energies of each object in a system to get the total kinetic energy. After the collision, the calculation is the same: total kinetic energy is still 0.090 J. So the collision is, in fact, elastic.

2-d Collisions

Example 5: Maggie, of mass 50 kg, glides to the right on a frictionless frozen pond with a speed of 2.5 m/s. She collides with a 20-kg penguin. After the collision, the directions of the penguin's and Maggie's motion is shown in the following figure.

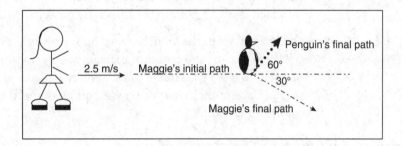

Strategy: When objects move in both an *x*- and a *y*-direction after a collision, analyze the collision with momentum conservation *separately* in each direction.

You will not likely be asked to do quantitative analysis of a two-dimensional collision, but you do need to understand conceptually how momentum conservation works here. Be able to explain how you would carry out the analysis of momentum conservation in each direction, and be able to answer simple qualitative questions.

For example, who has a greater magnitude of momentum in the *y*-direction after collision? Before the collision, there was no momentum in the *y*-direction. After the collision, the total *y*-momentum must also be zero. Since both the penguin and Maggie are moving in the *y*-direction, their momentums must be equal and opposite so as to subtract to zero. The answer is neither—both the penguin and Maggie have the same amount of *y*-momentum.

What about the *y*-component of their velocities? We've already established that they have the same *y*-momentum, which is equal to mass times *y*-velocity. Since Maggie has the bigger mass, she must have the smaller *y*-component of velocity.

Is momentum conserved in the *x*-direction? Of course it is. The total momentum before collision is all due to Maggie's movement: (50 kg)(2.5 m/s) = 125 N·s, all in the *x*-direction. After collision, the total *x*-momentum is also 125 N·s. The *x*-component of the penguin's momentum after collision is just his momentum *mv* times the cosine of 60°; Maggie's *x*-momentum is her momentum times the cosine of 30°. In this problem, the only way to get values for these components is to do some complicated algebra, which is beyond the scope of AP Physics 1. But you should be able to explain everything about this collision in words, as discussed here.

Motion of the Center of Mass

KEY IDEA

FACT: The center of mass of a system of objects obeys Newton's second law.

Two common examples illustrate this fact:

Example: Imagine that an astronaut on a spacewalk throws a rope around a small asteroid, and then pulls the asteroid toward him. Where will the asteroid and the astronaut collide?

Answer: at the center of mass. Since no forces acted except due to the astronaut and asteroid, the center of mass must have no acceleration. The center of mass started at rest, and stays at rest, all the way until the objects collide.

Example: A toy rocket is in projectile motion, so that it is on track to land 30 m from its launch point. While in the air, the rocket explodes into two identical pieces, one of which lands 35 m from the launch point. Where does the first piece land?

Answer: 25 m from the launch point. Since the only external force acting on the rocket is gravity, the center of mass must stay in projectile motion, and must land 30 m from the launch point. The two pieces are of equal mass, so if one is 5 m beyond the center of mass's landing point, the other piece must be 5 m short of that point.

Finding the Center of Mass

Usually the location of the center of mass (cm) is pretty obvious . . . the formal equation for the cm of several objects is

$$Mx_{cm} = m_1x_1 + m_2x_2 + \cdots$$

Multiply the mass of each object by its position, and divide by the total mass M, and voila, you have the position of the center of mass. What this tells you is that the cm of several equal-mass objects is right in between them; if one mass is heavier than the others, the cm is closer to the heavier mass.

> Practice Problems

1. A 2-kg coconut falls from the top of a tall tree, 30 m above a person's head. The coconut strikes and comes to rest on the person's head. Justify all answers thoroughly.

   (a) Calculate the magnitude of the momentum of the coconut just before it hits the person in the head.

   (b) Calculate the magnitude and direction of the impulse experienced by the coconut in colliding with the person's head.

   (c) The person's head experienced a force of 10,000 N in the collision. How long was the coconut in contact with the person's head?
   (A) Much more than 10 seconds
   (B) Just a bit more than one second
   (C) Just a bit less than one second
   (D) Much less than 1/10 second

   (d) In a different situation, explain how it could be possible for an identical coconut dropped from the same height to hit the person's head, but produce *less* than 10,000 N of force.

2. A car on a freeway collides with a mosquito, which was initially at rest. Justify all answers thoroughly.

   (a) Did the total momentum of the car-mosquito system increase, decrease, or remain the same after the collision?
   (b) Did the momentum of the mosquito increase, decrease, or remain the same after the collision?
   (c) Did the momentum of the car increase, decrease, or remain the same after the collision?
   (d) Which changed its speed by more in the collision, the car or the mosquito? (Or did they change speed by the same amount?)
   (e) Which changed its momentum by more in the collision, the car or the mosquito? (Or did they change momentum by the same amount?)
   (f) Which experienced a greater impulse in the collision, the car or the mosquito? (Or did they experience the same impulse?)
   (g) Which experienced a greater magnitude of net force during the collision, the car or the mosquito? (Or did they experience the same net force?)

3. Car A has a mass of 1,500 kg and travels to the right with a speed of 20 m/s. Car B initially travels to the left with a speed of 10 m/s. After the vehicles collide, they stick together, moving left with a common speed of 5 m/s. Justify all answers thoroughly.

   (a) Calculate the mass of Car B.
   (b) This collision is not elastic. Explain why not.
   (c) Describe specifically a collision between these two cars with the same initial conditions, but which is *not* elastic, and in which the cars bounce off one another.
   (d) Is the collision elastic when Car B remains at rest after the collision?

❱ Solutions to Practice Problems

1. (a) Momentum is mass times speed. To find the coconut's speed, use kinematics with $v_0 = 0$, $a = 10$ m/s per second, and $\Delta x = 30$ m. The equation $v_f^2 = v_0^2 + 2a\Delta x$ solved for v_f gives 24 m/s. Multiplying by the 2-kg mass gives a momentum of 48 N·s.[8]

   (b) Impulse is the change in momentum and is in the direction of the net force experienced by an object. The coconut's momentum after colliding with the head is zero—the coconut comes to rest. So its change in momentum, and thus the magnitude of the impulse it experiences, is 48 N·s. The direction of this impulse is upward, because the net force on the coconut must be opposite its speed in order to slow it down.

   (c) Impulse is also equal to force times the time interval of collision. Setting 48 N·s equal to $(10{,}000$ N$)(\Delta t)$, we find the time interval of collision is 48/10,000 of a second—much less than 1/10 second, even without reference to a calculator.

   (d) The impulse-momentum theorem says that $\Delta p = F\Delta t$. Solving for force, $F = \frac{\Delta p}{\Delta t}$. Here the momentum change has to be the same no matter what—the coconut will be traveling 24 m/s and will come to rest on the person's head. But if the person is wearing a soft helmet, or if the coconut has a rotten spot on it somewhere, then the time of collision could be larger than before. Since Δt is in the denominator of the force equation, a bigger time interval of collision leads to a smaller force on the coconut (and therefore on the person's head).

2. (a) Momentum is conserved when no forces are exerted, except for those on and by objects in the system. Here the only forces are of the car on mosquito and mosquito on car. Therefore, momentum was conserved. That means that the total momentum of the car-mosquito system remains the same.

---

[8] If you used units of kg·m/s, that's fine, too.

(b) The mosquito went from rest to moving freeway speeds after it hit the car. The mosquito's mass didn't change.[9] Momentum is mass times speed, so the mosquito's momentum increased.

(c) Since total momentum of the car-mosquito system doesn't change, and the mosquito gained momentum, the car has to lose that same amount of momentum.

(d) The mosquito's speed went from, say, zero to 60 miles per hour. While the car must lose the same amount of momentum that the mosquito gained, the car's mass is so much larger than the mosquito's that the car's speed will hardly change. And you knew that, because a car hitting a mosquito on the freeway doesn't cause the car to stop.

(e) The momentum change is the same for both, because total momentum remains unchanged. Any momentum gained by the mosquito must be lost by the car.

(f) Impulse is the same thing as momentum change, so the same for both.

(g) Newton's third law says the force of the mosquito on the car is equal to the force of the car on the mosquito. So they're equal.

3. (a) Before the collision, Car A has a momentum of 30,000 N·s to the right. If we call the mass of Car B "M_B," then Car B has momentum of M_B(10 m/s) to the left. Afterward, the total momentum is (M_B + 1,500 kg)(5 m/s) to the left. Let's call right the positive direction. Then the relevant equation for conservation of momentum is $30,000 - 10M_B = -5(1,500 + M_B)$, where I've left off the units so the algebra is clearer. Solve for M_B to get 7,500 kg. This makes sense—Car B was initially moving slower; yet after the collision, the cars moved off together in the direction Car B was going. Car B must therefore have more momentum than Car A initially and more mass because it was going slower.

(b) "Elastic" means that the kinetic energy (= $\frac{1}{2}mv^2$) of all objects combined is the same before and after collision. Before collision, Car A had 300 kJ of kinetic energy, and Car B had 375 kJ, for a total of 675 kJ before the collision.[10] After collision, the kinetic energy of the combined cars is 112 kJ. Kinetic energy was lost in the collision. (Note that it's legitimate to remember that collisions in which objects stick together can never be elastic.)

(c) Imagine that Car B keeps moving left, but much slower, say, 1 m/s. Momentum is conserved in a collision, regardless of whether the collision is elastic or not. The total momentum of Car A before collision is 30,000 N·s to the right; the total momentum of Car B before collision is 75,000 N·s to the left. This gives a total momentum of 45,000 N·s to the left before collision. If Car B moves 1 m/s after collision, it has 7,500 N·s of momentum to the left, leaving 37,500 N·s to the left for Car A. Dividing by Car A's 1,500-kg mass, Car A is found to be moving 25 m/s after the collision.

Now check total kinetic energy after collision. Car A has 469 kJ of kinetic energy and Car B has 4 kJ of kinetic energy, for a total of 473 kJ. Before the collision the total kinetic energy was 675 kJ, as calculated in (b). Therefore, kinetic energy is lost and the collision is inelastic. The whole point here is that not all collisions in which cars bounce are elastic.

(d) We need a total of 675 kJ afterward in order to have an elastic collision. Conservation of momentum means that the total momentum after collision is 45,000 N·s to the left. Since Car A is the only moving car, it has all that momentum. Dividing by Car A's 1,500-kg mass, we find Car A moving 30 m/s. Only Car A has kinetic energy, too; its kinetic energy is $\frac{1}{2}mv^2 = 675$ kJ, so the collision is elastic.

---

[9] . . . though its mass was likely redistributed around the windshield a bit.

[10] No, the total is not −75 kJ. Kinetic energy is a scalar, meaning it cannot have a direction; and kinetic energy cannot be negative. The total kinetic energy of a system is the sum of all the kinetic energies of the constituent objects, regardless of which way the objects are moving.

❯ Rapid Review

- In any system in which the only forces acting are between objects in that system, momentum is conserved. This effectively means that momentum is conserved in *all* collisions.

- The center of mass of a system of objects obeys Newton's second law.

- The impulse-momentum theorem is $\Delta p = F \cdot \Delta t$.

- The impulse-momentum theorem is always valid, but it is most useful when objects collide.

- The only time when momentum of a system is *not* conserved is when a force is exerted by an object that's not in the system.

CHAPTER 13

Work and Energy

IN THIS CHAPTER

Summary: An object possesses kinetic energy by moving. Interactions with other objects can create potential energy. Work is done when a force acts over a distance parallel to that force. When work is done on an object (or on a system of objects), kinetic energy can change. This chapter shows you how to recognize the different forms of energy and how to use them to make predictions about the behavior of objects.

Definitions

✪ **Kinetic energy** is possessed by any moving object. It comes in two forms:

  1. Translational kinetic energy is

$$\tfrac{1}{2}mv^2$$

  It exists when an object's center of mass is moving.

  2. Rotational kinetic energy is

$$\tfrac{1}{2}I\omega^2$$

  It exists when an object rotates.

✪ **Gravitational potential energy** is energy stored in a gravitational field. Near a planet, the formula is

$$GPE = mgh$$

where h is the vertical height above a reference position. A long way from a planet, the formula is

$$GPE = -G\frac{M_1 M_2}{d}$$

where d is measured from the planet's center.

☉ **Elastic potential energy,** also known as spring potential energy, is energy stored by a spring, given by

$$SPE = \tfrac{1}{2}kx^2$$

☉ **Internal energy** can refer to two somewhat different ideas. Both refer to the concept that multi-object systems can store energy depending on how the objects are arranged in the system.

   ☉ *Microscopic internal energy* is related to the temperature of the object. As the object warms up, energy can be stored by the vibrations of molecules.

   ☉ *Internal energy of a two-object system* is just another way of saying "potential energy."

☉ **Mechanical energy** refers to the sum of potential and kinetic energies.

☉ **Work** is done when a force acts on something that moves a distance parallel to that force.

☉ **Power** is defined as energy used per second, or work done per second.

Energy

The cart pictured above has gravitational potential energy with respect to the location of the motion detector, because the cart is vertically higher than the detector. If the cart were released from rest, it would speed up toward the detector. It would be tempting to try to use the kinematics equations to determine the cart's maximum speed. However, since the track is curved, the cart's acceleration will be changing throughout its motion. Whenever acceleration changes, kinematics as studied in Chapter 10 are invalid. The methods of energy conservation, as described in this chapter, must be used.

The College Board's curriculum guide for AP Physics 1 makes much of the difference between **objects** and **systems**. A system is just a collection of objects. In your class, you might well have talked about an object's kinetic and potential energies. The thing is, the exam development committee doesn't like that language. Sure, an object can have kinetic energy, just by moving. But a single object technically cannot "have" potential energy.

Why not? Potential energy is always the result of an interaction between objects in a system. For example, gravitational potential energy (equation: *mgh*) exists only if an object is interacting with the Earth. The Earth-object system stores the potential energy, not just the object itself. Similarly, an object attached to a spring *cannot* store potential energy; the spring-object system stores the energy.

Look, I'm going to talk about objects "having" potential energy. It's okay with me if you talk about a block on a spring "having" potential energy because the spring is compressed. You'll still get pretty much everything right on the exam. Just know that the block only "has" potential energy because of its interaction with the spring; and that potential energy is sometimes referred to as the "internal energy of the block-spring system."

Work

FACT: Work is done when a force is exerted on an object[1] and that object moves parallel to the direction of the force.

The relevant equation is work = force times parallel displacement:[2]

$$\boxed{W = F\Delta x_{\parallel}}$$

When a force is exerted in the same direction as the object's motion, the work done is considered to be a positive quantity; when a force is exerted in the opposite direction of the object's motion, the work done is considered to be a negative quantity. The *net* work on an object is the algebraic sum of the work done by each force.

Example 1: A string applies a 10-N force to the right on a 2-kg box, dragging it at constant speed across the floor for a distance of 50 cm.

Let's calculate the work done by each force acting, and the net work done on the box. Start by sketching a free-body diagram for the box.

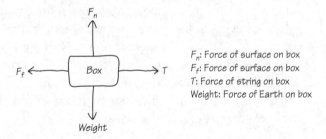

F_n: Force of surface on box
F_f: Force of surface on box
T: Force of string on box
Weight: Force of Earth on box

Strategy: Whenever you are calculating work done by a force with the equation $W = F\Delta x_{\parallel}$, always sketch the direction of the force and displacement vectors.

Consider each force separately. Start with the 10-N tension in the string. This force acts to the right. The displacement of the box is 50 cm (i.e., 0.50 m) to the right.

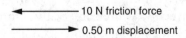

Since the force is in the same direction as the displacement, the work done by the tension is just 10 N times 0.50 m = +5 J.

Now consider the friction force. Since the box moves at constant speed, we know the left force (friction) equals the right force (tension); so the friction force has an amount of 10 N.

---

[1] Or on a system of objects—if a force is exerted on a system of objects and the system's center of mass moves parallel to the force, work was done.

[2] Or, equivalently, the equation is displacement times parallel force, which may sometimes be a more convenient expression.

Since the force is in the *opposite* direction of displacement, the work done by the friction force is 10 N times 0.50, with a negative sign. Thus, the work done by friction is –5 J. What about the force of gravity? The 20-N weight of the box points downward.

20 N weight   0.50 m displacement

Since no component of the weight is parallel to the displacement, the force of the Earth does zero work on the box.

Similarly, the normal force is straight upward while the displacement is to the right; since no component of the normal force is parallel to the displacement, the normal force does no work on the box.

> **Exam Tip from an AP Physics Veteran**
> If a force acts at an angle to the displacement, just break that force into components. The component perpendicular to the displacement does no work. The component parallel to the displacement can be multiplied by the displacement to get the work done.

Finding the Net Work

You can calculate the net work on the box in two ways:

1. First, determine the net force using a free-body diagram, like we showed in Chapter 11. Then, multiply the component of the net force that's parallel to the displacement by the displacement, just like you would when finding the work done by any force. In Example 1, the net force is zero; so there is no net work done on the box.
2. First, determine the work done by each force separately. Then, add the work done by each force algebraically (i.e., including negative signs). In Example 1, add the +5 J done by the tension to the −5 J done by friction (and the 0 J done by the normal force and the weight) to get zero net work.

Conservative Versus Nonconservative Forces

FACT: A "conservative" force converts potential energy to other forms of mechanical energy when it does work. Thus, a conservative force does not change the mechanical energy of a system.

The amount of work done by a conservative force depends only on the starting and ending positions of the object; that is, it's "path independent." The only conservative forces that you need to deal with on the AP Physics 1, Algebra-Based Exam are gravity and springs. When a spring does work on an object, energy is stored in the spring that can be recovered and converted back to kinetic energy. The sum of the potential and kinetic energy of the object-spring system is constant.

Conversely, a "nonconservative" force can change the mechanical energy of a system. Friction is the most common example: Work done by friction on an object becomes microscopic internal energy in the object, raising the object's temperature. That microscopic internal energy *cannot* be recovered and converted back to kinetic energy. Other nonconservative forces might include, for example, the propeller of an airplane—it does work on the airplane to increase the airplane's mechanical energy.

The Work-Energy Theorem

In your textbook, you'll see the work-energy theorem written as "net work = change in kinetic energy." That's certainly true—*net* work done on an object must change the object's kinetic energy. The tricky part is, net work must include work done by all forces, conservative and nonconservative.

I think it's easier to separate conservative and nonconservative forces. Work done by a nonconservative force (W_{NC}) changes the total mechanical energy of a system ($KE + PE$). I write the work-energy theorem as follows:

$$W_{NC} = (\Delta KE) + (\Delta PE)$$

Generally, the potential energy involved will be either that due to a spring, or due to a gravitational field. The kinetic energy includes *both* translational kinetic energy ($\frac{1}{2}mv^2$) and rotational kinetic energy[3] ($\frac{1}{2}I\omega^2$).

> **Example 2:** An archer pulls an arrow of mass 0.10 kg attached to a bowstring back 30 cm by exerting a force that increases uniformly with distance from 0 N to 200 N.

The AP exam could ask all sorts of questions about this situation. Before you start doing any calculation, categorize the problem. There are only three ways to approach a mechanics problem: kinematics/Newton laws, momentum, and energy. There's no collision, so momentum is unlikely to be useful. The problem talks about a force, but that force is *changing*. A changing force means a changing acceleration, which means that kinematics equations are not valid. Only the work-energy theorem will be useful.

The only types of potential energy used in AP Physics 1 are due to gravity (mgh) and due to a spring ($\frac{1}{2}kx^2$). Which is involved here? The example says that the force of the string varies "uniformly," which means that the force gets bigger as the distance stretched gets bigger, just like a spring. So treat the bowstring just like a spring.

Mistake: An interesting question here might be "how much work does the archer do in pulling back the bowstring?" And you'd be tempted to use the definition of work, $W = F\Delta x_{\parallel}$. But, no, since the force of the archer on the string is changing, this equation for work is not simple to apply. Instead, you should use the entire work-energy theorem.

To find the work done by the archer in pulling back the bowstring, write the work-energy theorem, considering the time from when he starts pulling until the maximum extension. Since the arrow is at rest before the archer starts pulling, and is *still* at rest when the string is pulled all the way back, the change in kinetic energy is zero. The potential energy of a spring is zero at the equilibrium position and is $\frac{1}{2}kx^2$ at full extension. The work done by the archer is a nonconservative force, since it changes the mechanical energy of the string-arrow system. We get

$$W_{NC} = (0) + (\tfrac{1}{2}kx^2 - 0)$$

But this isn't solvable yet—we know the distance x the archer pulled to be 0.30 m (i.e., 30 cm). But what is k, the spring constant of the "spring"? Use the equation $F = kx$ when the bow is fully extended. The problem says the maximum force the archer pulls with is 200 N when the string is extended 0.30m. Plugging into $F = kx$ and solving for k gives $k = 670$ N/m.[4]

Now the work done by the archer is $\frac{1}{2}(670 \text{ N/m})(0.30 \text{ m})^2 = 30$ J.

---

[3] See Chapter 14 for further discussion of rotational kinetic energy.

[4] No, *not* 666.6666666666 N/m. Use two significant figures, unless you want your 10th-grade chemistry teacher to have heart palpitations.

The AP exam could certainly ask for this calculation. Or, the exam might ask, "If the archer instead pulls back 60 cm, what will happen to the work done by the archer?" The work-energy theorem still applies, the kinetic energy terms still go away, and the work done is still $\frac{1}{2}kx^2$. The spring constant is a property of a spring (or in this case, a bowstring). So k doesn't change. We doubled the displacement from equilibrium, x. Since the variable x is squared, then we don't multiply the work done by a factor of two when we double x; we multiply the work done by a factor of 2^2 (i.e., by a factor of four). The archer has to do four times as much work.

How about finding out how fast the arrow would be traveling when the archer shoots it? We cannot use kinematics with a varying net force or a varying acceleration. Use the work-energy theorem again; except this time, let the problem start when the archer released the bowstring, and end when the string gets back to the equilibrium position and the arrow is released. Now, since no nonconservative forces act,[5] the equation becomes

$$0 = (0 - \tfrac{1}{2}mv^2) + (\tfrac{1}{2}kx^2 - 0)$$

The kinetic energy goes from zero to something; while we don't know the value of the arrow's final kinetic energy, we know the equation for that kinetic energy is $\frac{1}{2}mv^2$. The potential energy goes from $\frac{1}{2}kx^2$ to zero, because for a spring, $x = 0$ is by definition the equilibrium position.

Whenever all the forces acting are conservative, mechanical energy is conserved. This means that energy can be changed from potential to kinetic or back, but the total mechanical energy must remain the same always. Here the initial potential energy was 30 J—that's the same $\frac{1}{2}kx^2$ calculation that we did above. These 30 J of potential energy are entirely converted to kinetic energy. So set $30\text{ J} = \frac{1}{2}mv^2$ and solve for v. (Use the 0.10-kg mass of the arrow for m.) The speed is 24 m/s.

When you are asked to do a calculation, it's worth asking: Is the answer reasonable? One m/s is about 2 miles per hour.[6] This arrow was traveling in the neighborhood of 50 mph—about the speed of a car, but less than the speed of a professional baseball pitch.[7]

Exam Tip from an AP Physics Veteran

If the spring were instead hanging vertically instead of vibrating horizontally, this problem would be *solved the same way*. When you have a vertical spring, define the equilibrium position $x = 0$ as the place where the mass would hang at permanent rest. Then, $F = kx$ gives the *net* force on the hanging object, rather than just the force applied by the spring; and you can use $PE = \frac{1}{2}kx^2$ (not mgh) to calculate the object's potential energy.

Power

Whether you walk up a mountain or whether a car drives you up the mountain, the same amount of work has to be done on you. (You weigh a certain number of newtons, and you have to be lifted up the same distance either way!) But clearly there's something different

---

[5]The force of the bowstring is a conservative force, because the potential energy it stores is part of the mechanical energy of the bowstring-arrow system.

[6]For those of you who didn't grow up in America, 1 m/s is a bit less than 4 km/hr.

[7]For those of you who are uncomfortable with the World's Greatest Sport, this is less than the speed of a tennis player's serve.

about walking up over the course of several hours and driving up over several minutes. That difference is power.

> Power: energy/time

Power is, thus, measured in units of joules/second, also known as watts. A car engine puts out hundreds of horsepower, equivalent to maybe 100 kilowatts, whereas you'd work hard to put out a power of just a few hundred watts.

› Practice Problems

Note: An additional drill involving graphical analysis of a mass on a spring is available in Chapter 18.

1. A 0.5-kg cart released from rest at the top of a smooth incline has gravitational energy of 6 J relative to the base of the incline.

   (a) Calculate the cart's speed at the bottom of the incline.

   (b) When the cart has rolled halfway down the incline, the potential energy of the cart-earth system will be:
   (A) Greater than 3 J
   (B) Less than 3 J
   (C) Equal to 3 J
   Justify your answer.

   (c) When the cart has rolled halfway down the incline, the cart's kinetic energy will be
   (A) Greater than 3 J
   (B) Less than 3 J
   (C) Equal to 3 J
   (D) Unknown without knowledge of the cart's speed
   Justify your answer.

   (d) When the cart has rolled halfway down the incline, the cart's speed will be:
   (A) Half of its speed at the bottom
   (B) Greater than half of its speed at the bottom
   (C) Less than half of its speed at the bottom

   (e) A 1.0-kg cart is released from rest at the top of the same incline. At the bottom, it will be moving
   (A) Faster than the 0.5-kg cart
   (B) Slower than the 0.5-kg cart
   (C) The same speed as the 0.5-kg cart

2. A 0.1-kg stone sits at rest on top of a compressed vertical spring. The potential energy stored in the spring-earth-stone system is 40 J. The spring is released, throwing the stone straight up into the air a distance much greater than the distance the spring had been compressed.

   (a) How much kinetic energy will the stone have when it first leaves the spring?

   (b) How much gravitational energy, relative to the spot where the stone was released, will the stone have when it reaches the peak of its flight?

   (c) Calculate the height above the release point to which the stone travels.

   (d) Suggest something we could change about this situation that would cause the stone to reach a height double that calculated in Part (c).

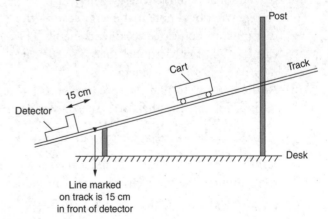

3. In the laboratory, a motion detector records the speed of a cart as a function of time, stopping its reading when the cart is 15 cm in front of the detector at the line marked on the track. The cart is released from rest at the position shown.

   (a) The kinetic energy of the cart at the line marked on the track is equal to the gravitational energy mgh of the cart at its initial position. On the preceding diagram, draw and label the distance you would measure for the height h of the cart.

(b) Explain in some detail how commonly available laboratory equipment could be used to measure the labeled height h.

(c) If the height h were doubled in a second trial, the motion detector would read
   (A) The same speed as in the first trial
   (B) Two times the speed in the first trial
   (C) Four times the speed in the first trial
   (D) $\sqrt{2}$ times the speed in the first trial
   Justify your answer.

4. Student A lifts a 50-N box from the floor straight up to a height of 40 cm in 2 s. Student B lifts a 40-N box straight up from the floor to a height of 50 cm in 1 s.

(a) Compared to Student A, Student B does
   (A) The same work but develops more power
   (B) The same work but develops less power
   (C) More work but develops less power
   (D) Less work but develops more power
   Justify your answer.

(b) Now Student A instead lifts the 50-N box from the floor diagonally, moving the box 40 cm to the right and 40 cm upward in the same 2 s.
   (A) Compared to the work he did originally, does Student A do more, less, or the same work?
   (B) Compared to the power he developed originally, does Student A develop more, less, or the same power?

› Solutions to Practice Problems

1. (a) Here gravitational energy is converted to kinetic energy. ("Smooth" generally means friction is negligible.) Kinetic energy at the bottom will be 6 J, which is equal to $\frac{1}{2}mv^2$. Plug in the 0.5-kg mass of the cart and solve for v to get 4.9 m/s.

(b) Gravitational potential energy is mgh. Since the h term is in the numerator and not squared or square rooted, cutting h in half cuts the whole equation in half as well; so the cart's gravitational potential energy will be 3 J.

(c) Any gravitational potential energy lost by the cart must be converted to kinetic energy. The cart lost 3 J of gravitational energy, so the cart now has 3 J of kinetic energy.

(d) At the bottom, to find the speed we set 6 J $= \frac{1}{2}mv^2$. Solving for the cart's speed, we get $v = \sqrt{\dfrac{2 \cdot (6\ \text{J})}{m}}$. We're going to cut that 6 J term in half. Since the 6 J is under the square root, though, we don't cut the speed in half; instead, we multiply the speed by $\dfrac{1}{\sqrt{2}}$. If you don't see why that gives a speed greater than half the speed at the bottom, try carrying out the entire calculation—you should get 3.5 m/s.

(e) The energy conversion is the same—we're setting gravitational energy (mgh) at the top

equal to kinetic energy ($\frac{1}{2}mv^2$) at the bottom. Notice the mass on both sides—the mass cancels and so doesn't affect the result. Thus, the speed is the same for either cart. Again, feel free to do the calculation with $m = 1.0$ kg to get 4.9 m/s again.

2. (a) No forces external to the spring-earth-stone system act on the block. Therefore, mechanical energy is conserved. The 40 J of potential energy is converted to the stone's kinetic energy, or 40 J.

(b) Again, mechanical energy is conserved. The 40 J of kinetic energy are now converted entirely to 40 J of gravitational energy.

(c) That 40 J of gravitational energy at the peak can be set equal to mgh. Solve for h to get 40 m.

(d) The energy conversion here is spring energy → gravitational energy. Mathematically, that's $\frac{1}{2}kx^2 = mgh$. Solving for h, $h = \frac{kx^2}{2m}$. To double the height, we could use a spring with double the spring constant of the original spring, because k is unexponented[8] in the numerator. We could compress the spring 1.4 times its original compression, since when the x in the numerator is squared, that would multiply the whole expression by 2. We could use a

---

[8] If "unexponented" is a word...

rock of mass 0.05 kg; with m in the denominator, halving the mass doubles the entire expression. (Okay, I suppose we could go to some new planet where g is 5 N/kg. If you will fund that trip, I'll give you credit for that answer.)

3. (a) In the equation mgh, h represents the vertical distance above the lowest position or some reference point. Here the reference point is the line on the track. The motion detector reads the front of the cart, so h must be measured to the front of the cart, not the middle or back. See above for the answer.

   (b) Use a meterstick, obviously, but it's not an easy measurement to make. First, measure the vertical distance from the desk to the line on the track 15 cm in front of the detector. Then measure the vertical distance from the desk to the track directly under the front of the cart; then subtract the two distance measurements. You can get more accurate measurements if you use a bubble level and plumb bob to ensure the table is horizontal and the measurements are vertical. (If you want to measure along the track the distance from the front of the cart to the line, use an angle measurer to get the angle of the track, then use trigonometry.)

(c) The energy conversion here is gravitational energy → kinetic energy. In equations, that's $mgh = \frac{1}{2}mv^2$. Solve for v to get $v = \sqrt{2gh}$. The variable h is in the numerator but under the square root, so doubling h multiplies the speed by the square root of 2, choice D.

4. (a) The work done by the student is equal to the change in the box's gravitational potential energy—that's mgh. The time it takes the student to lift the box doesn't depend on time at all. Plugging in, we find that Student A does (5 kg)(10 N/kg)(0.40 m) = 20 J of work on the box. Student B does (4 kg)(10 N/kg)(0.50 m) = 20 J of work, also. Now, power is work divided by the time it takes to do that work. Since they do the same amount of work, whoever takes less time to do the work develops more power. That's Student B. So the answer is choice A.

   (b) (A) As above, the work done by Student A on the box is mgh. Here h represents the vertical height above the lowest position. Since that vertical height is still 40 cm, Student A has done the same work. (You could also recognize that the horizontal displacement is not parallel to the box's weight, or to the force Student A applied to lift the box.[9])
   (B) Since the work done by Student A is the same as before, and it took the same amount of time, the power (= work/time) is the same.

› Rapid Review

- Work is done when a force is exerted on an object, and that object moves parallel to the direction of the force.

- A "conservative" force converts potential energy to other forms of mechanical energy when it does work. Thus, a conservative force does not change the mechanical energy of a system.

- The only types of potential energy used in AP Physics 1 are due to gravity (mgh) and due to a spring ($\frac{1}{2}kx^2$).

- The work-energy theorem can be written as $W_{NC} = (\Delta KE) + (\Delta PE)$, where W_{NC} is the work done by a nonconservative force.

- Whenever the force on an object is not steady, energy conservation methods must be used to solve the problem. The most common of these situations are curved tracks, springs, and pendulums.

---

[9]The force Student A applies on the box is straight up, at least while the box is moving at constant speed. Once the box starts moving horizontally, no force in that direction is necessary to continue its motion—that's Newton's first law.

CHAPTER 14

Rotation

IN THIS CHAPTER

Summary: When an object rotates, the rotation obeys rules similar to those of a moving object. Most equations and concepts have analogues for rotation. Whereas mass describes an object's resistance to a change in speed, *rotational inertia* describes an object's resistance to a change in rotational speed. Rotational inertia depends on mass as well as on the distribution of that mass.

Definitions

- ✪ **Centripetal acceleration** is the name given to an object's acceleration toward the center of a circle. "Centripetal" simply means "toward the center."
- ✪ **Torque** occurs when a force applied to an object could cause the object to rotate.
- ✪ The **lever arm** for a force is the closest distance from the fulcrum, pivot, or axis of rotation to the line on which that force acts.
- ✪ Everything covered in the previous review chapters is sufficient to describe "translational" motion. When an object rotates around a central point, or when an object is itself rotating as it moves, then we need some additional concepts. Just know that each of these rotational quantities is not truly new. Each rotational quantity should be treated exactly the same way as its translational analogue: for example, if you know how to deal with linear momentum, then angular momentum applies the same ideas to rotating objects.

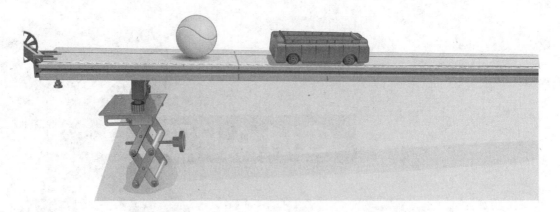

The ball rolling down the ramp in the preceding figure has translational kinetic energy because it is moving. It also has rotational kinetic energy because it is spinning. The ball is losing gravitational energy because it is changing its vertical height; that loss of potential energy is converted into a gain in kinetic energy because no nonconservative forces act on the ball.

Circular Motion

Example 1: A car of mass 1,000 kg travels at constant speed around a flat curve that has a radius of curvature of 100 m. The car is going as fast as it can go without skidding.

Does this car have an acceleration? Why yes, it does, even though it moves at constant speed. Its acceleration along its direction of motion is zero, because the car isn't speeding up or slowing down. However, its direction of motion is always changing; acceleration is technically the change in an object's vector *velocity* each second, and a change in the direction of motion is a change in velocity.

FACT: When an object moves in a circle, it has an acceleration directed toward the center of the circle. The amount of that acceleration is

$$\frac{v^2}{r}$$

Strategy: When an object is moving in a circle, often a standard Newton's second law approach is correct. Draw a free-body diagram, and then write $F_{net} = ma$ in each direction.

Draw a free-body diagram of this car as it moves. It's most useful to view this car from behind; let's say the car is turning to the right, so that the center of the circular motion is in the place indicated.

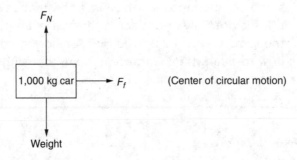

The forces are as follows:

F_N is the normal force of the road on the car.
Weight is the force of the Earth on the car.
F_f is the frictional force of the road on the car.

Wait, why is friction acting to the right? Shouldn't friction act opposite the direction of motion?

Ah. There certainly could be friction or air drag acting backwards, opposite the direction of motion; but with the car moving at constant speed, that would have to be canceled by a forward engine force.[1] Since we know the car moves at constant speed, that's probably not particularly relevant to the problem.

When a car goes around a flat curve, some sort of force must act toward the center of the circle—otherwise, the centripetal acceleration couldn't exist. How do we know it's friction in this case? Imagine the car were moving forward on a slick, flat sheet of ice. The car couldn't go around a curve at all, then; turning the wheels would do nothing. On an asphalt road, it's the static frictional force of the asphalt on the tires that pushes the car toward the center of the circle.

No matter what kind of question you're asked about this situation, the next step is to use Newton's second law in both the vertical and horizontal directions. Vertically, the car's acceleration is zero; the car isn't burrowing into the road or lifting off the road. Horizontally, we don't have a numerical value for the acceleration, but we know its equation: $\frac{v^2}{r}$.

$$F_N - weight = 0$$
$$F_f = m\frac{v^2}{r}$$

The first equation tells us that the normal force on the car is equal to the car's weight of 10,000 N. In order to calculate the friction force on the car, we'd need to know one of two pieces of additional information. On one hand, if we know the car's speed, we can use the second equation to calculate F_f. On the other hand, since we know the normal force, if we knew the coefficient of static friction between the car's tires and the road, we could calculate the friction force using $F_f = \mu F_n$.

Strategy: You cannot allow yourself to become angry or frustrated when you don't have enough information to complete a calculation. Sometimes, an AP Physics 1 problem will be deliberately concocted to ask, "What additional information would you need to solve this problem?" (Remember, actual calculation on the exam will be rare.) Or, often, some seemingly necessary information will be omitted, because it will turn out that the omitted information is irrelevant.

For example, an excellent problem using this situation might *not* give the mass of the car but instead give the car's speed and ask what minimum coefficient of friction would be necessary for the car to round the curve. Pretend, say, that the car's speed is 20 m/s.

---

[1]Technically, this would be a force of static friction between the tires and the road, but that's a different day's lesson.

I can't do that. I need the mass to calculate the force of friction.

Well, true, if you needed a value for the force of friction, but that's not the question. We want the coefficient of friction.

Yeah, I know. The equation is $F_f = \mu F_n$. I need the mass to calculate the friction force, *and* since the normal force is equal to the weight, I need the mass to calculate that, too. This isn't possible.

When you're stuck with a calculation that you think needs a value that wasn't given, try just making up that value. It's likely that the unknown value will cancel out. Or, if you want to be more elegant, assign a variable to the unknown value.

Let the mass be m. The equations we wrote from the free-body diagram show that the friction force is $m\frac{v^2}{r}$. The normal force is the weight of the car, or the car's mass times the gravitational field g of 10 N/kg. Now use the equation for friction force:

$$F_f = \mu F_n$$
$$m\frac{v^2}{r} = \mu\,(mg)$$

Look at that: solve for μ, and the masses cancel. You can plug in the 20-m/s speed and the 100-m radius to get $\mu = 0.4$. A car of *any* mass can go around this curve, as long as the coefficient of friction is at least 0.4.[2]

Torque

FACT: The torque τ provided by a force is given by the equation

$$\boxed{\tau = Fd_\perp}$$

I write the symbol "$\perp$" by the d to emphasize that the distance we want is the perpendicular distance from the line of the force to the fulcrum.[3] Usually that's an easy distance to visualize.

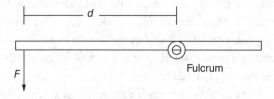

---

[2]That makes perfect sense—ever see those yellow signs warning of the appropriate speed for going around a curve? They just say, "Curve: 40 mph." They certainly *don't* say something silly like "Curve: go 10 mph for every 500 kg in your vehicle."
[3]The "fulcrum" is the point about which an object rotates, or could rotate.

What if a force isn't acting perpendicular to an extended object, like the force F on the pivoted bar that follows?

Example 2:

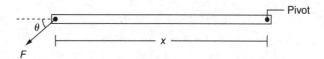

The easiest way to find the torque applied by this force is to break the force F into vertical and horizontal components.

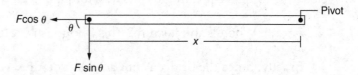

The vertical component of F applies a torque of $(F\sin\theta)x$. The horizontal component of F does not apply any torque, because it could not cause the bar to rotate. The total torque provided by the force F is just $(F\sin\theta)x$.

Lever Arm

This distance $d_\perp$ is sometimes referred to as the "lever arm" for a force. By definition, the lever arm for a force is the closest distance from the fulcrum to the line on which that force acts.

An alternative method of determining the torque applied by the force in Example 2 would be to find the lever arm instead of breaking F into components. Extend the line of the force in the diagram—now it's easy to label the lever arm as the closest distance from the pivot to the line of the force. By trigonometry, you can figure out that the lever arm distance is equal to $x\sin\theta$. No matter how you look at it, then, the torque provided by F is still $(F\sin\theta)x$.

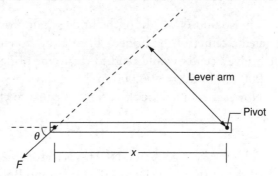

Calculations with Torque

You may be asked to calculate a force or a torque when an extended object experiences multiple forces, but generally only when that object is in equilibrium—that is, when up forces equal down forces, left forces equal right forces, and counterclockwise torques equal clockwise torques.

Example 3: Bob is standing on a bridge. The bridge itself weighs 10,000 N. The span between supports A and B is 80 m. Bob, whose mass is 100 kg, stands 20 m from the center of the bridge as shown.

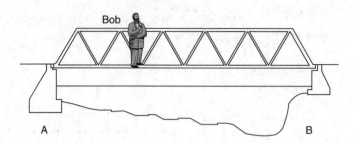

Generally, a problem with a bridge, plank, or some sort of extended object will ask you to describe or solve for the forces supporting the bridge. The approach is to make a list of torques acting in each direction, clockwise and counterclockwise, and then set the counterclockwise torques equal to the clockwise torques.

Aarrgh. Where's the fulcrum? This bridge isn't rotating anywhere!

Exactly. Since the bridge is not actually rotating, you can choose anywhere you like as the fulcrum. It's easiest in this case to choose one of the supports as the fulcrum, because then that support provides zero torque, and the lever arm for that force would be zero.

Let's choose support A as the fulcrum. What torques do we see?

The force of support B (I'll call it F_B) provides a torque equal to $F_B(80 \text{ m})$, because support B is 80 m from support A. This torque is *counterclockwise*, because pushing up on the bridge pivoted at A would rotate the bridge this way: ↺.

The weight of Bob provides a clockwise torque of $(1{,}000 \text{ N})(20 \text{ m}) = 20{,}000 \text{ m} \cdot \text{N}$. (We don't use 100 kg, because that's a mass, not a force; the force acting on the bridge is due to Bob's weight.)

Exam Tip from an AP Physics Veteran
In a torque problem with a heavy extended object, just pretend that the object's weight is all hanging at the object's center of mass.

The 10,000-N weight of the bridge itself provides a torque. Pretend that all 10,000 N act at the center of the bridge, 40 m away from each support. A weight pulling down at the bridge's center would tend to rotate the bridge clockwise. The torque we want here is $(10{,}000 \text{ N})(40 \text{ m}) = 400{,}000 \text{ m} \cdot \text{N}$, clockwise.

Now, set counterclockwise torques equal to clockwise torques:

$$F_B(80 \text{ m}) = 20{,}000 \text{ m} \cdot \text{N} + 400{,}000 \text{ m} \cdot \text{N}$$

Solve for F_B to get 5,300 N. This is reasonable because support B is supporting *less* than half of the 11,000-N weight of the bridge and Bob. Because Bob is closer to support A, and otherwise the bridge is symmetric, A should bear the majority of the weight—and it does.

Rotational Kinematics

An object's "rotational speed" says how fast the object rotates—that is, how many degrees or radians it rotates through per second. Rotational speed is generally given by the lowercase Greek variable omega, ω. An object's "rotational acceleration" α describes how much the rotational speed changes in one second. The variable θ represents the total angle through which an object rotates in some time period.

Just like position x, speed v, and acceleration a are related through the kinematics formulas given in Chapter 10, rotational angle, speed, and acceleration are related by the same formulas:

$$1. \quad \omega_f = \omega_0 + \alpha t$$
$$2. \quad \Delta\theta = \omega_0 t + \tfrac{1}{2}\alpha t^2$$
$$3. \quad \omega_f^2 = \omega_0^2 + 2\alpha\Delta\theta$$

It is highly unlikely that you'll be asked to actually make much of a calculation with these equations. Rather, you might be asked to rank rotating objects by their angular speed or acceleration; or you might be asked, "Is it possible to calculate…." The general approach to a calculation should be identical to that for nonrotational kinematics: Make a chart with the five variables in it. If you can identify a value for three of the five variables, the problem is solvable.

Rotational Inertia

Just like "inertia" refers to an object's ability to resist changes in its motion, "rotational inertia"[4] refers to an object's ability to resist changes in its rotational motion. Two things affect an object's ability to resist rotational motion changes: the object's mass and how far away that mass is from the center of rotation.

There are three ways to figure out something's rotational inertia:

1. For a single "point" particle that is moving in a circle around an axis, its rotational inertia is given by the equation $I = mr^2$. Here, m is the mass of the particle, and r is the radius of the circle.
2. For an object with some kind of structure, like a spinning ball, a disk, or a rod, a formula for its rotational inertia will generally be given if you need it.
3. For a system consisting of several objects, you can add together the rotational inertia of each of the objects to find the total rotational inertia of a system.

Example 4: Three meter-long, uniform 200-g bars each have a small 200-g mass attached to them in the positions shown in the diagram. A person grips the bars in the locations shown and attempts to rotate the bars in the directions shown.

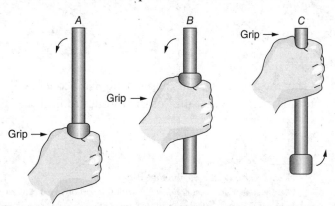

---

[4]The AP Physics 1, Algebra-Based Exam will always use the term "rotational inertia," usually represented by the variable I. Many textbooks and teachers will use the older term "moment of inertia" to refer to the same quantity. Don't be confused.

It's possible that you might be asked to calculate the rotational inertia of one of these gripped rods. If so, in the problem statement you'd be given the formula to calculate the rotational inertia of a rod: $\frac{1}{12}ML^2$ when pivoted in the center, and $\frac{1}{3}ML^2$ when pivoted at the end.[5] You know that the rotational inertia of the small mass is mr^2, where r is the distance from the mass to the grip. In each situation, add the rotational inertia of the rod to the rotational inertia of the small mass.

For Grip A, the rod's rotational inertia is $\frac{1}{3}ML^2 = \frac{1}{3}(0.2 \text{ kg})(1 \text{ m})^2 = 0.067 \text{ kg}\cdot\text{m}^2$. The small mass contributes nothing to the rotational inertia, because it is not rotating—the r term in $I = mr^2$ is zero. Thus, the total rotational inertia is $0.067 \text{ kg}\cdot\text{m}^2$.

For Grip B, the rod is pivoted in the center, so its rotational inertia is $\frac{1}{12}ML^2 = 0.017 \text{ kg}\cdot\text{m}^2$. The small mass isn't rotating. So the total rotational inertia is just $0.017 \text{ kg}\cdot\text{m}^2$.

Finally, for Grip C, the rod's rotational inertia is $\frac{1}{3}ML^2 = \frac{1}{3}(0.2 \text{ kg})(1 \text{ m})^2 = 0.067 \text{ kg}\cdot\text{m}^2$. The small mass's rotational inertia is $(0.2 \text{ kg})(1 \text{ m})^2 = 0.20 \text{ kg}\cdot\text{m}^2$. Thus, the total rotational inertia is the sum of both contributions, $0.27 \text{ kg}\cdot\text{m}^2$.

Calculations aren't usually the point, though. This situation is just begging to become a ranking task: without any specific values for the masses or lengths of the items, rank the grips by their rotational inertia. As long as we know that the small mass is equal to the mass of the rod, and that the rods are equal in length, then the ranking can be done. You can see that the small mass contributes nothing to the rotational inertia in A and B without calculation.

You can see that Grip A provides a greater rotational inertia than Grip B, *even without knowing the formulas $\frac{1}{12}ML^2$ and $\frac{1}{3}ML^2$*. Reason from the properties of an object that contribute to its rotational inertia: mass, and how far away that mass is from the axis of rotation. The rods have the same mass in A and B. But Rod A has much more mass that is far away from the grip; Rod B has more mass closer to the grip. Therefore, Rod B will be easier to rotate, and Rod A will have more rotational inertia.

Then, of course, Grip C combines the "worst" of both worlds: just the rod by itself provides the same rotational inertia as in Grip A, but the mass is also contributing to the rotational inertia. The final ranking would be $I_C > I_A > I_B$.[6]

Newton's Second Law for Rotation

Just as linear acceleration is caused by a net force, *angular* acceleration is caused by a net *torque:*

$$\boxed{\tau_{net} = I\alpha}$$

Only the net torque can cause an angular acceleration. If more than one force is applying a torque, then use the sum[7] of the torques to find the angular acceleration.

---

[5] Here, L represents the length of the bar.

[6] Okay, you *do* need to get comfortable with this sort of verbal explanation of concepts that refers to equations and facts but doesn't make direct calculation. If you are confused on this sort of problem, it is okay to make up values for whatever you need, and calculate. I don't at all recommend memorizing all the different formulas for rotational inertia of a rod, sphere, hoop, disk, etc. But if you happen to remember them, it's fine to use them.

[7] Or, if the torques are acting in opposite directions, use the difference.

Example 5: A turntable of known mass and radius is attached to a motor that provides a known torque. Using the torque of the motor and the rotational inertia of the turntable in Newton's second law for rotation, then, using rotational kinematics, a student predicts that it should take 5.0 s for the turntable to speed up from rest to its maximum rotational speed. When the student measures the necessary time, though, he discovers that it takes 6.8 s to reach maximum rotational speed.

First, you should be able to describe how to perform such a measurement in your laboratory. There's a bazillion ways of doing so: the idea is to make many measurements of rotational speed until that rotational speed doesn't change. Rotational speed could be measured with a video camera and a protractor, by running the video frame-by-frame to see how many degrees the turntable advances per frame. Or tape a tiny piece of paper to the edge of the turntable, and have that paper trigger a few photogates; you can measure the angle between the photogates, and the photogates will tell you how much time it took for the turntable to traverse that angle.

This problem is setting up for you to figure out why the prediction didn't match the measurement.[8] The most obvious issue is that the torque provided by the motor might not be the *net* torque on the turntable. Friction in the bearings of the turntable could easily provide a torque in the opposite direction to that provided by the motor. Thus, the real value for net torque will be *lower* than the value the student used. And, by $\tau_{net} = I\alpha$, the real angular acceleration will be lower; finally, by $\omega_f = \omega_0 + \alpha t$, a smaller angular acceleration to get to the same final speed means that the time t will be longer than predicted.

Angular Momentum

The rotational analogue of the impulse-momentum theorem involves torque and angular momentum rather than force and linear momentum:

$$\boxed{\Delta L = \tau \cdot \Delta t}$$

Here τ is the net torque acting on an object, and Δt is the time during which that torque acts. The change in the object's angular momentum is ΔL.

An object's angular momentum can be calculated using three methods:

1. For a single "point" particle that is moving in a circle around an axis, its angular momentum is given by $L = mvr$. Here, r represents the radius of that circle.
2. For a single "point" particle that is moving in a straight line,[9] its angular momentum is also given by $L = mvr$; but in this case r represents the "distance of closest

---

[8]Please don't automatically say "human error." There's no such thing as "human error," and using that phrase is basically an automatic *wrong* on the AP exam.

[9]Angular momentum must always be defined with respect to some central axis of rotation. For most rotating objects, that axis is obvious. For a particle moving in a straight line, you have to say what position you're calculating angular momentum for, but the particle can still have angular momentum.

approach" from the line of the particle's motion to the position about which angular momentum is calculated, as shown below.

3. For an extended object with known rotational inertia I, angular momentum is given by $L = I\omega$.

For most problems, you can reason by analogy to the linear impulse-momentum theorem. Just as a force applied for some time will change an object's linear momentum, a torque applied for some time will change an object's angular momentum. Just as the area under a force versus time graph gives the change in an object's linear momentum, the area under a torque versus time graph gives the change in an object's angular momentum.

Conservation of Angular Momentum

FACT: In any system in which the only torques acting are between objects in that system, angular momentum is conserved. This effectively means that angular momentum is conserved in *all* collisions, but also in numerous other situations.

Example 6: A uniform rod is at rest on a frictionless table. A ball of putty, whose mass is half that of the rod, is moving to the left, as shown. The ball of putty collides with and sticks to the rod.

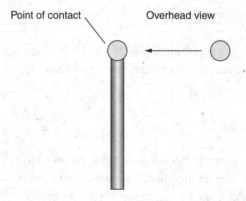

Point of contact   Overhead view

Exam Tip from an AP Physics Veteran
Usually, the fulcrum or axis of rotation is obvious. But when an object is not forced to pivot at some specific position, if it rotates it will most likely rotate about its center of mass.

Start with what quantities are conserved for the putty-rod system. It's a collision, in which the only forces involved are the force of the putty-on-rod and rod-on-putty. Therefore, linear momentum is conserved. Similarly, the putty applies a torque to the rod because it pushes on the rod at a position away from its center of mass. But the only torques involved are provided by objects in the system, so angular momentum is also conserved.

This collision cannot be elastic because the putty sticks to the rod; so kinetic energy was not conserved. Mechanical energy was also not conserved because the kinetic energy of the putty was not stored as potential energy in a spring or gravitational field. Of course, the sum of *all* forms of energy was conserved, because whatever kinetic energy was lost by the putty-rod system was converted to microscopic internal energy, and thus the temperature of the putty-rod will increase.

Where's the center of mass? Using the equation from Chapter 12, call $x = 0$ the top of the rod. Pretend the rod is 1 m long and 1 kg in mass. Then the putty is 0.5 kg in mass. So $m_{putty} (0) + m_{rod} (0.5 \text{ m}) = m_{total} (x_{cm})$.[10] Plugging in the masses, you get $x = 0.33$ m.

But the problem emphatically did *not* say that the rod was 1 m long.

Right. Whatever the rod's length, its center of mass is one-third of the way down the rod.

> **Exam Tip from an AP Physics Veteran**
> When you're asked about the center of mass speed, you can ignore all angular stuff. In that case, just treat the collision as if these were carts colliding.

Again, you can make up values to find the speed of the center of mass after collision. If the putty's initial speed were 1 m/s, then the total momentum before collision is $0.5 \text{ N} \cdot \text{s}$. By conservation of momentum, that's also the total momentum after collision, but the mass of the combined objects after collision is 1.5 kg. The speed of the center of mass would be 0.33 m/s. But since the initial speed wasn't given, you can only definitively say that the speed of the center of mass after collision will be one-third of the speed of the putty before collision.

Conservation of Angular Momentum Without Collisions

FACT: Angular momentum is conserved any time an object, or system of objects, experiences no net torque.

Example 7: A person stands on a frictionless turntable. She and the turntable are spinning at one revolution every two seconds.

Sure, the person can wiggle and exert a torque on the turntable. But this torque is internal to the person-turntable system. The person thus cannot change the angular momentum of the person-turntable system.

This doesn't mean that she can't change her angular speed. What if she throws her arms way out away from her body?[11] Her rotational inertia would change, because she'd have the same total mass but more of that mass would be far away from the center of rotation. Her angular momentum can't change. By $L = I\omega$, to keep a constant L with a bigger I, the angular speed ω must decrease. This is the physical basis for how figure skaters can control their spinning.

---

[10]It's (0.5 m) because the center of mass of the rod by itself must be halfway down the rod.

[11]AP reader Matt Sckalor quite reasonably asks, "After she throws the first arm, what part of her body does she use to throw the other arm?" Perhaps I should say she "extends" her arms.

Example 8: A planet orbits a sun in an elliptical orbit.

You won't have to deal with elliptical orbits in the sense of making calculations, or using Kepler's laws and Physics C-style calculations. But you can understand that angular momentum of a planet orbiting a sun must be conserved. Since the force of the sun on a planet is always on a line toward the sun itself, this force cannot provide any torque—there's no lever arm. With no torque exerted on a planet, that planet cannot change its angular momentum. Treat the planet as a point particle; its angular momentum is $L = mvr$, where r is the distance from the sun. Whenever r is big, v must be small to keep L constant. The farther away the planet is from the sun, the slower it moves.

Rotational Kinetic Energy

FACT: When an object is rotating, its rotational kinetic energy is

$$\tfrac{1}{2}I\omega^2$$

In Example 6, the putty-rod system has *both* rotational *and* linear kinetic energy after the collision. The total kinetic energy is then the sum of $\tfrac{1}{2}mv^2$, where v is the speed of the center of mass, plus the rotational kinetic energy.

When an object rotates, the work-energy theorem still applies. The kinetic energy terms each include the addition of rotational and linear kinetic energy. In Example 6, work is done by a nonconservative force (the force of the rod on the putty). To find out how much work was done, set $W_{\mathrm{NC}} = \Delta KE + \Delta PE$. This situation doesn't involve a spring or a changing vertical height, so $\Delta PE = 0$. The kinetic energy was originally just $\tfrac{1}{2}mv^2$ for the putty; after the collision, the kinetic energy is as discussed in the previous paragraph, the speed of the center of mass plus the rotational kinetic energy.

› Practice Problems

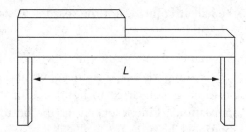

1. A uniform wooden block has a mass m. On it is resting half of an identical block, as shown above. The blocks are supported by two table legs, as shown.

   (a) Which table leg, if either, should provide a larger force on the bottom block? Answer with specific reference to the torque equation.

   (b) In terms of given variables and fundamental constants, what is the force of the right-hand table leg on the bottom mass?

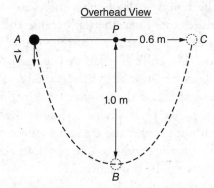

Overhead View

2. A small ball of mass m moving on a frictionless horizontal surface is attached to a rubber band whose other end is fixed at point P. The ball moves along the dotted line in the preceding figure, stretching the rubber band. When it passes Point A, its velocity is v_A directed as shown.

   (a) Is the angular momentum of the ball about Point P conserved between positions A and B?

   (b) Is the linear momentum of the ball conserved between positions A and B?

   (c) Describe a system in this problem for which mechanical energy is conserved as the ball moves from A to B.

   (d) Explain why the net force on the ball at Point B is not $\frac{mv_A^2}{(1.0 \text{ m})}$.

3. A smooth, solid ball is released from rest from the top of an incline, whose surface is very rough. The ball rolls down the incline without slipping.

   (a) Describe in words the energy conversion for the ball from its release until it reaches the bottom of the incline.

   (b) Is the mechanical energy of the ball-Earth system conserved during its roll?

   (c) This ball is replaced by a new ball, whose surface and mass are identical to the first ball, but which is predominantly hollow inside. Describe any differences in its roll down the incline without slipping, with explicit reference to forms of energy.

› Solutions to Practice Problems

1. (a) Call the force of the left support F_L, and the force of the right support F_R. Consider the middle of the bottom block as the fulcrum. Then one clockwise torque acts: $F_L \cdot (L/2)$. Two counterclockwise torques act, though: $F_R \cdot (L/2)$ and $(1/2)m \cdot (1/4)L$. The point is that if you have to add something to the torque provided by the right support to get the torque provided by the left support, the left support thus provides more torque. Because the supports are the same distance from the center, the left support provides more force, too.

   (b) You certainly could use the reasoning in Part (a) with the fulcrum in the center, along with the total support force equaling $1.5Mg$ (vertical equilibrium of forces). However, it's much easier mathematically to just call the left end of the rod the fulcrum. Then the counterclockwise torque is $F_R \cdot L$. The clockwise torque is $(1/2)mg \cdot (L/4) + mg \cdot (L/2)$. Set these equal and play with the fractions to get $F_R = (\frac{1}{8} + \frac{1}{2})mg = \frac{5}{8}mg$.

2. (a) Angular momentum is conserved when no torques external to the system act. Here the system is just the ball. The only force acting on the ball is the rubber band, which is attached to Point P. The force applied by the rubber band can't have any lever arm with respect to P and thus provides no torque about point P, so the ball's angular momentum about point P can't change. Angular momentum is conserved.

(b) Linear momentum is conserved when no forces external to the system act. Here the system is just the ball. The rubber band is external to the system and applies a force; therefore, linear momentum is *not* conserved.

(c) Mechanical energy is conserved when no force external to the system does work. The rubber band does work on the ball, because it applies a force and stretches in a direction parallel to the force it produces. Consider the rubber band part of the system. The post at Point P still applies a force to the ball–rubber band system, but since the post doesn't move, that force does no work on the ball–rubber band system. Any kinetic energy lost by the ball will be stored as elastic energy in the rubber band. The mechanical energy of the ball–rubber band system is conserved.

(d) The general form of this equation is fine—the ball's path at Point P is, at least in the neighborhood of P, approximately circular. The ball experiences a centripetal acceleration at Point B, and centripetal acceleration is v^2/r. The problem is that if the r term is 1.0 m, then the v term must represent the speed at Point B. With angular momentum conserved, the total of mvr must always be the same. The ball's mass doesn't change. The distance r from Point P gets bigger from A to B, so the speed

must get smaller. The equation given uses the given variable v which represents the speed of the ball at Point A, not the speed at B, and so is invalid.

3. (a) Gravitational energy at the top (because the ball is some vertical height above its lowest position) is converted to both rotational and translational kinetic energy at the bottom—rotational because the ball will be spinning, and translational because the ball's center of mass will move down the incline.

(b) Mechanical energy is conserved when no nonconservative forces act. Here the Earth's gravitational field can give the ball kinetic energy, but since the Earth is part of the system and since the gravitational force is conservative, that still allows for conservation of mechanical energy. Friction is a nonconservative force, but here friction does no work.

(c) The hollow ball of the same mass will have greater rotational inertia, because the mass is concentrated farther from the center of rotation. The ball's gravitational energy before the rolling begins is the same as the previous scenario, because the height of the incline is the same. The total kinetic energy at the bottom will not change; the question is how much of that kinetic energy will be rotational, and how much will be translational.

Rotational KE is $\frac{1}{2}I\omega^2$; the angular speed ω depends on the translational speed v. (The faster the ball is moving, the more it's rotating, too.) Therefore, rotational kinetic energy depends on v^2. Translational kinetic energy also depends on v^2 in the formula $\frac{1}{2}mv^2$. The hollow ball has bigger I. The speed v must be lower for the hollow ball so that $\frac{1}{2}I\omega^2 + \frac{1}{2}mv^2$ adds to the same value for both balls.

❯ Rapid Review

- When an object moves in a circle, it has an acceleration directed toward the center of the circle. The amount of that acceleration is $\frac{v^2}{r}$.

- The torque τ provided by a force is given by the equation $\tau = Fd_\perp$.

- In any system in which the only torques acting are between objects in that system, angular momentum is conserved. This effectively means that angular momentum is conserved in *all* collisions, but also in numerous other situations.

- Angular momentum is conserved any time an object, or system of objects, experiences no net torque.

- When an object is rotating, its rotational kinetic energy is $\frac{1}{2}I\omega^2$.

CHAPTER 15

Gravitation

IN THIS CHAPTER

Summary: The force on an object due to gravity is mg, where m is mass and g is the gravitational field. The gravitational field produced by an object of mass m is $G\dfrac{M}{d^2}$, where d is the distance from the object's center. Want to be sure you know the difference between a gravitational field, a gravitational force, and the universal gravitation constant? This chapter explains these concepts.

Definitions

- ✪ The **gravitational field** g near a planet tells how much 1 kg of mass weighs at a location. Near Earth's surface, the gravitational field is 10 N/kg.
- ✪ The **gravitational force** of a planet on any other object in the planet's gravitational field is mg, where m is the mass of the object experiencing the force.
- ✪ **Newton's gravitation constant** is the universal constant $G = 6 \times 10^{-11}$ N·m²/kg².
- ✪ The **free-fall acceleration** (sometimes imprecisely called the **acceleration due to gravity**) near a planet is, by an amazing coincidence of the universe, equal to the gravitational field near that planet. Near Earth, then, the free-fall acceleration is 10 m/s per second because the gravitational field is 10 N/kg.

The gravitational force is the weakest of the fundamental forces in nature. However, when enormous amounts of mass congregate—as in a star or a planet—the gravitational force becomes dominant. The picture as follows gives a hint of the scales involved in studying stars and planets—it's the Earth and the moon, but drawn to approximately the proper scale. Sure, the Earth seems humongous, especially when you're caught in traffic. But *all* planets and stars seem small when the distances between them are considered.

Earth   Moon

The word *gravity* by itself is an ambiguous term. Begin this chapter by carefully reading the differences between all the various things that could be referred to by the word *gravity*. See the four preceding definitions, each of which relate to the word.

Determining the Gravitational Field

The gravitational field is a vector quantity—this means it has an amount and a direction. The direction is always toward the center of the Earth (or whatever is creating the gravitational field).

FACT: The amount[1] of gravitational field depends on two things: the mass of the planet creating the field (*M*) and the distance you are from that planet's center (*d*). The relevant equation for the gravitation field *g* produced by a planet is

$$g = G\frac{M}{d^2}$$

Some books, and probably even the AP exam, will use the variable *r* for the distance from the planet's center. That's fine, but know that this *r* does *not* necessarily stand for the radius of the planet—it means the distance from the planet's center.

Example 1: A 20-kg rover sits on newly discovered Planet *Z*, which has twice the mass of Earth and twice the diameter of Earth.

You do not get a table of astronomical information on the AP Physics 1, Algebra-Based Exam. Nevertheless, you might well be asked to calculate the gravitational field near the surface of Planet *Z*. How can that be done without knowing the mass of Planet *Z*? You're expected to be fluent in semiquantitative reasoning.

Even though you don't know the value of the mass of the Earth, you know that the mass of Planet *Z* is twice Earth's mass. Whatever the exact mass, the numerator in the gravitational field equation will double for Planet *Z*.

The surface of a planet is one planet-radius away from the planet's center; so here, *d* means the radius of the planet. Planet *Z*'s diameter is twice Earth's, which also means *Z*'s radius is twice Earth's. The *d* term in the denominator is doubled; because *d* is squared, the entire denominator is multiplied by 2^2, which is 4.

---

[1]The exam will refer not to the "amount," but to the "magnitude" of a vector quantity. Just translate in your head.

Combining these effects of mass and radius, the numerator is multiplied by 2, the denominator multiplied by 4, so the entire gravitational field of the Earth is multiplied by one-half. We know Earth's gravitational field—that's 10 N/kg. Planet Z produces a gravitational field of 5 N/kg at the surface. No calculator is necessary.

The formula shows that the gravitational field produced by a planet drops off rapidly as you get far from the planet's center: if you double your distance from the planet's center, then you cut in one-fourth the value of the gravitational field.

This seems easy enough, but think about reality for a moment. Just how often do you double your distance from the center of the Earth? The radius of the Earth is about 4,000 miles. Even when you fly in an airplane, you're no more than about seven miles above the surface; so your distance from the center of the Earth is *still* about 4,000 miles.

The point is, unless you're an astronaut, the gravitational field near the surface of a planet is a constant value. Don't be tricked by the d^2 in the denominator—that only matters when you're considering objects in space.

Determining Gravitational Force

FACT: The weight of an object—that is, the gravitational force of a planet on that object—is given by *mg*.

That 20-kg rover would weigh 200 N on Earth (20 kg times 10 N/kg). But on Planet Z, the rover weighs only 100 N (that's 20 kg times 5 N/kg).

A weight of 100 N means that Planet Z pulls the rover downward with 100 N of force. What about the force of the rover on Planet Z? That's got to be so small it's negligible, right?

Wrong. Newton's third law says that the force of Planet Z on the rover is equal to the force of the rover on Planet Z. The rover pulls up on Planet Z with a force of 100 N.

Now, as you might suspect, you'd never notice or measure any effect from the rover's 100-N force on Planet Z. Planet Z is enormously massive—in the neighborhood of 10^{24} kg. By $F_{net} = ma$, you can calculate that the *acceleration* provided to the planet is immeasurably small.[2] It's the force that's the same, and the acceleration that's different.

Force of Two Planets on One Another—Order of Magnitude Estimates

Example 2: The Earth has a mass of 6.0×10^{24} kg. The sun has a mass of 2.0×10^{30} kg. The Earth orbits the sun in a circle of radius 1.5×10^{11} m.

FACT: The gravitational force of one object on another is given by

$$F = \frac{Gm_1m_2}{d^2}$$

---

[2]And the rover's force on the planet is certainly not the *net* force on the planet, so this $F_{net} = ma$ calculation is silly anyway.

So it seems straightforward, if calculator intensive, to calculate the force the sun exerts on the Earth (or vice versa). Just plug in the numbers. But that's *not* a likely AP Physics 1 exercise! No one cares whether you can use the buttons on your calculator correctly.

Instead, you might be asked, "Which of the following is closest to the force of the sun on the Earth?"

(A) 10^{12} N
(B) 10^{22} N
(C) 10^{32} N
(D) 10^{42} N

Look how far apart these answer choices are. Don't use a calculator—instead make an *order of magnitude estimate*. Plug in just the powers of 10, and the answer will leap off the page. Leaving out the units of each individual term for simplicity, in the equation $F = \dfrac{Gm_1 m_2}{d^2}$ we have

$$\frac{(10^{-11})(10^{24})(10^{30})}{(10^{11})^2}$$

That's easy to simplify without a calculator—add exponents in the numerator, and then subtract the exponents in the denominator.

$$\frac{(10^{43})}{(10^{22})} = 10^{21}\,\text{N}.$$

But that's not one of the choices.

The only reasonable choice, though, is (B) 10^{22} N. The others are at least a factor of a billion too big or too small. Sure, you could have spent five minutes plugging in the more precise values into your calculator,[3] getting 3.3×10^{22} N as the answer. The order of magnitude estimate is as precise as would ever be necessary on the AP Physics 1 Exam, and it's a lot easier, too.

Gravitational Potential Energy

Near the surface of the Earth, the potential energy provided by the gravitational force is

$$\boxed{PE_{gravity} = mgh}$$

That's plenty good enough for calculations with everyday objects.

However, if you're talking about objects way out in space, the gravitational potential energy possessed by two objects near one another is given by

$$\boxed{PE_{gravity} = G\frac{M_1 M_2}{d}}$$

---

[3]And then spend another 10 minutes swearing at the calculator because you left out a parenthesis, or you forgot to type a negative sign, or you forgot a decimal.

This equation is usually written with a negative sign; that negative sign simply indicates that this potential energy is *less* than zero; and in outer-space situations, zero potential energy means the objects are infinitely far away from each other.

This gravitational potential energy can be converted into kinetic energy—if two planets move toward one another due to their mutual gravitational attraction, you might be able to figure out how fast they move by calculating the gravitational potential energy possessed before and after they move. Any lost potential energy was converted into kinetic energy.

Gravitational and Inertial Mass

Example 3: Neil Armstrong had a mass of 77 kg when he went to the moon. The gravitational field on the Moon is one-sixth that on Earth.

The term "mass" is often colloquially defined as the amount of "stuff" in an object. You're likely to see an AP question of the form, "What was Neil Armstrong's mass on the Moon?" The answer is, still 77 kg. Sure, Neil's weight on the Moon was smaller than his weight on Earth, because the gravitational field on the Moon is smaller, but since he didn't cut off his leg or go on a starvation diet, his mass didn't change.

FACT: Gravitational mass indicates how an object responds to a gravitational field.

FACT: Inertial mass indicates how an object accelerates in response to a net force.

FACT: In every experiment ever conducted, an object's gravitational mass is equal to its inertial mass.

The AP exam requires you to distinguish between the two meanings of mass. Simply put, if there's acceleration involved, you're talking about inertial mass. You'll be asked to design experiments to measure each type of mass.

So let's say you want to figure out who has more *gravitational* mass, you or Neil Armstrong. Just put each of you on a balance scale—the one with the bigger scale reading has more gravitational mass. You could use a spring scale, too—whoever compresses the springs more experiences more gravitational force in the same gravitational field, and so has more gravitational mass.

But to figure out experimentally who has more *inertial* mass, you'd put each of you in an identical buggy. Speed up each buggy using the same net force for the same amount of time. Whichever of you has sped up by more—that is, whoever experienced the greater acceleration under the same net force—has the smaller inertial mass.

And if your experiment gives contradictory results—say, that Neil has more inertial mass but that you have more gravitational mass—then you should reject that result as ridiculous. An exam question might pose just this type of situation in which you have to reject impossible results.[4]

---

[4]Well, if you really have repeatable and unassailable results of this nature, you should publish. I guarantee you'll win a Nobel Prize for your work, which is a bit more likely to earn college credit than a 5 on the AP exam.

› Practice Problems

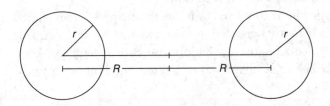

1. Two stars, each of mass M, form a binary system. The stars orbit about a point a distance R from the center of each star, as shown in the diagram above. The stars themselves each have radius r.

   (a) In terms of given variables and fundamental constants, what is the force each star exerts on the other?

   (b) In terms of given variables and fundamental constants, what is the magnitude of the gravitational field at the surface of one of the stars due only to its own mass?

   (c) In terms of given variables and fundamental constants, what is the magnitude of the gravitational field at the midpoint between the stars?

   (d) Explain why the stars don't crash into each other due to the gravitational force between them.

2. A space shuttle orbits Earth 300 km above the equator.

   (a) Explain why it would be impractical for the shuttle to orbit 10 km above the Earth's surface (about 1 km higher than the top of Mount Everest).

   (b) A "geosynchronous orbit" means that the shuttle will always remain over the same spot on Earth. Explain and describe the calculations you would perform in order to determine whether this orbit is geosynchronous. You should not actually carry out the numerical calculations; just describe them in words and show them in symbols.

   (c) The radius of Earth is 6,400 km. At the altitude of the space shuttle, what fraction of the surface gravitational field g does the shuttle experience?

   (d) When the shuttle was on Earth before launch, the shuttle's mass (not including any fuel) was 2×10^6 kg. At the orbiting altitude, what is the shuttle's mass, not including fuel?

3. A satellite is in circular orbit around an unknown planet. A second, different satellite also travels in a circular orbit around this same planet, but with an orbital radius four times larger than the first satellite.

   (a) Explain what information must be known in order to calculate the speed the first satellite travels in its orbit.

   (b) Compared to the first satellite, how many times faster or slower is the second satellite's speed?

   (c) Bob says:
   "The gravitational force of the planet on a satellite in circular orbit depends inversely on the orbital radius squared. Since the second satellite's orbital radius is four times that of the first satellite, the second satellite experiences one-sixteenth the gravitational force that is exerted on the first satellite."
   Explain what is wrong with Bob's explanation.

4. A spacecraft is positioned between the Earth and the Moon such that the gravitational forces on the spacecraft exerted by the Earth and the Moon cancel.

   (a) Is this position closer to the Moon, closer to the Earth, or halfway in between?

   (b) Are the gravitational forces on the spaceship (the force exerted by the Moon, and the force exerted by the Earth) a Newton's third law force pair?

› Solutions to Practice Problems

1. (a) The term in the denominator of Newton's law of gravitation refers to the distance between the centers of the two stars. That distance is given as $2R$. So the answer is $G\dfrac{M^2}{(2R)^2}$ or $G\dfrac{M^2}{4R^2}$. Notice you must use the notation given in the problem—this means a capital R here. (The M is squared because the equation for gravitational force multiplies the masses of the stars applying and experiencing the force. Since the masses of both stars are the same, you get $M \cdot M = M^2$.)

    (b) When calculating gravitational field at the surface of a star, the term in the denominator is the star's radius. That's r here. So $G\dfrac{M}{r^2}$. (The M is *not* squared here because the field is produced by a single star, not an interaction between two stars.)

    (c) The left-hand star provides a field of $G\dfrac{M}{R^2}$ at the location of the midpoint, pointing toward the left-hand star. The right-hand star also provides a field of $G\dfrac{M}{R^2}$, pointing toward the right-hand star. These fields with the same amount but opposite direction cancel out when they add as vectors, producing a net gravitational field of zero at the midpoint.

    (d) The direction of a force is not the same as the direction of an object's motion. Here, at any time a star is moving along an orbit, tangent to the radius of the orbit. The force applied by the other star will always be toward the center of the orbit, perpendicular to the direction of the star's motion. When a force is applied perpendicular to an object's velocity, the result is circular motion. The centripetal force changes the direction (not the amount) of the star's speed, but the force itself always changes direction so that it is pulling toward the center of the circular motion.

2. (a) The shuttle must be above the atmosphere in order to maintain a circular orbit without continually burning fuel. If the Earth had no atmosphere, then a satellite could orbit at any distance from the surface that's greater than the tallest mountain. But air resistance in the atmosphere does work on the shuttle, reducing its mechanical energy. At 300 km above the surface, though, the shuttle is above the atmosphere and experiences no forces in or against the direction of travel.

    (b) This question requires a calculation: the force on the shuttle is $G\dfrac{M_{earth}M_{shuttle}}{d^2}$, where d is the distance from the center of the Earth to the location of the shuttle. Since this force is a centripetal force, we can set it equal to $\dfrac{M_{shuttle}v^2}{d}$, where v is the speed of the shuttle in orbit. If the orbit is geosynchronous, that doesn't mean that the shuttle goes the same speed as a position on Earth, it means that the *period* of the orbit is 24 hours—it goes around the Earth in the same time as a location on the surface does.

    To determine the period of the orbit, set the speed equal to the orbit's circumference ($2\pi d$) divided by the period, which I'll call T. Here's how our equation looks now:

    $$G\frac{M_{earth}M_{shuttle}}{d^2} = \frac{M_{shuttle}\left(\dfrac{2\pi d}{T}\right)^2}{d}.$$

    There is lots of algebra here, but notice that all values are things that can be looked up: G, the mass of the Earth, the mass of the shuttle (which cancels anyway), and d, which is the radius of the Earth plus 300 km. Solve this equation for T. If the value of T turns out to be 24 hours, then the orbit is geosynchronous; if not, the orbit is not geosynchronous.[5]

    (c) Your first instinct might be that you need the mass of the Earth to answer this question, because the equation for the gravitational field is $G\dfrac{M}{R^2}$. On one hand, we could calculate the mass of Earth knowing that the gravitational field near the surface is 10 N/kg—just plug in the given value of R and G from the table of information. That will work. It's more elegant to solve in variables: The fraction we want is

$$\frac{G\dfrac{M}{(6700 \text{ km})^2}}{G\dfrac{M}{(6400 \text{ km})^2}}.$$

The G and M cancel, whatever their value. Work the improper fraction to get that the gravitational field 300 km above the surface is $\dfrac{(6400 \text{ km})^2}{(6700 \text{ km})^2} = 91\%$ of g at the surface.

(d) Mass is the amount of "stuff" in an object. It doesn't matter where that object is in the universe: 1 kg of mass is 1 kg of mass. Unless the shuttle loses a wing, its mass is still 2×10^6 kg.

3. (a) Set the gravitational force on the satellite equal to the formula for centripetal force:

$$\frac{GM_{planet}M_{satellite}}{d^2} = \frac{M_{satellite}v^2}{d}.$$

We'll want to be able to solve for v. The mass of the satellite cancels, and G is a universal constant. But we'll need to know d, the distance of the satellite's orbit from the center of the planet. And we'll need to know the mass of the planet or the period of the orbit.

(b) When we solve for v, we get $v = \sqrt{\dfrac{GM_{planet}}{d}}.$ The second satellite has four times the orbital radius, which is represented by d. Multiplying

by four in the denominator under the square root multiplies the whole expression by one-half. The second satellite's speed is one-half as large.

(c) The equation for the force of the planet on the satellite is $F = G\dfrac{M_{planet}M_{satellite}}{d^2}$. Sure, Bob is right about the inverse square dependence on d, but he's assumed that the satellites have the same masses as each other. If they do, Bob is correct; if not, then, the mass of the satellite shows up in the numerator of the force equation.

4. (a) The relevant equation here comes from setting the forces on the spacecraft (of mass m) equal:

$$G\frac{M_{earth}m}{d_{earth}^2} = G\frac{M_{moon}m}{d_{moon}^2}.$$

The mass of the spacecraft cancels, as does the G. Since the mass of the Earth is bigger than the mass of the Moon, the equation shows that the distance of this location from Earth d_{earth} must be larger than the distance of the location from the Moon d_{moon}. The location is closer to the Moon.

(b) A Newton's third law force pair cannot act on the same object. The force of the Moon on the spacecraft is paired with the force of the spacecraft on the Moon; the force of the Earth on the spacecraft is paired with the force of the spacecraft on the Earth.

› Rapid Review

- The amount of gravitational field depends on two things: the mass of the planet creating the field (M) and the distance you are from that planet's center (d). The relevant equation for the gravitation field g produced by a planet is $g = G\dfrac{M}{d^2}$.

- The weight of an object—that is, the gravitational force of a planet on that object—is given by mg.

- The gravitational force of one object on another is given by $F = \dfrac{Gm_1m_2}{d^2}$.

- Gravitational mass indicates how an object responds to a gravitational field.

- Inertial mass indicates how an object accelerates in response to a net force.

- In every experiment ever conducted, an object's gravitational mass is equal to its inertial mass.

---

[5]If you do all the plugging and chugging—which is *not* necessary—you'll find that the orbit is not geosynchronous. Geosynchronous orbits are somewhere in the 35,000-km range above Earth's surface.

CHAPTER 16

Simple Harmonic Motion

IN THIS CHAPTER

Summary: This chapter introduces basic properties of waves, especially of sound waves. You'll define wave speed, frequency, and wavelength, and relate them through $v = \lambda f$. Although a wave moves through a material, the pieces of the material themselves do not move. Rather, they tend to oscillate in simple harmonic motion. This chapter describes exactly what that means.

Definitions

- ✪ The **period** is the time for one cycle of simple harmonic motion.
- ✪ The **frequency** of simple harmonic motion is the number of times an object goes back and forth in one second.
- ✪ The unit of frequency is the Hz, which means "per second."
- ✪ The **amplitude** is the distance from the midpoint of simple harmonic motion to the maximum displacement.
- ✪ The **spring constant** k, measured in units of newtons per meter (N/m), is related to the stiffness of a spring.
- ✪ A **restoring force** is any force that always pushes an object toward an equilibrium position.

Simple Harmonic Motion

Simple harmonic motion refers to a back-and-forth oscillation whose position-time graph looks like a sine function. The typical examples are a mass vibrating on a spring, and a pendulum.

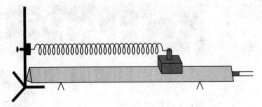

Example: A cart of mass 0.5 kg is attached to a spring of spring constant 30 N/m on a frictionless air track, as shown. The cart is stretched 10 cm from the equilibrium position and released from rest.

FACT: The period T of an object on a spring in simple harmonic motion is given by

$$T = 2\pi \frac{\sqrt{m}}{\sqrt{k}}$$

Of course, the AP exam will not likely ask, "What is the period of this oscillation?" Rather, it might ask for the specific effect that doubling the mass of the cart would have on the period. Since the m term is in the numerator of the period equation, a bigger mass means a larger (longer) period of oscillation. Since the m is under a square root, doubling the mass multiplies the period by the square root of 2.

What if the amplitude of the motion were doubled? How would that affect the period? Since you don't see an A in the equation for the period, the period would not change. This is a general result for all simple harmonic motion and wave problems: The amplitude does not affect the period.[1]

FACT: The frequency and period are inverses of one another.

Once you know by being told or by doing the calculation that the period of this cart on a spring is 0.81 s, you can use your calculator to do 1 divided by 0.81 s, giving a frequency of 1.2 s.

FACT: The amount of restoring force exerted by a spring is given by

$$F = kx$$

---

[1] There are exceptions for simple and physical pendulums once the amplitude reaches large enough values, but the AP exam will not likely ask much about these situations.

The force of the spring on the cart is therefore greatest when the spring is most stretched, but zero at the equilibrium position. And since $a = F_{net}/m$, the acceleration likewise changes from lots at the endpoints to nothing at the middle.

This means that you cannot use kinematics equations with harmonic motion. A kinematics approach requires constant acceleration. Instead, when a problem asks for the speed of a cart somewhere, use conservation of energy.

FACT: The spring potential energy is given by

$$PE_{spring} = \frac{1}{2}kx^2$$

The energy stored by the spring is thus largest at the endpoints and zero at the equilibrium position. There, the spring energy is completely converted to the kinetic energy of the cart. Where is the cart's speed greatest, then? At the equilibrium position, of course, because kinetic energy is $\frac{1}{2}mv^2$—largest kinetic energy means largest speed.

To calculate the value of the maximum speed, write out the energy conversion from the endpoint of the motion to the midpoint of the motion: spring potential energy is converted to kinetic energy. Translated into equations, you get $\frac{1}{2}kx^2 = \frac{1}{2}mv^2$. Plug in values, and solve for the speed. Here, you get 0.77 m/s (i.e., 77 cm/s).[2]

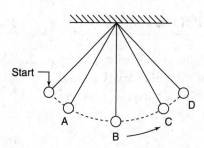

Example 2: The pendulum shown in the preceding figure is released from rest at the start position. It oscillates through the labeled positions A, B, C, and D.

Treat a pendulum pretty much the same way as a spring. It's still in harmonic motion; it still requires an energy approach, not a kinematics approach, to determine its speed at any position.

FACT: The period T of a pendulum is given by

$$T = 2\pi \frac{\sqrt{L}}{\sqrt{g}}$$

---

[2]Don't forget to convert the maximum distance from equilibrium to 0.1 meters before plugging into the equation.

As always, it's unlikely you're going to plug in numbers to calculate a period. Among the gazillion possibilities, you might well be asked to rank the listed positions in terms of some quantity or other. Here are some ideas:

Rank the lettered positions from greatest to least by the bob's gravitational potential energy. Gravitational potential energy is *mgh*; the bob always has the same mass, and *g* can't change, so the highest vertical height has the greatest gravitational potential energy. Ranking: $D > C = A > B$.

Rank the lettered positions from greatest to least by the bob's total mechanical energy. Total mechanical energy means the sum of potential and kinetic energies. Here, with no nonconservative force like friction acting, and no internal structure to allow for internal energy, the total mechanical energy doesn't change. The ranking is as follows: $(A = B = C = D)$.

Rank the lettered positions from greatest to least by the bob's speed. Since gravitational potential energy is converted to kinetic energy, the bob moves fastest when the gravitational potential energy is smallest. Ranking: $B > C = A > D$.

The gravitational field at the surface of Jupiter is 26 N/kg and on the surface of the Moon, 1.6 N/kg. Rank this pendulum's period near Jupiter, the Moon, and Earth. Since *g* is in the denominator of the period equation, the lowest gravitational field will have the greatest period; so $T_{\text{Moon}} > T_{\text{Earth}} > T_{\text{Jupiter}}$. The ranking by frequency would be just the opposite—because frequency is the inverse of period, a bigger *g* leads to a smaller period but a bigger frequency.

› Practice Problems

1. You want to build a pendulum clock using a heavy ball on the end of a light cable that has 1 second between its "tick" and its "tock"; that is, 1 second should elapse while the pendulum swings from one side to the other.

   (a) What is the period of this pendulum?
   (b) How long do you make the cable?
   (c) Suppose the cable stretches a bit from the weight on the end. Will the clock run ahead or behind a precise clock? Explain.

2. The period of a mass-on-a-spring system is doubled, while still using the same spring.

   (a) By what factor does the frequency of the mass-on-a-spring system increase or decrease?
   (b) By what factor does the mass attached to the spring increase or decrease?

› Solutions to Practice Problems

1. (a) Period is the time for one complete back-and-forth cycle of simple harmonic motion. Here it takes 1 second for the ball to go one side to the other; so it takes 2 seconds to go all the way back to the starting position, creating a full cycle. The period is 2 s.

   (b) The period of a pendulum is $T = 2\pi \frac{\sqrt{L}}{\sqrt{g}}$.

   Solve for *L* to get $L = T^2 g / 4\pi^2$. Plug in the 2 s period, 10 N/kg for *g*, and you get 1.1 m.

   (c) In the equation for period, length is in the numerator. So a longer length will mean a longer period as well. This means what the clock thinks is a second is really a bit longer than a second. Over a long time, while a precise clock counts, say, 3,600 seconds, this clock will count fewer than 3,600 seconds. Thus, the clock will run behind a precise clock.

2. (a) Frequency is the inverse of the period. When the period doubles, the frequency is cut in half.

(b) The relevant equation is $T = 2\pi \frac{\sqrt{m}}{\sqrt{k}}$. The spring constant doesn't change because it's the same spring. Since the mass term is in the numerator and square rooted, the mass should quadruple. Then, square rooting the factor of four increases the whole fraction by a factor of two.

› Rapid Review

- The period of a mass on a spring in simple harmonic motion is given by $2\pi \frac{\sqrt{m}}{\sqrt{k}}$.
- The frequency and period are inverses of one another.
- The amount of restoring force exerted by a spring is given by $F = kx$.
- The spring potential energy is given by $PE_{spring} = \frac{1}{2}kx^2$.
- The period of a pendulum is given by $2\pi \frac{\sqrt{L}}{\sqrt{g}}$.

Extra Drills on Difficult but Frequently Tested Topics

IN THIS CHAPTER

Summary: Included in this chapter are problems providing extra practice on frequently tested topics that students often find difficult:
✪ Springs and graphs
✪ Tension
✪ Inclined planes
✪ Motion graphs

If you have any extra time, spend it sharpening your AP Physics 1 skills working out these problems. Following each question set are detailed explanations that take you step by step to the solution.

How to Use This Chapter

Practice problems and tests cannot possibly cover every situation that you may be asked to understand in physics. However, some categories of topics come up again and again, so much so that they might be worth some extra review. And that's exactly what this chapter is for—to give you a focused, intensive review of a few of the most essential physics topics.

We call them "drills" for a reason. They are designed to be skill-building exercises, and as such, they stress repetition and technique. Working through these exercises might remind you of playing scales if you're a musician or of running laps around the field if you're an athlete. Not much fun, maybe a little tedious, but very helpful in the long run.

The questions in each drill are all solved essentially the same way. *Don't* just do one problem after the other . . . rather, do a couple, check to see that your answers are right,[1] and then, half an hour or a few days later, do a few more, just to remind yourself of the techniques involved.

Springs and Graphs

The Drill

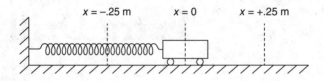

A 0.50-kg lab cart on a frictionless surface is attached to a spring, as shown in the preceding figure. The rightward direction is considered positive. The spring is neither stretched nor compressed at position $x = 0$. The cart is released from rest at the position $x = +0.25$ m at time $t = 0$.

1. On the axes below, sketch a graph of the kinetic energy of the cart as a function of position x.

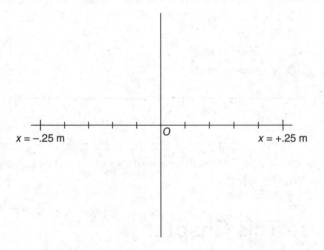

2. On the axes below, sketch a graph of the total mechanical energy of the cart-spring system as a function of position *x*.

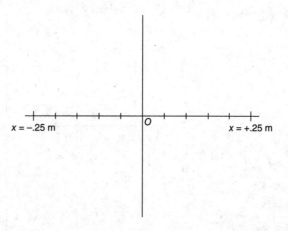

$x = -.25$ m   *O* $x = +.25$ m

3. On the axes below, sketch a graph of the speed of the cart-spring system as a function of position *x*.

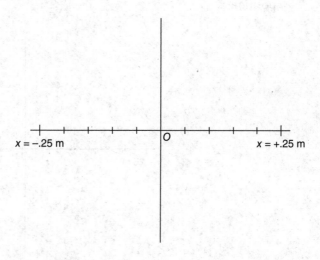

$x = -.25$ m   *O* $x = +.25$ m

4. On the axes below, sketch a graph of the force applied by the spring on the cart as a function of position *x*.

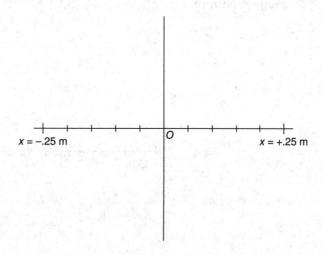

$x = -.25$ m   *O* $x = +.25$ m

5. On the axes below, sketch a graph of the force applied by the cart on the spring as a function of position x.

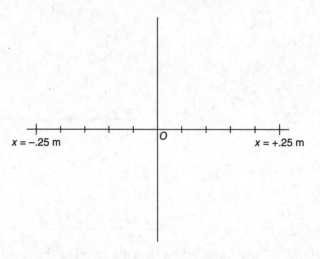

6. On the axes below, sketch a graph of the spring constant of the spring as a function of position x.

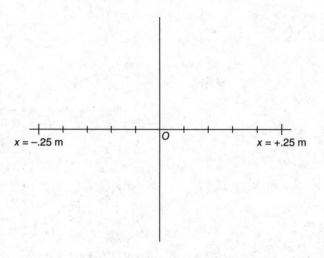

7. On the axes below, sketch a graph of the acceleration of the cart-spring system as a function of position x.

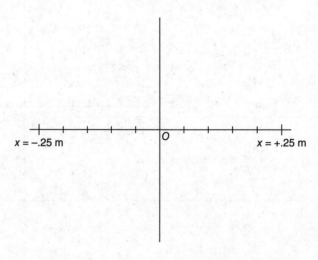

8. On the axes below, sketch a graph of the potential energy of the cart-spring system as a function of position x.

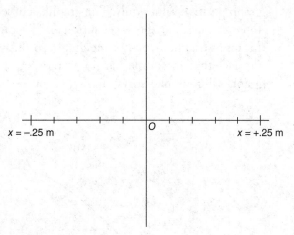

x = −.25 m   O   x = +.25 m

Answers with Explanations

1. Kinetic energy is zero at the endpoints, where the cart comes briefly to rest. At the midpoint, the cart-spring system's potential energy ($\frac{1}{2}kx^2$) is zero since $x = 0$. All the energy is kinetic at the midpoint. The graph is curved because the potential energy graph is curved; the kinetic and potential energy must add to the same value, since friction is negligible.

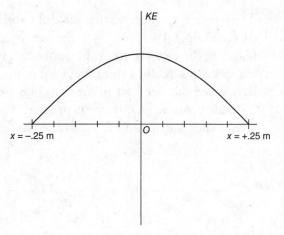

KE

x = −.25 m   O   x = +.25 m

2. Total mechanical energy of a system with no nonconservative forces doing work is conserved. Friction is negligible; gravity and the normal force do no work. The only relevant force is the spring force, which is conservative. Mechanical energy cannot change.

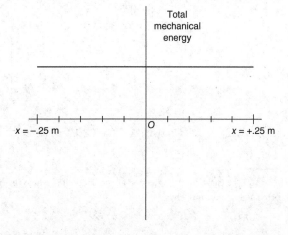

Total mechanical energy

x = −.25 m   O   x = +.25 m

3. The cart comes briefly to rest at both ends, so speed is zero there. At the midpoint, kinetic energy is greatest, so speed is as well: $KE = \frac{1}{2}mv^2$. Speed has no direction, so graph positive values only. The graph is curved—you can know that because the spring force changes, so the acceleration of the cart is not constant. Constant acceleration means a straight velocity-time graph, so this graph must be curved.[2] Or, you can know the fact that in simple harmonic motion, a position-time graph and a velocity-time graph will look like curvy sine functions.

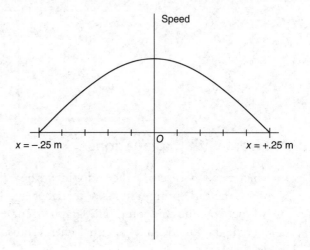

4. The relevant equation relating force of a spring to displacement of the spring is $F = kx$. At the midpoint where $x = 0$, the net force is zero as well. The amount of force gets bigger as the distance from the midpoint gets bigger. When the cart is far to the left, the spring pushes the cart to the right; so the force is positive when the distance is negative. When the cart is far to the right, the spring pushes the cart to the left; so the force is negative when the distance is positive. The graph is straight because the x is neither squared nor square rooted, but just to the first power.

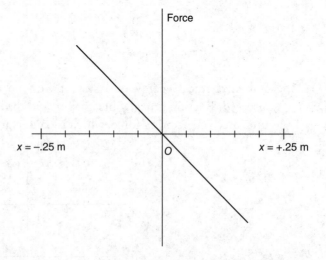

---

[2]And the curve must be steepest at the endpoints, where the net force $F = kx$ is greatest; that's where the speed must be changing most quickly.

5. By Newton's third law, the force of the cart on the spring is equal in magnitude and opposite in direction to the force of the spring on the cart. Just flip the direction of the answer to Question 4.

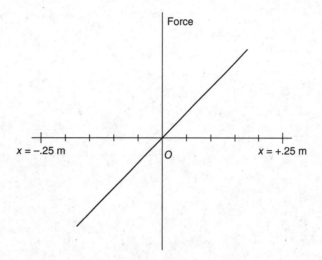

6. The spring constant of a spring is a property of the spring itself. Since the spring isn't replaced while the cart oscillates, the spring constant cannot change.

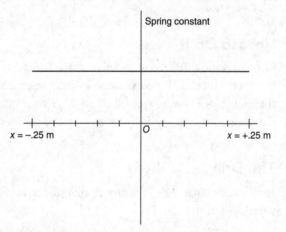

7. By Newton's second law, the net force on the cart is equal to *ma*. The acceleration graph should look exactly like the force of the spring on the cart graph. If we cared about the actual values on the graph, we'd divide the force by the cart's mass at each position. The problem says "sketch"—just the shape is necessary.

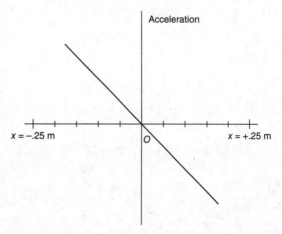

8. The relevant equation for the potential energy due to a spring is $PE = \frac{1}{2}kx^2$. At $x = 0$, the potential energy is also zero. The potential energy is largest at the endpoints. And the equation includes an x^2, so the graph is curved.

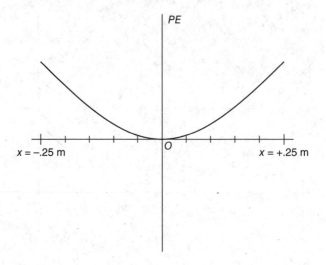

Tension

How to Do It

Use the following steps to solve these kinds of problems: (1) Draw a free-body diagram for each block; (2) resolve vectors into their components; (3) write Newton's second law for each block, being careful to stick to your choice of positive direction; and (4) solve the simultaneous equations for whatever the problem asks for.

The Drill

In the diagrams below, assume all pulleys and ropes are massless, and use the following variable definitions:

$$F = 10 \text{ N}$$
$$M = 1.0 \text{ kg}$$
$$\mu = 0.2$$

Find the tension in each rope and the acceleration of the set of masses.
(For a greater challenge, solve in terms of F, M, and μ instead of plugging in values.)

1. Frictionless

2. Frictionless

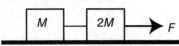

3. Frictionless

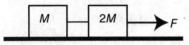

4. Coefficient of Friction μ

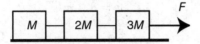

5.

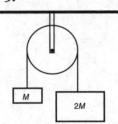

6.

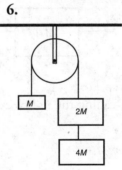

7. Frictionless

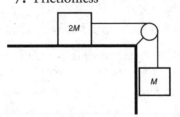

8. Frictionless

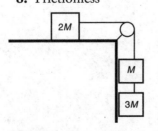

9. Frictionless

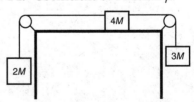

10. Coefficient of Friction μ

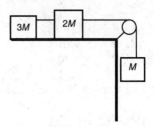

11. Coefficient of Friction μ

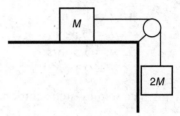

12. Frictionless

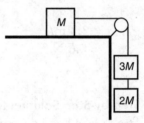

13. Frictionless

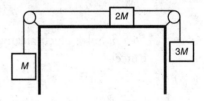

14. Coefficient of Friction μ

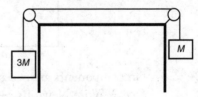

The Answers

1. $a = 10$ m/s^2
2. $a = 3.3$ m/s^2
   $T = 3.3$ N

See step-by-step solution below.

3. $a = 1.7$ m/s^2
   $T_1 = 1.7$ N
   $T_2 = 5.1$ N
4. $a = 1.3$ m/s^2
   $T = 3.3$ N
5. $a = 3.3$ m/s^2
   $T = 13$ N

See step-by-step solution below.

6. $a = 7.1$ m/s^2
   $T_1 = 17$ N
   $T_2 = 11$ N
7. $a = 3.3$ m/s^2
   $T = 6.6$ N

8. $a = 6.7$ m/s^2
   $T_1 = 13$ N
   $T_2 = 10$ N
9. $a = 1.7$ m/s^2
   $T_1 = 5.1$ N
   $T_2 = 8.3$ N
10. $a = 6.0$ m/s^2
    $T = 8.0$ N
11. $a = 8.0$ m/s^2
    $T_1 = 10$ N
    $T_2 = 4.0$ N
12. $a = 5.0$ m/s^2
    $T = 15$ N
13. $a = 3.3$ m/s^2
    $T_1 = 13$ N
    $T_2 = 20$ N
14. $a = 0.22$ m/s^2
    $T_1 = 20$ N
    $T_2 = 29$ N

Step-by-Step Solution to Problem 2

Step 1: Free-body diagrams:

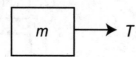 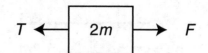

No components are necessary, so on to the next step.

Step 2: Write Newton's second law for each block, calling the rightward direction positive:

$$T - 0 = ma$$
$$F - T = (2m)a$$

Step 3: Solve algebraically. It's easiest to add these equations together, because the tensions cancel:

$$F = (3m)a, \text{ so } a = F/3m = (10 \text{ N})/3(1 \text{ kg}) = 3.3 \text{ m/s}^2.$$

To get the tension, just plug back into $T - 0 = ma$ to find $T = F/3 = 3.3$ N.

Step-by-Step Solution to Problem 5

Step 1: Free-body diagrams:

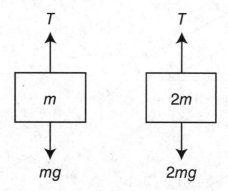

No components are necessary, so on to the next step.

Step 2: Write Newton's second law for each block, calling clockwise rotation of the pulley positive:

$$(2m)g - T = (2m)a$$
$$T - mg = ma$$

Step 3: Solve algebraically. It's easiest to add these equations together, because the tensions cancel:

$$mg = (3m)a, \text{ so } a = g/3 = 3.3 \text{ m/s}^2$$

To get the tension, just plug back into $T - mg = ma$: $T = m(a + g) = (4/3)mg = 13$ N.

Inclined Planes

How to Do It

Use the following steps to solve these kinds of problems: (1) Draw a free-body diagram for the object (the normal force is perpendicular to the plane; the friction force acts along the plane, opposite the velocity); (2) break vectors into components, where the parallel component of weight is $mg(\sin \theta)$; (3) write Newton's second law for parallel and perpendicular components; and (4) solve the equations for whatever the problem asks for.

Don't forget, the normal force is *not* equal to mg when a block is on an incline!

The Drill

Directions: For each of the following situations, determine:

(a) the acceleration of the block down the plane
(b) the time for the block to slide to the bottom of the plane

In each case, assume a frictionless plane unless otherwise stated; assume the block is released from rest unless otherwise stated.

1.

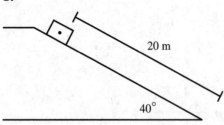

2.

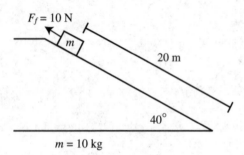

3.

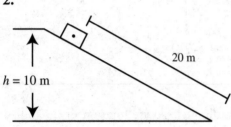

$m = 10$ kg

4.

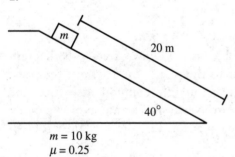

$m = 10$ kg
$\mu = 0.25$

5.

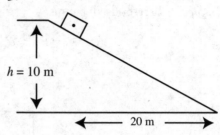

6.

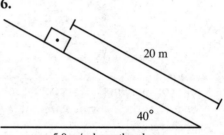

$v_o = 5.0$ m/s down the plane

7.

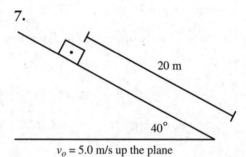

$v_o = 5.0$ m/s up the plane

8.

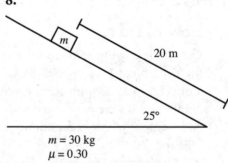

$m = 30$ kg
$\mu = 0.30$
$v_o = 3.0$ m/s up the plane

Careful—this one's tricky.

The Answers

1. $a = 6.3$ m/s², down the plane
   $t = 2.5$ s
See step-by-step solution below.

2. $a = 4.9$ m/s², down the plane
   $t = 2.9$ s

3. $a = 5.2$ m/s², down the plane
   $t = 2.8$ s

4. $a = 4.4$ m/s², down the plane
   $t = 3.0$ s

5. Here the angle of the plane is 27° by trigonometry, and the distance along the plane is 22 m.
   $a = 4.4$ m/s², down the plane
   $t = 3.2$ s

6. $a = 6.3$ m/s², down the plane
   $t = 1.8$ s

7. $a = 6.3$ m/s², down the plane
   $t = 3.5$ s

8. This one is complicated. Since the direction of the friction force changes depending on whether the block is sliding up or down the plane, the block's acceleration is *not* constant throughout the whole problem. So, unlike problem 7, this one can't be solved in a single step. Instead, in order to use kinematics equations, you must break this problem up into two parts: up the plane and down the plane. During each of these individual parts, the acceleration is constant, so the kinematics equations are valid.

   - up the plane:
     $a = 6.8$ m/s², down the plane
     $t = 0.4$ s before the block turns around to come down the plane

   - down the plane:
     $a = 1.5$ m/s², down the plane
     $t = 5.2$ s to reach bottom

   So, a total of $t = 5.6$ s for the block to go up and back down.

Step-by-Step Solution to Problem 1
Step 1: Free-body diagram:

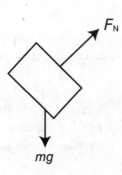

Step 2: Break vectors into components. Because we have an incline, we use inclined axes, one parallel and one perpendicular to the incline:

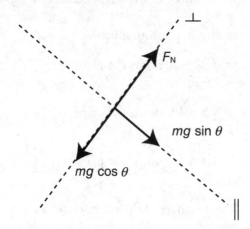

Step 3: Write Newton's second law for each axis. The acceleration is entirely directed parallel to the plane, so perpendicular acceleration can be written as zero:

$$mg \sin \theta - 0 = ma$$
$$F_N - mg \cos \theta = 0$$

Step 4: Solve algebraically for *a*. This can be done without reference to the second equation. (In problems with friction, use $F_f = \mu F_N$ to relate the two equations.)

$$a = g \sin \theta = 6.3 \text{ m/s}^2$$

To find the time, plug into a kinematics chart:

$$v_o = 0$$
$$v_f = \text{unknown}$$
$$\Delta x = 20 \text{ m}$$
$$a = 6.3 \text{ m/s}^2$$
$$t = ???$$

Solve for *t* using the second star equation for kinematics (**): $\Delta x = v_o t + \frac{1}{2}at^2$, where v_o is zero:

$$t = \sqrt{\frac{2\Delta x}{a}} = \sqrt{\frac{2(20\,\text{m})}{6.3\,\text{m/s}^2}} = 2.5\,\text{s}$$

Motion Graphs

How to Do It

For a position-time graph, the slope is the velocity. For a velocity-time graph, the slope is the acceleration, and the area under the graph is the displacement.

The Drill

Use the graph to determine something about the object's speed. Then play "Physics *Taboo*": suggest what object might reasonably perform this motion and explain in words how the object moves. Use everyday language. In your explanation, you may *not* use any words from the list below:

velocity
acceleration
positive
negative
increase
decrease
object
constant

1.

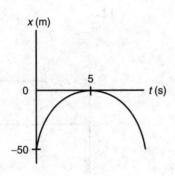

2.

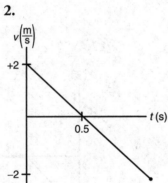

3.

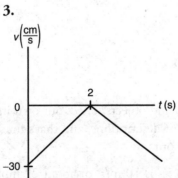

4.

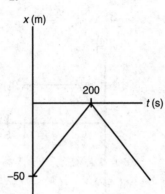

5.

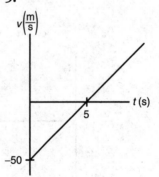

6.

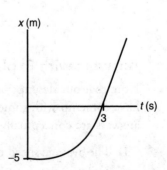

7.

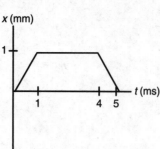

8.

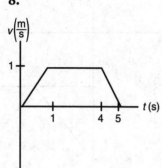

9.

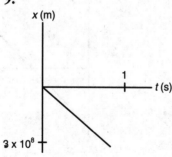

10.

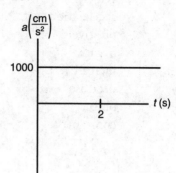

11.

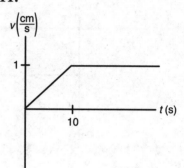

12.

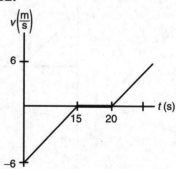

Answers with Explanations

Note that our descriptions of the moving objects reflect our own imaginations. You might have come up with some very different descriptions, and that's fine . . . provided that your answers are conceptually the same as ours.

1. The average speed over the first 5 s is 10 m/s, or about 22 mph. So:

Someone rolls a bowling ball along a smooth road. When the graph starts, the bowling ball is moving along pretty fast, but the ball encounters a long hill. So, the ball slows down, coming to rest after 5 s. Then, the ball comes back down the hill, speeding up the whole way.

2. This motion only lasts 1 s, and the maximum speed involved is about 5 mph. So:

A biker has been cruising up a hill. When the graph starts, the biker is barely moving at jogging speed. Within half a second, and after traveling only half a meter up the hill, the bike turns around, speeding up as it goes back down the hill.

3. The maximum speed of this thing is 30 cm/s, or about a foot per second. So:

A toy racecar is moving slowly along its track. The track goes up a short hill that's about a foot long. After 2 s, the car has just barely reached the top of the hill, and is perched there momentarily; then, the car crests the hill and speeds up as it goes down the other side.

4. The steady speed over 200 s (a bit over 3 minutes) is 0.25 m/s, or 25 cm/s, or about a foot per second.

A cockroach crawls steadily along the school's running track, searching for food. The cockroach starts near the 50-yard line of the football field; around three minutes later, the cockroach reaches the goal line and, having found nothing of interest, turns around and crawls at the same speed back toward his starting point.

5. The maximum speed here is 50 m/s, or over a hundred mph, changing speed dramatically in only 5 or 10 s. So:

A small airplane is coming in for a landing. Upon touching the ground, the pilot puts the engines in reverse, slowing the plane. But wait! The engine throttle is stuck! So, although the plane comes to rest in 5 s, the engines are still on . . . the plane starts speeding up backwards! Oops . . .

6. This thing covers 5 meters in 3 seconds, speeding up the whole time.

An 8-year-old gets on his dad's bike. The boy is not really strong enough to work the pedals easily, so he starts off with difficulty. But, after a few seconds he's managed to speed the bike up to a reasonable clip.

7. Though this thing moves quickly—while moving, the speed is 1 m/s—the total distance covered is 1 mm forward, and 1 mm back; the whole process takes 5 ms, which is less than the minimum time interval indicated by a typical stopwatch. So we'll have to be a bit creative:

In the Discworld novels by Terry Pratchett, wizards have developed a computer in which living ants in tubes, rather than electrons in wires and transistors, carry information. (Electricity has not been harnessed on the Discworld.) In performing a calculation, one of these ants moves forward a distance of 1 mm; stays in place for 3 ms; and returns to the original position. If this ant's motion represents two typical "operations" performed by the computer, then this computer has an approximate processing speed of 400 Hz times the total number of ants inside.

8. Though this graph *looks* like Problem 7, this one is a velocity-time graph, and so indicates completely different motion.

A small child pretends he is a bulldozer. Making a "brm-brm-brm" noise with his lips, he speeds up from rest to a slow walk. He walks for three more seconds, then slows back down to rest. He moved forward the entire time, traveling a total distance (found from the area under the graph) of 4 m.

9. This stuff moves 300 million meters in 1 s at a constant speed. There's only one possibility here: electromagnetic waves in a vacuum.

   Light (or electromagnetic radiation of any frequency) is emitted from the surface of the moon. In 1 s, the light has covered about half the distance to Earth.

10. Be careful about axis labels: this is an *acceleration*–time graph. Something is accelerating at 1,000 cm/s^2 for a few seconds. 1,000 cm/s^2 = 10 m/s^2, about Earth's gravitational acceleration. Using kinematics, we calculate that if we drop something from rest near Earth, after 4 s the thing has dropped 80 m.

   One way to simulate the effects of zero gravity is to drop an experiment from the top of a high tower. Then, because everything that was dropped is speeding up at the same rate, the effect is just as if the experiment were done in the Space Shuttle—at least until everything hits the ground. In this case, an experiment is dropped from a 250-ft tower, hitting the ground with a speed close to 90 mph.

11. 1 cm/s is ridiculously slow. Let's use the world of slimy animals:

    A snail wakes up from his nap and decides to find some food. He speeds himself up from rest to his top speed in 10 s. During this time, he's covered 5 cm, or about the length of your pinkie finger. He continues to slide along at a steady 1 cm/s, which means that a minute later he's gone no farther than a couple of feet. Let's hope that food is close.

12. This one looks a bit like those up-and-down-a-hill graphs, but with an important difference—this time the thing stops not just for an instant, but for five whole seconds, before continuing back toward the starting point.

    A bicyclist coasts to the top of a shallow hill, slowing down from cruising speed (~15 mph) to rest in 15 s. At the top, she pauses briefly to turn her bike around; then, she releases the brake and speeds up as she goes back down the hill.

STEP 5

Build Your Test-Taking Confidence

AP PHYSICS **1** Practice Exam 1

AP PHYSICS **1** Practice Exam 2

How Long Should My Answers Be on the AP Physics 1 Exam?

Quick answer: probably shorter than you think.[1]

Below is a variety of AP Physics 1 prompts, and how I would suggest structuring your answer. Please note that while I do grade the exams every year, I am writing here in the role of independent observer. I am not a representative of the College Board. These are my own simplified instructions to my own students, which may not be perfect in all situations.

Yet, as you can tell from reading this book, learning physics is much better done through simple guidelines rather than legalisms. If you want the legalisms, go to the College Board's course and exam description and look at the AP Central page where they go into great detail about the requirements for a paragraph response. But you don't want or need to see such detail.

On my last day of class before the exam, I remind students of the types of prompts below and my guidelines for the length of the response required. Then I let go, and wish them the best, as I wish to you as you embark on the practice exams . . .

"Briefly explain" or "Briefly justify": Answer in one sentence.

"Derive an expression": Use variables only; start with an equation from the equation sheet or a fundamental principle. It will help to annotate your work with words, but complete sentences are not necessary. Full credit can usually be earned without words at all as long as the mathematics is communicated clearly.

"Describe a procedure": Two to three sentences, never more. Say what you will measure and what equipment you'll use to measure it. And stop writing.

"Explain" or "Justify your answer": About two sentences, or perhaps one sentence with reference to an equation.

"Answer in a clear, coherent, paragraph-length response": Five sentences; four is often enough. Do not repeat the question in the answer. Get to the point.

For all responses except mathematical derivations: Use sentences with subjects and verbs, but without fluff.

Don't fear for the lost point. Students tend to write page-long essays because they fear that the reader will "take off" if they miss one small detail. But those students miss the bigger picture. Running out of time on question 5 could cost them seven points, while writing an extra page may in their imaginations earn one point. And writing that extra page is far more likely to lose credit for an incorrect statement than to gain credit.

Please don't be afraid. Answer each question briefly and confidently. If you have to guess, guess briefly. Believe it or not, AP readers know when you're just writing random crap because you have no idea how to approach a problem. And rubrics are written such that they are unlikely to award credit for baloney.

Kick butt on the practice tests that follow . . .

---

[1] This advice is adapted from the *Jacobs Physics* blog post of May 1, 2017, by Greg Jacobs.

Practice Exam 1

SECTION I
ANSWER SHEET

1 (A) (B) (C) (D)
2 (A) (B) (C) (D)
3 (A) (B) (C) (D)
4 (A) (B) (C) (D)
5 (A) (B) (C) (D)
6 (A) (B) (C) (D)
7 (A) (B) (C) (D)
8 (A) (B) (C) (D)
9 (A) (B) (C) (D)
10 (A) (B) (C) (D)
11 (A) (B) (C) (D)
12 (A) (B) (C) (D)
13 (A) (B) (C) (D)
14 (A) (B) (C) (D)
15 (A) (B) (C) (D)
16 (A) (B) (C) (D)
17 (A) (B) (C) (D)

18 (A) (B) (C) (D)
19 (A) (B) (C) (D)
20 (A) (B) (C) (D)
21 (A) (B) (C) (D)
22 (A) (B) (C) (D)
23 (A) (B) (C) (D)
24 (A) (B) (C) (D)
25 (A) (B) (C) (D)
26 (A) (B) (C) (D)
27 (A) (B) (C) (D)
28 (A) (B) (C) (D)
29 (A) (B) (C) (D)
30 (A) (B) (C) (D)
31 (A) (B) (C) (D)
32 (A) (B) (C) (D)
33 (A) (B) (C) (D)
34 (A) (B) (C) (D)

35 (A) (B) (C) (D)
36 (A) (B) (C) (D)
37 (A) (B) (C) (D)
38 (A) (B) (C) (D)
39 (A) (B) (C) (D)
40 (A) (B) (C) (D)
41 (A) (B) (C) (D)
42 (A) (B) (C) (D)
43 (A) (B) (C) (D)
44 (A) (B) (C) (D)
45 (A) (B) (C) (D)
46 (A) (B) (C) (D)
47 (A) (B) (C) (D)
48 (A) (B) (C) (D)
49 (A) (B) (C) (D)
50 (A) (B) (C) (D)

AP Physics 1 Practice Exam 1

SECTION I

(Multiple-Choice Questions)
Time: 90 minutes

Directions: The multiple-choice section consists of 50 questions. You may write scratch work in the test booklet itself, but only the answers on the answer sheet will be scored. You may use a calculator, the equation sheet, and the table of information.

A Note About Timing: The multiple-choice section below includes questions about waves and circuits, which were moved from AP Physics 1 to AP Physics 2. We leave the questions here for now, in case you need them for your class.

If you'd like an authentic 2022 AP Physics 1 experience, skip the grayed-out questions and limit yourself to 60 minutes, not 90 minutes. (That's a little less than two minutes per question, which is the exact right pace!)

Questions 1–45: Single-Choice Items

Directions: Choose the single best answer from the four choices provided and grid the answer with a pencil on the answer sheet.

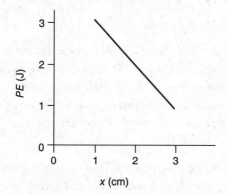

1. A system of objects contains total mechanical energy of 4 J. When only one of these objects moves several centimeters to the right (along the x-axis), the system's potential energy changes according to the graph above. What is this moving object's kinetic energy when it is located at $x = 3$ cm?

   (A) 3 J
   (B) 2 J
   (C) 1 J
   (D) 0 J

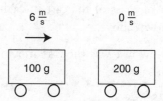

2. Two carts collide elastically on a smooth track. Before the collision, the 100 g cart moved to the right with speed 6 m/s, while the 200 g cart was at rest, as shown above. Which of the following is correct about the velocities of the carts immediately after collision?

	100 g cart	200 g cart
(A)	zero	6 m/s, right
(B)	2 m/s, left	4 m/s, right
(C)	2 m/s, right	4 m/s, right
(D)	6 m/s, left	zero

3. Spring scales are used to measure the net force applied to an object; a sonic motion detector is used to measure the object's resulting acceleration. A graph is constructed with the net force on the vertical axis and the acceleration on the horizontal axis. Which of the following quantities is directly measured using the slope of this graph?

   (A) Gravitational mass
   (B) Weight
   (C) Velocity
   (D) Inertial mass

GO ON TO THE NEXT PAGE

Questions 4 and 5 refer to the information below:

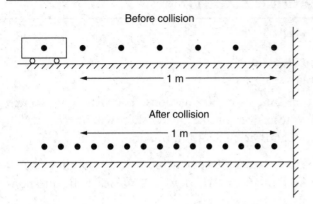

In the laboratory, a 0.5-kg cart collides with a fixed wall, as shown in the preceding diagram. The collision is recorded with a video camera that takes 20 frames per second. A student analyzes the video, placing a dot at the center of mass of the cart in each frame. The analysis is shown above.

4. About how fast was the cart moving before the collision?

(A) 0.25 m/s
(B) 4.0 m/s
(C) 0.20 m/s
(D) 5.0 m/s

5. Which of the following best estimates the change in the cart's momentum during the collision?

(A) 27 N·s
(B) 13 N·s
(C) 1.3 N·s
(D) 2.7 N·s

6. At time $t = 0$, a cart is located 10 cm to the right of a black spot drawn on a track. The cart is moving left at a speed of 30 cm/s, with an acceleration of 50 cm/s^2 to the right. Where is the cart located after 1 s?

(A) 15 cm to the right of the black spot
(B) 5 cm to the left of the black spot
(C) 15 cm to the left of the black spot
(D) 5 cm to the right of the black spot

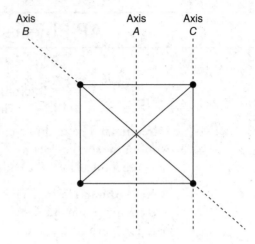

7. Four identical lead balls with large mass are connected by rigid but very light rods in the square configuration shown in the preceding figure. The balls are rotated about the three labeled axes. Which of the following correctly ranks the rotational inertia I of the balls about each axis?

(A) $I_B > I_A = I_C$
(B) $I_A > I_C = I_B$
(C) $I_C > I_A > I_B$
(D) $I_C > I_A = I_B$

8. In the laboratory, a cart experiences a single horizontal force as it moves horizontally in a straight line. Of the following data collected about this experiment, which is sufficient to determine the work done on the cart by the horizontal force?

(A) The magnitude of the force, the cart's initial speed, and the cart's final speed
(B) The mass of the cart and the distance the cart moved
(C) The mass of the cart, the cart's initial speed, and the cart's final speed
(D) The mass of the cart and the magnitude of the force

GO ON TO THE NEXT PAGE

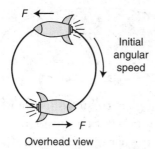

Overhead view

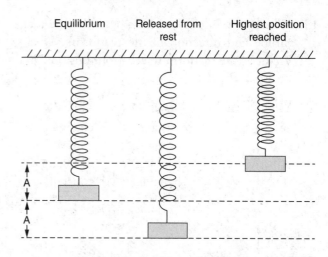

9. A wheel on a frictionless air track is initially spinning clockwise while its center of mass is at rest. Next, two small rocket engines fire for the same short time interval. Each rocket applies an identical force F in the directions shown. Which of the following is correct about how the angular momentum L about the wheel's center changes and about how the linear momentum p in the horizontal direction changes?

	$\underline{L}$	$\underline{p}$
(A)	decreases	does not change
(B)	increases	does not change
(C)	increases	increases
(D)	decreases	increases

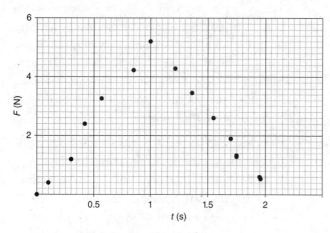

10. In the laboratory, a 3-kg cart experiences a varying net force. This net force is measured as a function of time, and the data collected are displayed in the graph above. What is the change in the cart's momentum during the interval $t = 0$ to $t = 2$ s?

(A) 5 N·s
(B) 10 N·s
(C) 15 N·s
(D) 30 N·s

11. A block is attached to a vertical spring. The block is pulled down a distance A from equilibrium, as shown above, and released from rest. The block moves upward; the highest position above equilibrium reached by the mass is less than A, as shown. When the mass returns downward, how far below the equilibrium position will it reach?

(A) Greater than the distance A below equilibrium
(B) Less than the distance A below equilibrium
(C) Equal to the distance A below equilibrium
(D) No distance—the block will fall only to the equilibrium position

Questions 12 and 13 refer to the following information:

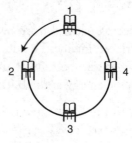

A platform rotates counterclockwise at a constant angular speed in a vertical circle, as shown above. The platform remains horizontal.

12. Which of the following correctly ranks the normal force of the platform on an object sitting on the platform at each of the four labeled locations?

(A) $1 = 2 = 3 = 4$
(B) $1 = 4 > 2 = 4$
(C) $1 > 2 = 4 > 3$
(D) $3 > 2 = 4 > 1$

GO ON TO THE NEXT PAGE

13. Which of the following best describes the magnitude and direction of the platform's velocity vector as the platform travels from position 1 to position 2?

Velocity vector	Magnitude	Direction
(A)	constant	changing
(B)	constant	constant
(C)	changing	changing
(D)	changing	constant

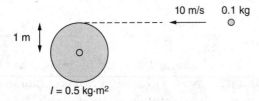

1 m

10 m/s   0.1 kg

$I = 0.5$ kg·m²

14. A disk of radius 1 m and rotational inertia $I = 0.5$ kg·m² is free to rotate, but initially at rest. A blob of putty with mass 0.1 kg is traveling toward the disk with a speed of 10 m/s, as shown in the preceding figure. The putty collides with the outermost portion of the disk and sticks to the disk. What is the angular momentum of the combined disk-putty system after the collision?

(A) 5 kg·m²/s
(B) 1 kg·m²/s
(C) 0.5 kg·m²/s
(D) 0 kg·m²/s

15. A 1-kg object is released from rest at the top of a rough-surfaced incline. The object slides without rotating to the bottom of the incline. The object's kinetic energy at the bottom must be

(A) Equal to the block's gravitational potential energy when it was released, because total mechanical energy must be conserved.
(B) Equal to the block's gravitational potential energy when it was released, because the gain in kinetic energy compensates for the mechanical energy lost to thermal energy on the rough incline.
(C) Less than the block's gravitational potential energy when it was released, because the gravitational potential energy was converted both to thermal energy and to kinetic energy.
(D) Less than the block's gravitational potential energy when it was released, because the work done by the friction force must be greater than the block's gain in kinetic energy.

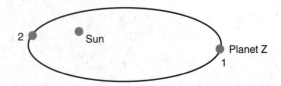

2   Sun   Planet Z   1

16. Extrasolar planet Z orbits its sun in an ellipse. As the planet moves from position 1 to position 2, does the angular momentum of the planet about the sun's center change?

(A) No, because the sun does not apply a torque on the planet.
(B) Yes, because in the equation $L = mvr$, the r term changes.
(C) No, because in the equation $L = I\omega$, neither I nor ω for the planet changes.
(D) Yes, because the torque of the sun on the planet changes.

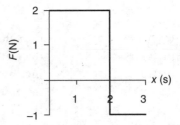

17. A cart is initially at rest on a smooth, horizontal track. A student applies a horizontal force to the cart. The force of the student on the cart as a function of time is shown in the graph above. How does the speed of the cart change during the 3 s time interval shown?

(A) The speed increases, and then decreases while the cart continues in the same direction.
(B) The speed increases, and then decreases while the cart reverses direction.
(C) The speed increases throughout.
(D) The speed decreases throughout.

18. The radius of Mars is about half that of Earth; the mass of Mars is about one-tenth that of Earth. Which of the following is closest to the gravitational field at the surface of Mars?

(A) 10 N/kg
(B) 4 N/kg
(C) 2 N/kg
(D) 0.5 N/kg

GO ON TO THE NEXT PAGE

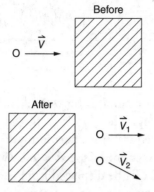

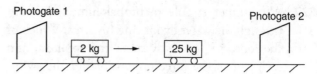

19. In an experiment, a marble rolls to the right at speed v, as shown in the top diagram. The marble rolls under a canopy, where it is heard to collide with marbles that were not initially moving. Such a collision is known to be elastic. After the collision, two equal-mass marbles are observed leaving the canopy with velocity vectors $\vec{v}_1$ and $\vec{v}_2$ directed as shown. Which of the following statements justifies why the experimenter believes that a third marble was involved in the collision under the canopy?

(A) Before collision, the only marble momentum was directed to the right. After the collision, the combined momentum of the two visible marbles is still to the right. Another marble must have a leftward momentum component to conserve momentum.

(B) Before collision, the only marble momentum was directed to the right. After the collision, the combined momentum of the two visible marbles has a downward component; another marble must have an upward momentum component to conserve momentum.

(C) Before collision, the only marble kinetic energy was directed to the right. After the collision, the combined kinetic energy of the two visible marbles is still to the right. Another marble must have a leftward kinetic energy component to conserve kinetic energy.

(D) Before collision, the only marble kinetic energy was directed to the right. After the collision, the combined kinetic energy of the two visible marbles has a downward component; another marble must have an upward kinetic energy component to conserve kinetic energy.

20. In the laboratory, two carts on a track collide in the arrangement shown in the preceding figure. Before the collision, the 2-kg cart travels through photogate 1, which measures its speed; the 0.25-kg cart is initially at rest. After the collision, the carts bounce off one another. Photogate 2 measures the speed of each cart as it passes.

A student is concerned about his experimental results. When he adds the momentum of both carts after collision, he gets a value greater than the momentum of the 2-kg cart before collision. Which of the following is a reasonable explanation for the discrepancy?

(A) The track might have been slanted such that the carts were moving downhill.

(B) Human error might have been involved in reading the photogates.

(C) Friction might not have been negligible.

(D) The collision might not have been elastic.

	Wheel Structure	Wheel Mass	Wheel Radius
Wagon A	solid disk, $I = \frac{1}{2}MR^2$	0.5 kg	0.1 m
Wagon B	solid disk, $I = \frac{1}{2}MR^2$	0.2 kg	0.1 m
Wagon C	hollow hoop, $I = MR^2$	0.2 kg	0.1 m

21. Three wagons each have the same total mass (including that of the wheels) and four wheels, but the wheels are differently styled. The structure, mass, and radius of each wagon's wheels are shown in the preceding chart. In order to accelerate each wagon from rest to a speed of 10 m/s, which wagon requires the greatest energy input?

(A) Wagon A
(B) Wagon B
(C) Wagon C
(D) All require the same energy input

GO ON TO THE NEXT PAGE

22. A swimmer is able to propel himself forward through the water by moving his arms. Which of the following correctly states the applicant and recipient of the force responsible for the swimmer's forward acceleration?

(A) The force of the surrounding water on the swimmer's arms
(B) The force of the swimmer's arms on the swimmer's torso
(C) The force of the swimmer's arms on the surrounding water
(D) The force of the swimmer's torso on the swimmer's arms

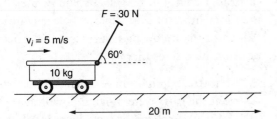

23. A 10-kg wagon moves horizontally at an initial speed of 5 m/s. A 30-N force is applied to the wagon by pulling the rigid handle, which is angled 60° above the horizontal. The wagon continues to move horizontally for another 20 m. A negligible amount of work is converted into thermal energy. By how much has the wagon's kinetic energy increased over the 20 m?

(A) 300 J
(B) 600 J
(C) 125 J
(D) 63 J

24. A moving 1.5-kg cart collides with and sticks to a 0.5-kg cart, which was initially at rest. Immediately after the collision, the carts each have the same _____ as each other.

(A) Velocity
(B) Kinetic energy
(C) Mass
(D) Linear momentum

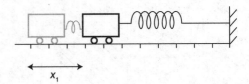

25. A cart on a smooth horizontal track is attached to a spring. The cart is displaced a distance x_1 from its equilibrium position and released from rest; its maximum speed is measured. How far must the cart be displaced from equilibrium and released from rest in order to double the cart's maximum speed?

(A) $2x_1$
(B) $\sqrt{2}x_1$
(C) $2\sqrt{2}x_1$
(D) $4x_1$

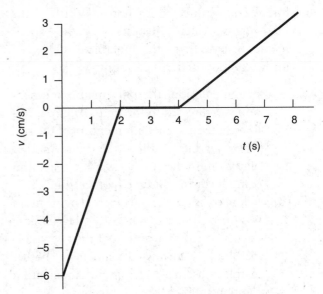

26. A cart moves according to the velocity-time graph shown above. When does the cart return to its initial position?

(A) The cart does not return to its initial position during the 8 s interval shown.
(B) At time $t = 8$ s.
(C) Between times $t = 2$ s and 4 s.
(D) When the cart returns to its initial position cannot be determined from this graph.

GO ON TO THE NEXT PAGE

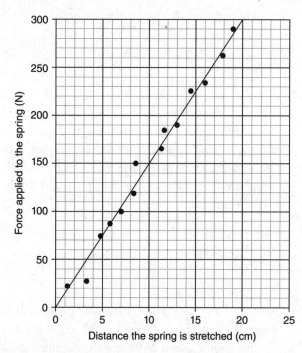

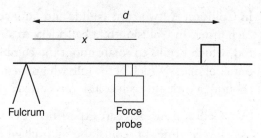

27. A force probe is used to stretch a spring by 20 cm. The graph of the force as a function of distance shown in the preceding figure is produced and used to determine the amount of work done in stretching the spring 20 cm. The experimenter reports the result as 3,000 N·cm. Which of the following is a reasonable estimate of the experimental uncertainty on this measurement?

    (A) 3,000 ± 3 N·cm
    (B) 3,000 ± 30 N·cm
    (C) 3,000 ± 300 N·cm
    (D) 3,000 ± 3,000 N·cm

28. Two carts moving in opposite directions collide and stick together. Which of the following statements correctly indicates how to determine the direction of motion of the combined carts after collision?

    (A) The carts will move in the direction in which the more massive cart was moving before collision.
    (B) The carts will move in the direction in which the cart with greater speed was moving before collision.
    (C) The carts will move in the direction in which the cart with greater magnitude of momentum was moving before collision.
    (D) The carts will move in the direction in which the cart with greater kinetic energy was moving before collision.

29. In the laboratory, a long platform of negligible mass is free to rotate on a fulcrum. A force probe is placed a fixed distance x from the fulcrum, supporting the platform. An object of fixed mass is placed a variable distance d from the fulcrum. For each position d, the force probe is read. It is desired to determine the mass of the object from a graph of data. Which of the following can determine the object's mass?

    (A) Plot the reading in the force probe times x on the vertical axis; plot the gravitational field times d on the horizontal axis. The mass is the slope of the line.
    (B) Plot the reading in the force probe on the vertical axis; plot the distance d on the horizontal axis. The mass is the area under the graph.
    (C) Plot the reading in the force probe on the vertical axis; plot the distance d multiplied by the distance x on the horizontal axis. The mass is the y-intercept of the graph.
    (D) Plot the reading in the force probe times d on the vertical axis; plot the distance x on the horizontal axis. The mass is the slope of the line divided by the gravitational field.

GO ON TO THE NEXT PAGE

30. In Collision A, two carts collide and bounce off each other. In Collision B, a ball sticks to a rigid rod, which begins to rotate about the combined center of mass. Which of the following statements about quantities in each collision is correct?

(A) Collision A: each cart experiences the same force, time of collision, and change in kinetic energy. Collision B: the ball and the rod each experience the same torque, time of collision, and change in rotational kinetic energy.

(B) Collision A: each cart experiences the same force, time of collision, and change in linear momentum. Collision B: the ball and the rod each experience the same torque, time of collision, and change in angular momentum.

(C) Collision A: each cart experiences the same force, time of collision, and change in kinetic energy. Collision B: the ball and the rod each experience the same torque, time of collision, and change in angular momentum.

(D) Collision A: each cart experiences the same force, time of collision, and change in velocity. Collision B: the ball and the rod each experience the same torque, time of collision, and change in angular velocity

31. It is known that a lab cart is moving east at 25 cm/s at time $t_1 = 0.10$ s, and then moving east at 15 cm/s at $t_2 = 0.20$ s. Is this enough information to determine the direction of the net force acting on the cart between t_1 and t_2?

(A) Yes, since we know the cart is slowing down, its momentum change is opposite the direction of movement, and the net force is in the direction of momentum change.

(B) No, because we don't know whether forces such as friction or air resistance might be acting on the cart.

(C) No, because we don't know the mass of the cart.

(D) Yes, since we know the cart keeps moving to the east, the net force must be in the direction of motion.

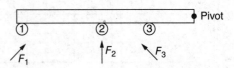

32. A rigid rod is pivoted at its right end. Three forces of identical magnitude but different directions are applied at the positions 1, 2, and 3 as shown, where F_1 and F_3 make 45° angles with the vertical. Which of the following correctly ranks the torques τ_1, τ_2, and τ_3 provided by the forces F_1, F_2, and F_3?

(A) $\tau_1 > \tau_2 > \tau_3$
(B) $\tau_3 > \tau_2 > \tau_1$
(C) $\tau_2 > \tau_1 > \tau_3$
(D) $\tau_2 > \tau_1 = \tau_3$

33. A block hanging vertically from a spring undergoes simple harmonic motion. Which of the following graphs could represent the acceleration a as a function of position x for this block, where $x = 0$ is the midpoint of the harmonic motion?

(A)

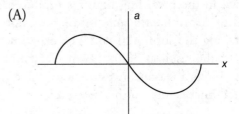

(B)

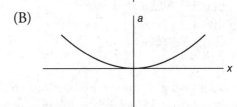

(C)

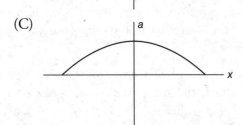

(D)

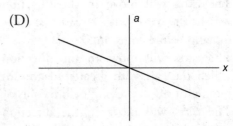

34. A textbook weighs 30 N at sea level. Earth's radius is 6,400 km. Which of the following is the best estimate of the textbook's weight on a mountain peak located 6,000 m above sea level?

(A) 60 N
(B) 15 N
(C) 30 N
(D) 7.5 N

35. The mass of the Earth is 5.97×10^{24} kg. The Moon, whose center is 3.84×10^{8} m from the Earth's center, has mass 7.35×10^{22} kg. Which of the following is the best estimate of the gravitational force of the Earth on the Moon?

(A) 10^{39} N
(B) 10^{29} N
(C) 10^{19} N
(D) 10^{9} N

36. A children's toy consists of a cart whose very light wheels are attached to a rubber band. This rubber band can wind and unwind around the axle supporting the wheels.

This toy is given a shove, after which the toy rolls across a flat surface and up a ramp. It is observed that the toy does not go a consistent distance up the ramp—in some trials it ends up higher than in other trials, even though the shove imparts the same kinetic energy to the cart each time. Which of the following is a reasonable explanation for this phenomenon?

(A) Depending on how the rubber band is initially wound, more or less potential energy can be transferred from the rubber band to the kinetic energy of the car's motion.
(B) The normal force on the cart's wheels will be different depending on how much the rubber band winds or unwinds.
(C) How much energy is transferred from kinetic energy to gravitational potential energy depends on the vertical height at which the cart ends up.
(D) Some of the cart's initial kinetic energy will be dissipated due to work done by friction.

37. A man stands on a platform scale in an elevator. The elevator moves upward, speeding up. What is the action-reaction force pair to the man's weight?

(A) The force of the elevator cable on the man
(B) The force of the man on the scale
(C) The force of the elevator cable on the elevator
(D) The force of the man on the Earth

38. A tape timer makes a mark on a strip of paper every 2/100 of a second. What is the frequency at which this tape timer produces marks?

(A) 0.02 Hz
(B) 5 Hz
(C) 50 Hz
(D) 500 Hz

39. A table supports a wooden block placed on the tabletop. Which fundamental force of nature is responsible for this interaction, and why?

(A) The electric force, because the protons in the nuclei of the top atomic layer of the table repel the nuclei in the bottom atomic layer of the wood.
(B) The gravitational force, because by $F = GMm/r^2$, the force of the table on the wood at that close range is sufficient to balance the force of the Earth on the wood.
(C) The electric force, because the outer electrons in the top atomic layer of the table repel the outer electrons in the bottom atomic layer of the wood.
(D) The strong nuclear force, because the protons in the nuclei of the top atomic layer of the table repel the nuclei in the bottom atomic layer of the wood.

GO ON TO THE NEXT PAGE

40. A solid sphere ($I = 0.06$ kg·m^2) spins freely around an axis through its center at an angular speed of 20 rad/s. It is desired to bring the sphere to rest by applying a friction force of magnitude 2.0 N to the sphere's outer surface, a distance of 0.30 m from the sphere's center. How much time will it take the sphere to come to rest?

(A) 4 s
(B) 2 s
(C) 0.06 s
(D) 0.03 s

41. Which of the following force diagrams could represent the forces acting on a block that slides to the right while slowing down?

(A)
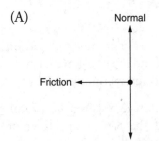

(B)
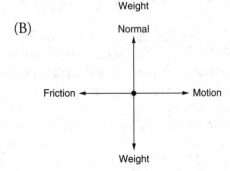

(C)
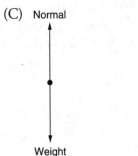

(D)
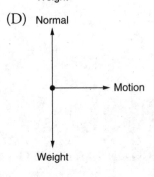

Questions 42–43: Two carts are initially at rest next to each other on a smooth horizontal track. Cart A's mass is three times cart B's mass. Cart B releases a spring, pushing cart A such that both carts move away from each other.

42. Which statement below is correct about the carts' kinetic energies?

(A) Cart B has nine times the kinetic energy of cart A.
(B) Cart B has three times the kinetic energy of cart A.
(C) Cart B has the same kinetic energy as cart A.
(D) Cart B has one-third the kinetic energy as cart A.

43. Which statement below is correct about the net force experienced by cart A while it is being pushed by the spring?

(A) It is nine times the net force experienced by cart B.
(B) It is three times the net force experienced by cart B.
(C) It is equal to the net force experienced by cart B.
(D) It is one-third the net force experienced by cart B.

44. A block of mass m is attached to a spring of force constant k. The mass is stretched a distance A from equilibrium and released from rest. At a distance x from the equilibrium position, which of the following represents the kinetic energy of the block?

(A) $\frac{1}{2}kA^2 - \frac{1}{2}kx^2$
(B) $\frac{1}{2}m\,A\sqrt{k/m}^2$
(C) $\frac{1}{2}kA^2 + \frac{1}{2}kx^2$
(D) $\frac{1}{2}kx^2$

GO ON TO THE NEXT PAGE

45. A man stands with his hands to his sides on a frictionless platform that is rotating. Which of the following could change the angular momentum of the man-platform system?

(A) The man catches a baseball thrown to him by a friend.

(B) The man thrusts his arms out away from his body.

(C) The man thrusts his arms out away from his body, and then quickly brings his arms back to his side again.

(D) The man jumps straight up in the air and lands back on the platform.

Questions 46–50: Multiple-Correct Items

Directions: Identify *exactly two* of the four answer choices as correct and grid the answers with a pencil on the answer sheet. No partial credit is awarded; both of the correct choices and none of the incorrect choices must be marked for credit.

46. A device claims to behave as an ideal spring. Which of the following methods could provide evidence of whether the claim is correct? Select two answers.

(A) Hang an object from the spring, and set that object in oscillation. Use a motion detector to graph the object's velocity versus time. Observe if the graph is sinusoidal for any amplitude of oscillation.

(B) Pull the spring several distances measured from the spring's unstretched position with a force probe. Graph the force probe reading versus the distance stretched; observe whether this graph is linear.

(C) Hang an object of known mass m from the spring, and set that object in oscillation. Use frame-by-frame video analysis to measure the object's speed v at several positions. Graph the object's momentum mv versus the position where the speed was measured; observe whether this graph is horizontal.

(D) Hang an object from the spring. Stretch the spring several measured distances, release the object from rest, and use a photogate to measure the object's maximum speed. Graph the maximum speed versus the distance stretched; observe whether this graph is linear.

47. A small cart sits on a heavy inclined track, as shown above. Both the cart and the track are on wheels, such that friction between all surfaces is negligible. The cart is released from rest. Which of the following is a correct explanation for why the heavy track moves backward while the cart slides down the track? Select two answers.

(A) The track exerts a normal force on the cart, which causes the cart to have a horizontal acceleration to the right. By Newton's third law, the cart exerts an equal force on the track, causing the track to have a horizontal acceleration to the left.

(B) The velocity of the two-object system must be conserved. Since the system began with zero velocity, the total velocity must be zero throughout. Thus the rightward velocity component of the cart must be canceled by a leftward velocity component of the track.

(C) No external forces act on the cart-track system, so the horizontal position of the system center of mass must remain at rest. The cart has a rightward velocity component, so the cart must have a leftward velocity component.

(D) The kinetic energy of the two-object system must be conserved. Since the system began with zero kinetic energy, the total kinetic energy must be zero throughout. Since the cart has kinetic energy to the right, the track must have kinetic energy to the left.

GO ON TO THE NEXT PAGE

48. A student of mass 50 kg stands on a scale in an elevator. The scale reads 800 N. Which of the following could describe how the elevator is moving? Select two answers.

(A) Moving downward and slowing down
(B) Moving downward and speeding up
(C) Moving upward and speeding up
(D) Moving upward and slowing down

49. Two pendulums are constructed from the same length of string. One has a 50 g bob on the end; one has a 100 g bob on the end. Both are released from rest from the same small angle. Which of the following quantities are the same for the two pendulums? Select two answers.

(A) Maximum speed
(B) Maximum kinetic energy
(C) Period
(D) Maximum acceleration

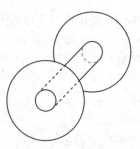

50. The device shown in the preceding figure consists of two wheels connected by a thick axle. A force can be applied to the axle by pulling a rope at several positions along the axle. Assuming the spool does not slip on the table, which of the pictured applied forces would cause rotation to the right of the device's wheels? Select two answers.

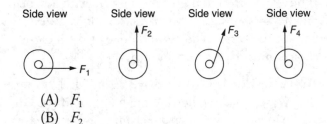

(A) F_1
(B) F_2
(C) F_3
(D) F_4

AP Physics 1 Practice Exam 1

SECTION II

(Free-Response Questions)
Time: 90 minutes

Directions: The free-response section consists of five questions. Budget approximately 20 to 25 minutes each for the first two longer questions; the next three shorter questions should take about 12 to 17 minutes each. Explain all solutions thoroughly, as partial credit is available. On the actual test, you will write the answers in the test booklet; for this practice exam, you will need to write your answers on a separate sheet of paper.

A Note About Timing: In this free-response test, the last question is about a topic that's been moved to AP Physics 2. If you'd like the authentic 2022 exam experience, just do Questions 1–4. The rule of thumb for AP Physics 1 is that problems should take about 2 minutes per point. So, instead of 90 minutes, limit yourself to about 75 minutes to finish.

1. (12 points)

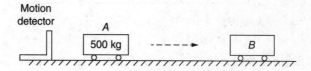

In Experiment 1, two carts collide on a negligible-friction track: Cart A with mass 500 g, and Cart B with unknown mass. Before the collision, Cart B is at rest. Adhesive is attached to the carts such that after the collision, the carts stick together. The speeds of Cart A before collision and after collision are measured using the sonic motion detector, as shown in the diagram.

(a) In one trial, the motion detector is turned on, Cart A is given a shove, the carts collide, and then the detector is turned off. The detector produces the velocity-time graph shown as follows. On the graph, indicate with a circle the portion of the graph that represents the collision occurring. Explain how you figured this out.

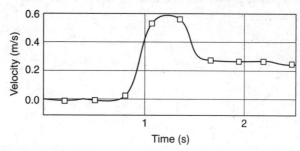

(i) Use the graph to estimate the speed of Cart A before the collision.
(ii) Use the graph to estimate the speed of Cart A after the collision.

(b) In numerous trials, the speeds of Cart A before and after the collision are measured. You are asked to construct a graph of this data whose slope can be used to calculate the mass of Cart B.

(i) What should you graph on each axis?
(ii) Explain in several sentences how you will use the slope of this graph to calculate the mass of Cart B. Be specific both about the calculations you will perform, and about why those calculations will produce the mass of Cart B.

GO ON TO THE NEXT PAGE

(c) In Experiment 2, the adhesive is removed such that the carts bounce off of one another. The motion detector is again positioned to read the speed of Cart A before and after collision.

   (i) Describe an experimental procedure by which the speed of Cart B after collision can be measured. You may use any equipment available in your physics laboratory, but you may *not* use a second sonic motion detector.

   (ii) The masses of Carts A and B are now both known; the speeds of both carts before and after collision have been measured. Explain how you could determine whether the collision in Experiment 2 was elastic. Be sure to describe specifically the calculations you would perform, as well as how you would use the results of those calculations to make the determination.

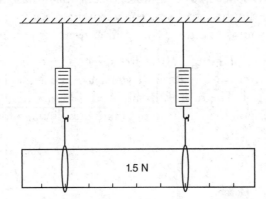

2. (12 points)

A uniform meterstick, which weighs 1.5 N, is supported by two spring scales. One scale is attached 20 cm from the left-hand edge; the other scale is attached 30 cm from the right-hand edge, as shown in the preceding diagram.

(a) Which scale indicates a greater force reading? Justify your answer qualitatively, with no equations or calculations.

(b) Calculate the reading in each scale.

(c) Now the right-hand scale is moved closer to the center of the meterstick but is still hanging to the right of center. Explain your answers to the following in words with reference to your calculations in (b).

   (i) Will the reading in the left-hand scale increase, decrease, or remain the same?

   (ii) Will the reading in the right-hand scale increase, decrease, or remain the same?

(d) Now the scales are returned to their original locations, as in the diagram. Where on the meterstick could a 0.2-N weight be hung so as to increase the reading in the right-hand spring scale by the largest possible amount? Justify your answer.

3. (7 points)

Space Probe A orbits in geostationary orbit directly above Mars's equator, 17,000 km above the surface. Identical Space Probe B sits on the surface of Mars.

(a) Which probe, if either, has a greater speed? Justify your answer.

(b) Which probe, if either, has the greatest acceleration toward the center of Mars? Justify your answer.

(c) Consider the list of gravitational forces below:

1. The force of Mars on Space Probe A
2. The force of Mars on Space Probe B
3. The force of Space Probe A on Mars
4. The force of Space Probe B on Mars
5. The force of Space Probe A on Space Probe B
6. The force of Space Probe B on Space Probe A

(i) Rank the magnitudes of the six gravitational forces listed above from greatest to least. If two or more quantities are the same, indicate so clearly in your ranking.

Greatest _____ _____ _____ _____ _____ _____ *Least*

(ii) Justify your ranking.

4. (7 points)

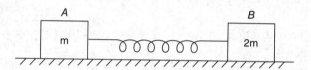

Two blocks, Block A of mass m and Block B of mass $2m$, are attached together by a spring. The blocks are free to move on a level, frictionless surface. The spring is compressed and then the blocks are released from rest.

Consider two different systems. One system consists *only* of Block A; the other system consists of both blocks and the connecting spring. In a clear, coherent, paragraph-length response, explain whether kinetic energy, total mechanical energy, and/or linear momentum is conserved in each of the systems described.

5. (7 points)

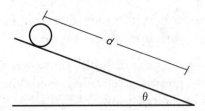

A uniform solid cylinder of mass m is released from rest from the top of an incline of angle θ, as shown in the diagram. The cylinder rolls a distance d down the incline without slipping. The cylinder has speed v after rolling the distance d.

(a) In terms of given variables and fundamental constants, derive an expression for the cylinder's rotational kinetic energy at the bottom of the incline.

(b) In another experiment, a hollow cylindrical shell is released from rest from the top of the same incline. Will this hollow cylindrical shell be moving faster, slower, or the same speed as v when it has rolled the same distance d without slipping? Justify your answer.

(c) Next, a solid block of mass m is released from rest from the top of the same incline. This block slides, without rolling, the same distance d. The block has speed v after rolling the distance d. Which of the following is correct about the objects at the bottom of the incline? Choose one, and justify your answer.

____ The work done by friction on the block is zero.

____ The work done by friction on the block is greater than the rotational kinetic energy of the solid cylinder.

____ The work done by friction on the block is less than the rotational kinetic energy of the solid cylinder.

____ The work done by friction on the block is equal to the rotational kinetic energy of the solid cylinder.

Solutions: AP Physics 1 Practice Exam 1

SECTION I

(Multiple-Choice Questions)

Questions 1–45: Single-Choice Items

1. **A**—Mechanical energy is defined as potential plus kinetic energy, which is 4 J in this case. At position $x = 3$ cm, the potential energy read off the vertical axis is 1 J. So the remaining 3 J must be kinetic energy.

2. **B**—In all collisions, including elastic collisions, momentum must be conserved. Here, the total momentum before collision is (100 g)(6 m/s) + 0. So the total momentum after collision must also be 600 g·m/s to the right. Momentums in the same direction add, so choice C doesn't work—that would give 1,000 g·m/s. Choice A gives 1200 g·m/s to the right. Choice D does give 600 g·m/s for the total momentum, but to the left, not to the right. So choice B is correct: momentums in opposite directions subtract to the total, giving 800 − 200 = 600 g·m/s to the right.

3. **D**—The relevant equation connecting force and mass is $F = ma$. The slope is the vertical axis divided by the horizontal axis, or $F/a = m$. So the slope is mass—but why inertial not gravitational mass? Inertia is defined as an object's resistance to acceleration. If acceleration is involved, you're talking inertial mass. Gravitational mass would involve the weight of an object in a gravitational field.

4. **B**—The dots divide the 1-meter distance into five parts. In the time between dots, the cart travels 1/5 of a meter, or 0.2 m. The time between dots is 1/20 of a second, or 0.05 s. At constant speed, the speed is given by distance/time: 0.20 m/0.05 s = 4 m/s.

5. **D**—Initially, the cart's mass is 0.5 kg and speed is 4 m/s, so the cart's momentum is $mv = 2$ N·s. In the collision, the cart loses that 2 N·s in order to stop briefly and then gains more momentum in order to speed up again. So the momentum change must be more than 2 N·s. How much more? After collision, the cart is moving slower

than 4 m/s because the dots are closer together, so the cart's momentum is less than 2 N·s. The cart's momentum change is (2 N·s) + (something less than 2 N·s); the only possible answer is 2.7 N·s.

6. **D**—The formula for displacement is $v_0 t + \frac{1}{2}at^2$. Let's use the right direction as positive, so that the initial speed to the left is −30 m/s. Using cm/s and cm/s^2 as common units, we get that the displacement of the cart is $(-30)(1) + \frac{1}{2}(50)(1)^2$. This works out to −5 cm, or 5 cm to the left *of the original position*. Since the cart was originally 10 cm right of the black spot, the cart ends up 5 cm to the right of the black spot.

7. **D**—The rotational inertia of a point mass is MR^2, where R is the distance from the mass to the axis of rotation. Pretend the side of the square is of length 2 m, and that each mass is 1 kg. For axis A, each mass has rotational inertia (1 kg) (1 m)^2 = 1 kg·m^2. With four masses total, that's 4 kg·m^2. For axis B, each mass is $\sqrt{2}$ m from the axis (the diagonal of the square is $2\sqrt{2}$ m, each mass is half a diagonal from the axis). Each mass has (1 kg)$(\sqrt{2}$m$)^2$ = 2 kg·m^2. Two masses make a total of 4 kg·m^2. And for axis C, the masses are each 2 m from the axis, so they each have (1 kg) × (2 m)^2 = 4 kg·m^2. With two masses, that's a total of 8 kg·m^2. So this would be ranked axis C, followed by equal axes A and B.

8. **C**—The work done by the force is force times distance; but that's not an option. The other option to find work is that work done by a nonconservative force is equal to the change in an object's potential and kinetic energy. There's no potential energy change, because the surface is horizontal. The kinetic energy $(\frac{1}{2}mv^2)$ change can be determined by knowing the mass and the speed change.

9. **A**—When a (net) torque is applied opposite the direction of motion, an object's angular speed slows down. Here, both engines apply torques in the counterclockwise direction, but the motion

was initially clockwise; so the angular speed slows, and so does angular momentum by $L = I\omega$. As for linear momentum, the two rocket engines apply forces in opposite directions, left and right. Thus, the forces on the wheel are balanced, and the linear momentum does not change.

10. **A**—Change in momentum is also known as impulse and is equal to force times time interval. On this graph, the multiplication of the axes means to take the area under the graph. Each segment of the data looks like it represents a straight line, making a big triangle. The area of a triangle is ½(base)(height). That's ½(5 N)(2 s) = 5 N·s.

11. **B**—If friction and air resistance are negligible, a mass on a spring oscillates about the equilibrium position, reaching the same maximum distance above and below. In this case, since the mass doesn't get all the way to position A at the top, mechanical energy was lost (to friction or air resistance or some nonconservative force). Thus, without some external energy input, the mass won't reach its maximum position at the bottom, either—at the bottom it will have no kinetic energy, so all the energy will be potential, and we've already established that some total mechanical energy was lost.

12. **D**—At all positions, the free-body diagram on the sitting object looks the same: normal force up, weight down. The object's acceleration always points toward the center of the platform. Acceleration is in the direction of unbalanced force. So at position 3, the forces are unbalanced upward, meaning the normal force is greater than the object's weight, and at position 1, the forces are unbalanced downward, meaning the normal force is less than the object's weight. At positions 2 and 4, the forces are unbalanced to the left or right—this means a friction force of the platform on the object must act, but the *vertical* forces on the object are balanced because the acceleration has no vertical component. So at 2 and 4, the normal force is equal to the object's weight.

13. **A**—The "magnitude" of the velocity simply means how fast an object is moving. The object's speed doesn't change, so the magnitude of the velocity is constant. The direction of the velocity indicates which way the object is moving. At position 1 the object moves left, while at position 2 the object moves down—so the direction is changing.

14. **B**—In a collision, momentum—including angular momentum—is conserved. The question might as well be asking, "What is the angular momentum of the two objects before the collision?" And since the disk is at rest initially, the question is asking the even easier question, "What is the angular momentum of the putty before collision?" The axis of rotation is the center of the disk. The putty is a point mass; the angular momentum of a point mass is mvr with r the distance of closest approach to the axis. That's (0.1 kg)(10 m/s)(1 m) = 1 kg·m²/s.

15. **C**—Mechanical energy is not conserved because of the work done by the nonconservative friction force provided by the rough-surfaced incline. The object starts with only gravitational potential energy, because it is higher than its lowest position and at rest. This gravitational energy is converted to thermal energy via the friction force, and to kinetic energy because the object speeds up.

16. **A**—The force of the sun on the planet always acts on a line directly toward the sun's center. This creates no lever arm for a torque to be exerted by the equation torque = force times lever arm. And by the impulse-momentum theorem applied to rotation—$\Delta L = \tau t$—no torque means no change in angular momentum. (Because L doesn't change, the planet's speed is greater at position 2 than at position 1, contrary to what choice C asserts.)

17. **A**—When the (unbalanced) force acts in the same direction as motion, the cart speeds up; when the force acts opposite the direction of motion, the cart slows down. Since the cart starts from rest, initially the cart speeds up. Then at the 2 s mark, the force changes direction—let's say the force starts acting to the left rather than to the right. But the cart was already moving right. So this leftward force slows the cart down. The cart would only reverse direction if the total impulse on the cart (equal to the cart's total change in momentum) were to the left. Impulse is area under the graph. Since the area above the graph is greater, the net impulse is to the right, so the cart ends up moving right not left.

18. **B**—The gravitational field at the surface of a planet is $g = G\dfrac{M}{r^2}$. The numerator for Mars is 1/10 that of Earth, reducing the gravitational field by 1/10. The denominator for Mars is $(1/2)^2 = 1/4$ that of Earth, increasing the gravitational field by a factor of 4 (because a smaller denominator means a bigger fraction). The overall gravitational field is multiplied by 4/10. On Earth, the gravitational field is 10 N/kg, so on Mars, $g = 4$ N/kg.

19. **B**—Choices C and D are wrong because kinetic energy doesn't have a direction. Choice A is wrong because momentum conservation does not require a leftward momentum component—since the initial momentum was all to the right, the final momentum should be to the right. It's the vertical momentum that's the problem. Since the vertical momentum was zero to start with, any vertical momentum after collision must cancel out.

20. **A**—Choice B is ridiculous—scientists should never refer generically to "human error." Significant friction should reduce, not increase, the speed (and thus the momentum) measured by Photogate 2. The elasticity of a collision refers to kinetic energy conservation, not momentum conservation—even inelastic collisions must conserve momentum. If the track is slanted downhill to the right, then the carts speed up; conservation of momentum won't be valid between Photogates 1 and 2 because the downhill component of the gravitational force is a force external to the two-cart system.

21. **A**—The energy input must be enough to change the translational kinetic energy of the cart *and* to change the rotational kinetic energy of the wheels. Since the wheels are all of the same radius, they will rotate with the same angular speed when the wagon reaches 10 m/s. Whichever wheels have the largest rotational inertia will therefore require the largest energy input to get to the same speed. Calculating, wagon A has the largest rotational inertia of 0.0025 kg·m².

22. **A**—Choice C is not correct because if the *swimmer* is accelerating, the responsible force must act on the swimmer, not on something else. That force can act on any part of the swimmer's body. But a force provided by the swimmer himself on the swimmer himself won't accelerate him—that's like pulling yourself up by your own bootstraps. Choices B and D do not consider a force external to the swimmer. The answer is A: the Newton's third law force pair to the force of the swimmer's arms on the water.

23. **A**—The work-energy theorem says that the work done by a nonconservative force is equal to the change in potential energy plus the change in kinetic energy. Since the wagon is on a horizontal surface, the potential energy change is zero; the work done by the 30-N pulling force is the change in the wagon's KE. Work is force times parallel displacement, so we don't use 30 N in this formula, we use the component of the 30-N force parallel to the 20-m displacement. That's $(30\text{ N})(\cos 60°)(20\text{ m}) = 300$ N.

24. **A**—Yes, momentum is conserved. That means the carts combined have the same momentum as they did in sum before the collision. And sure, if we were solving for the speed after collision, we'd combine the masses together for the calculation, but that doesn't mean that the carts both have the same mass—one cart is 1.5 kg, and the other 0.5 kg. The problem asks what is the same for each cart in comparison to the other. Since the carts are stuck together, they must move together. They have the same velocity as one another.

25. **A**—The energy conversion here is from spring potential energy at maximum displacement, to kinetic energy when the maximum speed occurs. Therefore, the equation that solves for the maximum speed v is $½kx_1{}^2 = ½mv^2$. Solving, $x_1 = \sqrt{\dfrac{m}{k}}\,v$. Since k and m don't change when we change x_1, the relationship between x_1 and v is linear—no squares or square roots. Doubling v means doubling x_1.

26. **B**—The area under a velocity-time graph represents displacement. The cart returns to its initial position when displacement is zero, so when the (negative) area from 0–2 s is equal to the (positive) area from 4–8 s. The area of the triangle in the first 2 seconds is $½(2)(6) = 6$ cm. The area of the triangle between 4 s and 8 s is $½(4)(3) = 6$ cm. So the cart moves 6 cm in one direction, then back 6 cm in the other direction after 8 s. (While it is true that the position of a cart cannot be determined from a velocity-time

graph, the displacement can. We can't figure out whether the cart is near the left end of the track or near the right end of the track; but we *can* figure out how far the cart has moved from its starting point.)

27. **C**—The work done by the spring is the area under a force-distance graph because work = force times distance. Using the best-fit line drawn as the top of a triangle, the area is $(1/2) \times (300 \text{ N})(20 \text{ cm}) = 3{,}000$ N·cm.* Now, put your ruler along the data points. Try to draw another line that's still a reasonable best fit, but is a bit shallower. Where does that line intersect the 20-cm position? It intersects at a point probably not much below 280 N, maybe even 290 N. The smallest possible work done, given this data, would be area = $(1/2)(280 \text{ N})(20 \text{ cm}) = 2{,}800$ N·cm, which is 200 N·cm short of the 3,000 N·cm original estimate. That's closest to Choice C. If you've done a lot of in-class lab work, you might have noticed that your data often look about as scattered as shown in the graph; and that anything you calculate is never much closer to a known value or to your classmates' calculations than 5 or 10 percent. Here, Choice B works out to an uncertainty of 1 percent; Choice D is 100 percent. So C is the reasonable choice.

28. **C**—Total momentum is always conserved in a collision. In this case, the carts' momentums in opposite directions subtract to the total, meaning the total momentum is in the direction of whichever cart had greater momentum to start with. After the collision, because the carts stick together, the total momentum is just the total mass times the combined speed, in the direction of motion.

29. **A**—Since the platform itself is of negligible mass, only two torques act on the platform: counterclockwise by the force of the force probe (F_P), and clockwise by the downward force of the object (mg). Torque is force times distance from a fulcrum, so set these torques equal: $F_P(x) = mg(d)$. Solving for the mass, we get $\frac{F_p x}{gd}$. Plot the numerator on the vertical, the denominator on the horizontal, and the slope is the mass m.

---

*The units are N·cm rather than joules because a joule is a newton times a meter, not a newton times a centimeter.

30. **B**—The problem says nothing about the collision being "elastic"; therefore, the change in kinetic energy of any sort does not have to be the same for each object. Velocity is never conserved in a collision—momentum is—so Choice D is ridiculous. Newton's third law demands that the force of one cart on another is the same, and so also the torque on each object about the center of mass.

31. **A**—Net force includes the contributions of all forces, including friction or air resistance; and net force is in the direction of *acceleration*, not of motion.

32. **A**—Torque is force times distance from a fulcrum, but that force must be perpendicular to the rod. So in this case, the force used in the equation will be the vertical component, which includes a sine 45° term for F_1 and F_3. The sine of 45° is 0.7; call the length of the rod L, so F_2 is a distance $L/2$ from the pivot, and F_3 is about $L/4$ from the pivot. So $\tau_1 = 0.7FL$. $\tau_2 = 0.5FL$. $\tau_3 = (0.7 \cdot 0.25)FL$.

33. **C**—The weight of the textbook is GMm/d^2, where M and m are the masses of Earth and the textbook. These don't change on a mountain. The d term will change, because d represents the distance between the textbook and Earth's center. But that will change the denominator of the weight equation from $(6{,}400 \text{ km})^2$ to $(6{,}406 \text{ km})^2$; in other words, not to the two digits expressed in the answers. No need to use the calculator. You can see that the choices require the weight to either stay the same, double, or be cut in half. The weight of the textbook remains 30 N.

34. **A**—The amplitude is measured from the midpoint to the peak or trough of a wave. Waves A and B are each two "bars" above the midpoint, while C is only one bar above the midpoint.

35. **C**—Use the equation $F = G\dfrac{M_1 M_2}{d^2}$ but just use the power of 10 associated with the value—the answer choices are so far separated that more precision would be useless. $F = \dfrac{(10^{-11})(10^{22})(10^{24})}{(10^8)^2}$. Add exponents in the numerator because everything is multiplied together: $F = \dfrac{(10^{35})}{10^{16}}$. Now

subtract exponents for the division problem: $F = 10^{19}$ N.

36. A—Choice B is wrong—the normal force on the flat surface is equal to the cart's weight, regardless of the rubber band. Choice C is true but does not explain different heights in each trial—the problem said that the kinetic energy provided to the cart was the same every time. Choice D may or may not be true but is irrelevant in any case—even if kinetic energy is lost to work done by friction, neither the force of nor the coefficient of friction changes in different trials, so that can't explain different heights. Now, the rubber band, though, that can change things. If it's initially wound and able to unwind as the cart moves, it can transfer some of its elastic potential energy to kinetic energy of the cart. Or, if it's initially unwound, it will require some kinetic energy in order to wind up again and store elastic potential energy.

37. D—The man's weight is the force of the Earth on the man. The Newton's third law force pair is then the force of the man on the Earth.

38. C—Frequency, whether in simple harmonic motion or not, is the inverse of the period. Here the period of the tape timer's oscillations is 2/100 of a second—that's the time it takes for the timer to oscillate once. So the frequency is 100/2 Hz, which is 50 Hz.

39. C—Choice B is ridiculous because not only is gravity the weakest of the fundamental forces, it makes no sense that the gravitational force of the maybe 100-kg table is similar to the gravitational force of the 10^{24}-kg Earth in the equation $F = G \dfrac{M_1 M_2}{d^2}$. Choices A and D are ridiculous because the protons are about 10^5 (100,000) times smaller than the diameter of an atom—any interactions between atoms have to involve the electrons at the outside of the atoms, not protons far away in the center.

40. B—This is a calculation using $\tau_{net} = I\alpha$. The net torque on the sphere is force times distance from the center, or $(2.0 \text{ N})(0.30 \text{ m}) = 0.60$ m·N. Now the angular acceleration can be calculated: $(0.60 \text{ m·N}) = (0.06 \text{ kg·m}^2)(\alpha)$, so $\alpha = 10$ rad/s per second. Use the definition of angular accel-

eration: the sphere loses 10 rad/s of speed each second. It started with 20 rad/s of speed, so after 1 s it has 10 rad/s of speed; after 2 s it will have lost all its speed.

41. A—There's no such thing as the "force of motion," so motion does not belong on a force diagram. The block slows down, so the block has acceleration in the opposite direction of motion, or left. That means there must be a leftward force.

42. B—Total momentum before the spring is released is zero. So the total momentum after the spring is released is also zero. This means the carts must have equal momentums in opposite directions, so the individual momentums subtract to a total of zero. The momentum formula is mv. Cart A has three times the mass, so it must have ⅓ the speed of cart B. Now, the formula for kinetic energy is ½mv^2. Since for cart A the mass is multiplied by 3 and the speed is multiplied by ⅓ (and the number ½ isn't changed, it's multiplied by 1!), cart A's kinetic energy is changed by a factor of $(1)(3)(⅓)^2$, which is a factor of ⅓. Cart A has ⅓ the kinetic energy as cart B, which is what choice B says.

(Alternate solution: If you know that the formula for kinetic energy can be written in terms of momentum as $K = p^2/2m$, then the solution is much quicker. The momentums are the same, so multiplying cart A's mass by 3 in the denominator decreases cart A's kinetic energy by a factor of 3.)

43. C—By Newton's third law, the force of cart B on cart A is equal to the force of cart A on cart B.

44. A—Here use the work-energy theorem, $W_{NC} = \Delta PE + \Delta KE$. The change in kinetic energy is what we're looking for, since the block began at rest. The only force doing work is the spring force, and that's a conservative force, so $W_{NC} = 0$. What we want, then, is the change in the block's potential energy, or the initial and final potential energies subtracted from one another. The potential energy of a block on a spring is ½kx^2. What values do we use for x here? The initial and final positions are used. At first the block is at position $x = A$. At the end, the block is at a distance called x from equilibrium.

45. A—Angular momentum can only change when a torque that's *external* to the man-platform system acts; that is, when a torque is applied by something that isn't the man or the platform. The force of the baseball on the man acting anywhere but precisely at the center of the man's rotational motion will provide a torque, and thus change the man-platform's angular momentum. The other choices all involve interactions only between the man and the platform.

Questions 46–50: Multiple-Correct Items (You must indicate both correct answers; no partial credit is awarded.)

46. A and **B**—An object on an ideal spring oscillates in simple harmonic motion, and simple harmonic motion means that a velocity-time graph looks like a sine curve—this is choice A. An ideal spring obeys the formula $F = kx$, where k is a constant value for that particular spring. So k would be the slope of a force versus position graph.

47. A and **C**—For choice A, by Newton's third law, the force of the track on the cart is equal to the force of the cart on the track. For choice C, no external force on the system means no acceleration of the center of mass, and that means no change in the center of mass speed—which was zero to begin with. Choice B is incorrect because velocity is never a conserved quantity (though horizontal total momentum is conserved here). Choice D is incorrect because kinetic energy is not conserved in this case, and even more important, kinetic energy does not have a direction.

48. A and **C**—A free-body diagram would include the student's 500-N (50 kg·g) weight downward, and the scale's 800-N force upward. (No, there's no "force of the elevator." The elevator isn't in contact with the student.) So the net force is upward; and the acceleration is in the direction of the net force, also upward. Upward acceleration could mean one of two things: speeding up and moving upward, or slowing down and moving downward.

49. A and **C**—The pendulums have different initial potential energies because they have different masses in the equation $GPE = mgh$. Since that potential energy is converted to kinetic energy at the bottom, they have different maximum kinetic energies, too. However, if you set initial gravitational energy equal to maximum kinetic energy and solve for speed, you get $v = \sqrt{2gh}$. Since the pendulums are released from the same height h, they have the same maximum speed. Period of a pendulum is independent of mass in the equation $T = 2\pi \dfrac{\sqrt{L}}{\sqrt{g}}$.

50. A and **D**—The key is knowing where the "fulcrum," or the pivot for rotation, is. Here, that's the contact point between the surface and the wheel. Now look at the line of the force. In F_1, the line of force is pulling right above the pivot point, and that causes clockwise, or forward, rotation. For F_2, the line of force is pulling up to the right of the pivot, and that causes counterclockwise, or backward, rotation. F_3's line of force is going exactly through the pivot point, so it will cause no rotation at all. F_4 pulls up with a line of force to the left of the pivot. This produces clockwise, or forward, rotation.

Solutions: AP Physics 1 Practice Exam 1

SECTION II
(Free-Response Questions)

Obviously your solutions will not be word-for-word identical to what is written below. Award points for your answer as long as it contains the correct physics, and as long as it does *not* contain incorrect physics.

Question 1

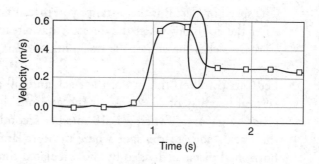

Part (a)

1 point for a correct circle on the diagram.

1 point for a correct explanation: When the carts collide, the moving cart must lose speed. The vertical axis of the velocity-time graph indicates speed. The circled portion of the graph is the only place where the vertical axis value drops rapidly, as the cart's speed must drop in the collision.

(i) **1 point** for answer: 0.60 m/s (or thereabouts—anywhere between, say, 0.55 m/s and 0.60 m/s is fine.)

(ii) **1 point** for answer: 0.25 m/s (or thereabouts—anything between, say, 0.22 m/s and 0.29 m/s is fine.)

Part (b)

(i) **1 point:** The easiest answer is to put the speed of Cart A before collision on the vertical axis; and to put the speed of Cart A after collision on the horizontal axis. There are other answers that will work.

(ii) **3 points:** Award one or two points of partial credit for correct but incomplete physics. For example, writing and using an expression for momentum conservation should earn a point, even if the rest of the explanation doesn't follow properly.

Conservation of momentum means the total momentum before the collision equals the total momentum after the collision. Before the collision, the total momentum is that of Cart A: $m_A v_A$. After the collision, the total momentum is $(m_A + m_B)v'$ where v' is the speed of Cart A (and, because they stick together, the speed of Cart B, too). Set these momentum expressions equal:

$$m_A v_A = (m_A + m_B)v'.$$

This equation can be solved for the y-axis variable divided by the x-axis variable:

$$\frac{v_A}{v'} = \frac{(m_A + m_B)}{m_A}.$$

So, to get the mass of Cart B, I'd determine the slope of the line on the graph, and set that equal to $\frac{(m_A+m_B)}{m_A}$. The mass of Cart A is given as 500 g, so I'd plug that in and solve for m_B.

Part (c)

(i) **2 points:** Award one point for a partially correct description, two points for a complete and correct description.

Three ideas occur, but many are possible:

- Measure the distance that Cart B has to travel to the end of the track. When the carts collide, start a stopwatch; when Cart B hits the end of the track, stop the stopwatch. The speed of Cart B is the distance you measured divided by the time on the stopwatch.
- After the collision, when the detector has already read the speed of Cart A but before Cart B reaches the end of the track, lift up Cart A. Now the detector can read Cart B's speed.
- Let Cart B roll off the end of the track and fall to the floor as a projectile. Measure the vertical height y of the track off the ground; the time t that the cart was in the air is given by $y = \frac{1}{2}gt^2$, where g is 10 m/s per second. Measure the horizontal distance from the track's edge to the spot where the cart landed. Then the speed of the cart is this horizontal distance divided by the calculated time of flight.

(ii) **2 points:** Award one point for a partially correct description, two points for a complete and correct description.

"Elastic" means that the total kinetic energy of the two carts was the same before and after collision. Before the collision, the only kinetic energy is that of Cart A: $\frac{1}{2}m_A v_A^2$. After the collision, the total kinetic energy is the sum of the kinetic energy of both carts, where each cart's kinetic energy is given by $\frac{1}{2}mv^2$. Compare the total kinetic energy after collision to Cart A's kinetic energy before collision. If these values are equal, the collision was elastic. If the kinetic energy after the collision is less than the kinetic energy before collision, the collision was *not* elastic.

Question 2

Part (a)

2 points: Award one point for a partially correct description, two points for a complete and correct description. Consider the center of the meterstick as the fulcrum; then the weight of the meterstick provides no torque. The oppositely directed torques applied by each scale must be equal, because the meterstick is in equilibrium. Torque is force times distance from the fulcrum; since the right-hand scale's torque calculation includes a smaller distance from the fulcrum, the right-hand scale must apply more force in order to multiply to the same torque.

Part (b)

4 points: Full credit for a complete and correct answer. Award three points partial credit for a correct approach with incorrect answers. Award two points for a correct approach and correct answer for one of the scales, but not the other. Award at least one point if the answer involved some use of torque equilibrium.

For this calculation, consider the left-hand scale as the fulcrum—that way, the left-hand scale provides no torque, and we only have to solve for one unknown variable. Set counter-clockwise torques equal to clockwise torques, with T_2 the reading in the right-hand scale.

The weight of the meterstick provides the clockwise torque; the right-hand scale provides the counterclockwise torque.

$$** \; (T_2)(50 \text{ cm}) = (1.5 \text{ N})(30 \text{ cm})$$

Solve for T_2 to get $T_2 = 0.9$ N
Next, the sum of the scale readings has to be the 1.5 N weight of the meterstick:

$$0.9 \text{ N} + T_1 = 1.5 \text{ N}$$

Giving $T_1 = 0.6$ N

Part (c)

(i) **2 points:** Award one point for a partially correct description, two points for a complete and correct description.

Look at the starred calculation in Part (b). By moving the right-hand scale closer to the center, the scale will be less than 50 cm from the left-hand scale; but the meterstick's center will still be 30 cm from the fulcrum. So when we solve for T_2, we're dividing (1.5 N) (30 cm) by a smaller value, giving a bigger T_2 reading.

But the question asks for the reading in the left-hand scale, which adds to T_2 to the same 1.5 N. A bigger T_2 adds to a smaller T_1 to get 1.5 N. Answer: decrease.

(ii) **2 points:** Award one point for a partially correct description, two points for a complete and correct description.

See Part (i): T_2, the reading in the right-hand scale, will increase.

Part (d)

2 points: Award one point for a partially correct description, two points for a complete and correct description.

Again, start from the equilibrium of torques using the left-hand scale as the fulcrum:

$$(T_2)(50 \text{ cm}) = (1.5 \text{ N})(30 \text{ cm})$$

Hanging a 0.2-N weight would provide a clockwise torque that would add to the torque applied by the meterstick's weight on the right of this equation. Algebraically, T_2 is increased by adding to the numerator of the right side of this equation. We want to add the biggest possible torque.

Torque is force times distance from the fulcrum. We want, then, the largest possible distance from the fulcrum, which would be the right-hand edge of the meterstick, 80 cm from the left-hand scale.

Question 3

Part (a)
1 point for *both* a correct answer *and* a correct justification.

Probe A. The probe's speed is the circumference of its circular motion divided by its period of revolution. We already established that the period is the same for each. Probe A has a bigger orbital radius, meaning a larger circumference of its circular motion, meaning a greater speed.

Part (b)
2 points: Award one point for the correct answer with a partially correct justification; award both points for the fully correct answer and justification.

Probe A. The centripetal acceleration is $\dfrac{v^2}{r}$. The problem is that Probe A has both a larger speed v and a larger orbital radius r. In order to answer the question, it's necessary to replace the speed v by circumference over period, $v = \dfrac{2\pi r}{T}$. Now the acceleration is $\dfrac{\left(\dfrac{2\pi r}{T}\right)^2}{r} = \dfrac{4\pi^2 r}{T^2}$.

Okay, now we know: both probes have the same orbital period T, and r is in the numerator. The bigger-radius orbit—Probe A—has the greater acceleration.

Part (c)

(i) **1 point** for correct ranking

$$\textit{Greatest} \qquad 2 = 4 > 1 = 3 > 5 = 6 \qquad \textit{Least}$$

(ii) **3 points:** Award one point for justifying all three sets of force pairs set equal. Award one more point for justifying act least one correct portion of the ranking. Award the third point for justifying a second correct portion of the ranking.

By Newton's third law, the three force pairs can be immediately set equal: that's #1 with #3, #2 with #4, and #5 with #6. Next, we know that the force of Mars on either probe is given by $F = G\dfrac{Mm}{r^2}$, where M and m are the masses of Mars and the probe, respectively. Since the probes are identical, the numerator is the same for both #1 and #2, but the distance of the probe from Mars's center is smaller for Probe B. Therefore, Probe B experiences more force, and force #2 is greater than force #1. As for force #5, Mars is an enormous planet, many times more massive than Earth even. There's no way that the product of the space probes' masses can ever approach Mars's mass, meaning that the numerator of the force equation must be way smaller for force #5.

Question 4

The paragraph response must discuss kinetic energy, total mechanical energy, and linear momentum for each of the two systems. For each of these three quantities in each system, award one point for correctly explaining whether it is conserved and correctly justifying why it is or isn't conserved. For example:

1 point: In system A, kinetic energy is *not* conserved. When the blocks are released, Block A speeds up away from Block B. Kinetic energy depends on mass and speed only. Since Block A's speed increases without changing its mass, kinetic energy cannot remain constant.

1 point: In system A, total mechanical energy is *not* conserved. Since the system consists only of Block A, there is no interaction with another object that would allow for the storage of potential energy. The force of the spring on Block A would be a force external to the system, and the spring does work on Block A because Block A moves parallel to the spring force; when a net force external to the system does work, mechanical energy is not conserved.

1 point: In system A, linear momentum is *not* conserved. Either the reasoning for system A's kinetic energy or total mechanical energy can be extended here. Linear momentum depends on mass and speed, and Block A's speed changes without changing mass. Or, the spring force is external to the system, and momentum is only conserved in systems on which no net external force acts.

1 point: In system B, kinetic energy is *not* conserved. Kinetic energy is a scalar, so kinetic energy of a system of objects is just the addition of the kinetic energies of all the objects in the system. Both blocks speed up, so both blocks are increasing their kinetic energy, increasing the system's kinetic energy.

1 point: In system B, total mechanical energy *is* conserved. No force external to the spring-blocks system does work, so mechanical energy is conserved. The kinetic energy gained by the blocks was converted from potential energy stored in the spring.

1 point: In system B, linear momentum *is* conserved. No force external to the spring-blocks system acts, so linear momentum is conserved. Here even though Block B gains linear momentum, momentum is a vector—its gain of momentum is canceled by the momentum gained by Block A in the opposite direction.

Add 1 point if the paragraph correctly states whether each quantity is conserved in each system, regardless of whether the justifications are legitimate.

Question 5

Part (a)

1 point for recognizing that the initial gravitational potential energy is converted into both rotational and translational kinetic energies.

> **1 point** for setting gravitational potential energy to mgh (using any height variable, even d) and translational kinetic energy to $\frac{1}{2}mv^2$.

> **1 point** or recognizing that the vertical height traveled is $d\sin\theta$.

(Alternate solution for the first two points)

1 point for recognizing both that rotational kinetic energy is $\frac{1}{2}I\omega^2$ AND that the rotational inertia for a solid cylinder is $\frac{1}{2}mR^2$. This is an alternate solution because this inertia formula is not given on the exam and is not necessary for this derivation. But if you knew this formula and use it correctly, you would get credit.)

> **1 point** for combining the equations above using the relationship $\omega = v/R$).

Part (b)

1 point for recognizing that the rotational inertia of the hollow cylinder is greater than the rotational inertia of the solid cylinder (you don't have to say why here, but the reason is because the hollow cylinder's mass is distributed farther from the axis of rotation than the solid cylinder's mass is).

> **1 point** for recognizing that a different amount of the gravitational potential energy is converted to rotational energy than before, changing the amount of energy available for translational kinetic energy, which is what affects linear speed v.

Part (c)

1 point for checking the correct box, that the work done by friction on the block is equal to the rotational kinetic energy of the solid cylinder.

> **1 point** for a correct justification, that the gravitational energy and translational kinetic energies are the same for both the cylinder and the block, and so whatever energy wasn't converted from gravitational to translational must be the same.

Scoring the Practice Exam

Remember that the raw percentage score necessary to obtain a 5, 4, 3, or 2 is not a fixed number. The scores are scaled each year so regardless of whether the questions on that year's exam are hard or easy, the meaning of each score is similar year after year after year. What you see below is merely my best educated guess at a reasonable score conversion. I'll even use this very score conversion in my own classes. But I don't guarantee the accuracy of the chart any more than I guarantee Arsenal to win the Premier League.

Multiple-Choice Raw Score: Number Correct _____ (50 points maximum)

Free Response: Problem 1 _____ (12 points maximum)

Problem 2 _____ (12 points maximum)

Problem 3 _____ (7 points maximum)

Problem 4 _____ (7 points maximum)

Problem 5 _____ (7 points maximum)

Free-response total: _____ (45 points maximum)

The final score should represent half multiple-choice, half free-response. So, multiply the free response score by 1.11, and add that score to the multiple choice to get the total.

Total score: _____ (100 points maximum)

Approximate Score Conversion Chart (only a guesstimate; see above)

Raw Score	AP Grade
70–100	5
55–69	4
40–54	3
25–39	2
0–24	1

Practice Exam 2

SECTION I
ANSWER SHEET

1 Ⓐ Ⓑ Ⓒ Ⓓ
2 Ⓐ Ⓑ Ⓒ Ⓓ
3 Ⓐ Ⓑ Ⓒ Ⓓ
4 Ⓐ Ⓑ Ⓒ Ⓓ
5 Ⓐ Ⓑ Ⓒ Ⓓ
6 Ⓐ Ⓑ Ⓒ Ⓓ
7 Ⓐ Ⓑ Ⓒ Ⓓ
8 Ⓐ Ⓑ Ⓒ Ⓓ
9 Ⓐ Ⓑ Ⓒ Ⓓ
10 Ⓐ Ⓑ Ⓒ Ⓓ
11 Ⓐ Ⓑ Ⓒ Ⓓ
12 Ⓐ Ⓑ Ⓒ Ⓓ
13 Ⓐ Ⓑ Ⓒ Ⓓ
14 Ⓐ Ⓑ Ⓒ Ⓓ
15 Ⓐ Ⓑ Ⓒ Ⓓ
16 Ⓐ Ⓑ Ⓒ Ⓓ
17 Ⓐ Ⓑ Ⓒ Ⓓ

18 Ⓐ Ⓑ Ⓒ Ⓓ
19 Ⓐ Ⓑ Ⓒ Ⓓ
20 Ⓐ Ⓑ Ⓒ Ⓓ
21 Ⓐ Ⓑ Ⓒ Ⓓ
22 Ⓐ Ⓑ Ⓒ Ⓓ
23 Ⓐ Ⓑ Ⓒ Ⓓ
24 Ⓐ Ⓑ Ⓒ Ⓓ
25 Ⓐ Ⓑ Ⓒ Ⓓ
26 Ⓐ Ⓑ Ⓒ Ⓓ
27 Ⓐ Ⓑ Ⓒ Ⓓ
28 Ⓐ Ⓑ Ⓒ Ⓓ
29 Ⓐ Ⓑ Ⓒ Ⓓ
30 Ⓐ Ⓑ Ⓒ Ⓓ
31 Ⓐ Ⓑ Ⓒ Ⓓ
32 Ⓐ Ⓑ Ⓒ Ⓓ
33 Ⓐ Ⓑ Ⓒ Ⓓ
34 Ⓐ Ⓑ Ⓒ Ⓓ

35 Ⓐ Ⓑ Ⓒ Ⓓ
36 Ⓐ Ⓑ Ⓒ Ⓓ
37 Ⓐ Ⓑ Ⓒ Ⓓ
38 Ⓐ Ⓑ Ⓒ Ⓓ
39 Ⓐ Ⓑ Ⓒ Ⓓ
40 Ⓐ Ⓑ Ⓒ Ⓓ
41 Ⓐ Ⓑ Ⓒ Ⓓ
42 Ⓐ Ⓑ Ⓒ Ⓓ
43 Ⓐ Ⓑ Ⓒ Ⓓ
44 Ⓐ Ⓑ Ⓒ Ⓓ
45 Ⓐ Ⓑ Ⓒ Ⓓ
46 Ⓐ Ⓑ Ⓒ Ⓓ
47 Ⓐ Ⓑ Ⓒ Ⓓ
48 Ⓐ Ⓑ Ⓒ Ⓓ
49 Ⓐ Ⓑ Ⓒ Ⓓ
50 Ⓐ Ⓑ Ⓒ Ⓓ

AP Physics 1 Practice Exam 2

SECTION I

(Multiple-Choice Questions)
Time: 90 minutes

Directions: The multiple-choice section consists of 50 questions. You may write scratch work in the test booklet itself, but only the answers on the answer sheet will be scored. You may use a calculator, the equation sheet, and the table of information.

A Note About Timing: The multiple-choice section below includes questions about waves and circuits, which were moved from AP Physics 1 to AP Physics 2. We leave the questions here for now, in case you need them for your class.

If you'd like an authentic 2022 AP Physics 1 experience, skip the grayed-out questions and limit yourself to 60 minutes, not 90 minutes. (That's a little less than two minutes per question, which is the exact right pace!)

Questions 1–45: Single-Choice Items

Directions: Choose the single best answer from the four choices provided and grid the answer with a pencil on the answer sheet.

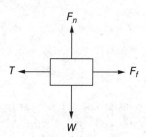

Questions 1 and 2 refer to the following information:
A person pulls on a string, causing a block to move to the left at a constant speed. The free-body diagram shows the four forces acting on the block: the tension (T) in the string, the normal force (F_n), the weight (W), and the friction force (F_f). The coefficient of friction between the block and the table is 0.30.

1. Which is the Newton's third law force pair to T?

   (A) The force of the block on the string
   (B) The force of the block on the table
   (C) The force of the table on the block
   (D) The force of friction on the block

2. Which of the following correctly ranks the four forces shown?

   (A) $T > F_f > W = F_n$
   (B) $W = F_n > T = F_f$
   (C) $W = F_n > T > F_f$
   (D) $W = F_n = T = F_f$

GO ON TO THE NEXT PAGE

3. A block on a rough horizontal surface is given an initial shove to the right. Which of the following is a reasonable graph of the block's kinetic energy as a function of position after the shove?

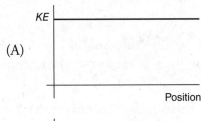

(A)

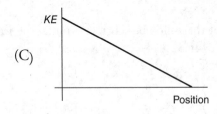

(B)

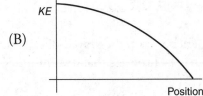

(C)

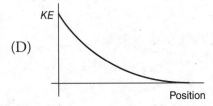

(D)

4. A car and a truck are both moving east on a straight road. Both vehicles enter an intersection simultaneously. At the moment when they enter the intersection, the car is moving with a speed of 2 m/s and an eastward acceleration of 5 m/s². The truck is moving with a speed of 5 m/s and an eastward acceleration of 2 m/s². Which of the following statements is correct about whether the vehicles are passing one another?

(A) It is unknown which vehicle is passing the other as they enter the intersection, but the car will pass the truck farther along the road.

(B) The car is passing the truck as they enter the intersection.

(C) It is unknown which vehicle is passing the other as they enter the intersection, but the truck will pass the car further along the road.

(D) The truck is passing the car as they enter the intersection.

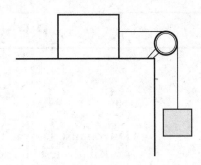

5. A light rope connects two blocks over an ideal pulley, as shown above. Friction on the table is negligible. The block on the table has much greater mass than the hanging block. Which of the following is the best estimate of the magnitude of the acceleration of the two-block system?

(A) Just about ½g
(B) Slightly greater than zero
(C) Slightly greater than g
(D) Slightly less than g

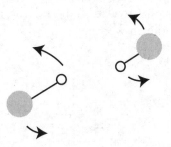

6. A device consists of a heavy sphere and a light sphere connected by a thin, light rod. This device is launched upward and to the right so that it undergoes projectile motion while spinning, as shown in the diagram. Consider the heavy sphere, the light sphere, and the device's center of mass. Does each of these trace a parabolic path during the projectile motion?

	Heavy sphere	Light sphere	Device center of mass
(A)	yes	yes	no
(B)	no	no	yes
(C)	yes	yes	yes
(D)	no	no	no

GO ON TO THE NEXT PAGE

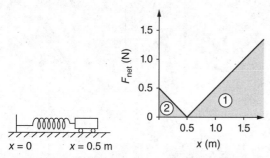

x = 0   x = 0.5 m

7. A cart attached to a spring initially moves in the x direction at a speed of 0.40 m/s. The spring is neither stretched nor compressed at the cart's initial position ($x = 0.5$ m). The figure shows a graph of the magnitude of the net force experienced by the cart as a function of x, with two areas under the graph labeled. Is it possible to analyze the graph to determine the change in the cart's kinetic energy as it moves from its initial position to $x = 1.5$ m?

(A) No, the cart's mass must be known.
(B) Yes, subtract area 2 from area 1.
(C) Yes, add area 2 to area 1.
(D) Yes, determine area 1.

8. A horse is attached to a cart that is at rest behind him. Which force, or combination of forces, explains how the horse-cart system can accelerate from rest?

(A) The forward static friction force of the ground on the horse is greater than any friction forces acting backward on the cart, providing a forward acceleration.
(B) The forward force of the horse on the cart is greater than the backward force of the cart on the horse, providing a forward acceleration.
(C) The force of the horse's muscles on the rest of the horse-cart system provides the necessary acceleration.
(D) The upward normal force of the ground on the horse is greater than the horse's weight, providing an upward acceleration.

9. Two carts are released from rest from the same height on frictionless inclines. At the bottom of the incline, Cart A is launched straight upward, while Cart B is launched at an angle less than 90° above the horizontal. Which cart (if either) reaches a greater maximum height after launch, and which cart (if either) has greater kinetic energy at its maximum height?

	Greater maximum height	Greater kinetic energy at maximum height
(A)	same	Cart B
(B)	same	same
(C)	Cart A	Cart B
(D)	Cart A	same

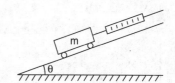

10. In the laboratory, a cart of mass m is held in place on a smooth incline by a rope attached to a spring scale, as shown in the figure. The angle of the incline from the horizontal θ varies between $0°$ and $90°$. A graph of the reading in the spring scale as a function of the angle θ is produced. Which of the following will this graph look like?

(A)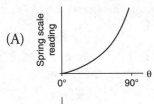

(B)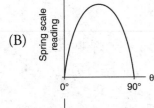

(C)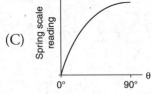

(D)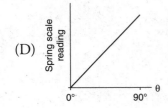

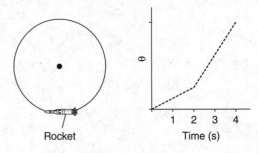

Rocket   Time (s)

Questions 11 and 12 refer to the following information: A bicycle wheel of known rotational inertia is mounted so that it rotates around a vertical axis, as shown in the first figure. Attached to the wheel's edge is a rocket engine, which applies a clockwise torque τ on the wheel for a duration of 0.10 s as it burns. A plot of the angular position θ of the wheel as a function of time t is shown in the graph.

11. In addition to the wheel's rotational inertia and the duration of time the engine burns, which of the following information from the graph would allow determination of the net torque the rocket exerts on the wheel?

(A) The area under the graph between $t = 0$ s and $t = 3$ s

(B) The change in the graph's slope before and after $t = 2$ s

(C) The vertical axis reading of the graph at $t = 3$ s

(D) The vertical axis reading of the graph at $t = 2$ s

GO ON TO THE NEXT PAGE

12. Which of the following graphs sketches the angular acceleration α of the wheel as a function of time?

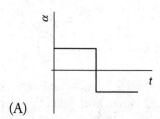

(A)

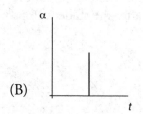

(B)

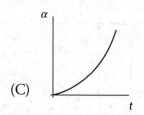

(C)

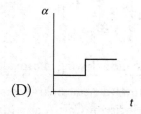

(D)

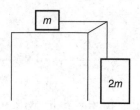

Questions 13 and 14 refer to the following information:
Two objects of mass m and $2m$ are connected by a light rope over an ideal pulley, as shown above. Friction is negligible. The objects are released from rest.

13. Which of the following is correct about the acceleration of the block of mass $2m$?

(A) 9.8 m/s²
(B) 3.3 m/s²
(C) 4.9 m/s²
(D) 6.6 m/s²

14. Which of the following correctly compares the accelerations of the two blocks?

(A) The blocks have equal accelerations, because the blocks change speed by the same amount in every time interval.
(B) The block of mass m has greater acceleration, because it experiences a greater tension from the rope.
(C) The block of mass m has greater acceleration, because it does not experience a leftward force.
(D) The blocks have equal accelerations, because the net force on each block is the same.

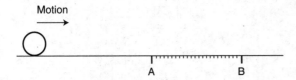

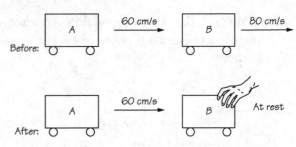

15. A ball slides to the right without rotating on a horizontal surface, as shown. The surface is frictionless except for the region between position A and position B, which is rough. Which of the following correctly indicates how the ball's center of mass speed and the ball's rotational speed about its center change from positions A and B?

	Center of mass speed	Angular speed
(A)	decreases	decreases
(B)	does not change	decreases
(C)	decreases	increases
(D)	decreases	does not change

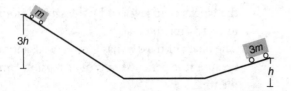

16. Two carts are released from rest on negligible-friction inclines. Cart A has mass $3m$ and is released from height h. Cart B has mass m and is released from height $3h$. The carts continue onto the smooth flat surface, collide, and stick together. Which of the following statements regarding the movement after collision is correct?

(A) The carts *will* be moving after collision, because they have different kinetic energies right before collision.

(B) The carts *will not* move after collision, because they have the same kinetic energies right before collision.

(C) The carts *will* be moving after collision, because they have different magnitudes of momentum in opposite directions right before collision.

(D) The carts *will not* be moving after collision, because they have the same magnitudes of momentum in opposite directions right before collision.

17. Two carts, each of mass 0.5 kg, move to the right at different speeds as shown in the diagram above. Next, a student stops Cart B with his hand. By how much has the linear momentum of the two-cart system changed after the student stops Cart B?

(A) 0.4 N·s
(B) 0.1 N·s
(C) 0.3 N·s
(D) 0.7 N·s

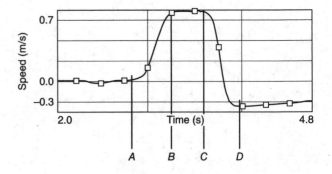

Questions 18 and 19 refer to the following information:

A student pushes Cart A toward a stationary Cart B, causing a collision. The velocity of Cart A as a function of time is measured by a sonic motion detector, with the resulting graph shown in the figure.

18. At which labeled time did the collision begin to occur?

(A) A
(B) B
(C) C
(D) D

GO ON TO THE NEXT PAGE

19. What additional measurements, in combination with the information provided in the graph, could be used to verify that momentum was conserved in this collision?

   (A) The mass of each cart and Cart B's speed after the collision
   (B) The force of Cart A on Cart B, and Cart B's speed after the collision
   (C) The mass of each cart only
   (D) The force of Cart A on Cart B only

20. A car of mass m initially travels at speed v. The car brakes to a stop on a road that slants downhill, such that the car's center of mass ends up a vertical height h below its position at the start of braking. Which of the following is a correct expression for the increase in the internal energy of the road-car system during the braking process?

   (A) $\frac{1}{2}mv^2 - mgh$
   (B) $\frac{1}{2}mv^2$
   (C) 0
   (D) $\frac{1}{2}mv^2 + mgh$

21. An object traveling east on a flat surface with decreasing speed has an acceleration directed

   (A) nowhere; the object's acceleration is zero
   (B) west, only
   (C) east, only
   (D) east or west

22. A student pushes a puck across a table, moving it from position $x = 0$ to position $x = 0.2$ m. After he lets go, the puck continues to travel across the table, coming to rest at position $x = 1.2$ m. When the puck is at position $x = 1.0$ m, which of the following is a correct assertion about the net force on the puck?

   (A) The net force is in the negative direction, because the puck is moving in the positive direction but slowing down.
   (B) The net force is down, because the puck is near the Earth, where gravitational acceleration is 10 m/s² downward.
   (C) The net force is in the positive direction, because the student's push caused the puck to speed up in the positive direction.
   (D) The net force is zero, because the student's push in the positive direction must equal the force of friction in the negative direction.

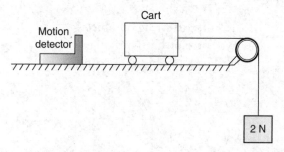

23. In an experiment, a cart is placed on a flat, negligible-friction track. A light string passes over a nearly ideal pulley. An object with a weight of 2.0 N hangs from the string. The system is released, and the sonic motion detector reads the cart's acceleration. Can this setup be used to determine the cart's inertial mass?

   (A) Yes, by dividing 2.0 N by the acceleration, and then subtracting 0.2 kg.
   (B) No, because only the cart's gravitational mass could be determined.
   (C) Yes, by dividing 2.0 N by the acceleration.
   (D) No, because the string will have different tensions on either side of the pulley.

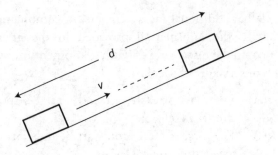

24. An object hangs by a string from a car's rearview mirror, as shown in the figure above. The car is speeding up and moving to the right. Which of the following diagrams correctly represents the forces acting on the object?

(A) T: Force of string on object
W: Force of Earth on object
F_o: Force of object on string

(B) T: Force of string on object
W: Force of Earth on object
F_o: Force of object on string

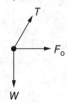

(C) T: Force of string on object
W: Force of Earth on object
F_o: Force of object on string

(D) T: Force of string on object
W: Force of Earth on object

25. A block is given an initial speed v up a rough incline, as shown above. The block travels up the incline a distance d, comes instantaneously to rest, and returns to its initial position. Let t_1 be the time it takes for the block to travel up the ramp the distance d; let t_2 be the time it takes for the block to return from the top of the ramp to the block's initial position. Which of the following is correct about the relationship between t_1 and t_2?

(A) t_2 will be equal to t_1 in all ramp inclines.
(B) t_2 will be greater than t_1 for all ramp inclines.
(C) t_2 will be greater than t_1 for some ramp inclines, less than t_1 for others.
(D) t_2 will be less than t_1 for some ramp inclines, equal to t_1 for others.

GO ON TO THE NEXT PAGE

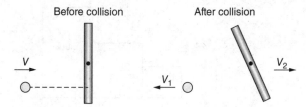

Before collision   After collision

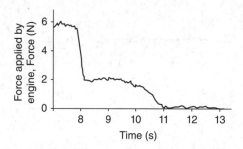

Questions 26 and 27 refer to the following information:
A small ball of mass m moving to the right at speed v collides with a stationary rod, as shown in the preceding figure. After the collision, the ball rebounds to the left with speed v_1, while the rod's center of mass moves to the right at speed v_2. The rod also rotates counterclockwise.

26. Which of the following equations determines the rod's change in angular momentum about its center of mass during the collision?

(A) $I\omega$, where I is the rod's rotational inertia about its center of mass, and ω is its angular speed after collision.

(B) Iv_2/r, where I is the rod's rotational inertia about its center of mass, and r is half the length of the rod.

(C) mv_1d, where d is the distance between the line of the ball's motion and the rod's center of mass.

(D) mv_1r, where r is half the length of the rod.

27. Is angular momentum about the rod's center of mass conserved in this collision?

(A) No, the ball always moves in a straight line and thus does not have angular momentum.

(B) No, nothing is spinning clockwise after the collision to cancel the rod's spin.

(C) Yes, the only torques acting are the ball on the rod and the rod on the ball.

(D) Yes, the rebounding ball means the collision was elastic.

Questions 28 and 29 refer to the following information:
A model rocket with a mass of 100 g is launched straight up. Eight seconds after launch, when it is moving upward at 110 m/s, the force of the engine drops as shown in the force-time graph above.

28. Which of the following is the best estimate of the impulse applied by the engine to the rocket after the $t = 8$ s mark?

(A) 100 N·s
(B) 20 N·s
(C) 5 N·s
(D) 50 N·s

29. Which of the following describes the motion of the rocket between $t = 8$ s and $t = 10$ s?

(A) The rocket moves upward and slows down.
(B) The rocket moves downward and speeds up.
(C) The rocket moves upward at a constant speed.
(D) The rocket moves upward and speeds up.

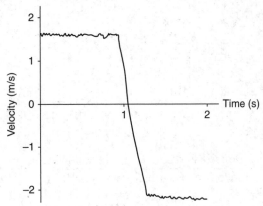

30. The velocity-time graph shown here represents the motion of a 500-g cart that initially moved to the right along a track. It collided with a wall at approximately time (t) = 1.0 s. Which of the following is the best estimate of the impulse experienced by the cart in this collision?

(A) 3.6 N·s
(B) 0.5 N·s
(C) 0.2 N·s
(D) 1.8 N·s

31. The Space Shuttle orbits 300 km above Earth's surface; Earth's radius is 6,400 km. What is the gravitational acceleration experienced by the Space Shuttle?

(A) Zero
(B) 4.9 m/s^2
(C) 9.8 m/s^2
(D) 8.9 m/s^2

32. A person stands on a scale in an elevator. He notices that the scale reading is less than his usual weight. Which of the following could possibly describe the motion of the elevator?

(A) It is moving downward and slowing down.
(B) It is moving upward and slowing down.
(C) It is moving upward at a constant speed.
(D) It is moving downward at a constant speed.

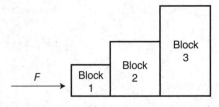

33. Three blocks of different size but the same density are pushed along a rough horizontal surface by a force F, as shown. Which of the following forces must have equal magnitudes?

(A) The friction force of the surface on Block 3, and the contact force of Block 2 on Block 3.
(B) The contact force of Block 2 on Block 3, and the contact force of Block 3 on Block 2.
(C) The friction force of the surface on Block 3, and the friction force of the surface on Block 2.
(D) The contact force of Block 3 on Block 2, and the contact force of Block 1 on Block 2.

34. A satellite orbits the moon in a circle of radius R. For the satellite to double its speed but maintain a circular orbit, what must the new radius of its orbit be?

(A) ½R
(B) 4R
(C) ¼R
(D) 2R

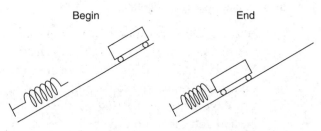

35. A 0.5 kg cart begins at rest at the top of an incline, 0.06 m vertically above its end position. It is released and allowed to travel down the smooth incline, where it compresses a spring. Between the positions labeled "Begin" and "End" in the preceding figure, the work done on the cart by the earth is 0.30 J; the work done on the cart by the spring is −0.20 J. What is the cart's kinetic energy at the position labeled "End"?

(A) 0.80 J
(B) 0.10 J
(C) 0.50 J
(D) 0.40 J

GO ON TO THE NEXT PAGE

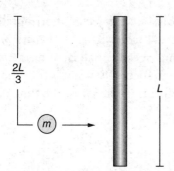

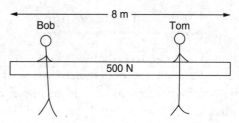

Questions 36 and 37 refer to the following information:
A rigid rod of length L and mass M sits at rest on an air table with negligible friction. A small blob of putty with a mass of m moves to the right on the same table, as shown in overhead view in the figure above. The putty hits and sticks to the rod, a distance of $2L/3$ from the top end.

36. How will the rod-putty system move after the collision?

    (A) The system will have no translational motion, but it will rotate about the rod's center of mass.
    (B) The system will move to the right and rotate about the rod-putty system's center of mass.
    (C) The system will move to the right and rotate about the rod's center of mass.
    (D) The system will have no translational motion, but it will rotate about the rod-putty system's center of mass.

37. What quantities, if any, must be conserved in this collision?

    (A) Linear momentum only
    (B) Neither linear nor angular momentum
    (C) Angular momentum only
    (D) Linear and angular momentum

38. Bob and Tom hold a rod with a length of 8 m and weight of 500 N. Initially, Bob and Tom each hold the rod 2 m from the its ends, as shown in the figure. Next, Tom moves slowly toward the right edge of the rod, maintaining his hold. As Tom moves to the right, what happens to the torque about the rod's midpoint exerted by each person?

    (A) Bob's torque decreases, and Tom's torque increases.
    (B) Bob's torque increases, and Tom's torque decreases.
    (C) Both Bob's and Tom's torque increases.
    (D) Both Bob's and Tom's torque decreases.

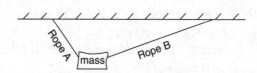

39. An object of mass m hangs from two ropes at unequal angles, as shown in the preceding figure. Which of the following makes correct comparisons between the horizontal and vertical components of the tension in each rope?

    (A) Horizontal tension is equal in both ropes, but vertical tension is greater in Rope A.
    (B) Both horizontal and vertical tension are equal in both ropes.
    (C) Horizontal tension is greater in Rope B, but vertical tension is equal in both ropes.
    (D) Both horizontal and vertical tension are greater in Rope B.

GO ON TO THE NEXT PAGE

Questions 40 and 41 refer to the following information: Block *B* is at rest on a smooth tabletop. It is attached to a long spring, which in turn is anchored to the wall. Identical Block *A* slides toward and collides with Block *B*. Consider two collisions, each of which occupies a duration of about 0.10 s:

Collision I: Block *A* bounces back off of Block *B*.
Collision II: Block *A* sticks to Block *B*.

40. In which collision, if either, does Block *B* move faster immediately after the collision?

(A) In collision I, because block *A* experiences a larger change in momentum, and conservation of momentum requires that Block *B* does as well.

(B) In collision I, because Block *A* experiences a larger change in kinetic energy, and conservation of energy requires that Block *B* does as well.

(C) In neither collision, because conservation of momentum requires that both blocks must have the same momentum as each other in each collision.

(D) In neither collision, because conservation of momentum requires that both blocks must change their momentum by the same amount in each collision.

41. In which collision, if either, is the period and frequency of the ensuing oscillations after the collision larger?

(A) Period and frequency are the same in both.

(B) Period is greater in collision II, and frequency is greater in collision I.

(C) Period and frequency are both greater in collision I.

(D) Period and frequency are both greater in collision II.

42. Two balls are projected horizontally off of a 0.50 m tall table. Ball A, of mass *m*, has initial horizontal speed *v*. Ball B, of mass 2*m*, has initial horizontal speed 2*v*. What is the ratio of the time that Ball A is in the air to the time that Ball B is in the air?

(A) 4
(B) 2
(C) $\sqrt{2}$
(D) 1

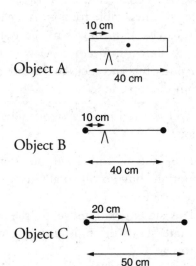

43. Three equal-mass objects (A, B, and C) are each initially at rest horizontally on a pivot, as shown in the figure above. Object A is a 40 cm long, uniform rod, pivoted 10 cm from its left edge. Object B consists of two heavy blocks connected by a very light rod. It is also 40 cm long and pivoted 10 cm from its left edge. Object C consists of two heavy blocks connected by a very light rod that is 50 cm long and pivoted 20 cm from its left edge. Which of the following correctly ranks the objects' angular acceleration about the pivot point when they are released?

(A) A = B > C
(B) A > B = C
(C) A < B < C
(D) A > B > C

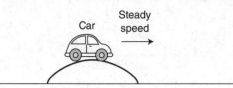

44. A car travels over a circular-shaped bump in the road, as shown. The car moves at a steady speed over the bump, but does not lose contact with the road. Which of the following is correct about the normal force of the road on the car when the car is at the top of the bump?

(A) It is equal to the weight of the car.
(B) It is less than the weight of the car, but not zero.
(C) It is greater than the weight of the car.
(D) It is zero.

45. An object of mass m is attached to an object of mass $3m$ by a rigid bar of negligible mass and length L. Initially, the smaller object is at rest directly above the larger object, as shown in the figure above. How much work is necessary to flip the object 180°, such that the smaller and larger objects switch positions?

(A) $2\pi mgL$
(B) $4mgL$
(C) $4\pi mgL$
(D) $2mgL$

Questions 46–50: Multiple-Correct Items

Directions: Identify **exactly two** of the four answer choices as correct, and grid the answers with a pencil on the answer sheet. No partial credit is awarded; both of the correct choices, and none of the incorrect choices, must be marked for credit.

46. Which of the experiments listed here measure inertial mass? **Select two answers.**

(A) Attach a fan that provides a steady 0.2 N force to a cart. Use a sonic motion detector to produce a velocity-time graph as the cart speeds up. The cart's mass is 0.2 N divided by the slope of the velocity-time graph.

(B) Hang an object from a spring and cause the object to oscillate in simple harmonic motion. Use a stopwatch to determine the period of the motion. The object's mass is this period squared, divided by $4\pi^2$, divided by the spring's force constant.

(C) Place an object on one side of a two-pan balance scale. On the other pan, place objects with previously calibrated masses. The object's mass is equal to the amount of calibrated mass on the other plate when the plates balance.

(D) Hang a spring from a clamp, then hook an object on the spring. Use a ruler to measure how far the spring stretched once the object was attached. This distance multiplied by the force constant of the spring determines the object's weight. Use 10 N/kg to convert this weight to mass.

47. An object on a spring vibrates in simple harmonic motion. A sonic motion detector is placed under the object. Which of the following determines the period of the object's oscillation? **Select two answers.**

(A) The maximum slope on a position-time graph divided by the maximum slope on a velocity-time graph

(B) The maximum vertical axis value on a position-time graph divided by the maximum vertical axis value on a velocity-time graph

(C) The time between positive maxima on a velocity-time graph

(D) The time between positive maxima on a position-time graph

48. Two carts on a negligible-friction surface collide with each other. Which of the following is a correct statement about an elastic collision between the carts? Select two answers.

(A) Some of the kinetic energy of the two-cart system is converted to thermal and sound energy.
(B) The carts bounce off of each other.
(C) Linear momentum is conserved.
(D) The carts stick together.

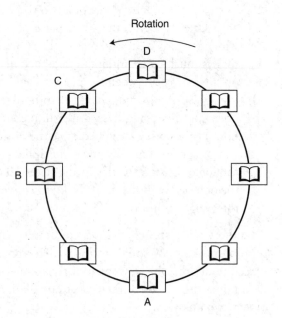

Rotation

49. A platform spins counterclockwise at constant speed in a vertical circle, as shown. The platform always remains horizontal. A book sits on the platform and does not move relative to the platform. At which positions is the friction force of the platform on the book horizontal and nonzero? Select two answers.

(A) A
(B) B
(C) C
(D) D

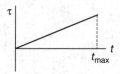

50. The net torque τ on an object of rotational inertia I is shown as a function of time t. At time t_{max}, the object has speed ω and angular acceleration α. Which of the following methods correctly determine the change in the object's angular momentum? Select two answers.

(A) Multiply I by α/t_{max}.
(B) Multiply the average torque by t_{max}.
(C) Calculate the area under the line on the graph.
(D) Multiply I by ω.

AP Physics 1 Practice Exam 2

SECTION II

(Free-Response Questions)
Time: 90 minutes

Directions: The free-response section consists of five questions. Budget approximately 20 to 25 minutes each for the first two longer questions; the next three shorter questions should take about 12 to 17 minutes each. Explain all solutions thoroughly, as partial credit is available. On the actual test, you will write the answers in the test booklet; for this practice exam, you will need to write your answers on a separate sheet of paper.

A Note About Timing: In this free-response test, the last question is about a topic that's been moved to AP Physics 2. If you'd like the authentic 2022 exam experience, just do Questions 1–4. The rule of thumb for AP Physics 1 is that problems should take about 2 minutes per point. So, instead of 90 minutes, limit yourself to about 75 minutes to finish.

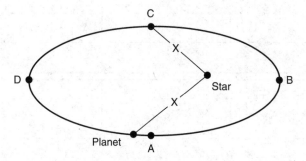

1. (7 points)

A planet of mass m is in elliptical orbit around a star whose mass M is much greater than the planet's mass, as shown above. Four positions in the planet's orbit are labeled. At positions A and C, the planet's center is a distance X away from the star's center.

(a) In terms of given variables and fundamental constants, determine the magnitude of torque with respect to the planet's center exerted by the sun on the planet when the planet is at position A.
Briefly justify your answer.

(b) Rank the locations shown in the diagram according to the magnitude of the planet's angular momentum, with respect to the planet's center, at each position. If the planet has the same magnitude of angular momentum at multiple locations, indicate this clearly in your ranking.

Greatest angular momentum _____ *Lowest angular momentum*
Justify your ranking.

(c) Rank the locations shown in the diagram according to the planet's speed at each position. If the planet has the same speed at multiple locations, indicate this clearly in your ranking.

Greatest speed _____ *Lowest speed*
Justify your ranking.

GO ON TO THE NEXT PAGE

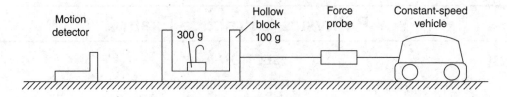

2. (12 points)

In the laboratory, a student connects a toy vehicle to a hollow block with a string. The hollow block has a mass of 100 g and contains an additional 300-g object. The vehicle is turned on, causing it to move forward along a table at a constant speed. A force probe records the tension in the string as a function of time, and a sonic motion detector reads the position of the cart as a function of time. The positioning of the probes is shown in the diagram above. The data collected are shown below.

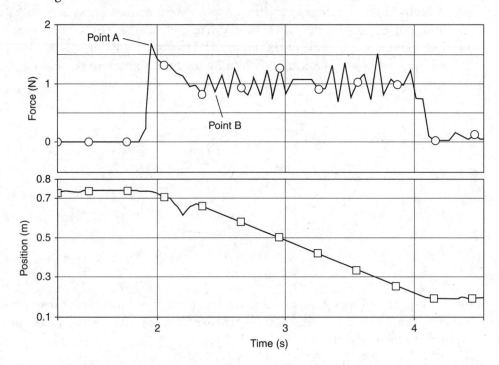

(a) Explain briefly why the force reading marked point A on the graph is significantly different from the reading marked point B on the graph.

(b) i. Calculate the impulse applied by the string on the block.

  ii. A student in the lab contends, "The block moved at a constant speed, so it has no change in momentum and should thus experience no impulse." Evaluate the validity of this student's statement with reference to the answer to part (i).

Now the student is asked to determine whether the coefficient of kinetic friction between the block and the table depends on the block's speed.

(c) Describe an experimental procedure that the student could use to collect the necessary data, including all the equipment he or she would need.

(d) How should the student analyze the data to determine whether the coefficient of friction depends on the block's speed? What evidence from the analysis would be used to make the determination?

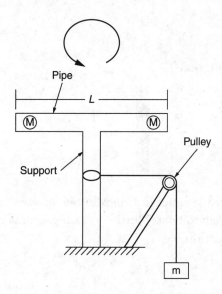

3. (12 points)

An object of mass m is attached via a rope to the stem of the device, as shown in the figure above. The top portion of the device includes two rocks, each with a mass of M, located near the end of a hollow horizontal pipe of length L. The rotational inertia of the pipe itself and the cylindrical support is assumed to be negligible compared to that of the rocks inside the pipe. As the object falls from rest, the device begins to rotate.

(a) Explain why the tension in the hanging rope is not equal to mg.

(b) Can the angular acceleration of the device be calculated given the tension in the rope T and the other information provided in the description? If so, explain in several sentences how the calculation could be performed. If not, explain in several sentences why not, including what additional measurements would be necessary and how those measurements could be performed. In either case, you should not actually do the calculations, but provide complete instructions so that another student could use them.

(c) Derive an expression for the rotational inertia of the device. If you need to define new variables to represent easily measurable quantities, do so clearly.

(d) How would replacing the hanging object with a new object with a mass of $2m$ affect the angular acceleration of the device? Answer with specific reference to the equation you derived in (c).

(e) Explain how the reasonability of the assumption that the rotational inertia of the pipe and the support is negligible in the calculation of the device's rotational inertia could be justified. You may use either a theoretical or an experimental approach to your justification.

4. (7 points)

A spring is attached vertically to a table. Undisturbed, the spring has a length of 20 cm. In procedure A, a block with a mass of 400 g is placed gently on top of the spring, compressing it so its length is 15 cm. In procedure B, a student pushes the block farther down, such that the spring has a length of 10 cm, and then releases the block from rest. The block is projected to height h.

 Consider a system consisting of the block, the spring, and Earth. Define the potential energy of this system as zero when the spring has a length of 15 cm.

(a) i. Calculate the work done by the student on the block-spring-Earth system in procedure B.
    ii. Justify your choice of equations in your calculation, as well as any distance values you used.

(b) Now the same spring is used with a block whose mass is 800 g. In procedure C, the 800-g block is placed gently on top of the spring, compressing it to a length of 10 cm. In procedure D, a student pushes the block 5 cm farther down and releases it from rest. In terms of h, how high will this 800-g block be projected? Justify your answer.

5. [paragraph response] (7 points)

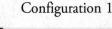

Configuration 1   Configuration 2

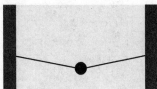

An object can be supported by two symmetric strings in one of two ways, as shown above. In which configuration are the strings more likely to break? Justify your answer, referencing physics principles in a clear, coherent, paragraph-length explanation.

Solutions: AP Physics 1 Practice Exam 2

SECTION I

(Multiple-Choice Questions)

Questions 1–45: Single-Choice Items

1. **A**—The tension is the force of the string acting on the block. Newton's third law says that since the string pulls on the block, the block pulls equally on the string. (The answer is NOT for force of friction: Newton's third law force pairs can never act on the same object.)

2. **B**—Since the block has no acceleration, left forces equal right forces, and up forces equal down forces. The equation for a force of friction is $F_f = \mu F_n$. Since the coefficient of friction μ is less than 1, the friction force must be less than the normal force.

3. **C**—The initial kinetic energy is converted to work done by friction on the block. The formula for that work is force times distance, Fx. So the work done on the block is related to the position x to the first power—that means the work done as a function of position would increase as a straight line. Similarly, then, the kinetic energy of the block will *decrease* as a straight line.

4. **D**—Speed tells how fast an object is moving; acceleration has nothing to do with speed, but rather tells how an object's speed is changing. Here, the truck's greater speed means it is passing the car—5 m/s means the truck moves faster than the 2 m/s car right now. It's true that a while later, the car will catch up with the truck, because the car's speed is changing more than the truck's is each second. Eventually, the car will move faster than the truck. We know, however, what is happening now, as the vehicles enter the intersection—the truck has greater speed, so the truck passes the car.

5. **B**—Conceptually, imagine a hippopotamus on the table, attached to a paperclip over the pulley. Even with truly zero friction between the hippopotamus and the table, the hippopotamus would hardly speed up at all—her acceleration would be close to zero. Mathematically, you can set system acceleration equal to net force over total mass. The net force is mg, the weight of the paperclip. The total mass is $m + M$, the weight of the paperclip and hippopotamus together. Plug in any reasonable values for the masses, and you see you get an acceleration nowhere close to g, or even $\frac{1}{2}g$.

6. **B**—An object is in free fall if it experiences only the force of Earth, and objects in free fall trace a parabolic path. The only external force applied on the device-spheres system is the gravitational force of Earth, which is applied at the center of mass. This force causes no torque; so the device continues to spin around its center of mass. The device-spheres system is in projectile motion, meaning its center of mass traces a parabolic path. The individual spheres are rotating about this center of mass, so they are not tracing a parabola.

7. **D**—The work done by the net force is the area under the graph. Since the cart only moved from position $x = 0.5$ m to $x = 1.5$ m, area 1 is the work done by the net force. By the work-energy theorem, work done by the net force is the change in an object's kinetic energy. (Yes, the mass must be known to determine the values of the initial and final kinetic energy; however, the question asks only for the *change* in kinetic energy.)

8. **A**—To evaluate the acceleration of the horse-cart system, you can only consider the forces applied by objects external to the system. This eliminates Choices B and C, which discuss forces of the system on itself. Choice D is ridiculous because the horse remains on the ground. Choice A is correct: the ground pushes forward on the horse's hooves because the horse's hooves push backward on the ground.

9. **C**—The carts have the same kinetic energy at launch because they convert the same amount of gravitational energy to kinetic energy. But since Cart B is launched at an angle, its horizontal acceleration is zero, and thus it must have horizontal velocity throughout its flight. Thus, it

cannot lose all its kinetic energy. Cart A comes to rest at its peak, so it does lose all its kinetic energy. Cart A goes to a greater maximum height because it converts all its launch kinetic energy to gravitational energy, while Cart B converts only some of its kinetic energy to gravitational energy.

10. **C**—The cart is in equilibrium, so the spring scale's force is equal to the component of the cart's weight that acts parallel to the plane. That component is $mg \sin\theta$. Thus, the graph of spring scale reading vs. θ should be a sine function, as in Choice C. Choice B is wrong because that's what a sine function looks like all the way to 180°; here, the angle of the incline only goes to 90°.

11. **B**—Newton's second law for rotation says $\tau_{net} = I\alpha$, where α is the angular acceleration, or change in the wheel's angular velocity per time. To find the wheel's angular velocity, look at the slope of the angular position versus time graph. The slope changes after the torque is applied; so the change in the slope is the change in the angular velocity, which (when divided by the 0.10 s duration of the rocket firing) gives the angular acceleration.

12. **B**—Angular acceleration is the change in angular speed in each second. To find angular speed, take the slope of the angular position versus time graph shown. This slope is constant for two seconds, then it changes to another constant slope. Therefore, there is no angular acceleration during the time when the slope doesn't change—with no change in angular speed, there's no acceleration. The only change in angular speed comes at the moment the slope changes, so that's the only time when there's any angular acceleration.

13. **D**—Looking at the system as a whole, the net force is $2mg$, and the system mass is $3m$. By Newton's second law, the acceleration is net force/mass, or $2mg/3m = 2/3g$. The acceleration is not automatically g because the object of mass $2m$ is not in free fall—it's attached to a rope.

14. **A**—Acceleration is defined as how much an object changes speed in one second. The objects are attached—so if one speeds up, the other speeds up, too, by the same amount.

15. **C**—The rough surface provides a force on the ball to the left. The ball is already moving to the right, so the net force opposite the direc-

tion of motion decreases the ball's linear speed. However, the ball wasn't rotating to start; then the friction force provides a clockwise torque around the ball's center. Therefore, the ball's rotation speeds up in the clockwise direction.

16. **C**—Momentum (not kinetic energy) is conserved in all collisions, including collisions in which the carts stick together. The carts having different momentums in opposite directions means the two-cart system has a total momentum before collision; by conservation, the system likewise has a total momentum after collision, meaning the stuck-together objects must have a velocity. Kinetic energy is in fact the same for both carts because the same amount of gravitational potential energy converts to kinetic energy, but that is irrelevant to the collision. For two objects with the same kinetic energy, it can be shown that the higher speed has the greater momentum because the speed in the kinetic energy formula is squared.

17. **A**—The initial momentum of the system is $(0.5 \text{ kg})(0.6 \text{ m/s}) + (0.5 \text{ kg})(0.8 \text{ m/s}) = 0.7 \text{ N·s}$. After Cart B is stopped, the momentum of the system is just $(0.5 \text{ kg})(0.6 \text{ m/s}) = 0.3 \text{ N·s}$. So, the change in momentum is 0.4 N·s.

18. **C**—The graph represents the speed of Cart A, the one that's initially moving. So right before the collision, the vertical axis of the graph must be nonzero. Right after the collision, the vertical axis must quickly either decrease or perhaps become negative if the cart changed directions. That's what happens in the tenth of a second or so after the time labeled C.

19. **A**—Conservation of momentum requires that the total momentum of the two-cart system be the same before and after the collision. You already know Cart A's speed and direction of motion before and after the collision by looking at the vertical axis of the graph; so the mass of Cart A will give us Cart A's momentum before and after the collision. You know Cart B has no momentum before the collision. But you need both Cart B's mass AND its velocity after the collision to finish the momentum conservation calculation.

20. **D**—"Increase in the internal energy of the road-car system" is a fancy way of saying "work done

by the car's brakes to stop the car." Without the brakes, the car would have gained mgh of mechanical energy in dropping the height h, giving it a total mechanical energy of $\frac{1}{2}mv^2 + mgh$. The brakes convert all of that mechanical energy to internal energy.

21. **B**—When an object slows down, its acceleration is opposite the direction of its motion. Here the object moves east, so acceleration is west.

22. **A**—The motion after the push is finished is toward more positive x, so it is in the positive direction. The puck is slowing down. When an object slows down, its acceleration and its net force are in the direction opposite the motion. (Choice C would be correct at a position at which the student were still pushing the puck, but at $x = 1.0$ m, the student had already let go, so the puck was slowing down.)

23. **A**—The net force on the cart-object system is 2.0 N. Dividing 2.0 N by the acceleration gives the mass of the entire cart-object system, not just the mass of the cart; so subtract the 0.2 kg mass of the object from the whole system mass to get the cart mass. This is actually inertial mass, because it uses the equation $F_{net} = ma$; Newton's second law defines inertial mass as resistance to acceleration.

24. **D**—All of the diagrams have the object's weight correct. Any other force acting on the object must be provided by something in contact with that object. The only thing making contact with the object is the string, so add the force of the string on the object. That's it. The force of the object on the string doesn't go on this diagram, because this diagram only includes forces acting ON the object, not exerted by the object.

25. **B**—The equation $d = \frac{1}{2}at^2$ applies to both the up and down motion. The distance d is the same both up and down the ramp. Solving for t, the time it takes to travel the distance d depends inversely on the acceleration—less acceleration, more time. Now, consider the unbalanced force acting on the block. On the way up, both friction and a component of gravity act down the incline. But on the way down, friction acts opposite gravity's component, partially balancing these forces. Thus, the net force and the

acceleration are smaller on the way down than on the way up. This gives greater time on the way down. The forces are unbalanced the same way regardless of the angle of the incline.

26. **A**—The rod starts from rest, so its final angular momentum is the same as its change in angular momentum. Although the equation $\omega = v/r$ is valid for a point object moving in a circle, it does not apply to a rotating rod; thus, Choice B is wrong. Choice C gives the final angular momentum of the ball, which is not the same as the angular momentum change of the rod because the ball does NOT start from rest.

27. **C**—Choice C states the fundamental condition for angular momentum conservation, which is correct here. The ball does have angular momentum about the rod's center of mass before and after the collision, because its line of motion does not go through the rod's center of mass. Whether or not the collision is elastic has to do with conservation of mechanical energy, not angular or linear momentum.

28. **C**—Impulse is the area under a force-time graph. From $t = 8$ s to $t = 10$ s, the area is an approximate rectangle of 2 N times 2 s, giving 4 N·s. Add an approximate triangle from $t = 10$ s to $t = 11$ s, which has the area $\frac{1}{2}(2$ N$)(1$ s$) = 1$ N·s. That gives a total of 5 N·s.

29. **D**—The force of the engine on the rocket during this time is 2 N upward. The weight of the rocket is 1 N (that is, 0.1 kg times the gravitational field of 10 N/kg). So the net force is still upward during this time. Since the rocket was already moving upward, it will continue to move upward and speed up.

30. **D**—Impulse is change in momentum. The initial momentum was something like (0.5 kg)(1.6 m/s) = 0.8 N·s to the right. The cart came to rest, changing its momentum by 0.8 N·s, then sped back up, again changing momentum by (0.5 kg)(2 m/s) = 1.0 N·s. Thus, the total momentum change is about 1.8 N·s.

31. **D**—The gravitational acceleration is given by GM/d^2, where d is the Space Shuttle's distance to Earth's center. You don't know values for G and M, nor do you need to know them. You do know that at Earth's surface, 6,400 km from the

center, the gravitational acceleration is 9.8 m/s². To calculate using this equation at the height of the Space Shuttle, the numerator remains the same; however, the denominator increases from (6,400 km)² to (6,700 km)², a difference of about 8%. (Try it in your calculator if you don't believe me.) Thus, the gravitational acceleration will decrease by about 8%, giving Choice D. (Yes, things seem "weightless" in the Space Shuttle. That's not because $g = 0$ there, but because everything inside the shuttle, including the shuttle itself, is in free fall, accelerating at 8.9 m/s per second toward the center of Earth.)

32. **B**—The scale reading is less than the man's weight; that means that the net force is downward. By Newton's second law, the person's acceleration is downward, too. Downward acceleration means either moving down and speeding up, or moving up and slowing down. Only Choice B works.

33. **B**—The force of Block 2 on Block 3 and the force of Block 3 on Block 2 are a Newton's third law force pair, so they must be equal. There's no indication that any block is in equilibrium; therefore the forces on any given block could be balanced *or* unbalanced.

34. **C**—In circular motion around a planet, the centripetal force is provided by gravity: $\frac{mv^2}{d} = G\frac{Mm}{d^2}$. Solving for the radius of the satellite's circular orbit, we get $d = \frac{GM}{v^2}$. The numerator of this expression doesn't change, because the mass of the planet M and Newton's gravitation constant G don't change. The satellite's speed v is doubled. Since the v term is squared, that increases the denominator by a factor of 4. So the radius of orbit d is now ¼ as much as before.

35. **B**—Consider the cart alone, which as a single object has no internal energy or potential energy. Thus, any work done on the cart will change the cart's kinetic energy. The cart began with no kinetic energy at all. Earth increased the cart's kinetic energy by 0.30 J, as stated in the problem; the spring decreased the cart's kinetic energy by 0.20 J. A gain of 0.30 J and a loss of 0.20 J leaves 0.10 J of kinetic energy.

36. **B**—Conservation of linear momentum requires that the center of mass of the system continue to move to the right after the collision. The rotation will be about the combined rod-putty center of mass. To understand that, imagine if the putty were really heavy. Then after the collision, the rod would seem to rotate about the putty, because the center of mass of the rod-putty system would be essentially at the putty's location. In this case, you don't know whether the putty or the rod is more massive, but you do know that when the two objects stick together, they will rotate about wherever their combined center of mass is located.

37. **D**—No unbalanced forces act here other than the putty on the rod and the rod on the putty. (The weight of these objects is canceled by the normal force.) Thus, linear momentum is conserved. No torques act on the rod-putty system except those due to each other; thus, angular momentum is conserved. It's essentially a fact of physics that in a collision between two objects, both linear and angular momentum must be conserved.

38. **C**—The net torque on the rod must be zero, because the rod doesn't rotate. Therefore, whatever happens to Bob's torque must also happen to Tom's torque—these torques must cancel each other out. That eliminates Choices A and B. The forces provided by Bob and Tom must add up to 500 N, the weight of the rod. Try doing two quick calculations: In the original case, Bob and Tom must each bear 250 N of weight and are each 2 m from the midpoint, for 500 N·m of torque each. Now put Tom farther from the midpoint—say, 3 m away. For the torques to balance, $F_{Bob}(2 \text{ m}) = F_{Tom}(3 \text{ m})$. The only way to satisfy this equation and get both forces to add up to 500 N is to use 300 N for F_{Bob} and 200 N for F_{Tom}. Now, the torque provided by each is (300 N)(2 m) = 600 N·m. The torque increased for both people.

39. **A**—The object is in equilibrium, so left forces equal right forces. Thus, the horizontal tensions must be the same in each rope. Rope A pulls at a steeper angle than Rope B, but with the same amount of horizontal force as Rope B. To get to

that steeper angle, the vertical component of the tension in Rope A must be larger than in Rope B.

40. **A**—There's no indication that energy must be conserved in collision I. However, momentum is always conserved in a collision. When Block A bounces, its momentum has to change to zero and then change even more to go back the other way. Since Block A changes momentum by more in collision I, Block B must as well because conservation means that any momentum change by Block A must be picked up by Block B. Choices C and D are wrong because, among other things, they use conservation of momentum to draw conclusions about two separate collisions; momentum conservation means that total momentum remains the same before and after a single collision, not in all possible collisions.

41. **B**—The period of a mass-on-a-spring oscillator is $T = 2\pi\sqrt{\dfrac{m}{k}}$. The important part here is that the mass term is in the numerator—a larger mass means a larger period. More mass oscillates on the spring in collision II, so collision II has a greater period. Frequency is the inverse of the period, so the period is smaller in collision II.

42. **D**—Vertical and horizontal motion are treated separately. The vertical direction determines the time in the air. Vertically, both objects have the same initial speed of zero, the same distance traveled, and the same acceleration g because they're in free fall. In the kinematic equation $\Delta x = v_0 t + \frac{1}{2}at^2$, all variables are the same for both, so the time of flight is also the same. Note that mass is not in this equation.

43. **D**—Angular acceleration is net torque divided by rotational inertia, $\alpha = \dfrac{\tau_{net}}{I}$. Imagine each object has total mass of 2 kg. Begin by comparing Objects A and B: To find the net torque on object A, assume the entire 20 N weight is concentrated at the dot representing the rod's center of mass. That's located 10 cm from the pivot, giving a net torque of 200 N·cm. For Object B, consider the torques provided by each block separately. The right block provides a torque of (10 N)(30 cm) = 300 N·cm clockwise; the left block provides a torque of (10 N)(10 cm) = 100 N·cm counterclockwise. That makes the net

torque 200 N·cm, the same as for Object A. But Object B has more rotational inertia, since its 2 kg of mass are concentrated farther away from the pivot than Object A's mass. So the denominator of the angular acceleration equation is bigger for Object B with the same numerator, which means A > B.

Now consider Object C. It experiences less net torque than A and B. Calculate (10 N)(30 cm) = 300 N·cm clockwise, and (10 N)(20 cm) = 200 N·cm counterclockwise for a net torque of 100 N·cm. And Object C has the same mass distributed even farther from the pivot point than either of the other two objects, giving C an even bigger rotational inertia. In the angular acceleration equation, Object C gives a smaller numerator and a bigger denominator than object B, meaning C < B. Put it all together to get A > B > C.

44. **B**—The free-body diagram of the car at the top of the bump includes the downward weight and the upward normal force. The car's acceleration is downward, because when an object moves in a circle its acceleration is toward the center of the circle. Thus, the forces are unbalanced downward. This makes the weight greater than the normal force. Because the car doesn't lose contact with the road, the normal force is not zero.

45. **D**—Consider the system consisting of the objects and Earth, with the location of the $3m$ mass being the zero of gravitational energy. The initial gravitational energy of the system is mgL. After the rotation, the final gravitational energy of the system is $3mgL$. That extra gravitational energy of $2mgL$ came from the work done on the system, meaning Choice D. If you want instead to think of work on the objects as force times distance, remember that the force of Earth on the objects acts straight down, not along a circle. So the distance term to use here is just L, not πL.

Questions 46–50: Multiple-Correct Items (You must indicate both correct answers; no partial credit is awarded.)

46. **A and B**—Choice A uses the equation $F_{net} = ma$, which essentially defines inertial (as opposed to gravitational) mass. Choice B measures inertial mass, because it measures mass as resistance to the acceleration caused by the spring force.

Choices C and D measure an object's behavior in a gravitational field; by definition, that's *gravitational*, not inertial, mass.

47. **C and D**—Though both speed divided by acceleration (as in Choice A) and position divided by speed (as in Choice B) give units of time, the time indicated has no relation to the period of the motion. The period is defined as the time for one complete cycle to happen. One complete cycle can be defined as the time for the object to get back to its extreme position, as in Choice D, or it can be defined as the time between the occurrences of maximum velocity in the same direction, as in Choice C.

48. **B and C**—Elastic means that mechanical energy is conserved in the collision, so the answer is not Choice A, which describes a loss of mechanical energy. Mechanical energy conservation requires that carts bounce, so Choice B is correct, but Choice D is not. Linear momentum is conserved in all collisions, elastic or not elastic.

49. **B and C**—The acceleration, and thus the net force, on the book must be toward the center because the book moves in a circle. At A and D, the center is located directly above or below the book, so the book experiences no horizontal component of acceleration or net force. However, at B and C the direction to the center has a horizontal component, meaning the net force has a horizontal component. The friction force of the platform on the book provides that horizontal force.

50. **B and C**—Change in angular momentum is $\tau \Delta t$, which means the area under a torque-time graph; thus, Choice C is correct. Since this graph is linear, the average torque multiplied by the maximum time is the same thing as the area under the graph, so Choice B is also correct. While Choice D describes a calculation of angular momentum, it does not correctly give the *change* in angular momentum, so you don't know whether the object had an initial angular momentum or not.

Solutions: AP Physics 1 Practice Exam 2

SECTION II
(Free-Response Questions)

Obviously your solutions will not be word-for-word identical to what is written below. Award points for your answer as long as it contains the correct physics and as long as it does *not* contain incorrect physics.

Question 1

Part (a)

1 point for the correct answer, zero torque.

1 point for a correct justification, explaining that the lever arm for this torque is zero (because the force of the sun on the planet is exerted directly at the planet's center).

Part (b)

1 point for the correct ranking (in any format), all are equal.

1 point for a correct justification, explaining that with no torque exerted on the planet, the angular momentum cannot change (by $\Delta L = \tau \Delta t$).

Part (c)

1 point for the correct ranking (in any format), $B > A = C > D$.

1 point for using the equation $L = mvr$.

1 point for recognizing that with constant L, a bigger distance from the sun r gives a smaller speed v.

(Alternate solution for the last two points: **1 point** for correctly referencing that the planet-sun system stores more energy when the objects are farther apart; **1 point** for relating the loss of potential energy to the gain in kinetic energy.)**Question 2**

Part (a)

The maximum coefficient of static friction is greater than the coefficient of kinetic friction. The graph shows the maximum force of static friction, when the block starts moving, to be 1.7 N; when the block is moving, the friction force drops to 1.0 N, which is appropriate for the lower kinetic friction force.

1 point for correctly explaining the difference between static and kinetic friction in this case.

Part (b)

(i) Impulse is the area under a force-time graph. The graph has an average force of about 1.0 N, and a time interval of about 2 s (from $t = 2$ s to $t = 4$ s). That's an impulse of 2 N·s.

1 point for using the area under the force versus time graph.

1 point for making reasonable estimates of time and force from the graph.

(ii) The student is incorrect. While it is true that the net impulse on an object is equal to the object's change in momentum, the graph shown does not include the net force. The graph shows the force of the string only. If you were to subtract the impulse provided by the friction force, you would get zero net impulse and thus zero change in momentum.

1 point for discussing the difference between the force of the string and the net force on the cart.

1 point for including no incorrect statements.

Part (c)

The student could use a set of toy carts, each of which moves at a different constant speed. The student should connect the carts to the block via the force probe and produce force-time graphs for each cart as the cart moves across the table. The constant speed traveled by each cart can be measured by placing a sonic motion detector in front of the cart.

3 points for a complete and correct description. Of these points, 1 or 2 could be holistically awarded for a partially complete and/or partially correct description.

Part (d)

The student should make a plot of the force of kinetic friction on the vertical axis versus speed on the horizontal axis. The speed of each cart would be determined by the slope of the position-time graph produced by the sonic motion detector. The force of kinetic friction would be measured by the force probe.

   The block is the same mass each time, which means it always experiences the same normal force; the coefficient of friction is the friction force divided by the normal force. So if the coefficient of friction changes, the force probe reading would change as well.

   If this graph is horizontal, then the force of friction and the coefficient of friction do not change with speed. If the graph is sloped, then we can conclude that the coefficient of friction *does* change with speed.

1 point for using a graph with a significant number of data points, or perhaps statistical analysis of multiple trials.

1 point for correctly relating the friction coefficient to the force probe reading with constant F_n.

2 points for a complete and correct analysis. One of these points can be holistically awarded for a partially complete and/or partially correct analysis.

Question 3

Part (a)

1 point: As the hanging object m falls, it speeds up. Its acceleration is therefore downward, and so is the net force acting on it. To get a downward net force, the downward gravitational force mg must be greater than the rope's tension.

Part (b)

4 points:
- **1 point** for using an applicable fundamental relationship such as $\alpha = \dfrac{\tau_{net}}{I}$ (or $a = r\alpha$).
- **1 point** for a correct discussion of how to get τ_{net} (or α).
- **1 point** for a correct discussion of how to estimate I (or a).
- **1 point** for a correct conclusion to answer the question.

The angular acceleration can be found by dividing the net torque on the device by its rotational inertia. The rotational inertia I of the device can be calculated based on the assumption that the pipe and the stem do not contribute; the device consists of two pointed masses, each a distance of $L/2$ from the center of rotation. The net torque on the device is Tr, where r is the radius of the support.

The only unknown information in all of this is the radius of the support r. So **no, the angular acceleration cannot be calculated** with the information provided unless r is measured with calipers.

(*Alternate solution:* The angular acceleration of the device α is related to the linear acceleration a of the falling mass by $a = r\alpha$. The radius of the support r must be measured with calipers. To get a, the distance the mass falls from rest d can be measured with a meterstick, and the time t to fall that distance can be measured with a stopwatch. Then kinematics can be used to calculate a. So **no, the angular acceleration cannot be calculated** with the information given here.)

Part (c)

1 point for clearly defining and correctly using any new variables.

1 point for a correct expression for I (or a).

1 point for a correct final answer.

As described in Part (b), let r be the radius of the support.

By Newton's second law for rotation, $\alpha = \dfrac{\tau_{net}}{I}$.

Using the net torque and rotational inertia explained in Part (b), $\alpha = \dfrac{Tr}{2M\left(\dfrac{L}{2}\right)^2}$.

(*Alternative solution, as described in Part [b]:* $\alpha = \dfrac{a}{r}$.

Falling from rest means zero initial velocity, so $d = \frac{1}{2}at^2$, with d and t defined as shown.

Algebraically, this makes $a = \dfrac{2d}{t^2}$.

Combining these two statements gives $\alpha = \dfrac{2d}{rt^2}$.)

Part (d)

1 point for describing the quantity in the equation in (c) that would be affected by the new mass.

1 point for describing with reference to the equation how that change would affect the acceleration.

While the tension in the hanging rope is not equal to the weight of the hanging object, increasing the hanging object's mass would increase the tension in the rope T. Since T is in the numerator of the equation for angular acceleration, and since the parameters in the denominator are unchanged, the angular acceleration would increase.

(*Alternative solution:* We would be able to measure that the hanging object falls the same distance in less time. Note that this is NOT because "heavier objects fall faster"; this is really a consequence of the reasoning already given, that the tension in the rope increases without changing the properties of the device. With a smaller t in the denominator and other variables unchanged, the angular acceleration would increase.)

Part (e)

2 points for a complete and correct solution. One of these points can be awarded for a partially complete or partially correct solution.

Using a calculational approach: You assumed that the rotational inertia of the device was wholly due to the two rocks as point objects, $2M(L/2)^2$. The rotational inertia of a cylinder rotating horizontally and vertically can be looked up, and the mass of the pipe and support can be measured. You could calculate the additional rotational inertia provided by the cylinder and support. If this additional rotational inertia is substantially less than $2M(L/2)^2$

such that the calculation of α would still come out approximately the same, then this additional inertia is negligible.

Using an experimental approach: Measure the angular acceleration of the device directly. This can be done with frame-by-frame video analysis or with a photogate set to measure the increase in angular velocity. If the angular acceleration measured matches that predicted by the equation in (c), then the assumption that the rotational inertia is due wholly to the point masses is reasonable. However, if the angular acceleration is measured to be noticeably smaller than that predicted in (c), then the rotational inertia of the pipe and support do contribute meaningfully to the calculation and are not negligible.

Question 4

Part (a)

(i) **1 point** for calculating the spring constant.

   1 point for using the calculated spring constant in a correct equation to determine the work done.

The spring constant of the spring can be determined by procedure A. The rock applies a 4 N force on the spring, compressing it 0.05 m. By $F = kx$, that gives a spring constant k of (4 N)/(0.05 m) = 80 N/m.

   The potential energy of the spring-block-Earth system is just $\frac{1}{2}kx^2$, where x is the distance from the position of the block after procedure A. (If you were talking about just the spring-block system, you would use the distance from the undisturbed position, but then you would have to consider the work done on the block-Earth system separately.) So in procedure B, the block-Earth system gains $\frac{1}{2}$(80 N/m)(0.05 m)^2 of potential energy, which is 0.10 J. That's how much work was done by the student.

(ii) **1 point** for correctly justifying the use of data from procedure A to get the spring constant.

   1 point for justifying use of $\frac{1}{2}kx^2$ as a change in potential energy of the correct system.

See above.

Part (b)

1 point for recognizing that the same potential energy is available to be converted to *KE*.

1 point for words or equations showing that the mass only shows up in the denominator of an expression for the height.

1 point for using an equation or conservation of energy reasoning to get $\frac{1}{2}$h.

The new spring-block-Earth system stores the same 0.10 J of potential energy: $\frac{1}{2}kx^2$, where x is the 0.05 m distance from the position of the block after procedure C. That 0.10 J is converted into kinetic energy, then to purely gravitational energy. Gravitational energy is mgh; the new height is $h_{new} = 0.10$ J/mg. Since this new mass is twice as much as before, and since height is in the denominator, the new height is half as much as h.

Question 5

1 point for appropriate free body diagram(s) or equivalent clear descriptions of forces acting on the object.

1 point for relating the tension in the rope to the likelihood that the string will break.

1 point for using horizontal and vertical components of the strings' tensions.

1 point for use of trigonometry (graphically, or with sines and cosines) relating the magnitude of the tension to the components of the tension.

1 point for an equivalence between the vertical tension components and the object's weight.

1 point for recognizing that the vertical components of tension must be the same in either configuration.

1 point for connecting identical vertical tensions with different horizontal tensions to show that configuration 1 gives the larger magnitude of tension.

Example of a good paragraph: In each configuration, the forces acting on the object are the two equal tensions T, and the object's weight. Equilibrium demands that the vertical tension components are together equal to the object's weight and that the horizontal tension components are equal to each other. No matter what the angle, the vertical components of tension must remain the same (because the weight of the object can't change). The vertical component is given by $T \sin \theta$, with angle θ measured from horizontal. To keep this vertical component the same no matter the angle, the tension must increase as the sine of the angle decreases. The angle θ is smaller in configuration 1; therefore, the tension is larger and the string is more likely to break.

Scoring the Practice Exam

Remember that the raw percentage score necessary to obtain a 5, 4, 3, or 2 is not a fixed number. The scores are scaled each year so regardless of whether the questions on that year's exam are hard or easy, the meaning of each score is similar year after year after year. What you see below is merely my best educated guess at a reasonable score conversion. I'll even use this very score conversion in my own classes. But I don't guarantee the accuracy of the chart any more than I guarantee Arsenal to win the Premier League.

Multiple-Choice Raw Score: Number Correct _____ (50 points maximum)

Free Response: Problem 1 _____ (12 points maximum)

Problem 2 _____ (12 points maximum)

Problem 3 _____ (7 points maximum)

Problem 4 _____ (7 points maximum)

Problem 5 _____ (7 points maximum)

Free-response total: _____ (45 points maximum)

The final score should represent half multiple-choice, half free-response. So, multiply the free response score by 1.11, and add that score to the multiple choice to get the total.

Total score: _____ (100 points maximum)

Approximate Score Conversion Chart (only a guesstimate; see above)

Raw Score	AP Grade
70–100	5
55–69	4
40–54	3
25–39	2
0–24	1

5 Minutes to a 5

120 Daily Questions and Activities in

5 Minutes a Day

INTRODUCTION

The AP Physics 1 Exam will pose five free-response problems, each with three to six subparts. While a few of these may require mathematical calculation in the response, most will not. You'll instead be asked to explain, justify, describe—that is, to *write*.

But the exam doesn't require essays in the sense that your English class does. A good response to an AP Physics question reasons directly from equations or from facts of physics. Although you must write sentences with subjects and verbs, the graders aren't evaluating the quality of your prose or the depth of your vocabulary. In my experience grading, the longer a student's response, the less likely it is to get full marks.

That's why we say "five minutes." Each of the following questions is intended to be answered by an experienced AP Physics student in about 5 minutes. Did it take you 6 minutes? That's probably okay. But if it took 12 minutes, either you're writing too much or you are taking too much time to recall the relevant facts and equations. To get through the entire AP free-response section without running out of time, you must practice responding concisely.

Rule of thumb: Use two to four sentences for a justification. Okay, a full paragraph response question can stretch to five sentences. But you don't have to write a book; just answer the question so the reader knows you understand the physics involved and then stop. If your teacher might have given you only three of four points because you missed something, well, no worries: since getting 70 percent of the available points generally earns a 5 on an AP Physics 1 Exam, you're golden.

How These Items Are Organized

As the *5 Steps to a 5: AP Physics 1* book explains, the AP exam is not organized by traditional physics chapters. Rather, the exam consists of the following:

- One-half Newton's laws, generally about the relationship between force (or torque) and motion
- One-half conservation laws, including energy and both linear and angular momentum

A single free-response question will often overlap these categories. For example, a collision problem generally suggests momentum conservation as the path to solution. Yet, the same problem might ask about the net force on the two-object system! Thus our five-minute items are arranged by category, not by specific physics topic, because that's how the exam is constructed.

How to Use These Items

AP Physics 1 is not a broad course! The official course and exam description for the 2022 exam and beyond suggests that it's appropriate to use somewhere between 102 and 124 class days for this course. And we have 120 activities in this section.

I don't suggest you start with question 1 on the first day of school, though. This is a *review* book! Do what your teacher assigns, watch the AP Daily videos, read the content chapters in the main portion of this book. Start there.

Then once you're comfortable with a topic based on your work in physics class, leaf through this section and try an item on that topic. All classes cover topics in different orders. So if you cover forces in equilibrium before motion, well, find the equilibrium questions first. If you cover waves first, head to the last questions first.

Don't do more than a couple in a day. Think of these items as lifting weights in preparation for athletics. Perhaps you can bench-press a 100-pound bar fifteen times before you tire. Great—do that once or twice a day, perhaps increasing the weight on the bar once it becomes easy; you'll be strong and fit when your season starts.

However, skipping your workouts for a month and then trying to cram 400 bench presses in a single day is not just silly, but impossible. Even if you skip workouts, 15 bench presses once or twice a day is still the limit that your body can handle.

Your brain works the same way. Don't try to cram 30 of these five-minute items into a single day. Even if you feel like you're behind in your studying, you'll do far better by picking one or two items each day than by cramming. Do each one carefully. Check the solution. If you got it pretty close to right on, great.

If you got it wrong, though, come back to that question in a week or two. Once you leave enough time, these problems will become as new. And since you've already tried it once, you should have the context to explain that problem well this time.

Check off each activity as it is completed.

1. ❑		31. ❑		61. ❑		91. ❑	
2. ❑		32. ❑		62. ❑		92. ❑	
3. ❑		33. ❑		63. ❑		93. ❑	
4. ❑		34. ❑		64. ❑		94. ❑	
5. ❑		35. ❑		65. ❑		95. ❑	
6. ❑		36. ❑		66. ❑		96. ❑	
7. ❑		37. ❑		67. ❑		97. ❑	
8. ❑		38. ❑		68. ❑		98. ❑	
9. ❑		39. ❑		69. ❑		99. ❑	
10. ❑		40. ❑		70. ❑		100. ❑	
11. ❑		41. ❑		71. ❑		101. ❑	
12. ❑		42. ❑		72. ❑		102. ❑	
13. ❑		43. ❑		73. ❑		103. ❑	
14. ❑		44. ❑		74. ❑		104. ❑	
15. ❑		45. ❑		75. ❑		105. ❑	
16. ❑		46. ❑		76. ❑		106. ❑	
17. ❑		47. ❑		77. ❑		107. ❑	
18. ❑		48. ❑		78. ❑		108. ❑	
19. ❑		49. ❑		79. ❑		109. ❑	
20. ❑		50. ❑		80. ❑		110. ❑	
21. ❑		51. ❑		81. ❑		111. ❑	
22. ❑		52. ❑		82. ❑		112. ❑	
23. ❑		53. ❑		83. ❑		113. ❑	
24. ❑		54. ❑		84. ❑		114. ❑	
25. ❑		55. ❑		85. ❑		115. ❑	
26. ❑		56. ❑		86. ❑		116. ❑	
27. ❑		57. ❑		87. ❑		117. ❑	
28. ❑		58. ❑		88. ❑		118. ❑	
29. ❑		59. ❑		89. ❑		119. ❑	
30. ❑		60. ❑		90. ❑		120. ❑	

NEWTON'S LAWS

Day 1

Two stones, of mass m and $2m$, are each launched straight up by a cannon. Upon leaving the cannon, the less massive stone has twice the speed of the more massive stone. Which stone, if either, reaches a higher maximum height, and how many times higher does it go? Justify your answer.

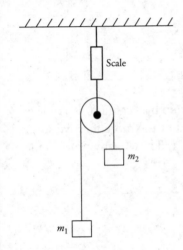

Scale

m_2

m_1

While doing an experiment with an Atwood's machine, two students hang the apparatus from a scale as shown. The hanging object m_2 has a larger mass than the hanging object m_1. The students are surprised to notice that when the objects are released from rest, the reading on the scale changes.

Explain why the scale reading changes. As part of your explanation, indicate whether the scale reading increases or decreases.

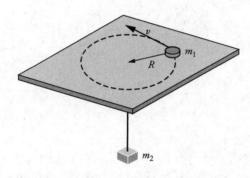

A hole is drilled in a board through which a string is run. On the board is object 1 of mass m_1. Hanging below the board is object 2 of larger mass m_2.

In the first experiment, object 1 is set into circular motion in such a way that the radius R of the circular motion does not change. In the second experiment, object 2 is placed on the board with the less massive object 1 hanging beneath.

How will the linear velocity v of object 2 in the second experiment compare to the linear velocity of object 1 in the first experiment?

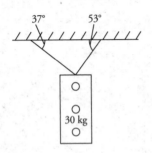

Two ropes support a 30-kg stoplight, as shown. A student is asked to find the tension in each rope. Note that this problem does NOT ask for a complete solution to the problem.

1. On the dot above that represents the traffic light, draw and label the forces (not components) that act on the stoplight.

2. Derive two equations that together can be solved for the tension in each rope. If you need to draw anything other than what you have shown in Part (1) to assist in your solution, use the space below. Do NOT add anything to the figure in Part (1).

3. In your derived equations, circle the variables that represent unknown quantities; place a checkmark beside the variables that represent given variables or fundamental constants.

Day 5

A horse pulls a cart with force F_H such that the cart and the horse move at constant speed in the forward direction. A friction force F_f acts on the cart in the backward direction.

A class of students is asked, "Are F_f and F_H a Newton's third law force pair?" Each student's response follows.

Abel says, "No, they are equal and opposite, but not a third law pair, because Newton's third law cannot apply to forces acting on the same object."

Baker says, "No, they are equal and opposite, but not a third law pair because Newton's third law doesn't apply to objects in equilibrium."

Charles says, "Yes, because these forces are equal and opposite."

Daniel says, "No, they're opposite but not equal: because the cart is able to move, F_H must be greater than F_f."

For each student's response, indicate whether the response is correct or incorrect. For any incorrect response, briefly explain which parts of the statement are correct and incorrect, and why.

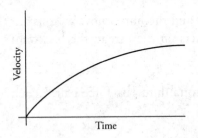

A lab cart moves according to the velocity-time graph shown above. The positive direction is to the right.

In a clear, coherent, paragraph-length response, describe how the cart moves and how the graph indicates the motion you describe. Include reference to the direction of motion and whether the cart is speeding up or slowing down.

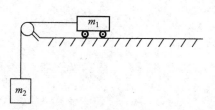

A cart of mass $m_1 = 0.50$ kg on a frictionless surface is connected by a string to a hanging object of mass $m_2 = 0.10$ kg. The system is released from rest.

Calculate the magnitude and direction of the cart's acceleration. Annotate your calculation with a description of your approach.

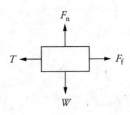

A person pulls on a string, causing a block to move to the left at the constant speed of 0.20 m/s. The force diagram above shows the four forces acting on the block: the tension T in the string, the normal force F_n, the weight W, and the friction force F_f. The coefficient of kinetic friction between the block and the table is 0.30.

Rank the magnitudes of these four forces, from greatest to least. If two or more forces have the same magnitude, indicate so in your ranking.

Largest force_____   _____   _____   _____ Smallest force

Justify your ranking.

Day 9

In an experiment, two baseballs are dropped from the top of a tall building. When the first baseball is dropped, a timer is started. After 1.0 second, the second baseball is dropped. Air resistance can be neglected.

As the baseballs fall, what happens to the difference between the two baseballs' speeds?

_____ It increases.

_____ It decreases.

_____ It remains the same.

Justify your answer.

As the baseballs fall, what happens to the distance between them?

_____ It increases.

_____ It decreases.

_____ It remains the same.

Justify your answer.

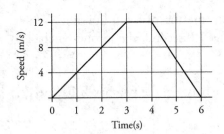

In the graph above, the speed of a small object as it moves along a horizontal straight line is plotted against time. Which of the following methods is correct for determining the average speed between 0 and 4 s? Choose one, and justify your answer.

(A) Read the vertical axis at $t = 4$ s.

(B) Read the vertical axis at the average time, which is $t = 2$ s.

(C) Read the vertical axis to see the object starts at 0 m/s and finishes at 12 m/s, so add these speeds and divide by 2.

(D) Divide the area under the graph from 0–4 s by 4 s.

Day 11

An alien visits Earth and discovers that she is able to jump incredibly high. The alien speculates that the free-fall acceleration g on Earth is different from that of her home planet. Her home planet is twice the diameter of Earth but made of material with the same density.

In terms of g, what is the free-fall acceleration on the alien's home planet?

A satellite is in circular orbit around an unknown planet. The satellite has a speed of 64 km/s, and the radius of its orbit (measured from the center of the planet) is 2,100 km. A second, identical satellite also has a circular orbit around this same planet, of radius 8,400 km.

Two students are discussing how the speed of the second satellite might be calculated:

Luis says, "The speed of the second satellite cannot be determined. We need to know the mass of the satellites and the unknown planet."

Marsha says, "But the mass of the unknown planet can be calculated using Newton's law of universal gravitation with the speed and radius of the first satellite. We have to do that first, but then we can calculate the speed of the second satellite."

Evaluate the arguments of Luis and Marsha. Indicate which statements they make are correct and incorrect.

Planets A and B are identical to each other. Planets C and D are each twice the mass of planets A and B, and are located the same distance from each other as A and B are.

Let F_{AB} represent the force of planet A on planet B; let F_{CD} represent the force of planet C on planet D. Is it possible to determine the ratio of forces F_{AB}/F_{CD}? Explain.

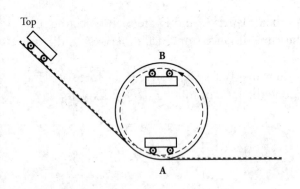

A cart is released from rest from the top of a frictionless track, as shown above. The cart goes around the vertical loop, never leaving the track.

At which of the two labeled positions, if either, is the normal force of the track on the cart greater?

___ The normal force is greater at point A.

___ The normal force is greater at point B.

___ The normal force is the same at both locations.

Justify your answer.

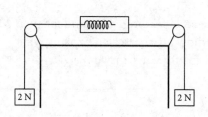

A spring scale is tied on both ends and connected to two 2-N objects via pulleys as shown in the diagram. Three students debate the reading on the spring scale.

- Student 1: The spring scale will read 2 N. There is a pull from one side of 2 N, and as a reaction, the other side will pull with 2 N. The reading will then equal 2 N.
- Student 2: No—the spring scale will equal zero. As you said, on each side there is a 2-N object pulling on the scale, but since these pulls are in opposite directions, the net force on the scale would equal zero.
- Student 3: You are both wrong. The scale reads how much force is exerted on the spring inside. Since there is a 2-N object pulling from each side, the spring scale will read 4 N.

Which aspects, if any, are correct in each student's reasoning?

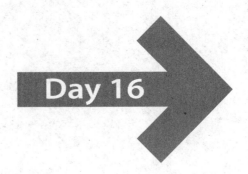
A student stands on a bathroom scale and records the scale reading. The student then pushes down on the bathroom sink while still standing on the scale. Explain what changes to the scale reading the student will observe. Justify your answer.

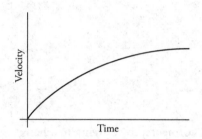

A lab cart moves according to the velocity-time graph shown above. The positive direction is to the right.

During the motion represented, is the magnitude of the object's acceleration increasing, decreasing, or remaining constant? Justify your answer.

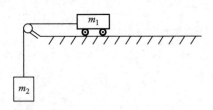

A cart of mass $m_1 = 0.50$ kg on a frictionless surface is connected by a string to a hanging object of mass $m_2 = 0.10$ kg.

In Experiment A, the system is released from rest. In Experiment B, a student gives the cart an initial push to the right to set it in motion.

(a) In which experiment, if either, is the magnitude of the cart's acceleration greater? Explain briefly.

(b) Is the direction of the cart's acceleration the same or different in each experiment? Explain briefly.

Day 19

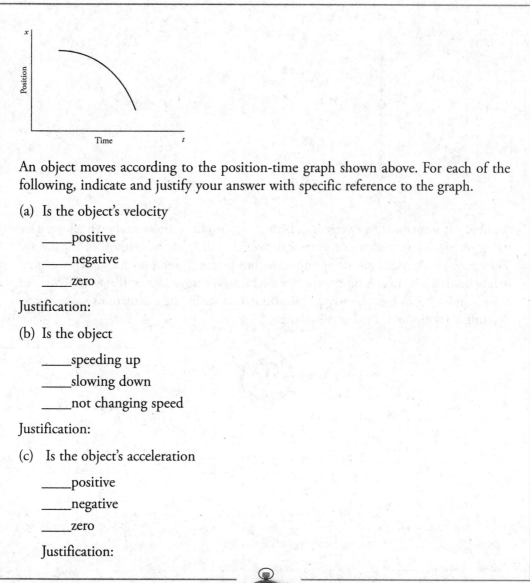

An object moves according to the position-time graph shown above. For each of the following, indicate and justify your answer with specific reference to the graph.

(a) Is the object's velocity

_____positive

_____negative

_____zero

Justification:

(b) Is the object

_____speeding up

_____slowing down

_____not changing speed

Justification:

(c) Is the object's acceleration

_____positive

_____negative

_____zero

Justification:

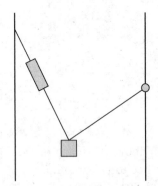

An object is suspended by two strings between two vertical poles as shown above. The string on the left is tied to a spring scale, which will read the tension in the string. The string on the right has no spring scale, but is free to slide up and down the pole to any desired position. A protractor is available to measure angles. If the string on the right is moved such that the string is horizontal, describe the calculations necessary to determine the value of the unknown mass.

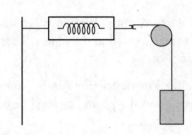

A spring scale is tied on one end to a vertical pole and connected to an object that weighs 2 N via a pulley, as shown in the diagram. Predict the reading on the spring scale. Justify your answer.

A 10-N object is at rest on a surface where the coefficient of static friction is 0.3 and the coefficient of kinetic friction is 0.1. A 2-N force is then applied to the object. Three students make predictions about the value of static friction.

- Student 1: The static frictional force is zero. Since the kinetic friction can be found by $f = F_N = 1$ N, the object will be accelerating due to the greater applied force. With the object in motion there is no static frictional force.

- Student 2: The static frictional force will equal 2 N. The maximum static frictional force can be found by $f = F_N = 3$ N. Since the maximum force has not been exceeded, the static frictional force will equal the applied force.

- Student 3: The static frictional force will equal 3 N. The frictional force can be found by $f = F_N = 3$ N. Since the applied force is less than 3 N, the object is not set into motion and held in place by 3 N of static friction.

Which student, if any, correctly predicts the value of static friction? Justify your answer.

In the laboratory, students drop tennis balls from rest at various heights h above the ground. They measure the time t necessary for the balls to hit the ground.

The students are asked to plot a linear graph of their data whose slope can be used to determine g.

(a) What should be graphed on each axis such that the graph is linear?

(b) How can the slope of the best-fit line be used to determine g?

Justify your answer to each question.

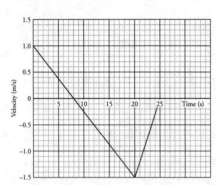

A lab cart moves according to the velocity-time graph shown above. A student is asked to determine the cart's displacement in the first 20 s of the cart's motion. His response—which is partially incorrect—is shown below.

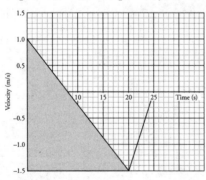

The cart's displacement is the area under the velocity-time graph from time $t = 0$ to $t = 20$ s. That area is shaded above in gray. The area of a triangle is ½(base)(height)—for this triangle, that's ½(20 s)(2.5 m/s) = **25 m**.

(a) Explain the error(s) in the student's solution.

(b) Does this student overestimate or underestimate the cart's displacement in the first 20 s of its motion? Explain your answer.

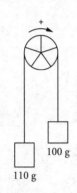

100 g

110 g

Two hanging objects are connected with light string passing over a pulley of mass 100 g, as shown above. The pulley consists of a massive ring with very light spokes.

In experiment 1, the pulley is given an initial clockwise angular velocity. The resulting angular velocity versus time graph is shown below.

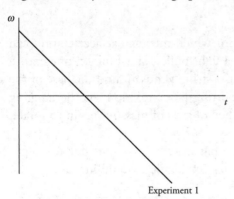

Experiment 1

In experiment 2, the same hanging objects are instead connected over a different pulley, which has the same mass and radius but is shaped like a uniform disk. The pulley is given the same initial angular velocity.

On the same axes, sketch what the angular velocity versus time graph should look like for experiment 2. Justify your answer.

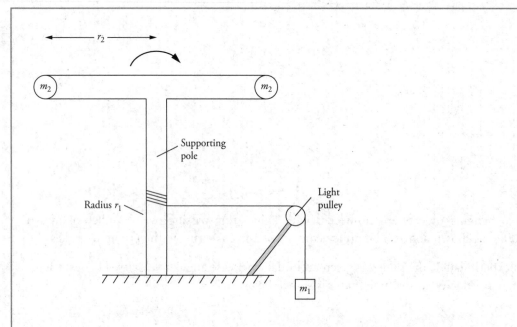

The diagram above shows a laboratory device for which the angular acceleration can be measured directly. A light string passes over a light pulley, attaching on one end to a hanging object of mass m_1. The other end of the string winds around the base of the device at radius r_1 from the center of the supporting pole's rotation. As the hanging object drops, the supporting pole and the attached objects of mass m_2 begin to rotate.

Describe two simple modifications to the device that would *increase* the device's angular acceleration. For each, explain why the angular acceleration would increase.

Day 27

A 500-g cart sits on a frictionless track.

In experiment 1, a student pulls the cart to the right via a string attached to a spring scale. The student pulls such that the reading on the spring scale remains constant at 1.0 N.

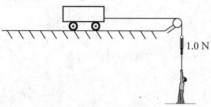

1.0 N

Note: Figure not drawn to scale.

In experiment 2, an object of weight 1.0 N is attached to the same string. The string is passed over a light pulley, as shown.

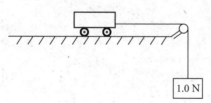

1.0 N

In which experiment, if either, is the cart's acceleration greater? Justify your answer.

Planet X has three times the gravitational field of Earth. A red ball is thrown upward on Earth; a blue ball is thrown upward on planet X with three times the initial speed of the red ball. Which ball, if either, goes higher? And how many times higher does it go, if applicable? Justify your answer.

Planets A and B are identical to each other. Planets C and D are each twice the mass of planets A and B, and are located the same distance from each other as A and B are.

(a) Let g_A represent the gravitational field at the surface of planet A; let g_B represent the gravitational field at the surface of planet B. Is it possible to determine the ratio of gravitational fields g_A/g_B? Explain.

(b) Let g_A represent the gravitational field at the surface of planet A; let g_C represent the gravitational field at the surface of planet C. Is it possible to determine the ratio of gravitational fields g_A/g_C? Explain.

For each prompt below, give a brief but specific description. Use normal, everyday language, without technical terms. In particular, do not use the words *positive* or *negative*.

(a) Describe an object that has zero velocity and zero acceleration.

(b) Describe an object that has nonzero velocity and zero acceleration.

(c) Describe an object that has zero velocity and nonzero acceleration.

(d) Describe an object that has nonzero velocity and nonzero acceleration.

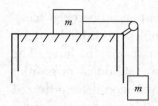

Two blocks, each of mass $m = 2$ kg, are attached via string over a light pulley, as shown above. The surface is frictionless. The blocks are released from rest.

(a) What is the magnitude of the acceleration of the top block after it is released?

(b) What is the direction of the acceleration of the top block after it is released?

A student designs an experiment to determine the linear relationship between acceleration and net force. The student sets up a cart on a frictionless horizontal surface, attached to a string that passes over a pulley, from which mass may be hung. The student varies the net force accelerating the cart by hanging additional mass from the string; the student measures the cart's acceleration with a motion detector placed behind the cart. The student plots the weight of the hanging objects versus the block's acceleration.

Describe at least one error in the student's lab design.

Day 33

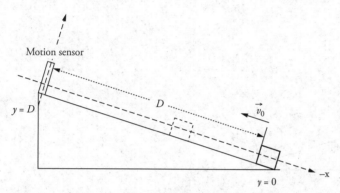

A box is moving up a frictionless incline with an initial velocity of v_0 as shown above. On the axes below, sketch position-time, velocity-time, and acceleration-time graphs for the period that the block slides up and back down the incline, reaching its highest point at time t_0. On the same graphs, create a second sketch of the position-, velocity-, and acceleration-time graphs if the experiment is repeated with friction present for the period that the block slides up and back down the incline, reaching its highest point at time t_0'. Explicitly label any intercepts, asymptotes, maxima or minima with algebraic expressions, given values, or fundamental constants as appropriate. Use a coordinate system with the origin at the base of the ramp, and the direction up the ramp considered positive.

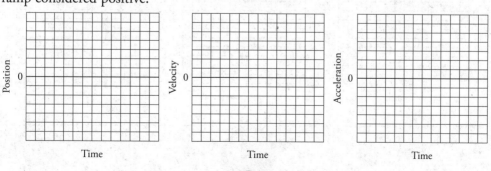

5 Minutes to a 5

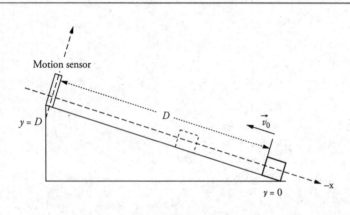

Motion sensor

$y = D$

D

$\vec{v}_0$

$y = 0$

$-x$

A box is moving up a frictionless incline with an initial velocity of v_0 as shown above. On the axes below, sketch position-time, velocity-time, and acceleration-time graphs. On the same graphs, create a second sketch of the position-, velocity-, and acceleration-time graphs for the same box if the angle of the incline to the horizontal is increased. Explicitly label any intercepts, asymptotes, maxima or minima with algebraic expressions, given values, or fundamental constants as appropriate.

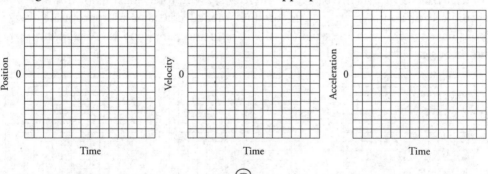

Position
0
Time

Velocity
0
Time

Acceleration
0
Time

A rocket attached to a rock begins at rest, then speeds up upward with an acceleration of 5 m/s². After 4 s, the rocket releases the rock. A group of students is asked to determine how much time it takes after the rock's release for the rock to begin moving downward. They brainstorm the four possible approaches to the solution, listed below.

(A) The rock's velocity is downward as soon as it's released.

(B) Set up constant acceleration kinematics equations with a final velocity equal to zero.

(C) Figure out when the downward forces on the rock exceed the upward forces.

(D) Figure out when the downward forces on the rock equal the upward forces on the rock.

    (a) Which is the correct method?

    (b) For one of the incorrect methods, identify the error in the reasoning, explaining why that method will not work.

A block of mass *m* is not touching a surface. A student pulls up on the block with a tension *T*, which is less than the weight of the block. Which way is the block moving? Choose one, and justify your answer.

(A) Down

(B) Up

(C) Nowhere; the block cannot move

(D) The block could be moving in any direction

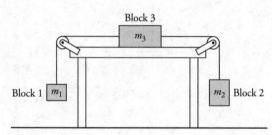

Note: Figure not drawn to scale.

Three blocks are attached by strings in a system as shown above. Block 2 has twice the mass of block 1. Block 3 has 3 times the mass of block 1. The system is moving at constant speed, with block 3 moving to the right.

Derive an expression for the coefficient of kinetic friction between block 3 and the table. Express your answer in terms of m_1, m_2, m_3, and fundamental constants as appropriate.

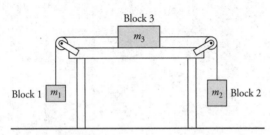

Note: Figure not drawn to scale.

Three blocks are attached by strings in a system as shown above. Block 2 has twice the mass of block 1. Block 3 has 3 times the mass of block 1. The system remains at rest.

(a) The dots below represent the three blocks. Draw free-body diagrams showing and labeling the forces exerted on each block. Draw the relative lengths of all force vectors to reflect the relative magnitudes of all forces.

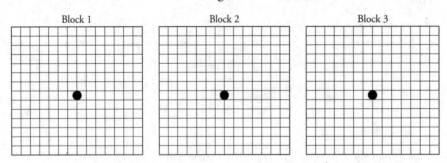

(b) What is the direction of the frictional force between block 3 and the table? Justify your answer.

An object has an acceleration of constant magnitude 4 m/s^2. Describe in detail three different possibilities of how this object could be moving.

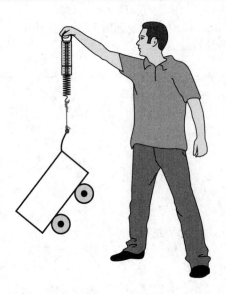

A student is asked to determine the weight of a lab cart with a spring scale. However, when he hangs the cart directly from the spring scale as shown, the scale doesn't work, because it reaches its maximum reading.

Describe how the student could use this spring scale—and other lab equipment, but no other scales—to measure the weight of the lab cart.

5 Minutes to a 5

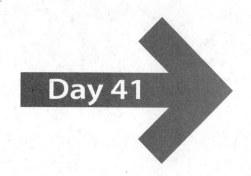

Day 41

A car traveling at highway speed collides with a bug, which was initially at rest. The bug sticks to the car after the collision.

Does the bug or the car experience a larger magnitude of acceleration during the collision? Justify your answer.

Day 42

An astronaut drops a ball from 4.0 m above the surface of the moon, where the gravitational field is 1.7 m/s².

(a) On the axes below, draw a velocity-time graph to scale representing the motion of this ball, starting when it was dropped. Label and scale the axes.

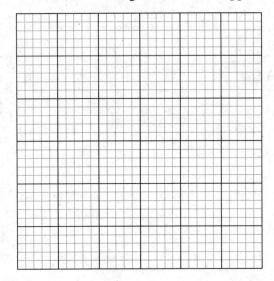

(b) Explain how to *use the graph* to estimate the time it takes for the ball to hit the moon's surface.

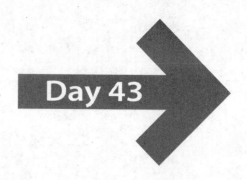

A disk initially at rest is subjected to a constant torque. On the axes below, graph the angular displacement, velocity, and acceleration of the disk as a function of time.

 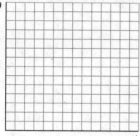 θ ... t

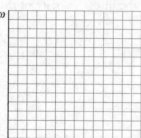 ω ... t

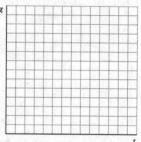 α ... t

An automobile speeds up due to a constant force. The tires do not slip on the road. On the axes below, plot graphs of the linear distance traveled versus the angular displacement of one of the wheels, and the linear velocity of the car versus the angular velocity of one of the wheels.

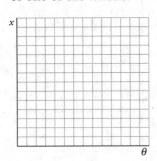

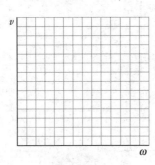

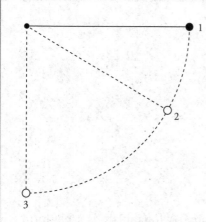

A pendulum is released from a horizontal position and swings through an arced path as shown above. On the diagram above, sketch a single vector to indicate the direction of the net force acting on the bob at locations 2 and 3. If there is zero net force at either location, clearly label as such by stating NONE.

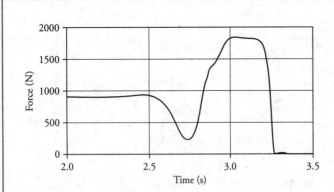

The graph above represents the reading in a force plate. (A force plate is a platform scale whose output can be graphed 20 times per second.) At time $t = 2$ s, a person stood at rest on the force plate. Then the person bent his knees and jumped vertically off of the scale.

At $t = 3$ s, determine the following. For each, explain how you made your determination.

(a) The total magnitude, in newtons, of the upward forces acting on the person

(b) The magnitude and direction of the net force on the person

(c) The total magnitude, in newtons, of the downward forces acting on the person

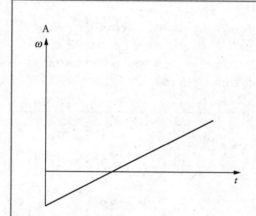

A graph of angular velocity versus time for an unknown object is shown above. Describe an object and its motion that could produce this graph.

A small boy on a sled is launched across a level, snowy surface with an initial speed of 7 m/s. Next, a large boy on the same sled is launched at the same speed across the same surface. In a clear, coherent, paragraph-length response, explain why both the small and the large boys travel the same distance before coming to rest.

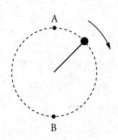

An object of mass *m* attached to a light string rotates at constant speed in a vertical circle, as shown above. Is the tension in the string greater at position A or at position B? (Or is the tension equal at both locations?) Justify your answer.

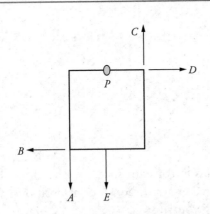

Five equal forces are applied to either the corners or edges of a square as shown in the diagram above. Rank the forces, from greatest to least, in terms of the greatest magnitude of torque about point P.

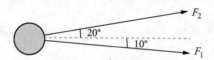

Note: Figure not drawn to scale.

An object is accelerated by two forces: F_1 at 10 degrees below the line of motion, and F_2 at 20 degrees above the line of motion, as shown above. For the object to accelerate directly to the right, does F_2 need to be greater than, less than, or equal to F_1? Justify your answer.

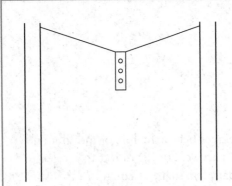

A student makes the following statement about a traffic light that is suspended on cables as shown above: "This appears to be shoddy workmanship. If the cables are pulled tighter, then they will be horizontal instead of sagging."

Do you agree or disagree with the student? Justify your answer.

A weightlifter is lifting a barbell over his head while standing on a scale. As the barbell is moving upward at a constant speed, the scale reading equals the weight of the barbell and weightlifter combined. During the time interval when the barbell slows to a stop, will the reading on the scale increase, decrease, or remain the same? Justify your answer.

Situation 1:

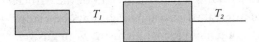

Two blocks on a frictionless surface are connected by a cord, as shown above. The block on the right is twice the mass of the block on the left. A second cord accelerates the system to the right. The two blocks then change position as shown below.

Situation 2:

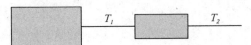

Describe any changes in the tensions of each cord if the masses change locations, as shown, but the system is to have the same acceleration.

5 Minutes to a 5

Day 55

A student observes that a bicycle wheel take 20 seconds to reach a top speed by a motor providing a constant torque. A second wheel that is the same size, but of greater mass, is placed on the same axle and brought to the same initial speed by the motor. Predict how the time it takes for the second wheel to reach top speed compares to that of the first. Justify your answer.

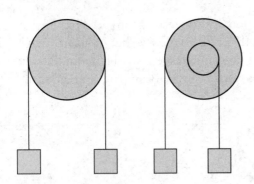

A light string passes over a pulley as shown above on the left. Two objects of equal mass are hung from each side of the string, and it is observed that the pulley stays at rest. The same objects are placed on a two-wheeled pulley, where the strings supporting the objects are wrapped around the pulley wheels. The object on the right is attached to a smaller wheel than the object on the left. Predict any changes in the motion of the new pulley system.

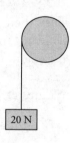

20 N

An object that weighs 20 N is attached to a string that is wrapped around a heavy, fixed pulley, as shown above, causing the pulley to accelerate. If the 20-N object is replaced by a rope pulling with a constant force of 20 N, predict how the angular acceleration of the pulley will change, if at all.

A monster truck is one that, among other modifications, has much larger wheels than the standard truck. An owner of a monster truck makes the following statement: "I can reach a greater top speed in the monster truck. The rotational speed of the engine is transferred directly to the rotational speed of the wheels. With larger wheels, at the same speed, more linear distance will be covered per rotation, resulting in a greater linear speed."

What, if anything, do you agree with in this statement?

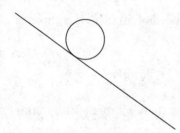

An iron hoop rolls without slipping down an incline.

(a) On the diagram above, indicate the forces (not force components) that act on the iron hoop. The tail of the arrow representing each force should begin at the point of that force's application.

(b) Which of the force(s) you drew will cause the hoop to have an angular acceleration about its center of mass? Justify your answer.

A race car completes one lap around a track at an average speed of 50 m/s. It completes a second lap at an average speed of 100 m/s.

(a) Explain why the car's average speed for both laps is NOT 75 m/s.

(b) Is the average speed for both laps greater than or less than 75 m/s? Justify your answer qualitatively.

CONSERVATION

Day 61

In the laboratory, a ball is released from height h_1, measured with a ruler. The ball hits the ground and rebounds to height h_2. The experiment is repeated for many different heights h_1, each time measuring h_2 and graphing the results on the axes as shown. Which of the following possible graphs of h_1 as a function of h_1, where the scale on each axis is identical, violate the law of energy conservation? Choose all that apply, and justify your answer.

Graph 1

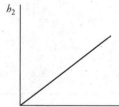

Graph 2

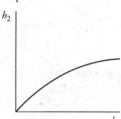

Graph 3

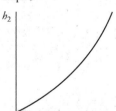

Graph 4

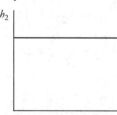

A 0.5-kg object hanging from a 25-N/m spring is pulled 5 cm from its equilibrium position and released from rest. Two students are asked to calculate the maximum speed of the object.

- Student 1 says: "Elastic potential energy is converted entirely into kinetic energy.

  $\frac{1}{2}kx^2 = \frac{1}{2}mv^2$
  Plug in $k = 25$ N/m, $x = 0.05$ m, $m = 0.5$ kg; solve for v.
  Answer is 0.35 m/s."

- Student 2 says: "Acceleration is F/m, which is kx/m, where $k = 25$ N/m, $x = 0.05$ m, and $m = 0.5$ kg. That gives 2.5 m/s/s.

  Then use the kinematics equation $v^2 = v_0^2 + 2ax$, where $v_0 = 0$ and $x = 0.05$ m. Solve for v.

  Answer is 0.50 m/s."

Which student, if either, do you agree with?

Two balls of equal mass are dropped onto a hard surface from the same height above the surface. Both balls are in contact with the surface for about the same amount of time in their respective collisions. After its collision, ball A rebounds from the surface with approximately the same speed it had right before contact; ball B nearly sticks to the surface, rebounding with hardly any speed at all.

Which ball experiences a greater force during its collision? Justify your answer.

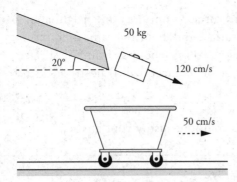

A 50-kg suitcase rolls down a chute and lands in a cart. Immediately before impact, the suitcase moves with a speed of 120 cm/s at an angle of 20° below the horizontal, as shown, while the cart moves to the right with a speed of 50 cm/s. Immediately after the collision, the suitcase is stuck inside the cart.

(a) Is the mechanical energy of the suitcase-cart system conserved during the collision? Justify your answer.

(b) Is the momentum of the suitcase-cart system in the vertical direction conserved during the collision? Justify your answer.

(c) Is the momentum of the suitcase-cart system in the horizontal direction conserved during the collision? Justify your answer.

Questions 1 and 2:

An archer shoots an arrow from his bow, whose bowstring acts exactly like a horizontal spring. Consider the time from when the archer releases the arrow until the time the arrow leaves the bow.

1. Is the work done by the bowstring on the arrow positive, negative, or zero? Explain.

2. Is the work done by Earth on the arrow positive, negative, or zero? Explain.

Question 3:

Now consider only the interval during which the archer pulls the arrow back, storing energy in the bow before releasing the arrow.

3. Is the force provided by the archer on the arrow constant or changing? Explain.

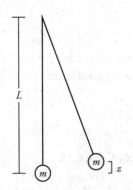

A ball of mass m is attached to a string of length L. The ball is pulled back and released from rest, a vertical distance of z above the lowest point.

(a) Derive an expression in terms of the given variables and fundamental constants for the speed of the ball at its lowest point. Circle the answer.

(b) As the starting point for the derivation in (a), did you use the kinematics equations with Newton's laws, or did you use the work-energy theorem? Explain briefly whether the approach you *did not* use would have been valid or invalid.

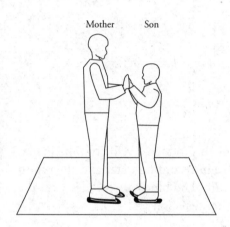

A mother and her son are initially at rest next to each other on an ice rink on which friction is negligible. The mother's mass is twice the son's mass. They push off of each other, causing them to glide apart.

Two students are discussing the quantities conserved in this collision. Each of the following statements is partially correct and partially incorrect. Identify the correct and incorrect parts, and explain why the incorrect parts are incorrect.

(a) Curtis says, "Linear momentum is conserved in this case. Even though the mother pushes with twice as much force as the son does, she will have only half of his speed after the collision, and by $p = mv$ they will have the same momentum as each other after the collision."

(b) Gregg says, "Kinetic energy is conserved in this case. The mother-son system begins with no speed and thus no kinetic energy. After the push, both have equal kinetic energy but in opposite directions; thus the system kinetic energy is zero, matching the system kinetic energy before collision."

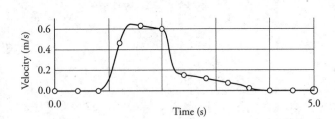

In the laboratory, you use a sonic motion detector to produce a velocity-time graph. The detector is located behind a blue cart. You begin recording data, and then push the blue cart toward an identical, stationary red cart. The blue cart collides with the red cart. Above is the graph produced by the motion detector.

(a) On the velocity-time graph, circle the graph immediately before the collision; draw an X on the graph immediately after the collision. Justify your choices.

(b) Did the carts stick together after the collision? Justify your answer with reference to the experimental data.

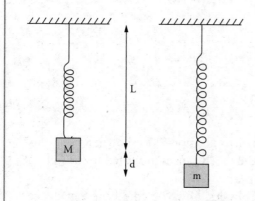

A cylinder of mass *m* is attached to a spring of spring constant *k* and length *L*. The cylinder initially hangs at rest. Next, the cylinder is pulled downward a distance of *d* from its resting position and released.

(a) Explain briefly how you know this cylinder's acceleration is not constant.

(b) Derive an expression in terms of given variables and fundamental constants for the maximum speed of the cylinder.

5 Minutes to a 5

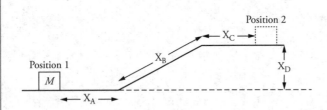

A block of known mass M moves from position 1 to position 2, as shown. The speeds of the block at positions 1 and 2 are known, as are the distances indicated in the figure.

Describe, as to another student at your level of physics, how you could show evidence for whether there is measurable friction between the surface and the block.

A child is standing in the center of a rotating platform and then walks toward the outside edge. Describe the change in the child-platform system, if any, of each of the following quantities. Justify your answers.

- Angular momentum
- Rotational inertia
- Angular velocity
- Rotational kinetic energy

An object attached to a spring oscillates horizontally in simple harmonic motion. Which of the following quantities is unchanged when the amplitude of the object's harmonic motion is doubled? Justify your answer.

(a) The period of oscillation

(b) The mass's maximum velocity

(c) The maximum potential energy stored in the spring-object system

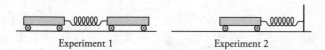

Experiment 1   Experiment 2

To demonstrate conservation of momentum, a teacher places two carts together with a spring between the carts. The spring is initially compressed. When the spring is released, both carts move away from each other with equal speeds due to their equal mass. The teacher then repeats the demonstration with the same spring, but now with only one cart and the spring between the cart and a rigid surface. What changes can you predict about the magnitude of the momentum of the cart when the spring is released in the second case as compared to the first case?

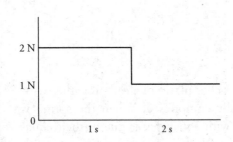

A 0.5-kg object is moving at a constant speed of 4 m/s and is subjected to a force, as shown above. What is the magnitude of the work done from 0 to 1s? Justify your answer with a calculation.

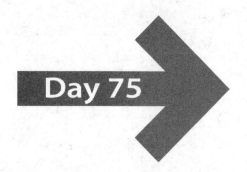

Can a normal force ever do work on an object? If so, describe such a situation. If not, explain why not.

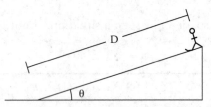

A skier of mass m starts from rest at the top of a hill that is inclined at an angle to the horizontal, as shown above. The hillside has a length D, and the coefficient of kinetic friction between snow and skis is μ.

For each of the following, choose one and justify your answer briefly.

1. Relative to the base of the hill, which of the following expressions gives the potential energy of the skier-Earth system?

   (A) $\dfrac{mgD}{\cos \theta}$

   (B) $\dfrac{mgD}{\sin \theta}$

   (C) $mgD \cos \theta$

   (D) $mgD \sin \theta$

   (E) mgD

2. Which of the following expressions gives the magnitude of the friction force on the skier while he moves down the incline?

   (A) $mg \sin \theta$

   (B) μmg

   (C) $\mu mg \cos \theta$

   (D) $\mu mg \sin \theta$

   (E) $mg \cos \theta$

3. Define the kinetic friction force on the skier as he slides down the incline as f. Which of the following expressions gives the work done on the skier by kinetic friction while the skier is on the incline?

   (A) $- \dfrac{fD}{\cos \theta}$

   (B) $- fD \sin \theta$

   (C) $- fD$

   (D) $- fD \cos \theta$

   (E) $- \dfrac{fD}{\sin \theta}$

John lowers an object of mass 100 g from head level to the floor at constant speed. Is the work done by John on the object positive, negative, or zero? Justify your answer.

Two identical balls are released simultaneously from the top of a table. Ball A is dropped from rest; ball B is given an initial shove so that it leaves the table moving horizontally. Both balls hit the ground at the same time, but they do *not* have the same speed when they arrive at the ground. With reference to energy, explain which ball has greater speed when it hits the ground, and why.

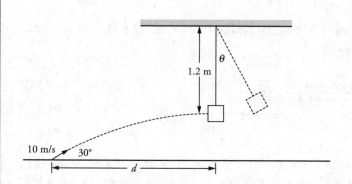

A dart is shot with an initial speed of 15 m/s at an angle of 30° from the horizontal. The dart, when at the top of its trajectory, strikes and sticks to a pendulum bob, swinging the pendulum to an angle θ.

The experiment is repeated with the projectile shot at the same speed and the angle increased to 60°. The pendulum height is changed such that the dart again strikes and sticks to the pendulum bob when the dart is at the top of its trajectory. Will the maximum amplitude of the pendulum swing be greater than θ, equal to θ, or less than θ? Justify your answer.

An object is compressed against a horizontal spring to location D and then released, as shown in the diagram below.

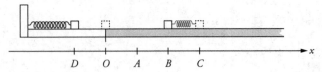

The block leaves the spring at position A. After sliding to position B, the block collides with an identical spring and stops at position C. There is friction between the block and the track between positions A and B, and no friction on any other portions of the track.

On the graphs below, sketch the total, kinetic, and potential energies as a function of location. You do not need to calculate values for the vertical axis, but the same vertical scale should be used for both quantities.

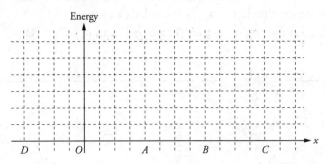

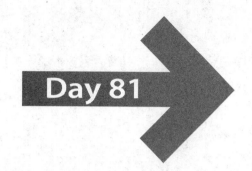

A flock of birds in flight (i.e., each bird is moving) may have a total momentum equal to zero.

(a) How is it possible for the flock's total momentum to be zero when each bird is moving? Explain briefly.

(b) Can the birds also have a total kinetic energy equal to zero? Explain briefly why or why not.

Day 82

An object attached to a spring oscillates horizontally in simple harmonic motion. Which of the following quantities is unchanged when the amplitude of the object's harmonic motion is doubled? Justify your answer.

(a) The frequency of oscillation

(b) The mass's acceleration at the equilibrium point

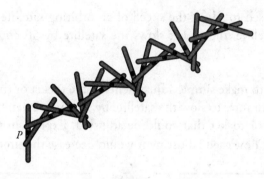

A rod—20 cm long, 0.060 kg in mass—slides across a low-friction air table. The rod rotates as it slides, as shown above.

You take high-speed video of the rod moving on the table. The video shows 1,000 frames per second and can be paused at any frame. A meterstick is clearly visible in the background for length measurements. The rotational inertia of a rod rotating about its center of mass in this manner is $\left(\frac{1}{12}\right)ML^2$, where M is the rod's mass and L is the rod's length.

Explain how to use the video to determine the angular momentum of the rod about point P (which is shown above). You need not actually make the determination, but you should state clearly what information you obtain from the video, how you obtain it, and how it will be used in a calculation to determine angular momentum.

A small rocket is used to adjust the speed of an orbiting satellite. By applying a force of 50 N to the satellite, the rocket slows the satellite by 50 cm/s. This process took 12 minutes.

An engineer wants to make simple adjustments to the rocket or the satellite such that it takes less than 12 minutes to slow the satellite by 50 cm/s. Briefly describe two properties of the satellite or rocket that could be adjusted. Explain in terms of the *impulse-momentum theorem* how each adjustment would decrease the time to slow the satellite.

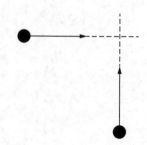

Two identical pucks, each of mass M, move with equal speeds v on a horizontal, frictionless surface. The direction of their velocities is illustrated in the figure above. The pucks collide and stick together.

1. In terms of given variables and fundamental constants, determine the magnitude of the linear momentum of the two-puck system before the collision. Explain how you made this determination.

2. After the collision, the magnitude of the linear momentum of the two-puck system is

   (A) Greater than the answer to (1)

   (B) Less than the answer to (1)

   (C) Equal to the answer to (1)

Choose one, and justify your choice.

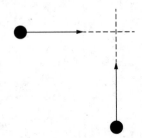

Two identical pucks, each of mass M, move with equal speeds v on a horizontal, frictionless surface. The direction of their velocities is illustrated in the figure above. The pucks collide and stick together.

1. In terms of given variables and fundamental constants, determine the kinetic energy of the two-puck system before the collision. Explain how you made this determination.

2. After the collision, the kinetic energy of the two-puck system is

   (A) Greater than the answer to (1)

   (B) Less than the answer to (1)

   (C) Equal to the answer to (1)

Choose one, and justify your choice.

A car traveling at highway speed collides with a bug, which was initially at rest. The bug sticks to the car after the collision.

Does the bug or the car experience a larger magnitude of impulse during the collision? Justify your answer.

Two carts, each of mass 0.5 kg, collide on a horizontal track. Before the collision, cart A is moving 3.0 m/s toward cart B. After the collision, cart A is moving at 2.0 m/s in the same direction as before the collision.

- Dexter says: "This can't be right. Momentum is always conserved in a collision. Cart A had a momentum of $mv = (0.5 \text{ kg})(3.0 \text{ m/s}) = 1.5$ Ns before the collision. After the collision, cart A has only 1.0 Ns of momentum. Momentum was lost, and so was not conserved."
- Teri replies: "That's because an external force acts on the two-cart system—they're on a track, so the force of the track is external to the system. Momentum is conserved only in a system in which no external force acts."

Both students' statements contain errors. Identify and correct the errors.

The dwarf planet Pluto goes around the sun in an elliptical orbit. Consider Pluto only. Is its angular momentum about the sun conserved? Justify your answer.

The body of a car is supported by several vertical springs. The car has mass 1,000 kg when empty. When two people, of combined mass 200 kg, sit in the car, the springs compress by 1.0 cm while the car remains at rest. A third 100-kg person, who is not in the car, pushes the car down an additional 1.0 cm and lets go, causing the car to oscillate in simple harmonic motion.

The equation $T = 2\pi\sqrt{\dfrac{m}{k}}$ can be used to calculate the period of the simple harmonic motion. What value of m should be used? Justify your choice.

A 75-kg student is standing in a 25-kg boat at rest in still water. The student then walks to the right at a speed v relative to the shore. Describe the subsequent motion of the boat in terms of v. Justify your answer.

A ball moving to the right as shown strikes a second identical ball at rest. The vectors shown are the velocity of the first ball before and after the collision. Draw a vector that represents the velocity of the second ball after the collision on the diagram below.

Justify your answer.

5 Minutes to a 5

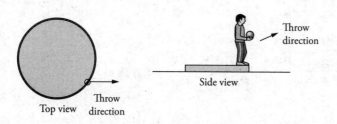

Top view   Throw direction

Throw direction   Side view

A man stands on the edge of a heavy disk made of ice, such that it can slide along the ground without friction. From the location indicated in the diagram, the man throws a ball at an angle above the horizontal.

From immediately before the throw to immediately after the throw, is the linear momentum of the disk-man-ball system in the horizontal direction conserved? Justify your answer.

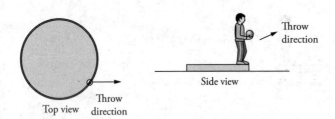

A man stands on the edge of a heavy disk made of ice, such that it can slide along the ground without friction. From the location indicated in the diagram, the man throws a ball at an angle above the horizontal.

From immediately before the throw to immediately after the throw, is the linear momentum of the disk-man-ball system in the vertical direction conserved? Justify your answer.

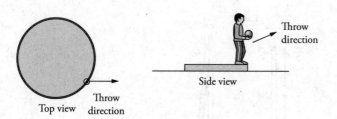

Top view   Throw direction

Side view   Throw direction

A man stands on the edge of a heavy disk made of ice, such that it can slide along the ground without friction. From the location indicated in the diagram, the man throws a ball at an angle above the horizontal.

From immediately before the throw to immediately after the throw, is the angular momentum of the disk-man-ball system about its center of mass conserved? Justify your answer.

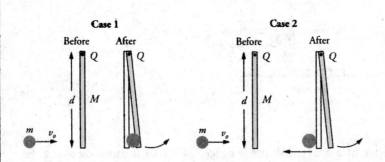

In two experiments, a ball collides with a rod. In case 1, a ball of mass m and velocity v_0 strikes a rod at the lower end and sticks to the rod as shown above. The rod is free to rotate around the fixed point Q. In case 2, the same ball again strikes the rod, but then rebounds without sticking to the rod. In a clear and coherent paragraph, predict in which situation, case 1 or 2, the rod will swing higher following the collision.

4 m/s →

← 9 m/s

A 1-kg ball changes its velocity as shown in the diagram above, from 4 m/s to the right to 9 m/s to the left.

(a) What is the magnitude of the ball's change in momentum?

(b) What is the magnitude of the ball's change in kinetic energy?

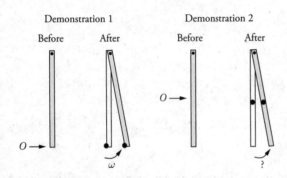

Demonstration 1

Before   After

Demonstration 2

Before   After

$O \rightarrow$

$O \rightarrow$

ω

$?$

In a physics demonstration, a ball strikes the end of a rod and sticks to the rod, which is fixed to a vertical pin. The rod is set into angular motion about the fixed pin with a velocity ω.

In a second demonstration, the ball strikes the same rod with the same initial speed, but this time strikes at the midpoint of the rod. A student makes the following prediction prior to the demonstration: "The rod will swing just as quickly as before with an initial angular velocity of ω. The ball has just as much linear momentum in the second collision. Momentum is conserved in each instance, so with the same initial momentum, the rod will swing just as high."

What, if anything, is wrong with this statement?

A grandfather clock consists of a pendulum, made of a metal, that keeps time based on the period of the pendulum. An owner of a grandfather clock notices that the clock runs slow during the warmer summer months. Describe the changes that have occurred in the pendulum to cause this to happen.

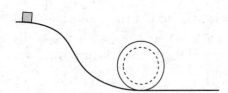

A student experiments with a box sliding down a hill with negligible friction into a loop, and finds the minimum initial height of the box necessary for the box to make it through the loop without falling. When the student repeats the experiment with a ball that rolls down the hill, she finds that the ball falls out of the loop and does not make it through. In a clear, concise paragraph, explain why the box makes it through the loop without falling, while the ball does not.

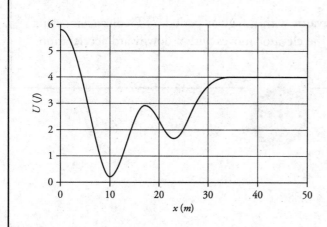

A particle's potential energy function is given in the graph above. The particle is moving to the left with 1 J of kinetic energy at the 40-m mark. Describe the subsequent motion of the particle.

A pendulum is oscillating in an elevator with a regular period T. Predict changes to the period of the pendulum when the elevator moves with a downward acceleration. Justify your answer.

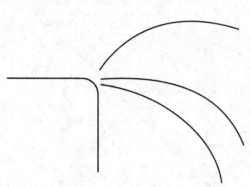

Diagram not to scale

Three identical balls are thrown from the top of a cliff, all with the same initial speed. The balls take three different trajectories: (a) one at an angle above the horizontal, (b) one thrown horizontally, and (c) one thrown at an angle below the horizontal.

Rank the three trajectories in terms of speed when they reach the ground.

_____   _____   _____

Fastest   Slowest

Justify your answer.

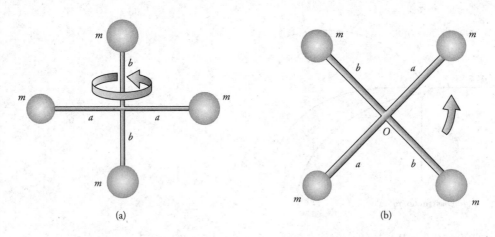

(a)   (b)

A mobile consists of four spheres of mass m attached to the end of rods of length L, as shown above. The mobile is set to rotate about two different axes. In the first instance, the mobile is rotated about an axis that passes through the rods. In the second instance, the mobile is rotated about an axis perpendicular to the plane that connects the two rods, passing through the page at point O in the diagram on the right. Two students make predictions about the kinetic energy of the mobile in each configuration when they are rotating at equal speeds.

- Student 1: "The mobile has different kinetic energies in each case. The rotational inertia is greater in the first case, with the axis through the rod, than in the second case, thereby increasing the rotational kinetic energy."
- Student 2: "The rotational kinetic energies are equal in each case. The axis of rotation passes through the center of the mobile, and the masses are at an equal distance from the axis, making the rotational inertias equal."

What, if anything, do you agree with in each student's statement?

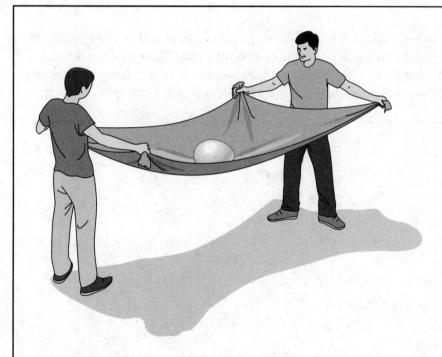

A classic physics demonstration involves throwing an egg against a bed sheet, loosely held by two people. The egg is caught in the sheet without breaking the egg. Explain why the egg does not break.

A bowling ball with speed v rolls toward a spring and rebounds with a momentum of equal magnitude to the initial momentum. The bowling ball is then rolled with initial speed v through long grass, which stops the ball completely. Predict how the magnitude of the impulse on the bowling ball differs from the spring to the grass.

An object falls freely from rest. As the ball falls, two students make statements explaining the physics involved with the ball falling.

- Student 1: "Momentum is not conserved as the object falls. The object experiences an impulse from the force of gravity acting on the object, which produces the change in momentum as the object accelerates."
- Student 2: "Momentum is conserved. The object falls because of an interaction of equal and opposite forces between the object and Earth."

Resolve these two arguments to describe the falling object in terms of momentum and gravitational force.

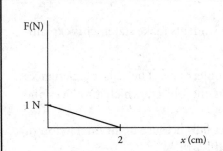

A toy gun consists of a spring that launches a dart. A graph of the force versus spring compression is given above for the spring inside the toy gun. A toy gun from a competitor will launch the same dart at twice the speed. Sketch on the graph a possible force versus spring compression for the competitor's toy gun.

Most Frisbees concentrate mass along the edge, or rim. Explain why having the mass concentrated at the edge, as opposed to having a uniform disk, aids in the stability of the Frisbee as it rotates and flies through the air. Make specific reference to torque and angular momentum.

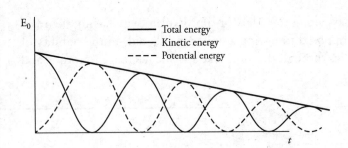

The graph above describes the energies involved in the motion of an unknown object. Describe a motion, providing as much detail as necessary, that would produce this graph.

A train car filled with oil is moving at a constant speed on a level track. After a period of time, a leak develops in the bottom of the train car, slowly releasing oil onto the ground directly beneath the car. Predict any changes to the motion of the train car. Justify your answer.

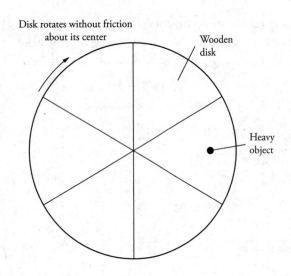

In the laboratory, a wooden disk of known mass M and radius R is initially rotating at an approximately constant angular speed. A heavy object is then dropped onto the wooden disk, sticking to the wooden disk where it was dropped. The experiment—both before and after the collision—is recorded on video at 100 frames per second. The sketch above shows the disk and the heavy object; notice that the size of the heavy object is much smaller than the disk's radius. The rotational inertia of the disk is $\frac{1}{2}MR^2$.

By collecting data from the video, the mass of the heavy object can be determined. Explain how to make that determination, including what information must be obtained from the video and how that information should be used.

5 Minutes to a 5

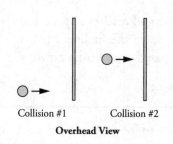

Collision #1   Collision #2

Overhead View

A ball is moving toward a uniform rod that is at rest on a frictionless surface. The ball strikes the rod at one end and rebounds from the rod, setting the rod into motion. In a second collision, the ball moves toward an identical rod, strikes the rod in the center, and rebounds. Predict any differences in the motion of the rod in the second collision compared to the first collision, explaining in terms of linear and angular momenta.

A 6-kg bowling ball rolls, starting from rest, down an incline and reaches a speed v at the bottom. A 12-kg bowling ball is then rolled from rest down the incline. Predict any changes in the speed of the 12-kg bowling ball as compared to the 6-kg bowling ball when it reaches the bottom. Justify your answer.

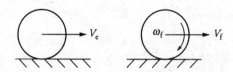

A bowling ball slides down a bowling lane with an initial speed v_0 without rotating. There is friction between the ball and the lane. Sometime later, the ball is rolling without slipping down the lane. Describe the changes in the translational and rotational energies of the ball between these two conditions, including the source of energy changes.

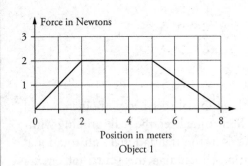

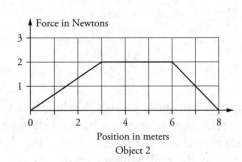

Object 1 ... Object 2

Two students are discussing the effect of a force on the motion of two identical objects. The force applied to each object is given by the graphs above.

- Student 1: "Object 1 will have the greater change in velocity. The force reaches its maximum value sooner, at the 2-m position, so the average acceleration is greater."
- Student 2: "Object 2 will have an equal final speed to that of object 1. The work done by each force can be found as the area under the curve, which is equal to each force. The work done equals the change in kinetic energy, so each object will have equal final speeds."

Identify the correct and incorrect aspects of each student's statement.

A student makes the following statement regarding a consequence of potential global warming: "With global warming, the mass of the polar ice caps will decrease due to melting. This mass will become liquid water, which will then be more uniformly spread over the surface of Earth. With this new distribution of mass, the rotational inertia of Earth will decrease, and by conservation of angular momentum, the angular speed, or rotation rate, of Earth will increase, thereby shortening the day."

What, if anything, is wrong with the above statement?

An object of mass M is hanging from a spring as shown above. A motion detector is placed below the object, producing graphs of position versus time. Three experiments are performed, producing the three graphs shown below.

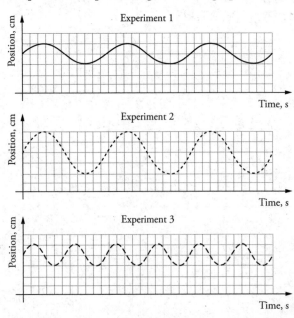

To produce the graph for experiment 1, the object was pulled down 1 cm and released from rest.

Describe what changes to the setup are necessary to produce the graphs in experiments 2 and 3.

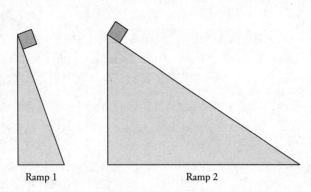

Ramp 1   Ramp 2

Two identical objects are simultaneously released from the top of two equally high frictionless ramps as shown.

Two students make predictions about the two objects' speeds at the bottom of the ramps.

- Student 1: "The object sliding down ramp 1 will have a greater velocity at the bottom. The acceleration of the object will be greater due to the larger component of gravity parallel to the surface that is accelerating the ball. With a larger acceleration, the object will achieve a greater final velocity."
- Student 2: "The object sliding down ramp 2 will have a greater velocity at the bottom. Although the acceleration is less due to the lesser incline, the acceleration is over a greater distance, producing a greater final speed."

Which aspects of each student's reasoning, if any, are incorrect?

Day 120

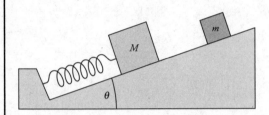

Two experiments are performed with an incline, an ideal spring, and two masses m and M, where the masses are such that $M > m$.

In experiment 1, mass m slides from rest and sticks to mass M, which is at rest in an equilibrium position on a spring. The blocks compress the spring and come to rest when the spring is compressed to a distance x.

In experiment 2, mass M slides from rest and sticks to mass m, which is at rest in an equilibrium position on the spring. The blocks compress the spring and come to rest when the spring is compressed to a distance x'.

Is x greater than, equal to, or less than x'?

Justify your answer.

Answers

Newton's Laws

Day 1

We have the speed of the stones upon leaving the cannon, when both stones are in free fall with acceleration 10 m/s per second, regardless of mass. Thus the smaller stone goes higher because it was launched with a greater initial speed.

How much higher does it go? Using kinematics equations with zero final velocity, the height as a function of initial speed becomes $x = v_0^2/2a$. Since the initial speed is squared and in the numerator, doubling the speed increases the maximum height by a factor of 4. The small stone goes four times higher than the large stone.

Day 2

The center of mass of the two-object system will be located closer to the falling, more massive object. As the more massive object falls, the center of mass of the system drops. As the center of mass was initially not moving, the center of mass therefore has a downward acceleration, and there must be a net downward force on the system. Therefore, the system's weight (the downward force of Earth on the objects) is greater than the upward force of the spring scale on the objects; so the scale reading drops when the objects are released.

Day 3

The centripetal force is produced by the hanging object. In the second experiment, there is less mass hanging, thus less centripetal force. The centripetal force can also be found by the product of the table mass (m_2 in the second experiment) and the centripetal acceleration. Given that there is more mass accelerating in the second experiment, the centripetal acceleration must then be less than in the first experiment. With the same radius of a

circle, to have less centripetal acceleration there must be less velocity by $a = \dfrac{v^2}{r}$.

Day 4

The stoplight is in equilibrium. Call the tension in the left rope T_1 and in the right rope T_2. Break these forces into components so that, for example, the horizontal component of T_1 is $T_1 \cos 37°$ and the vertical component of T_1 is $T_1 \sin 37°$. Set left forces equal to right forces and up forces equal to down forces to get the following.

$$\widehat{T_1} \cos 37° = \widehat{T_2} \cos 53°$$

$$\widehat{T_1} \sin 37° + \widehat{T_2} \sin 53° = mg$$

The variable m represents the 30-kg mass of the stoplight.

Day 5

Abel: Correct. Newton's third law says, for example, that the force of the horse on the cart is equal to the force of the cart on the horse—a third law force pair interchanges the objects applying and experiencing the force. Thus the forces in a third law pair cannot act on the same object.

Baker: Incorrect. Newton's third law applies in all situations, because a force requires an interaction between objects in order to exist.

Charles: Incorrect. Not all equal and opposite forces are a third law force pair. A force pair only involves the objects experiencing and creating the force, and so a force pair cannot cause an object to be in equilibrium.

Daniel: Incorrect. Same justification as for Charles's statement, except that in addition, movement has nothing to do with the magnitude of forces applied to an object; an object can move in any direction regardless of the forces applied to it. A net force causes acceleration, not velocity.

Day 6

The speed of a cart is indicated by the vertical axis of a velocity-time graph. Since the graph starts at a vertical axis value of zero, the cart begins at rest. Throughout the motion, the vertical axis value increases, so the cart speeds up the whole way, nearly reaching a constant speed at the end. The cart always moves to the right, because the vertical axis values are always positive.

Day 7

Consider the two-body system. The net force on the system is just the weight of the hanging object, $mg = 1.0$ N. The mass of the system is 0.60 kg. So using Newton's second law, $a = F_{net}/m = 1.0$ N/0.60 kg = 1.7 m/s per second.* Since the cart speeds up, its acceleration is in the direction of its motion—left.

---

* Units of m/s^2 are also acceptable. Units of m/s are not.

Day 8

The block is in equilibrium, because it moves at constant speed. Its acceleration is zero, so the net force is zero, meaning that up forces must equal down forces and left forces must equal right forces.

The equation for the force of friction says $F_f = \mu F_n$. Since the coefficient of friction μ is less than 1, the equation indicates that F_f is less than F_n.

Thus the final ranking is $F_n = W > F_f = T$.

Day 9

The speed difference between the two baseballs doesn't change. Both are in free fall, so both gain 10 m/s each second. When the second ball is dropped, the first ball is moving 10 m/s, and so the difference between their speeds is 10 m/s. Both get faster by the same amount each second and so maintain the same difference between their speeds.

The distance between them, however, increases. The first ball is always moving faster than the second ball; thus the first ball always goes a larger distance in 1 second than does the second ball. The second ball can never close the gap, because the second ball will never move faster than the first ball.

Day 10

Average speed is distance traveled divided by the time it takes to travel that distance. To get the distance traveled from a velocity-time graph, look at the area under the graph.

(Not that the problem asked, but the average speed calculated correctly is 30 m/4 s = 7.5 m/s. Method (A) gives the instantaneous speed at $t = 4$ s, 12 m/s; method (B) overestimates the average speed, giving 8 m/s, because the object spent more than half its time at a higher than average speed; method (C) underestimates the average speed, giving 6 m/s, also because the object spent more than half its time at a higher than average speed.)

Day 11

The free-fall acceleration is proportional to the mass and inversely proportional to the square of the radius, by $g = GM/r^2$. But we don't know directly about the planet's mass, just its density. So, we need to express g in terms of the planet's density, which I'll call ρ. Density is mass divided by volume, and volume depends on radius cubed. So get an r^3 term in the expression: multiply numerator and denominator by the planet's radius r to get $g = G\left(\dfrac{M}{r^3}\right)r = G\rho r$

Now it's clear: With G and density ρ unchanged on the new planet, doubling the planet's radius r will also double the gravitational field: **2g.**

Day 12

Luis is incorrect, contradicted by Marsha's correct first statement. For the first satellite, set $G\dfrac{Mm}{r^2} = m\dfrac{v^2}{r}$, where M is the mass of the central planet and m is the mass of the satellite. The speed v and the radius r are given in the problem statement. The satellite mass is unknown, but it cancels out. Thus Marsha is right that the mass of the central planet can be determined.

However, she is wrong that we have to calculate the planet's mass first in order to determine the second satellite's speed. Solving for v, $v = \sqrt{\dfrac{GM}{r}}$. Even though we don't know the mass m, we know it's the same for both satellites. The second satellite orbits with four times the radius of the first; since r is in the denominator and under the square root, the speed v is half (square root of ¼) as much for the second satellite as the first. So the speed is 32 km/s.

Day 13

Yes. The force between two planets is GMM/d^2. Here M is the planet's mass and d is the distance between the planets' centers. Thus we need to know how the masses and distances between planets C and D compare to those of planets A and B. We're told that C and D each have twice the mass of A and B, and they are the same distance apart, so we can solve for the force ratio.

Day 14

At point A, the normal force is up while the weight mg is down. Since acceleration is toward the center of the circle, start with the normal force to write $F_\mathrm{n} - mg = ma$. The normal force is $ma + mg$.

At point B, both the normal force and the weight are down, since the track is in contact with the cart from above. So we write $F_\mathrm{n} + mg = ma$. Here the normal force is $ma - mg$.

The speed at the bottom is larger than at the top (by conservation of energy), so the centripetal acceleration $a = v^2/r$ is also larger at the bottom. Thus, at point A, the normal force includes a larger term added to the weight of the cart; and at point B, the normal force expression has the weight subtracted from the term ma, which was smaller to begin with. The expression for F_n at point A must be bigger!

Day 15

- Student 1 is correct to say that the spring scale will read 2 N. However, the "other side" does not pull as a reaction; the 2-N pull from the other side is due to the 2-N weight.
- Student 2 is correct to say that the net force on the scale is zero. The student does not understand how the spring in the scale reacts to the pulls from each side and makes a reading.
- Student 3 is correct to say that the scale reads how much force is exerted on the spring inside.

Day 16

The student is in equilibrium, so the net force on the student must equal zero. Since the student is pushing down on the sink, the sink pushes up on the student as a reaction. With the introduction of this upward force from the sink, the normal force from the scale, which is the scale reading, will decrease and read a value less than the student's weight.

Day 17

The acceleration is the slope of the v-t graph. This slope begins steep, then gets shallow. So the acceleration starts off large and gets smaller. The acceleration decreases throughout the motion.

Day 18

(a) Once the student releases the cart after the push, the free-body diagram is the same in either experiment—the only net force on the two-object system is the weight of the hanging object. Net force has nothing to do with speed or with the direction of motion. By Newton's second law, $a = F_{net}/m$, since the net force on the system is the same in each experiment, the acceleration is also the same in each experiment.

(b) In experiment A, the cart's acceleration is left—the cart speeds up, so acceleration is in the direction of motion. In experiment B, since the cart is slowing down, its acceleration is opposite the direction of its motion, which is still to the left.

Day 19

(a) Velocity is determined by the slope of a position-time graph. The slope of the graph everywhere looks like a backslash (\\) and so is negative. Thus the velocity is always negative.

(b) Speed is the amount of velocity, determined by the steepness of the position-time graph. This graph gets steeper from A to B, so the object gains speed.

When an object speeds up (as this one does—see (b)), its acceleration is the same as its direction of motion. The object speeds up, as shown in (b). So its acceleration is negative.

Day 20

If the string on the right is horizontal, a free diagram would be as follows:

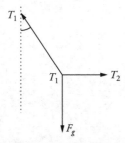

As such, the vertical component of tension in the string on the left, $T_1 \cos \theta$, must balance the weight.

The mass can be found by dividing the gravitational force by g.

Day 21

The spring scale will read 2 N. Although the *net* force on the scale is zero, the force in the spring must equal 2 N to hold the mass in equilibrium.

Day 22

Student 2 is correct. The calculation of static friction is an inequality. The value of 3 N found in this problem is the maximum value possible for static friction before motion begins. Since a lesser value is applied (2 N), the object is not set into motion, and with an acceleration of zero, the net force is equal to zero. The static friction is then 2 N to balance the applied force of 2 N.

Day 23

The relevant equation relating h and t comes from the constant-acceleration kinematics equations, with no initial velocity and an acceleration of g: $h = \frac{1}{2}gt^2$.

The students measured h, and that shows up in the equation directly, so they can put h on the vertical axis. They also measured t, but t doesn't show up directly; it shows up as t^2. So plot t^2 on the horizontal axis.

Then identify the values in $y = mx + b$:

$$\begin{pmatrix} h \\ y \end{pmatrix} = \begin{pmatrix} \frac{1}{2}g \\ m \end{pmatrix} \begin{pmatrix} t^2 \\ x \end{pmatrix} + b$$

The slope is $\frac{1}{2}g$. So take the slope, multiply by 2, and that's g.

Day 24

(a) The "area under a graph" refers to the area between the graph and the horizontal axis. In this graph, the horizontal axis is in the middle of the displayed portion of the graph, where velocity = 0. The student should be taking the area of *two* triangles—shown below—and then subtracting the two areas, because the top triangle indicates displacement in the positive direction, while the bottom triangle indicates displacement in the negative direction.

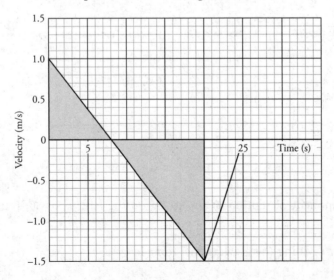

(b) The student is *overestimating* the cart's actual displacement. He's not accounting for the two different directions of motion—his calculation ends up giving the total distance traveled by the cart, not how far the cart ended up from its initial position.

Day 25

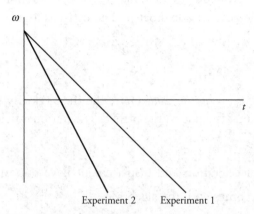

The net torque on the pulley does not change, since the weights of the hanging objects and the pulley's radius are unchanged. However, the rotational inertia of the pulley in experiment 2 is smaller—its identical mass is concentrated closer to the axis of rotation when shaped like a disk. In Newton's second law for rotation, $\tau = I\alpha$, constant net torque makes rotational inertia (I) and angular acceleration (α) inversely related. A smaller rotational inertia means the angular acceleration is larger.

Since angular acceleration is the slope of an angular velocity versus time graph, the slope should be steeper, as shown.

Day 26

The relevant equation is Newton's second law for rotation, $\tau = I\alpha$. To increase α, we must either decrease rotational inertia I or increase the net torque τ.

1. Increase the mass m_1 of the hanging object. This increases the force term in torque = force times lever arm, increasing the net torque on the device. (Another way to increase the net torque on the device would be to increase the radius r_1.)

2. Decrease the mass m_2 of the attached objects. This decreases the rotational inertia of the device, since now there's less mass to rotate. (Another way to decrease the rotational inertia of the device would be to shorten the distance r_2 from the attached objects to the pole.)

Day 27

In experiment 1, the tension in the string is measured to be 1.0 N; that's the only force on the 500-g (i.e., 0.5-kg) object, so we can apply Newton's second law to the cart: $a = (1.0\ \text{N})/(0.5\ \text{kg}) = 2.0\ \text{m/s/s}$.

In experiment 2, the tension in the string is *not* 1.0 N. Since the hanging object will speed up downward, it has a downward acceleration; thus the tension must be less than the hanging object's 1.0-N weight.

Answers

So consider the two-object system. The net force on this system is the weight of the hanging object, 1.0 N. The mass of this system is 0.5 kg plus the 0.1-kg mass of the hanging object. (On Earth, 1 kg weighs 10 N, so 0.1 kg weights 1.0 N.) By Newton's second law, $a = (1.0 \text{ N})/(0.6 \text{ kg}) = 1.7$ m/s/s.

Since in experiment 2 more mass is accelerating due to the same net force, the denominator in $a = F_{net}/m$ is larger, making the acceleration smaller. The cart has a greater acceleration in **experiment 1**.

Day 28

To determine the maximum height, use $v_f^2 = v_0^2 + 2ad$. Here, the final velocity of either ball is zero. The free-fall acceleration a is equal to the planet's gravitational field, and d represents that maximum height.

Solve for d to get $d = \dfrac{v_0^2}{2a}$. (Since the acceleration and displacement have opposite signs, that cancels the negative sign that comes with the algebra.)

The blue ball has a v_0 that is three times bigger, but also an a that is three times bigger. Those factors of three don't cancel out, though, because v_0 is squared in the numerator. For the blue ball, the maximum height d is multiplied by $(3)^2/(3)$, which is 3. The blue ball goes three times higher.

Day 29

(a) The gravitational field at the surface of a planet is given by GM/r^2. Here M is the planet's mass and r is the planet's radius. We're told that planets A and B are identical; thus their masses and radii are the same. All elements in the equation are known for both planets, so the ratio can be determined.

(b) As in (a), we need to know how the planets' masses M and their radii r relate. We know that planet C is twice planet A's mass, but we have no indication of either planet's radius or how the two radii compare. Thus we cannot determine the ratio of gravitational fields.

Day 30

(a) A boy sits still at his desk. (Zero velocity because he's not moving, zero acceleration because his velocity doesn't change.)

(b) A jet airplane cruises at steady speed. (Nonzero velocity because it moves, zero acceleration because its velocity doesn't change.)

(c) A ball that was thrown straight upward, at the instant when it reaches the peak of its flight. (Zero velocity because at that instant, the ball briefly isn't moving; nonzero acceleration because the ball is in free fall. Its velocity is changing, going from upward to downward.)

(d) A car on a highway entrance ramp, speeding up. (Nonzero velocity because it is moving, nonzero acceleration because its velocity is changing.)

Day 31

(a) Consider the entire system, and apply $F_{net} = ma$. The net force is the 20-N weight of the hanging block (because the normal force cancels the weight of the block on the table). The system mass is 4 kg. So $(20\ N) = (4\ kg)a$ gives an acceleration of 5 m/s/s.

(b) The top block speeds up while moving right. When an object speeds up, its acceleration is the same as its direction of motion. So acceleration is to the right.

Day 32

The mass of the system is not constant. The system is the cart and hanging masses. When mass is added to increase the accelerating force, the mass of the system is no longer a constant, meaning that the graph proposed would not be linear.

Day 33

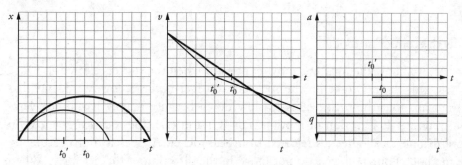

The thick lines indicate the behavior of the block without friction. Each graph is symmetric with respect to the time moving up and down the incline. The acceleration will be constant without friction and equal to $g \sin \theta$. The velocity function will then be linear due to the constant acceleration, beginning at the positive v_0 value. Constant accelerations will produce parabolic position paths.

With friction present, as indicated by the thinner lines, the acceleration will have a greater magnitude when the block is sliding up the incline than without friction. Friction will act against motion, which is down the incline while the block slides up. The frictional force is independent of speed and is constant, thus just added to the gravitational acceleration. When the block slides downhill, friction will now be up the incline, making the net acceleration less than the magnitude of gravitational acceleration. Due to the greater acceleration while the block slides up the incline, the highest point will be reached sooner than without friction.

Velocity will exhibit linear behavior up and down the incline due to the constant acceleration in these regions. Due to the greater acceleration up the incline, the slope of the velocity graph is greater while moving up the incline than when moving down.

The velocity will follow parabolic-like paths due to the constant accelerations up and down the inclines, with an extended parabolic shape while moving down the incline.

Day 34

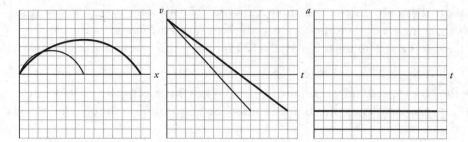

The acceleration is constant due to the constant slope of the incline, and is directed down the incline, and is thus negative. With the increased angle, the magnitude of acceleration will be greater. The velocity will have a slope equal to the magnitude of the acceleration, and with the steeper incline will reach the highest point and return to the base of the incline in less time. With constant accelerations, the position-time graphs will be parabolic, with the steeper inclined path returning to the base in less time.

Day 35

(a) (B) is the correct method.

(b) For (A), we know the rock was moving upward when the rocket released it. Once it's released, the net force on the rock does in fact become downward, but that only means that the rock begins to slow down because it now has an acceleration opposite its direction of motion. For (C) and (D), the rock experiences no upward force at all after it's released from the rocket. As if that didn't disqualify the method enough, objects do not move in the direction of the net force. When down forces are bigger than up forces, an object's acceleration is downward; it can still move upward while slowing down. And an object experiencing equal up and down forces can move in either direction, as long as it does so at constant velocity.

Day 36

The only forces acting on the block are the block's weight and the tension. Since the weight is larger, the net force is downward. But that does *not* mean that the block moves downward! The block has a downward acceleration. This could mean the block moves down while speeding up; this could mean the block moves up while slowing down; or it could mean that the block is moving, say, to the right while its path bends downward. The answer is **(D)**.

Day 37

The system is in equilibrium; thus the tension in the each rope is the weight of each hanging object. So block 3 has three horizontal forces acting: m_2g right, and m_1g and the friction force f left. Since m_2 is twice m_1, to equilibrate the top block the friction force must equal m_1g.

The normal force on block 3 is equal to the weight of block 3, which is three times the weight of block 1. Since the coefficient of friction can be found by $\mu = \dfrac{f}{F_N}$, the coefficient of friction is $\mu = \dfrac{m_1g}{3m_1g} = \dfrac{1}{3}$

Day 38

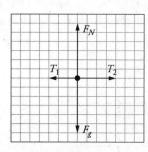
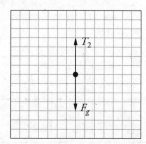

(a) With the blocks in static equilibrium, the sum of forces in each direction must equal zero. Thus the net force on any one block in both the horizontal and vertical directions must equal zero; from this it follows that the net force on the system will equal zero. The free-body diagrams demonstrate this with equal forces in both the horizontal and vertical directions.

(b) The tension force on block 2 will be twice the tension force on block 1; thus the tensions produce an unbalanced net force on block 3 to the right that is equal to the difference in the tensions, which is equal to the weight of block 1.

Day 39

1. The object could be speeding up, gaining 4 m/s of speed every second.

2. The object could be slowing down, losing 4 m/s of speed every second.

3. The object could be moving in a circle, where its speed and the circle's radius are related by $v^2/r = 4$ m/s/s.

Day 40

A multitude of solutions would work. (If you're not sure whether yours is correct, try it in the lab.) Here are a couple of ideas:

- Put the cart on an incline, and hold the scale parallel to the incline so that it measures the component of the cart's weight parallel to the incline. That component is the weight times the sine of the angle of the incline; solve to get the weight.
- Hang the cart from, say, four different ropes, spaced evenly along the cart. Attach three of these ropes to hooks on the ceiling; attach the other to the scale. The scale will read the tension in one rope. Multiply that by 4 to get the weight of the cart. (If the scale is still maxed out, add more ropes.)

Day 41

Two approaches:

- Acceleration is the change of speed per time. Both bug and car collide for the same amount of time. The car hardly changes its speed at all, while the bug goes from rest to near-highway speed. Thus the bug changes its speed by more in the same amount of time, meaning the bug has greater acceleration.
- Use Newton's second law, $F_{net} = ma$. Both bug and car experience the same force by Newton's third law. In this case, then, mass and acceleration are inversely related. The less massive bug experiences the larger acceleration.

Day 42

(a) See below—start from 0 m/s, and then have the vertical axis value rise by 1.7 m/s every second.

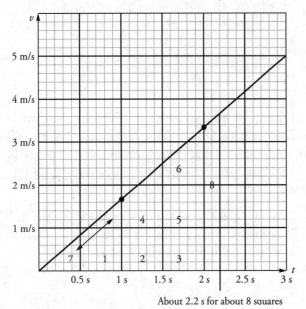

About 2.2 s for about 8 squares

(b) Distance is the area under the velocity-time graph. Each big square represents a distance of $(1 \text{ m/s})(0.5 \text{ s}) = 0.5$ m. Since the ball drops 4.0 m, there needs to be 8 big squares under the graph. Find the time on the horizontal axis when there are 8 big squares beneath the line drawn.

Day 43

A constant force will indicate a constant value of acceleration. The velocity will therefore have a constant slope of a value equal to the acceleration. The angular displacement graph will be parabolic with an increasing slope.

Day 44

For rolling without slipping, rotational kinematic quantities are related to translational kinematic quantities by $x = r\theta$ and $v = r\omega$, no matter what the object's acceleration. As such, both graphs are linear with a positive slope equal to the radius of the tire.

Day 45

In each position, there are two forces acting, the weight of the bob and the tension from the string. In position 2, the net force will point to the left, but not necessarily horizontally. The net force will *not* point tangent to the arced path. There must be a component of the net force that is tangent to the arc at point 2, which will cause the increase in speed of the falling pendulum bob, and there must also be a component that points along the string, which causes the centripetal acceleration that results in a circular path. If the net force was tangent to the arced path, there would be no centripetal acceleration.

At point 3, the net force is NOT zero. There are still the two forces previously identified, tension and weight. These forces both act vertically, and the bob is still turning in the arced path, so the net force must point to the center of the circle, or straight up.

Day 46

The person weighs 900 N. We know that because he was initially standing at rest on the force plate. The plate read 900 N from the vertical axis of the graph; that must be equal to his weight when he's in equilibrium.

At time $t = 3$ s, the scale reads 1,800 N. Still, the only forces acting on the person are his 900-N weight downward and the 1,800-N force of the scale upward.

(a) Only the scale is in contact with the person, and the scale pushes the person upward. The graph says the scale reads 1,800 N, so that is the total upward force on him.

(b) The up force is 1,800 N; the sole down force is his weight, 900 N. The net force is the difference between these, 900 N.

(c) The only down force acting is the force of Earth on the person; that is, his weight. That's 900 N.

Day 47

Many different scenarios could produce this graph, but the following key points must be noted:

- The angular acceleration is constant and positive, given that the slope of the velocity-time graph is constant and positive.
- The object must come to a stop and change direction, as the velocity is first negative, passes through zero, and becomes positive.
- The object has a positive velocity and is thus moving in the positive direction, for a longer period of time than the object has a negative velocity and is moving in the negative direction.

An example of a description: A ball is rolling up an incline, subject to the torque provided by gravity as it slows with a constant linear and angular acceleration directed down the incline. The ball stops on the incline and begins to speed up back down the incline, passing the starting point.

Or: Two objects of unequal mass hang from a pulley. Initially, the pulley is rotating toward the direction of the object with smaller mass, considered the negative direction here. Thus its net torque and angular acceleration are opposite the direction of rotation, slowing down the rotation. The pulley comes to rest, then begins to speed up its rotation in the other direction.

Day 48

The normal force of the surface on the sled is equal to the weight mg of the passenger and the sled because there is no vertical acceleration. The friction force is then μmg, where μ is the coefficient of friction between the sled and snow. Friction is the only horizontal force acting while the sled slows down, so it can be set equal to ma by

Newton's second law. The acceleration of the sled and boy can be solved for: $a = \mu g$. The masses cancel out—the acceleration does not depend on the mass of the person on the sled. By kinematics, the same initial and final velocities with the same acceleration must produce the same distance traveled by $v^2 = v_0^2 + 2ax$.

Day 49

The free-body diagram of the object at position A has two downward forces: mg and the tension T_A. By Newton's second law, $mg + T_A = ma$.

The free-body diagram at position B has one upward force (the tension) and one downward force (the weight). Since the acceleration is toward the center, the tension is the greater of these, so Newton's second law gives $T_B - mg = ma$.

The centripetal acceleration depends on speed and the circle's radius; since both speed and radius are the same at both positions, the acceleration is also the same at both positions. So solve the equations above for the tensions:

$T_A = ma - mg$
$T_B = ma + mg$

The tension is greater at the bottom, at position B.

Day 50

Torque is the product of the applied force and the lever arm (the shortest distance from the axis to the line of the force). The diagram below illustrates this for force A.

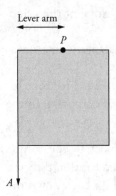

Consequently, force A and force C will produce equal torques. Forces D and E will produce zero torque—since the line of these forces goes straight through point P, no lever arm exists. Force B will produce the greatest torque, as its lever arm is twice that of force A or C.

To summarize,

$B > A = C > D = E = 0$

Day 51

F_2 will need to be less than F_1. Examine the condition if F_2 and F_1 are equal. F_2, with a larger angle to the path of motion (call this direction the horizontal), will have a greater component in the vertical direction than F_1. Thus the object would have a vertical component of acceleration in addition to the horizontal component. To reduce the vertical component, the overall force F_2 must be reduced, making F_2 less than F_1 to maintain a horizontal-only acceleration.

Day 52

You should disagree with the student. There is a vertical force acting down on the traffic light: gravity. To keep the traffic light suspended, there must be an upward force of equal magnitude applied on the traffic light, which is only possible through the cables. If the cables were somehow horizontal, then there would be no vertical component of tension from the cables, creating a net downward force on the traffic light. It is impossible for the cables to be perfectly horizontal.

Day 53

The system must be defined as the weightlifter and the barbell. On the system there are only two forces acting: the force of gravity, taken to be acting on the center of mass, and the normal force (which is directly measured by the scale). As the barbell is moving upward, the center of mass of the system is rising. If an acceleration is associated with the motion, then a net force must be acting on the system. Thus, as the barbell is moving at a constant speed, there is no acceleration on the system, making the scale reading equal to the weight of the system. As the barbell slows in the upward direction, there must be a net force down acting on the center of mass of the system. Since the gravitational force will remain constant, the scale reading must be less than the system weight, so the scale reading will decrease.

Day 54

Defining the system as both objects, to achieve the same acceleration in each instance, the same net force must be applied. The net force on the system is due to the cord on the right, thus T_2 will not change when the masses switch position. Following a similar argument, defining the system as the block on the left, in the second situation the net force on the system will be less, since a lesser mass is receiving the same acceleration. Thus T_1 will be less when the masses change position.

Day 55

The second wheel will take greater than 20 seconds to reach top speed. Each wheel is accelerated by an equal torque. Rotational inertia is proportional to the mass of the object, so the second wheel, with greater mass, will have a greater rotational inertia. By $\tau_{net} = I\alpha$, with the same torque applied to an object of larger rotational inertia, the angular acceleration will be less, therefore taking a greater time to reach top speed.

Day 56

The pulley will accelerate in the counterclockwise direction, as viewed above. A pulley will accelerate if there is a net torque acting on the pulley. Torque on a pulley can be found as the product of the applied force perpendicular to the radius (the hanging weight) and the radius. For the case on the left, each object produces a torque of equal magnitude, but in the opposite direction (clockwise for the object on the right, counterclockwise for the object on the left). The net torque, and therefore acceleration, is zero. In the second case, the applied force from each object is equal, but the force from the object on the right acts on a smaller radius; thus the torque is less. The larger torque from the object on the left is counterclockwise; thus the pulley accelerates in the counterclockwise direction.

Day 57

In the first instance, if the pulley is accelerating, then the 20-N weight is also accelerating (down). The net force on the weight is therefore directed downward, making the tension in the string less than 20 N. The torque that therefore accelerates the pulley is produced by a force that is less than 20 N. In the second instance, the torque that accelerates the pulley is produced by a force of exactly 20 N. The torque in the second case is therefore larger, and the angular acceleration of the disk in the second instance is greater.

Day 58

The driver is correct to say that at the same rotational speed, a larger wheel will cover a greater distance and thus produce a greater linear speed. Whether or not this is the outcome is uncertain, however, since the motor would need to deliver more power to get to this top rotation. The rotational inertia of the larger wheels is larger, requiring more torque to accelerate the wheels, thus more power from the engine. So the larger wheels do produce a greater speed at the same rotational rate, but the engine's top power could not achieve this same speed due to the greater rotational inertia of the wheels. The driver's explanation is inconclusive.

Day 59

(a)

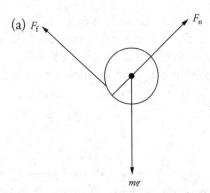

(b) An angular acceleration requires a net torque. A torque is applied by a force if the line of the force does not pass through the axis of rotation. Here, the normal force F_n and the weight mg both are applied directly through the center of the hoop. However, the friction force F_f is applied some distance from the center. So the friction force causes the angular acceleration.

Day 60

(a) Average speed is distance divided by time. The car went the same distance in each lap. So, the smaller average speed in the first lap means twice as much time was spent at the lower speed. When considering the whole race, then, the majority of time–2/3 of the total time–was spent at the lower speed. While both laps contribute equally to the total distance traveled, the first lap contributes most of the time in the denominator of the average speed formula.

(b) Since most of the time was spent at the lower speed, the average speed will be closer to the lower speed.

[The question doesn't ask, but if you want to calculate the average speed for the whole race, make up a distance – pretend the track is an unrealistic 100 m in length. Then the car spends 2 s in the first lap, and 1 s in the second lap for a total of 3 s. The average speed is total distance (200 m) divided by total time (3 s), 67 m/s.]

Conservation

Day 61

Graphs 3 and 4 violate energy conservation. The initial mechanical energy in the ball-Earth system before the drop is mgh_1, where m is the ball's mass. The mechanical energy after the bounce is mgh_2. Energy conservation allows this mechanical energy to be converted to other forms—say, thermal energy—during the bounce. But energy conservation does not allow for an increase in mechanical energy unless work is done on the system by an external force. Thus in graph 3 for high initial drop heights, h_2 is larger than h_1, making the final mechanical energy greater than the initial mechanical energy—that's a violation. Similarly, in graph 4 for low drop heights, h_2 is larger than h_1.

Day 62

Student 2's use of kinematics is valid only for constant acceleration. Here, the acceleration calculation using Newton's second law is correct, but only for the instant when the spring is stretched 5 cm. A moment later, when the spring is less stretched, the acceleration will be smaller. But the kinematics equation uses 2.5 m/s/s as the acceleration throughout, thus overestimating the final speed.

Student 1's approach is fully correct. Energy conservation applies whether or not acceleration is constant.

Day 63

Since it's a collision, it's likely that the impulse-momentum theorem is a good approach. That says $\Delta P = Ft$. In this case, the problem says the time of collision t is the same; so mathematically, whichever ball changes its momentum by more in the collision experiences more force. Both balls are dropped from the same height, so they hit the ground with the same speed; since they're of equal mass, they hit the ground with the same momentum.

Ball B loses all of that momentum upon hitting the ground. So does ball A. But ball A subsequently gains momentum in order to rebound. A's momentum thus changes by more than B's does, and A experiences more force in the collision.

Day 64

(a) Kinetic energy for this system is not conserved. Work is done by the cart on the suitcase when the two make contact; we know this because the suitcase changes its kinetic energy by slowing down. Mechanical energy would be conserved if this kinetic energy were stored in another form of mechanical energy such as a compressed spring. However, with no such storage mechanism, it becomes internal energy instead.

(b) Linear momentum in the vertical direction is not conserved. A net force external to the suitcase-cart system acts: that force is the normal force of the ground on the suitcase-cart system. (Alternatively: the system's center of mass initially has a downward component to its velocity, and after collision it has no vertical velocity at all. Thus the system's momentum vertically changed.)

(c) Linear momentum in the horizontal direction is conserved. No forces act horizontally except the force of the suitcase on the cart and its third law pair, the force of the cart on the suitcase. These forces are internal to the suitcase-cart system. With no net external force acting, the system's momentum must be conserved.

Day 65

1. **Positive.** The bowstring pushes in the same direction that the arrow moves; by definition that results in positive work. You could equivalently say that the arrow's kinetic energy increases, so the net work (equal to the work done by the string) must be positive.

2. **Zero.** The force of Earth on the arrow is downward; the motion of the arrow is horizontal. Since there is no component of the force of Earth parallel to the arrow's motion, the work done on the arrow is zero.

3. **Changing.** It is stated that the bow acts like a horizontal spring. The force of a spring increases as the spring is stretched or compressed. So the archer must apply more and more force as the bowstring is stretched to store energy in the bow.

Day 66

(a) Using the work-energy theorem, starting at the highest position and ending at the lowest point, the system is the ball-Earth.

$$W_{ext} = \Delta KE + \Delta PE + \Delta U$$

No work is done by external forces; no internal energy U is gained. The kinetic energy goes from 0 to $\frac{1}{2}mv^2$, where v is the speed we're looking for; the potential energy goes from mgz to 0. The equation simplifies to

$$mgz = \frac{1}{2}mv^2$$

And solving for v:

$$v = \sqrt{2gz}$$

(b) I used the work-energy theorem. Kinematics equations are not valid here. The free-body diagram for the ball looks different at the top than at the bottom. This means that the ball's acceleration changed, and the kinematics equations are only valid for constant acceleration situations.

Day 67

(a) Curtis is correct that linear momentum is conserved, that the mother has half the son's speed after the collision, and that they will have the same (magnitude of) momentum as each other after the collision.

Curtis is incorrect that the mother pushes with twice as much force as the son—Newton's third law requires that both exert the same force on each other.

(The two statements above are sufficient. However, Curtis is also displaying a clear misconception of what conservation means—he doesn't compare the system momentum before and after the push; he compares the son's momentum to the mother's momentum, both after the push. To provide evidence for momentum conservation here, he must show that the total momentum is the same both before and after the push—which it is, because the momentums in opposite directions subtract to zero after the push, and there was no movement and thus no momentum before the push. Any reference to this issue is also correct.)

(b) Gregg is correct that initially the mother-son system has no initial kinetic energy and that both the mother and son have kinetic energy after the collision.

Gregg is incorrect in every other statement. Kinetic energy has no direction, so it cannot subtract to zero or to anything else. Thus kinetic energy is NOT conserved here—the system went from zero to not-zero kinetic energy.

(The two statements above are sufficient. It's also legitimate to point out that the mother and the son do not have the same kinetic energy as each other after the push. As shown in (a), the mother and son have the same amount of momentum. Since kinetic energy is $p^2/2m$, the larger-mass mother has less kinetic energy than the son after the push.)

Day 68

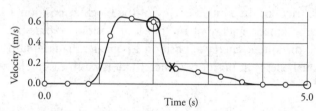

1. When the collision occurs, the blue cart must slow down. Speed on a velocity-time graph is determined by the vertical axis value. Between the circle and the X on the graph, the cart's speed decreased from 0.6 m/s to a bit less than 0.2 m/s in a couple of tenths of a second.

(Before that, the cart moved about 0.6 m/s for most of a second—that's not a collision. After the X, the blue cart slowed to rest over a couple of seconds—that's likewise not a collision. And at the $t = 1$ s mark, the cart's speed increases rapidly from 0 to 0.6 m/s. That's the person pushing the cart to get it started.)

2. The carts did *not* stick together. The carts are identical, and the red one is initially at rest. The total system momentum is mv, where m is the cart mass and v is the initial speed of the blue cart. This total momentum must be the same after collision. So if the carts did stick together, the system momentum would be $(2m)v_f$, where v_f is the combined speed after collision. Setting $mv = 2mv_f$, the final combined speed v_f is half of the initial blue cart speed v.

But that's not what the data says! The final speed of 0.2 m/s is only about a third of the initial 0.6 m/s speed. Thus the red cart must have moved after the collision.

Day 69

(a) The force of a spring is $F = kx$; the force depends on the distance the spring is stretched. So in this case, the net force on the cylinder is changing, so the acceleration is, too.

(b) Use the work-energy theorem on the cylinder-spring-earth system: $W_{ext} = \Delta KE + \Delta PE + \Delta U$

No work is done by external forces; no internal energy U is gained. The kinetic energy goes from 0 to $\frac{1}{2}mv^2$, where v is the speed we're looking for; the potential energy goes from $\frac{1}{2}kd^2$ to 0. The equation simplifies to

$$\frac{1}{2}kd^2 = \frac{1}{2}mv^2$$

And solving for v:

$$v = d\sqrt{\frac{k}{m}}$$

Day 70

Check whether the work-energy theorem requires a term for the work done by friction on the block. With no measurable friction, the kinetic energy of the block at position 1 ($\frac{1}{2}Mv^2$) should equal the sum of the kinetic energy of the block at position 2 plus the gravitational energy (Mgx_D) there. If the kinetic energy at position 1 is greater than the sum of the kinetic energy and gravitational energy at position 2, then friction was measurable.

Day 71

The angular momentum will remain constant. In the absence of a net external torque, angular momentum remains constant. Since the changes to the system are internal to the system, there is no change in angular momentum.

Rotational inertia will increase. As the child walks away from the axis of rotation, the rotational inertia of the system increases due to the movement of mass away from the axis of rotation.

The angular velocity will decrease. Since angular momentum remains constant and is the product of rotational inertia and angular velocity, with the increase in rotational inertia there must be a corresponding decrease in angular velocity by an equal factor.

The rotational kinetic energy will decrease. Rotational kinetic energy depends upon rotational inertia, which increases, and the square of angular velocity, which decreases. Rotational kinetic energy is more responsive to changes in velocity due to the velocity squared dependency. Since the velocity decreases by the same factor as the increase in rotational inertia, the kinetic energy will decrease due to the factor of velocity squared.

Day 72

(a) The period in simple harmonic motion depends only on mass and spring constant—not amplitude. So period is **unchanged.**

(b) To find maximum velocity, it's necessary to look at conservation of mechanical energy. Spring potential energy is converted to kinetic energy. Since the maximum potential energy increased, by conservation the maximum kinetic energy likewise increases. And velocity is related to kinetic energy, so maximum velocity increases, too.

(c) The potential energy of a spring is $\frac{1}{2}kx^2$. Here x represents the displacement of the spring from its equilibrium position. The amplitude is defined as the maximum displacement from equilibrium. So double A, double x in the formula, and maximum potential energy is changed.

Day 73

The momentum of the cart in the second case will be greater. Momentum is the product of mass and velocity. The mass of the cart will not change, so determining the relative velocities in the two cases will determine the relative momenta. In the each case, the spring will have the same amount of elastic potential energy that will be converted into kinetic energy of the carts or cart. In the first case, the potential energy is split between the two carts, whereas in the second case the potential energy is transferred entirely to the one cart. In the second case there is thus more kinetic energy in the lone moving cart, and therefore a greater velocity and momentum.

Day 74

The impulse given to the cart from 0 to 1 s is found by the product of force and time, or 2 N × 1 s = 2 Ns. The impulse equals the change of momentum of the object, or $Ft = \Delta mv$. Solving for velocity change, $\Delta v = \dfrac{Ft}{m} = \dfrac{2 \text{ Ns}}{0.5 \text{ kg}} = 4$ m/s. Since the initial velocity is given as 4 m/s, with a 4 m/s change in velocity, the final velocity at $t = 1$ s is 8 m/s. Work equals the change in kinetic energy, so $W = \Delta K = \dfrac{1}{2}m\left(v_f^2 - v_0^2\right) = \dfrac{1}{2}(0.5 \text{ kg})$ [(8 m/s)^2 − (4 m/s)^2] = 12 Nm.

Day 75

Work is done by a force on an object when that force and the object's direction of motion are in the same (or opposite) directions. A normal force, by definition, acts perpendicular to a surface. Thus if the object is moving along the surface, the normal force does no work—the normal force has no component in the direction of the object's motion.

However, consider an object on the floor of an elevator, which moves up. The normal force of the floor on the object is now in the same direction as the object moves. Thus the normal force does work on the object.

Day 76

1. Gravitational potential energy is generally defined as *mgh*, where *h* is the vertical distance above the reference position. Here, *h* is a component of the labeled distance *D*. Trigonometry shows this vertical distance to be *D sin θ*. Answer: **(D)**

2. The friction force is mF_n, where F_n is the normal force of the incline on the skier. The skier is in equilibrium in the direction perpendicular to the incline, so the normal force is equal to the component of the skier's weight perpendicular to the incline: *mg cos θ*. Answer: **(C)**

3. Work is force times the displacement parallel to that force. Here the force is given as *f*, and that friction force acts up the incline. The skier's displacement is *D* downward along the incline. Thus the friction force is directly opposite to the skier's displacement; no trig component is necessary, but the work done by the friction force will be negative. Answer: **(C)**.

Day 77

The object moves at constant speed and so is in equilibrium. Thus up forces equal down forces on the object. Gravity applies a downward force; to maintain equilibrium, John must apply an upward force equal to the object's weight.

The displacement of the object is downward; the force of John on the object is upward. When a force acts opposite to an object's displacement, that force does **negative** work.

Day 78

Consider the ball-Earth system. Ball A and ball B both convert the same amount gravitational potential energy *mgh* to kinetic energy, because they have the same mass and fall from the same height. However, ball B already had some kinetic energy to start with—so when it gains the same amount of kinetic energy that ball A does, ball B still has more kinetic energy. By $KE = \frac{1}{2}mv^2$, ball B thus moves faster.

Day 79

The maximum amplitude will be less. When the dart is at the top of its trajectory, the vertical component of velocity will be zero; thus the impact velocity of the dart will equal the horizontal component of the velocity. With the increase in launch angle, the horizontal component of velocity at the 60° angle is less than the horizontal component of velocity at the 30° angle. The impact velocity at 60° is therefore less than that at 30°. Momentum is conserved in the collision with the dart and the pendulum bob. Since the momentum of the system is equal to the momentum of the dart, the momentum of the dart-bob system after the collision is equal to the initial momentum of the dart, and thus proportional to the speed of the dart. With the lesser speed at 60° upon collision, the speed of the dart-bob system after the collision is less at 60°. Energy is conserved in the system after the collision, as the only force on the system is the conservative gravitational force. The kinetic energy of the dart-bob system will then be entirely converted to gravitational potential energy. With less kinetic energy in the 60° system, the bob will swing to a lower height due to the lesser potential energy.

Day 80

The potential energy while the spring is relaxing between D and O will exhibit a parabolic shape as shown, because position is squared in the equation for potential energy of a spring. There is no potential energy while the block is sliding on the horizontal surface from A to B. The potential energy will increase parabolically as the spring is compressed from positions B to C, but to a lesser maximum value, as there was energy lost to friction between A and B.

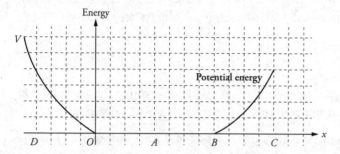

The total mechanical energy remains constant at first, because no external force acts on the block-spring system. But when the block is experiencing a constant friction force from A to C, the total energy decreases. The formula for work is force times distance, so the total energy will decrease linearly.

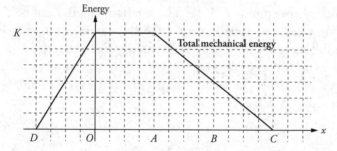

Total mechanical energy is potential plus kinetic energy. So draw the kinetic energy graph at each position so that it adds with the potential graph to the total graph.

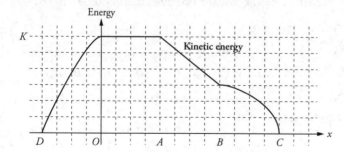

The maximum potential energy at position C should be less than at D by an amount equal to the kinetic energy lost by friction.

Day 81

(a) Momentum is a vector. Thus the total momentum of a system must account for the direction of each object's momentum. If, say, two birds are moving with equal momentum in opposite directions, then their momenta sum to zero. As long as each bird has a corresponding bird moving in the other direction—that is, as long as the center of mass of the whole flock is stationary—the total momentum of the flock is zero.

(b) The total kinetic energy of the flock cannot be zero. Kinetic energy is a scalar, meaning that it has no direction. Kinetic energy of objects within a system can never cancel.

Day 82

(a) Frequency is the inverse of period. Period of an object on a spring depends only on the object's mass and the spring constant. So frequency is **unchanged**.

(b) At the equilibrium point, the spring is unstretched and uncompressed. Thus the force of the spring on the oscillating object is zero. No other forces act on the object horizontally. Then by Newton's second law, no net force means no acceleration—regardless of the amplitude. Acceleration at equilibrium is **unchanged**.

Day 83

The relevant formula for angular momentum is $L = I\omega$. The rotational inertia can be found from $(1/12)ML^2$. To find the angular speed, forward the video frame-by-frame until the rod has undergone a full rotation. Find how many frames that took; divide by 1,000 to get the number of seconds that took. Then divide 6.3 by that number of seconds to get the angular speed in radians per second. (Since the rod went one full rotation, that's 2π radians, or about 6.3 radians.)

Day 84

The impulse-momentum theorem says $Ft = \Delta p$. For this problem, solve for the time t and include the full expression for the satellite's momentum $p = mv$. The equation becomes $t = \dfrac{m\Delta v}{F}$, where F is the force of the rocket on the satellite. The engineer wants a constant speed change of 50 cm/s. So:

1. Decrease the satellite's mass. Mass is in the numerator, so decreasing it while keeping other properties constant will also decrease t, the time for the satellite to change speed.

2. Increase the force of the rocket, which is in the denominator. Increasing the denominator will decrease the full expression for time.

Day 85

(a) $\sqrt{2}mv$. Each puck has momentum mv. Add the pucks' momentums as vectors. Since both pucks' momentums are perpendicular to one another, the magnitude of the resultant momentum is given by the Pythagorean theorem: $\sqrt{(mv)^2 + (mv)^2} = \sqrt{2}mv$.

(b) Equal to $\sqrt{2}mv$. In a collision—when no net external forces act on a system—momentum is conserved. Here the only net force on either puck is the force of the other puck. The system's momentum cannot change due to the collision.

Day 86

(a) Each puck has kinetic energy $\frac{1}{2}mv^2$. Kinetic energy is scalar, so just add them together: total kinetic energy is $\frac{1}{2}mv^2 + \frac{1}{2}mv^2 = \boldsymbol{mv^2}$.

(b) Kinetic energy is conserved only in an elastic collision. This collision cannot be elastic, as the pucks stick together. Thus kinetic energy must be lost, making the total less than mv^2. Choice **(B)**.

Day 87

Two options:

- Impulse is force times time. Both the car and bug collide for the same amount of time, as it's the same collision for both. Newton's third law demands that both experience the same force in the collision. So they experience the same impulse.
- Impulse is change in momentum. Since the only forces on the bug-car system are the internal forces of bug-on-car and car-on-bug, momentum is conserved. Any momentum lost by the car must be gained by the bug; they experience the same impulse.

Day 88

Dexter's major error is his understanding of what conservation of momentum in a collision means. Of course cart A can change its momentum . . . but the total momentum of the two-cart system cannot change. As long as cart B gains the 0.5 Ns of momentum that cart A lost, all is good.

Teri states the condition for momentum conservation incorrectly. Momentum is conserved when no *net* external force acts on a system. In this case, the only horizontal forces are internal—the force of each cart on each other. Vertically, the upward force of the track on the carts is canceled by the downward gravitational force of Earth on the carts; no net external force, so momentum is conserved.

Day 89

Angular momentum is conserved when no net external torque acts on a system. There is a net external force on Pluto—the gravitational force of the sun on Pluto. The question is, does that force provide a torque? The direction of the gravitational force is directly toward the sun. Thus the line of force passes through the axis of rotation (the sun). The lever arm for this force is zero, and therefore the force of the sun provides no torque. Pluto's angular momentum is conserved.

(You must go through the net external torque analysis. It's not sufficient to say "Pluto speeds up when closer to the sun so that angular momentum, equal to *mvr*, remains constant. Unless you know offhand the speeds and distances to plug in to verify that *mvr* doesn't change, you need to explain how Pluto experiences no net torque.)

Day 90

The *m* value is simply the amount of mass that is oscillating. That would be the body of the car and the two people inside the car—1,200 kg. Since the third person is not in the car and so is not vibrating, his mass doesn't count.

Day 91

There are no external forces acting on the boat along the direction of motion; as such momentum of the student-boat system must be conserved. Since the boat and student are initially at rest, the momentum of the system is zero. The student's momentum to the right $(75v)$ must equal the boat's momentum to the left $(25v')$ to keep a system momentum of zero. Since the student's mass is three times the boat's mass, the boat must have three times the speed to have a momentum of equal magnitude, so the boat will move to the left with a speed of $3v$.

Day 92

The momentum of the system is conserved since the forces in the collision are internal to the system. Since the balls are identical, they have equal mass. The net momentum of the system can then be represented by the initial velocity vector, which is 3 units to the right. The total momentum in the horizontal direction after the collision must then also equal 3 net units to the right. Since the horizontal component of the recoil vector is 1 unit to the left, the second ball's velocity vector must act 4 units to the right. Additionally, there is no initial velocity (or momentum) along the y-axis, so there must be zero momentum after the collision along the y-axis. The first ball has a momentum component of 1 unit in the negative y direction, so the second ball must have a y-axis component of 1 unit in the positive y direction.

Day 93

In the horizontal direction, the only forces acting on the disk, the man, or the ball are the forces of these items on each other. The only forces created by objects external to the system are the gravitational force of Earth and the normal force of the ground on the disk; these both act vertically, not horizontally. Thus, with no net external force on the system, linear momentum is conserved in the horizontal direction.

Day 94

In the vertical direction, there was initially no motion, thus no momentum. Immediately after the throw, however, the system has an upward vertical momentum—the ball's velocity has an upward vertical component, while the rest of the elements of the system don't move vertically. Thus the system went from zero momentum to nonzero momentum vertically; momentum vertically was *not* conserved.

Day 95

Angular momentum is conserved if no net external torque acts on a system. The force of the man on the ball—and the force of the ball on the man—each produce a torque, because these forces are not directed through the system's center of mass. However, these torques are applied by and experienced by objects in the system—they do not contribute to external torques.

The only external forces acting are the downward gravitational force of Earth on the system and the upward normal force of the ground on the system. Each of these provides no torque. So with no external torques applied to the system at all, angular momentum is conserved.

Day 96

In each instance, angular momentum is conserved since there will be no external torques on the system. The angular momentum of the system is equal to the initial angular momentum of the ball, or rmv. In the first instance, where the ball hits and sticks to the rod, the final angular momentum will be composed of an angular momentum of the ball and rod, which is in the same direction (counterclockwise) as the initial angular momentum of the ball. In the second instance, where the ball bounces off the rod, the final angular momentum is composed of the angular momentum of the ball, which is now in the opposite direction (clockwise), and the angular momentum of the rod, which will be in the same direction as the momentum of the system (counterclockwise). To have the same net counterclockwise angular momentum, the rod's angular momentum in the rebounding case must be greater than the rod's angular momentum in the case where the ball sticks to the rod. Therefore, in case 2, the rod has greater angular momentum and a greater angular velocity, leading to a greater kinetic energy. In the swing of the rod, energy will be conserved, and with a greater initial kinetic energy in case 2, the rod will swing to a greater height.

Day 97

(a) Momentum is a vector—it has direction. The ball's initial momentum is 4 N·s to the right; its final momentum is 9 N·s to the left. So the ball lost 4 N·s and then gained 9 more N·s, for a total change of **13 N·s**.

(b) Kinetic energy is a scalar—it does not have direction. Just subtract initial kinetic energy from final kinetic energy. The ball's initial kinetic energy is $\frac{1}{2}(1 \text{ kg})(4 \text{ m/s})^2 = 8$ J. The ball's final kinetic energy is $\frac{1}{2}(1 \text{ kg})(9 \text{ m/s})^2 =$ about 40 J. So the change in KE is 40 J – 8 J = **32 J**.

Day 98

The student is not recognizing the difference between linear momentum and angular momentum. To state that the ball has the same linear momentum in each instance is true, but linear momentum will not be conserved in the collision, due to the outside force from the pin that prevents the rod from translating. Angular momentum is conserved, which governs the initial rotational speed of the rod. The ball does not have the same angular momentum relative to the pin, or the rotation axis, in each case. Since the ball strikes halfway up the rod in the second case, closer to the axis of rotation, the ball (and therefore the system) has less angular momentum in the second case, and by conservation of angular momentum, the rod will have a smaller angular velocity after the collision.

Day 99

The period of a pendulum depends on the length of the pendulum and the acceleration of gravity. Since the acceleration of gravity won't change in a fixed location, the pendulum length must have changed. Period is proportional to the square root of the length, so the pendulum must be longer if the clock is running slow.

(A possible explanation is that metal expands as temperature increases, so the length of the pendulum is slightly longer due to thermal expansion, leading to the increased period. But this part is not necessary in your answer, as thermal expansion is not part of AP Physics 1.)

Day 100

Conservation of energy determines how fast the ball is at the top of the loop. The student has found the minimum potential energy possible to give the box enough kinetic energy at the top of the loop to make it through without falling.

If a ball is rolled instead of the sliding box, the ball will have the same initial gravitational potential energy. However, this energy will be converted to both translational kinetic energy (as with the box) *and* rotational kinetic energy. Since some of the available energy must go to rotational kinetic energy, there will not be enough translational kinetic energy to make it through the loop without falling.

Day 101

At the 40-m position, the object has a total of 4 J of potential energy, so the total energy is 5 J (4 J potential and 1 J kinetic). The particle will move to the left as long as the potential energy does not exceed the total energy. The potential energy does not reach 5 J until the $x = 5$ m mark. When the particle reaches that point, the particle is not in equilibrium and will begin to accelerate to the right and continue to move to the right until the potential energy equals the total energy of 5 J. Since there is no point to the right of $x = 5$ m where the potential energy equals 5 J, the particle will return to the original position with a kinetic energy of 1 J and continue to move to the right.

Day 102

The period of a pendulum depends upon the length and acceleration of gravity, as described by $T = 2\pi\sqrt{\dfrac{L}{g}}$, where g is the effective acceleration of gravity. In an elevator, the effective acceleration of gravity changes while the elevator accelerates. An easy

way to analyze the situation is to take the acceleration to the extreme—if the elevator itself was accelerating downward at g. If the elevator is accelerating downward at g, then relative to the elevator, the pendulum would have zero acceleration. As such, a downward acceleration would decrease the effective g, or acceleration of the pendulum. A decrease in the effective g of the pendulum would lead to an increase in the period of the pendulum.

Day 103

Each ball will have the same speed when reaching the ground and be ranked equally. Given that each ball is thrown from the same height, the potential energy of each ball is equal, since the balls are identical and also have the same mass. It is given that they have the same initial velocity and thus the same initial kinetic energy. Since each ball has an identical potential energy and kinetic energy, the total energy of each ball is the same. Thus when striking the ground, the balls will have the same kinetic energy and therefore the same speed.

Day 104

Student 1 is correct to say that the kinetic energies differ. However, with the axis through one of the rods, the rotational inertia of the first rod is very small, while the rotational inertia of the second rod is appreciable due to the distance of the two spheres from the axis of rotation.

Student 2 is only correct with observations about the location of the masses and the axis.

Rotational kinetic energy depends on mass and distance from the axis of rotation. Since the two rotations involve two different axes, there are two different rotational inertias. With equal masses, the configuration that puts the mass farther from the rotating axis will have the greater rotational inertia and therefore greater rotational kinetic energy since the speeds are the same, by $KE = \frac{1}{2}I\omega^2$. The configuration that has the mass farther from the rotating axis is the second configuration; thus the second rotation has a greater rotational kinetic energy.

Day 105

The egg's momentum will change from a nonzero value to zero when stopped by the bed sheet. To change the momentum of any object, an impulse is required, where impulse is the product of force and time. By stopping the egg in the bed sheet, as opposed to a more rigid surface like a basket or the wall, the impulse can consist of a relatively large time over which the stopping force is applied. With a large time, a smaller force is needed to produce the necessary impulse (force × time) to bring the momentum of the egg to zero, a force small enough such that the egg won't break.

Day 106

The bowling ball that bounces off the spring has twice the change of momentum as compared to the ball that stops in the grass. The ball on the spring will stop by experiencing an impulse opposite of the direction of initial motion, just as the ball in the grass does. The ball on the spring continues to feel an impulse in the same direction while the spring relaxes and rebounds the bowling ball. Since the final momentum is the same magnitude as the initial momentum, the change in momentum for the ball on the spring is twice that of the ball that stops in the grass. Since the impulse equals the change in momentum, the impulse from the spring on the ball is twice the impulse from the grass onto the ball.

Day 107

Both arguments can be accurate, depending on the how the system is defined. In the system that consists only of the falling object, the gravitational force is an external force. Momentum is then not conserved in a system that is defined as the object only, and the impulse from the gravitational force changes the momentum of the falling object.

When the object-Earth system is examined, the force of gravity is internal to the system. As student 2 states, Earth pulls on the object, but the object, by Newton's third law, pulls on Earth with an equal-magnitude force in the opposite direction. Since the force causing the change of momentum of the object is internal to the system, momentum is conserved. Thus, for as much momentum that the object gains while falling toward Earth, Earth will also gain an equal amount of momentum moving toward the object. This change in momentum of Earth is not measurable due to the extremely large mass of Earth.

Day 108

If the new spring launches an identical dart at twice the speed, then the dart has four times more kinetic energy, since kinetic energy is proportional to the square of speed. With four times more kinetic energy, the new spring must do four times more work on the dart, since the work from the spring will equal the change in kinetic energy of the dart. Any new force-distance relationship that has four times the area of the original force-distance graph would represent this. A sample solution is shown below.

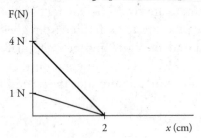

Day 109

To fly through the air in a stable path, without toppling, the Frisbee is designed to keep its balance by maintaining rotation about an axis. With mass concentrated toward the edges, this gives the Frisbee a large rotational inertia and therefore a large angular momentum. To change angular momentum, an external torque is necessary. To knock the Frisbee off its axis, or make it wobble, requires a change in angular momentum due to the change of the rotating axis. With the larger momentum, small torques from the air or gravity are not enough to immediately disturb the rotational state of the Frisbee.

Day 110

The motion described must involve an oscillatory motion, since kinetic energy and potential energy are continuously converted from one to the other, with a nonconservative force that is doing negative work on the object, reducing the total energy.

An example of an acceptable answer could be:

The graph is the energies of an object attached to the end of a horizontal spring on a surface with friction. The object begins at the equilibrium or unstretched position of the spring with kinetic energy. As the spring is either stretched or compressed, the system converts kinetic energy to potential energy, and then back again as the spring relaxes. While the oscillation occurs, there is friction between the mass and the surface, which does a net work on the system that reduces the total energy.

Day 111

The speed of the train car will remain constant. Defining the system as the car and oil, as the oil leaks from the car, the oil still has horizontal momentum. No forces have acted horizontally on the system; thus there is no change in the momentum of the system. Neither the oil nor the train will change the speed.

When the oil hits the ground and stops, the velocity of the center of mass of the oil-car system will decrease due to the friction between the oil and the ground, but this will not affect the speed of the car.

Day 112

Angular momentum for the disk-object system is conserved in this collision. Thus $I\omega = I'\omega'$—here I represents rotational inertia, ω represents angular speed, and the$'$ indicates quantities after collision. The rotational inertia of the disk is known; the angular speeds can be determined by counting how many frames the disk takes to make a full rotation, then dividing 6.3 radians (i.e., 2π radians) by the number of seconds it takes to make that full rotation.

So the rotational inertia I' of the system after collision can be calculated. Subtract that from the disk's rotational inertia to get the rotational inertia of just the heavy object. Since the heavy object can be treated as a point object—its radius is small compared to that of the disk—its rotational inertia is mr^2. Determine the radius r of its rotation by measuring on the video its distance from the disk's center. Then the object's mass m can be solved.

Day 113

In the first collision, the rod will move to the right as predicted by conservation of linear momentum. Angular momentum is also conserved in this collision. The ball has an angular momentum relative to the center of mass of the rod, which is the point about which the rod can rotate. (The equation for the angular momentum of a point mass is mvr, where r is the distance of closest approach to the axis of rotation.) Since angular momentum of the ball-rod system will be conserved, and the rebound of the ball changes the value of angular momentum of the ball, the angular momentum of the rod must also change, in this case going from zero before the collision to a nonzero value after the collision to keep the net momentum of the system a constant value.

In the second collision, the rod will again move to the right to conserve linear momentum. The rod will not rotate. Since the path of the ball takes it through the rotational axis of the rod, the angular momentum mvr of the ball is zero and thus of the system is zero. The angular momentum of the ball remains zero after the collision; so to conserve angular momentum, the rod must also have zero angular momentum and not rotate.

Day 114

The 12-kg bowling ball will have the same speed. In each case, energy is conserved. Gravitational potential energy will be converted to rotational kinetic energy and translational kinetic energy. Each of these energies is directly proportional to mass, making the final speed independent of the mass of the object, provided the bowling balls are the same structure with the same formula for rotational inertia (e.g., both are solid, as opposed to one being solid and one hollow).

Day 115

Examining the rotation of the ball: The friction between the ball and the lane as the ball slides produces a torque in the counterclockwise direction that starts the ball rotating. This torque does positive rotational work on the ball that increases the rotational kinetic energy.

Examining the translation of the ball: The friction force is in the opposite direction of motion. So friction does negative translational work, decreasing the translational kinetic energy of the ball.

Day 116

Student 1 is correct to observe that the maximum force is reached sooner with object 1, but then fails to examine the behavior of the force over the rest of the path, leading to false conclusions in the remainder of the argument.

Student 2 has made correct statements about the amount of work done being equal for each object, and the relationship between work and kinetic energy. The conclusion that the objects have equal final speeds cannot be drawn, however. The velocity changes will be equal due to the equal kinetic energy changes, but nothing is known about the initial velocity of each object, and particularly whether the initial velocities are equal. Thus no conclusion can be drawn about the final velocities.

Day 117

The student correctly describes the relationships between rotational inertia and angular velocity in instances where momentum is conserved, which it would be for Earth due to negligible external torques. However, the student is incorrect to state that the rotational inertia of Earth will decrease. The redistribution of mass from the poles will move mass farther away from Earth's rotational axis, thereby increasing the rotational inertia of Earth. Following a similar path of reasoning to that above, the rotational rate will decrease, thereby lengthening the day.

Day 118

Experiment 2 has a greater amplitude of oscillation with the same period. A greater amount of energy is thus required for experiment 2, which can be achieved by a greater initial position of the spring (a greater spring stretch distance).

Experiment 3 has an amplitude equal to experiment 1, but a shorter period. Spring oscillators have a period that is proportional to the square root of the mass and inversely proportional to the spring constant. To reduce the period, an object with less mass should be attached to the spring, or the spring could be replaced with one of larger spring constant.

Day 119

Student 1 is incorrect to state object 1 has the greater velocity and that the larger acceleration automatically produces a greater final velocity. The student has failed to consider the time of acceleration, or distance over which the acceleration will act.

Student 2 is incorrect to state that the greater distance is sufficient to overcome the lesser acceleration, producing a greater velocity at the bottom.

The object will have the same velocity in each case. The only work done on the objects is by gravity, which is a conservative force. Work done by conservative forces is path independent, meaning the steepness of the hill, or slope of the incline, is insignificant. The gravitational work done is dependent on the distance moved parallel to the gravitational field, which will be equal to the height of the incline. Equal work in each case produces equal changes in kinetic energy, and since the objects have the same mass, they will have the same final speed.

Day 120

x' is greater than x. The moving block M in experiment 2 will have the same speed as block m in experiment 1, but a greater kinetic energy due to its greater mass. When the system comes to rest, the kinetic energy has been stored in the spring as elastic potential energy. With a greater kinetic energy in experiment 2, there will be more elastic potential energy stored in the spring, and therefore a greater spring compression.

Appendixes

TABLE OF INFORMATION

You will be given this information as part of the AP Physics 1 Exam. It's worth checking out the official version of the table at https://www.collegeboard.org—they may use slightly different symbols and layout than you see here.

Constants

Gravitational field at Earth's surface	g	10 N/kg
Universal gravitation constant	G	6.7×10^{-11} N·m²/kg²

Trigonometry

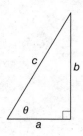

$\sin \theta = b/c$

$\cos \theta = a/c$

$\tan \theta = b/a$

Mechanics Equations

$v_f = v_0 + at$

$\Delta x = v_0 t + \dfrac{1}{2} at^2$

$v_f^2 = v_0^2 = 2a\Delta x$

$a = \dfrac{F_{net}}{m}$

$F_f = \mu F_n$

$p = mv$

$\Delta p = F \cdot \Delta t$

$KE = \dfrac{1}{2} mv^2$

$$KE_{\text{rotational}} = \frac{1}{2}I\omega^2$$

$$PE = mgh$$

$$PE = -G\frac{M_1M_2}{d}$$

$$PE = \frac{1}{2}kx^2$$

$$W = F\Delta x_{\parallel}$$

$$W_{\text{NC}} = (\Delta KE) + (\Delta PE)$$

$$a_c = \frac{v^2}{r}$$

$$I = \sum mr^2$$

$$\tau = Fd_{\perp}$$

$$\tau_{net} = I\alpha$$

$$\Delta L = \tau \cdot \Delta t$$

$$w = mg$$

$$g = G\frac{M}{d^2}$$

$$F = \frac{Gm_1m_2}{d^2}.$$

Wave and Simple Harmonic Motion Equations

$$T = 2\pi\frac{\sqrt{m}}{\sqrt{k}}$$

$$F_s = kx$$

$$T = 2\pi\frac{\sqrt{L}}{\sqrt{g}}$$

RECOMMENDED WEBSITES

It's certainly easy enough to search for physics tutorials, simulations, and example problems. But so much is available that quality control can be a major problem.

I'd suggest just a few sites as your home base for learning physics. I often assign problems in my class based on these sites. For some, I just say "please play with this site for 10 minutes for extra credit." Any way you choose to use them will be, well, useful. All of the sites below are free.

The Physics Classroom

- http://www.physicsclassroom.com/
  Click around to see better explanations for physics concepts than you'll find in any textbook, plus animations and solved sample problems. This is the place to go when you're starting a new topic and you need an overview.

PHET Interactive Simulations

- https://phet.colorado.edu/en/simulations
  These clever simulations are for exploring. Just click around. Discover how objects can move to the right even when the net force is to the left. Fool around applying torques to a turntable and making a ladybug crawl in all directions on the turntable. These will give you an instinct for physics concepts that are outside the realm of your direct experience.

The Physics Aviary

- http://www.thephysicsaviary.com/
  Is there a lab situation you don't have the equipment to set up live? (Like, for example, measuring the force of one planet on another with a spring scale?) Or do you not have the time in class to set up what you want? The Physics Aviary probably has a pretend lab setup that's the next best thing to an actual experiment. Click through their situations, including a huge number explicitly aligned to AP Physics 1. Pick an experiment; try graphing one value vs. another on graph paper, linearizing the graph, and figuring out the meaning of the graph's slope.

At Langel's, the extra cheese oozes and stretches beyond the mere constraints of slices. It takes a full 20 minutes before the cheese is congealed enough to hold the shape in which you cut it. But it's the sauce that makes Langel's the best pizza in the known universe. This deep-dish pizza does not come in layers, but rather mixed all about, which means that the sauce can be appreciated throughout every bite. The pepperoni is fine, but I actually recommend just getting a pure extra-cheese pie. You'll have enough for lunch right now, dinner tonight, and probably breakfast tomorrow. Too bad they don't deliver within a 1,200-km radius.

NOTES

5 Steps to Teaching AP Physics 1

TEACHER'S MANUAL

Greg Jacobs

AP Physics 1 Teacher at Woodberry Forest School in Virginia

Introduction to the *Teacher's Manual*

Nowadays teachers have no shortage of resources for their physics class. No longer limited to just the teacher and the textbook, teachers and students can look at online simulations, apps, computer-based homework, video lectures, and so on. Even the College Board itself provides so much material related to the AP exam that the teachers can easily become overwhelmed by an excess of information.

This book explains in straightforward language what a student needs to know for the AP Physics 1 exam—nothing more, nothing less.

The 5 Steps of Teaching AP Physics 1

This *Teacher's Manual* will take you through what I would consider the 5 steps of teaching an AP Physics 1 course. These 5 steps are:

▶ **Prepare a strategic plan for the course**

▶ **Hold an interesting class every day**

▶ **Evaluate your students' progress**

▶ **Get students ready to take the AP exam**

▶ **Become a better teacher every year**

I'll talk through each of these steps, some in more detail than others. Most of the suggestions and ideas are things that I've used in my own class, but that doesn't mean they're uniquely *mine*—physics teachers, like baseball pitchers, do best when they hear new things, try new things, adapt new things, and eventually make new things their own. I hope this *Teacher's Manual* inspires new ideas you can use in your own classroom.

And feel free to write to me with your own thoughts. I'm always collecting and trying out new teaching ideas for myself, so I'd love to hear from readers. My physics teaching blog at **jacobsphysics .blogspot.com** regularly updates with new ideas, most of which are inspired by correspondence and discussion with other physics teachers.

STEP 1

Prepare a Strategic Plan for the Course

By "strategic plan," I mean how your course is going to be structured from August to April. The obvious part of the strategic plan is which topics will be covered over what periods of time. While that is an important feature, there's much more to consider.

Begin Your Preparation by Grafting Topic Coverage onto Your Own School's Yearly Calendar

The AP Physics 1 exam includes eight major topic areas—the *5 Steps* book covers each of these as a separate content chapter. Course preparation begins by deciding how much time to spend in your initial coverage of each major topic.

A simple way to do this is to use the College Board's Physics 1 Course and Exam Description (CED). That document indicates the approximate number of class periods recommended for each unit. Now look at your own school calendar. Cross out "special" days when your class doesn't meet or when you know nothing will be accomplished. Label each remaining day of the school year with one of the eight units; now you have the beginnings of a plan.

Then Be Prepared to Actually Follow the Plan

Invariably, your calendar will tell you it's time to end, say, the study of Newton's laws and move in to energy. "But I know they don't truly get Newton's laws yet," you'll say. Perhaps you'll hear some pointed, passive-aggressive commentary from students, parents, or even colleagues: "You know, the school isn't gonna lose accreditation if you slow down a bit." Never mind; *move on.* Make the yearly plan nonnegotiable.

Yes, you will have students who still don't understand a topic when it's time to move along. That's OK. What makes you think that the portion of the class who isn't getting every problem right will suddenly have an epiphany the twelfth time you review a topic? And what about the students who are doing fine and are ready to keep going? They should not feel slowed down by their peers in what is billed as a college-level course.

Don't fret. "Review" is best done in context throughout the course. For example, when you talk about work done by friction, you likely will draw a free body diagram and calculate the force of friction. That right there is a review of Newton's laws. Do a problem with blocks colliding at the edge of a cliff, such that the blocks become projectiles after collision—and you've just done a kinematics review. It's amazing how students who back in September couldn't solve a projectile problem to save their lives suddenly figure it out when the projectile problem is in the context of new material. I've seen it happen every year without exception—those who initially seem hopeless figure things out the second or third time they are exposed to a topic.

Assign Test Dates in Advance, and Do Not Change Them for Anything Less Than the Apocalypse

I'll talk in Step 3 about the enormous utility of tests, how a test is the only event for which you

can be guaranteed to have the class's universal attention. It's therefore important to schedule tests carefully. By scheduling ahead of time in stone, you can avoid as many conflicts as possible. Don't schedule a test the Monday after the Super Bowl or the Friday before prom. But there's also no reason to postpone a test, other than the cancellation of school.

I discourage frequent "unit tests." Instead, I schedule a test once a month. Whatever you've covered from the first day of class up to the test date goes on the test. Students and parents will no doubt complain that such infrequent testing makes each test "high stakes." Good! That's kind of the point. The AP exam is a one-shot opportunity to earn college credit. By the time the AP exam happens, your students will have had experience with eight or so "high-stakes" practice tests, making the AP exam itself no big deal.

Don't Expect Students to Do More Than One or Two Problems Each Night

If you assign too much homework, it won't be done right and therefore will be worse than useless to your students' progress. This doesn't mean you have to assign work due every class meeting, though. As long as students are accountable for doing thorough work, you can have problems due every other day or even once a week. Let's say your overall plan involves 15 class days of work on kinematics. That means you can assign only 15–20 problems on kinematics. Better make 'em good!

So What Makes a Problem "Good," Anyway?

Homework problems should be similar in level and style to AP problems. Then, when it's time for the real exam, the students have the experience to know instinctively when they're overthinking or oversimplifying a question. Because you assign only two of these good problems per night, students can reasonably be expected to present a thorough, annotated solution rather than just "3/2 = 1.5 m/s/s."

You might be tempted to assign a bunch of straightforward plug-and-chug problems, such as "What is the acceleration of a 2-kg object experiencing a 3-N net force?" Perhaps you want students to gain experience solving new equations; perhaps you want your weaker students to build confidence. Nevertheless, assigning such problems is harmful, not helpful. Weak students develop a *false* sense of confidence—since they can do the baby problems, they reason, they can do some physics, so there's no need to work too much on those other problems. And even worse, the good students develop an unhealthy antipathy toward homework problems. Plug-and-chug problems, to most students, fall into the category of "busywork." So the good students tune out *all* the homework, assuming everything to be busywork.

Conversely, you might be tempted to challenge your top students by assigning some really tough, involved problems that are beyond the level of the AP exam. Don't! It's easy to think that those top students will enjoy the challenge—because *you* like a good challenge—but more likely they resent the burden of the additional work. And for the rest of the class, even one problem beyond the level of the AP exam frustrates them, making them doubt their own skill. Their learned hopelessness means they are likely to assume that an AP exam problem is beyond them, even when it's not.

How Do I Know What's AP Level?

When you have a chance, read and solve some of the official College Board released AP Physics 1 items. Use AP Classroom to get authentic items.

Then read the practice problems and the practice test in this book. That should give you an idea of the style and level of descriptive response questions your students will need to be prepared for. (Multiple-choice problems are perfectly good in-class and out-of-class assignments, as long as you demand that students justify their answers.)

Once the class starts, don't pull punches, especially with students who have reached a bit to be in the AP course. While I and the College Board encourage you to initially accept any student who is willing to do the work in your AP Physics 1 course, such an approach can turn into a disaster if students at the weaker end expect the class to slow down for them, or if they expect a route to high grades that doesn't involve performance on tests. The meaning of the AP grade—the 5, 4, 3, 2, 1 scale—is that it represents approximately an A, B, C, D, F in the equivalent college course. If someone is earning straight 1s on his tests, he should be getting Ds or Fs, not Bs. Ideally, though, I recommend counseling such a student into a general-level physics course once it's clear that they have little possibility of passing.[1]

What Should I Assign as Summer Work?

Nothing. Summer work for AP Physics 1 is a terrible idea. First of all, when does it get done? The night before class starts. What can be accomplished? Not much. You really want your students trying to learn about Newton's laws without your guidance?

The worst part of the summer assignment is that it sets you up for a worthless confrontation. In all their other AP courses, your students have summer assignments, most of which are far more integral to

---

[1] On this point many people disagree with me. The College Board will tell you that a student who gets a 1 on the AP exam still has gained valuable experience that will be useful to them in college. I say, why would you allow an overmatched batter to hurt the team and their own confidence by hitting .100 all year, when you could have put them on JV where they would have hit .300 and been a star? I've had many, many students throughout the decades who couldn't handle AP Physics the first time, but did well in a general course and then subsequently performed brilliantly in AP or actual college physics.

the course than anything you can do for summer physics. Therefore, most will show up resentful at having to do your work on top of everything else; and some will show up without the work at all. Now you have to make a decision: Do you ignore their failure, perhaps just giving them a slap on the wrist? That sends the message that you don't *really* care whether your students do the assigned work, meaning you've got a huge fight on your hands to get the students to take their problem sets seriously. Or do you bring the hammer down on the lazy bums who didn't do the summer work, giving them a horrible grade out of the gate? That would present yourself in the most hostile way possible on the first day of class. Why not save that battle for the regularly scheduled problem sets, which are crucial to developing an understanding of the active course material?

The chart below correlates the College Board's CED units and recommended class periods to the chapters in the *5 Steps* book.

TOPICS	PACING	*5 STEPS TO A 5*
Unit 1: Kinematics	19–22 class periods	Chapter 10, pp. 81–91
Unit 2: Dynamics	21–24 class periods	Chapter 11, pp. 93–103
Unit 3: Circular Motion and Gravitation	8–10 class periods	Chapters 14 and 15, pp. 127–150
Unit 4: Energy	22–25 class periods	Chapter 13, pp. 117–125
Unit 5: Momentum	14–17 class periods	Chapter 12, pp. 105–115
Unit 6: Simple Harmonic Motion	4–7 class periods	Chapter 16, pp. 151–155
Unit 7: Torque and Rotational Motion	14–19 class periods	Chapter 14, pp. 127–141

STEP 2

Hold an Interesting Class Every Day

Most class days in an AP Physics 1 course include some mix of this broad categorization of activities:

▶ **You presenting material to the class**

▶ **Lab work**

▶ **Independent/group work**

▶ **Quizzes**

▶ **Tests**

There's no way to plan each class to the minute before the school year starts. But you certainly can decide how you want to distribute these activities over a typical week.

A Basic Rule of Teaching: Your Students Don't Listen to You

Nothing personal—mine don't listen to me, either. There's no point in complaining about kids these days.[2] Deal with your students as they are, not as you think they ought to be. And they *are* inclined to tune out if you talk at them for more than a few minutes.

---

[2] I graduated high school in 1991. Kids in my day always listened, respected their elders, and absolutely never texted in class.

Don't feel like you need to "go over" every last little thing in class, because the class won't remember what you went over anyway. Here's where the *5 Steps* book comes in very handy. Chapter 4 lists all the facts that students need to know. Your students should know these facts cold. You don't have to say them or write them on the board; students can read them just fine out of the book. Go ahead and assign students to learn these facts, and quiz over them before you've said a word about them in class. In class, then, you assume knowledge of fundamental facts; you work with your students on applying the fundamentals to new situations. That's what physics is all about.

Give a Short Quiz Every Day

While students don't listen to you, they without question pay attention to quiz questions. Therefore, if there's a point you want to make about a common mistake on the homework, don't talk to the class about it; ask a pointed question about it on a daily quiz.

Quizzes can take any format you want. A colleague convinced me to use short-answer questions that can be either straight fact recall ("The slope of a velocity-time graph is _____") or a bit more open-ended ("On the homework problem for today, why was the normal force greater than the cart's weight?"). Multiple-choice questions have the advantage of quick-and-easy grading. A quiz could be word for word from a homework problem, thus ensuring that students didn't just copy their friend's or an online solution; or better yet you could change the situation from the homework slightly, by making the cart heavier or doubling its initial speed.

However the daily quiz is structured, it serves a multitude of purposes:

▶ **Any issues of students arriving late will vanish after a few daily quizzes.** Not in your seat when the bell rings? I'm not mad at you; you're not in trouble; you just don't get to take the quiz. Without confrontation or rancor, I've bought 5 extra minutes per class period.

▶ **The quiz provides a few quiet minutes for me to collect the students' homework individually while they are sitting in their seats.** I can find out immediately if someone is unprepared, without interrupting the flow of the class. I can also deal with the unprepared student immediately. Students know they can't hide missing homework.

▶ **Going over the quiz as soon as it's over is as good a content review as you can find.** Students care deeply about the answers, so they're willing to listen and engage in a way that wouldn't happen if you just said, "Let's go over the homework problems."

▶ **Try having students grade each other's quizzes.**[3] Then each student is paying double attention to the answers—the students are listening to see whether *they* got the answer right, *and* they're listening to see whether the paper they're grading should be marked right or wrong.

Sure, you might have to deal with some drama-mongering colleagues breathlessly wondering how you could be so cruel to your class as to give so many quizzes. Your response is to wonder, in return, why must a quiz be considered cruel? Is the football coach cruel because they have the team play football during practice? Is the soccer coach cruel because they run a 15-minute scrimmage at the end of each practice? So what's the problem with having students practice responding to physics questions every day? Isn't that exactly what we're *supposed* to be doing in a physics class? Keep giving your quizzes, and the complaints will become vanishing whispers in the wind.

---

[3] This will work even if the quizzes themselves count minimally or not at all to the students' course grades.

The *5 Steps to a 5 AP Physics 1: Elite Edition* provides excellent 5-minute quiz questions that can be used in your class. Many of these questions overlap multiple topic areas, so it's best to just thumb through and pick a question that your students can answer based on what they've learned so far. But here's a rough guide to which questions go with which *5 Steps* chapter:

UNIT	QUESTIONS IN THE *ELITE EDITION*
Unit 1: Kinematics	Days 1, 6, 9–10, 17, 19, 23–24, 30, 33–35, 39, 41–42, 60, 91
Unit 2: Dynamics	Days 2, 4–6, 8, 15–16, 18, 20–22, 25, 27, 31–32, 36–38, 40, 51–54
Unit 3: Circular Motion and Gravitation	Days 3, 11–14, 28–29, 45–46, 48–49
Unit 4: Energy	Days 61–62, 65–66, 69–70, 72, 74–78, 80, 82, 86, 101, 103, 108, 116, 119–120
Unit 5: Momentum	Days 63–64, 67–68, 73, 79, 81, 84–85, 87–88, 90, 92–94, 96–97, 105–107, 111–113
Unit 6: Simple Harmonic Motion	Days 99, 102, 110, 118
Unit 7: Torque and Rotational Motion	Days 26, 43–44, 47, 50, 55–59, 71, 83, 89, 95, 98, 100, 104, 109, 112, 114–115, 117

It's Fine to Use 1960s' Equipment for Laboratory Exercises

While I recommend using whatever technology you can lay your hands on for demonstrations, for lab work I think it's perfectly reasonable to minimize technology. The whole point of lab work is for students to get their hands dirty with experimental physics, to help them learn to be creative and rigorous in making direct measurements of physical quantities. If everything in lab is a preset app on a smartphone that automatically calculates whatever the students are measuring, much of that creativity is lost.

Perhaps you have enough motion detectors or photogates to give one setup to each group. Perhaps you have a class set of iPads with video analysis software. That's awesome. But if you don't, that's fine, too. You can do all sorts of AP Physics 1 experiments using only equipment that was available in 1960: masses, carts, stopwatches, pulleys, strings, batteries, resistors, metersticks,

spring scales, and so on. Just pick an equation from your text for which you can make direct measurements of two of the variables. Have the students measure and graph those variables, and you have created a laboratory exercise.

Are there other ways to do lab work? Sure. One different approach would be to pick one homework problem each week for which you have sufficient equipment for everyone to set it up live in class, just as you might set up a quantitative demonstration. Making the explicit link between problem solving and lab work is always a good idea if you can do it. Some teachers like to set up "stations," in which students are asked to make quick measurements of some quantity. After 20 minutes, students rotate to a new station, which uses similar equipment to ask for a different measurement. Any exercises that require your students to manipulate equipment with some degree of creativity work as AP Physics 1 labs.

Make All Graphs by Hand; Never Use a Graphical Analysis Program

Many students will certainly kvetch about making graphs by hand. "That's what Excel is for," they'll say. "You're just making me do busywork." No, not the case. How many of your students have ever had to take a piece of graph paper, create their own scales for the axes, plot the points, draw a best-fit, and take the slope with no aid other than a ruler and calculator? Probably none. Yet the AP exam expects students to do just that process, and to do it as just a small part of a 20-minute free-response problem.

Graphing by hand every week in lab not only gives your students practice to do well on the exam; it gives them visceral experience with analysis. For example, early on, students might try to record data from a voltmeter to four-figure precision. I don't object; I let them . . . because when they try to put that data on the graph, they realize for themselves that 4.318 volts looks exactly the same as 4.3 volts, but different from 4 volts. Or as they graph by hand, they see what looks like a linear pattern develop, but then they see for themselves that larger angles cause the graph to flatten. Later in the course, students will recognize for themselves how to collect data over an entire range of interest. But that recognition doesn't happen as easily if the computer just magically spits out a picture.

Dive into Real Physics from the First Moment of the First Day of Class

Within 10 minutes of arrival, I'm doing physics with both problem solving and experimentation. I introduce the definition of "equilibrium," showing with spring scales that up forces must equal down forces; left forces must equal right forces. By the second day of class, I've introduced the idea of a "normal" force, and I've shown what happens when forces act at angles.

What about reading the syllabus, discussing grading policies, and describing class rules? I don't understand the thought behind even *having* "class rules." Your students may not be adults in the eyes of the law, but if you want a relaxed, cooperative atmosphere in class, you absolutely must treat your students like adults. When adults come together for, say, a business conference or a national meeting, the event doesn't start with an authority figure reading a list of things that the attendees can and can't do. How would you react to such a start to a conference? I know I'd be thinking right away about how I could passive-aggressively stick it to the person trying to tell me what to do.

You see what I mean. Your students are generally juniors and seniors, and good students at that. They have plenty of experience taking high school classes. They can read, so give them the syllabus with a brief summary of grading policies and tell them to read it. Going over the syllabus and rules in class begs for an argument and leaves the students trying to figure out how to game their grade based on the rules you laid out. But doing physics leaves the students saying, "Cool," and asking questions like, "Wait, doesn't the block also apply a force to the table?"

If nothing else, you know that virtually every other teacher at your school is using the first day of class to read the syllabus and discuss policies. You will have an especially enthusiastic audience if you're the only teacher doing something active and content-related on the first day of school.

STEP 3

Evaluate Your Students' Progress

I'm a strong advocate of a "less is more" approach to teaching physics. You don't have to assign enormous amounts of work; you don't have to give tests every week; you don't have to assign any reading at all. One problem per night, a short quiz every day or two, and a test every month should be easily sufficient for your students to make appropriate progress. For one thing, such a small amount of assigned work will buy you a good bit of political capital, making students willing to work harder and without complaint. Even though the one problem each night requires a full page of presentation to answer three or four parts, students will compare their assignment favorably to math class's "Do problems 1–51 odd." They will be pleased that your expectations seem to them reasonable in scope (i.e., 20–40 minutes per night rather than the hours expected in other AP classes) and productive in nature (i.e., not perceived as busywork).

The more important reason to use a "less is more" philosophy is that by keeping the *amount* of work minimal, you can expect that work to be utterly brilliant.

Demand That Homework Problems Be Presented, Not Merely Answered

Doing a homework problem in physics is far more similar to writing a paragraph for English class, or even to doing an assignment for AP Studio Art, than to solving a math problem. It's not good enough to get the right answer or even just to show your work; a well-presented problem should provide an annotated, reasoned solution. The explanation of the reasoning behind the answer is more important than the answer itself.

Imagine an English teacher assigns a paper: Discuss, using textual evidence, the complexities of the relationship between Romeo and Juliet. Someone writes, as their entire paper, "He loved her." How well did this student meet the teacher's expectations? What grade is this student going to get? They'll complain, perhaps, that they don't deserve an F—because *the answer is exactly right.*

You may think I'm arguing ad absurdum, but have you not seen "solutions" to physics problems along these lines? A student whose answer to a physics problem is "$F = ma$, $30/6 = 5$ m/s/s" has in no way engaged with the problem, any more than "He loved her" has engaged with Shakespeare. You have every right, nay, every responsibility, to require more.

Another Basic Rule of Teaching: Trust, but Verify

Grading practice problems doesn't have to be a detailed process. Scores of some sort on practice problems must exist; otherwise, "less is more" devolves into just "less." First, know that this feedback doesn't have to count as a significant part of the final course grade. I've had good success for a while putting a score on the problems, calling in the students who get less than about half of the points for a required extra-help session to correct their mistakes. I'm transparent that homework or in-class work will not bring down the overall course grade unless they either don't do the problems to begin with or don't show up to redo the problems the right way when asked.

Note that the score you write doesn't have to be the result of a long, careful, rigorous process. Ideally, you're grading student work every couple of days. Unless you have no life beyond school, you must find a way to grade a stack of problems quickly.

Start by recognizing that there's little point in writing more than a word or two on anyone's problem set. The students almost definitely won't read what you're writing, at least not carefully. Your time is valuable; don't use it in noble yet fruitless endeavors.

I recommend grading work holistically. That means, look at the solution as a whole. Did the student apply the correct physics principle? Did they explain the important or tricky parts of the solution? Is the answer right? Is a conceptual portion of the problem justified with a fact, equation, or calculation, and is that justification clear and correct? Does the solution include words, equations, diagrams, and numbers?

If you answered yes to all of these, give the assignment full credit. If you have doubts about some of these issues, give the problem partial credit—exactly how much doesn't really matter. And if pretty much none of the questions can be answered in the affirmative, don't give the problem much credit at all.

"But won't the students argue about my grading?" At the beginning of the year, probably they will. *Don't engage* in a discussion about homework grades, especially during class. Answer any question about physics principles carefully and enthusiastically. But as soon as anyone asks about "points," stop talking and move on to something related to physics. Your students will quickly come to the realization that a point on one night's problem set, like a teensy drop of gasoline that didn't quite make it into the tank, is negligible and thus not worth worrying about. Especially once they realize that you won't even argue, they'll just drop the issue and move on.

Treat Tests as the Best Teaching Tool Ever Invented

Because your students care so much about their test grades, milk the tests for all their worth to firm up students' physics ability. A test can be visited and revisited at least three times: once is the test itself, and the two other times are when students do corrections on the problems they missed and when you ask targeted quiz questions about issues with which the class struggled. The process of giving and debriefing a test can be compared with a football team's treatment of a regular-season game. Perform on game day; then, win or lose, deconstruct what went right or wrong so that the next game is even better.

Start with an authentic test—ideally, a test identical in style and format to the AP exam itself. That means students are given a bit less than 2 minutes per multiple-choice item and 2 minutes per point on the free-response items. That means there will be few if any questions that ask merely for a one-step calculation, and certainly no questions at all like "Write the equation for net force in terms of acceleration."

Use the items released by the College Board (in AP Classroom); use the questions in this book's practice exam and some of those at the end of the chapters. Be careful about other test question sources, though. While every test has a few "hard" questions and a few "easy" questions, be sure that your tests mix difficulty levels so that the overall test is consistent with what you see in official released exams.

Make the test as long and broad as time allows. I use my extended lab period for testing once a month. This allows me to give nearly a half-length AP-style exam. If you don't have that kind of time available, try giving the multiple-choice section on one day, with the free response following on the next day.

Make the test cumulative, covering *all* the material you've covered this year. Otherwise, you give your class an excuse to forget or ignore old topics. Testing on the current unit only sends the message that the previous unit isn't important anymore, and then that attitude will bite your students when they prepare for the exam in April. When every test has several questions from previous topics as well as some free-response questions that integrate techniques from multiple topics, your students will spread their review time over the course of the year rather than trying to cram their review into an all-nighter on May 10.

Never, Ever, Allow Students to Ask Questions on a Test

Every year when I grade AP exams, I see students writing diatribes about how they don't understand the question, or that the question is unfair, or the sort of complaint that's generally accompanied by frustrated anger. Presumably these students have been in an AP class all year. So they can't answer one of the questions; why the hostility?

It's likely such students are not used to a testing situation without their teacher to rely on for guidance. Watch a colleague give a test in math or science class. How many times do you see students get stuck on a problem and *instantly* come to the teacher's desk to ask for help? Sure, a lot of the time the teacher might say something innocuous like, "Why don't you read the question again?," which gets the student unstuck so they can make progress on the test. I agree that such a teacher is not being unethical or dishonest in her testing. But that teacher *is* doing their students a tremendous disservice.[4]

When the AP exam presents a new and challenging situation, your students will not be able to ask you—or anyone else—a question to point them in the right direction. They will be on their own. They need practice in figuring out problems on their own. If students haven't had such practice, if they've always had the teacher show them how to start difficult problems on their in-class tests, then it's no wonder they get upset when their training wheels are yanked away on the biggest test of the year. And even if you never truly gave useful hints, just the fact that they cannot come to a teacher's desk to ask for "clarification" of a question will throw your students for a loop.

Prepare your students ahead of time for your no-questions-on-tests policy. A day or two before the test, go over testing procedures with the students. Pass out the cover sheet on which the number of questions is written, along with the time for each section and the AP table of information. Then explain: "Unless you are missing a page, you may not ask a question during the test. No exceptions."

But think why students ask questions. It's not true that most are desperately hoping you'll give them the answer. Most are genuinely confused, and when a smart student is confused, they quite reasonably assume that the issue is with the test question itself, not with their understanding. So the student comes to your desk to ask something like, "You didn't tell us the mass of the cart; shouldn't you do that, please?"

Well, as a physics teacher, you know that this student is missing something important. Either the mass isn't necessary to solve the problem, or perhaps the mass can be calculated or estimated through some indirect method. But no matter what your response, by allowing them to ask the question, you have defeated the point of the test question. Even saying "I think you can solve this

---

[4] And the teacher who actually does help, who talks the student through the problem, has in my mind breached testing decorum. That's comparable to a referee helping a quarterback read the defense: "Now, kid, you know they haven't covered your tight end the past three plays. You might want to throw there." How would you feel about that referee?

problem" implies to them—*and to the rest of the class*—that the mass isn't important. That's for the students to figure out for themselves, not for them to hear from you!

So ahead of time, you must give your students a strategy for when they think a problem is misstated. "While you *may not* ask me a question during the test, you may write anything you like on the test. If you think you need more information to solve a problem, tell me so in writing—and then make up the information and solve. If you think a multiple-choice item doesn't include the right answer or is ambiguous, write that down. Chances are, you're missing something; writing down your concern and moving on is the best approach to getting as much credit as possible. However, in the unlikely event that the question is poorly phrased, I will look at what you wrote and consider how to award credit fairly."

Proofread your tests rigorously. When you test, you're entering into a covenant with your students. They must, without help from you or their classmates, show you what they know so you can evaluate their physics knowledge. But in turn, *you* must write a test that fairly and clearly allows them to demonstrate that knowledge. If after every test you have to explain, "Yeah, number 4 wasn't stated clearly; I meant find the speed of cart A, but I said find the speed of cart B," then you'll lose your class's confidence.

Sure, mistakes happen. They've happened on the real AP exam; several released exams say "number 67 was not scored" or "since the problem as stated was not clear on this issue, either of two answers earned credit." If you screw up a question, be fair about it. Award credit for any reasonable approach, or just throw out a bad multiple-choice question. When you return the test, make sure your students know what happened and how

you're dealing with it. But if you have to correct a mistake more than once or twice in a year, you are not proofreading carefully enough.

Stick to your guns when students try to ask you questions anyway. I will bet my life savings[5] that, no matter how well you prepare your students for your first test, one of them will get up and try to ask you a question. "I know I can't ask questions, but . . . ," they'll say. *Cut them off.*

"Mr. Jones, are you missing a page? Did the copy machine mess up? Then what the heck are you doing up here, interrupting the rest of the class as they try to concentrate? Sit down, please, and consider apologizing to the class later for your disturbance."

It's worth fighting this battle. Once the students realize that they can't just go to you for hints, they will settle down and do great work. By the second test, you will be able to get enormous amounts of your own work done during that time. You can have colleagues or substitutes give tests on days you have to be gone. Most important, when it comes time for the real AP exam, your students will have the requisite confidence to deal with difficult and unusual problems, even though no help from the proctor is available.

How Do I Assign Test Grades?

I'm frequently asked how to "convert" an AP-style test to a standard high school grading scale. Generally, it takes about 65% of available points to get a 5; 50% to get a 4; 35% to get a 3; and 25% to get a 2. But a typical school scale tells us that 90% is an A and 80% is a B. I'll explain how I make the conversion. However, my method is not gospel; you need to be creative within the parameters of your class, your school, your personality.

---

[5] $134.95.

When students get their tests back, they see a grading sheet exactly like the one on page 206 of this book. You see the range of raw scores necessary to earn each AP score listed at the bottom. I circle the AP score of 5, 4, 3, 2, or 1. That's the first step toward building back confidence; students who thought they failed see a real AP score that they understand. And most did far, far better than they expected.

I do *not* communicate a letter grade yet. I make the students earn their letter grade through test corrections (see the next section). Students get back half the credit they lost for each problem corrected.

Finally, I use a "square root" curve[6] to convert to the school scale. The practical outcome is that with good corrections, a 5 on the AP scale becomes an A, a 4 becomes a B+ or B, and a 3 becomes a B or B−. But a lack of corrections means that even a 4 might become a D.

The exact method I use is not what's important, anyway. The important part is giving students tremendous incentive to make good corrections to the problems they missed. Do that by any means necessary.

Be Prepared for Tears After the First Test

I'm not exaggerating about smart students who have never earned below 90% on a test in their entire lives. The first AP Physics test will be, for a number of smart students, the first time ever that they don't get everything right. Many will feel that they failed the test, even if they got a 5 (in their mind, 65% is a failing grade, not an A). It doesn't matter how well you've explained the grading scale; I'm talking about a visceral, subconscious emotional reaction to a smart student's *perception* of failure.

You personally have to be strong to deal with the backlash. On one hand, I don't recommend engaging with sad and worried students. The more you try to comfort a student, the more upset that student will get. It's sufficient to say politely, "We'll see how you did tomorrow, when we start test corrections. Remember, we have eight tests this year, and this is only the first. Let's not discuss anything else until we have something concrete to work with." Just be as patient as you can with the emotionally shattered students. The few days after the first test are critical to rebuilding your students' confidence.

Test Corrections Are the Most Important Assignment You Can Give

There's nothing wrong with missing a test question. Your class will see that even the best students aren't getting perfect test scores. However, there is something very much wrong with fatalistically resigning oneself to missing test questions because physics is hard. The test exposes areas of physics that each student doesn't fully understand. It's now the student's job to use the test as an opportunity to improve their understanding.

For each multiple-choice question missed, a student is required to justify the answer thoroughly on a half page of unlined paper. For each lettered part missed on the free-response portion, a student is required to redo that part, and to answer any further questions I may pose.

Especially after the first test, I find it is worth a day of class time to allow students to collaborate on test corrections. Anyone may even ask me questions, and I will talk the student through the problem. However, there's a price for my help: when the next student asks about the same issue, I don't answer. Instead. I say, "Hey, good

---

[6] A "square root" curve takes the square root of a percentage and multiplies by 10 to get the score on the school scale. An 81% becomes an A: The square root of 81 is 9; 9 × 10 is 90; and 90 is an A. Continuing on, 64% is a B, and 49% is a C. I use this curve on all work, making it practically impossible for a student who does all the work to earn below a C, usually even a B−.

question. Jimbo here just asked me the same question. Jimbo, could you talk Kearney here through it?" The process of writing the correct answer, followed by explaining that answer to a classmate, generally improves physics understanding better than 10 of the best professor's best lectures.

Don't let students see their original response at first. Just hand back a clean copy of the test, and indicate which parts of which questions they missed. This way, they have to start from scratch, rather than spend half an hour trying to change just one word in their original answer. And this way, no one can just look at the best student's

answer! Even the top students will have to explain their understanding to their classmates, and that interaction is valuable to all concerned.

As the students do their corrections, you'll see their demeanor change from self-pitying sadness to gritty determination. Count how many times you see students hit themselves in the forehead, either figuratively or literally. They see quickly that half of their mistakes were silly things where they knew better but panicked under the pressure of the test, or where they did everything right except one little step. The corrections process allows students to see that the test wasn't nearly as impossible as they originally may have thought.

STEP 4

Get Students Ready to Take the AP Exam

Just like the swim team trains all season for the championship meet, your class is training all year for the AP exam. Some of the general principles of preparation are quite similar.

Early in the season, the swim team pushes very hard in practice. Maybe the team even takes a "training trip" during a school vacation, at which the swimmers exhaust themselves thoroughly during two rigorous practices—plus weightlifting—every day. This is the time when swimmers build their muscles, their technique, and their endurance.

But in the weeks leading up to the championship meet, the swimmers "taper." Practices become easier, as swimmers allow their bodies to recover from the rigor of the mid-season practices. It's critical that the swimmers still practice every day, but no longer are they *building* skill. Rather, they're *reinforcing* what they already have. They're

maintaining their muscle memory, maintaining their strength, keeping themselves rested and poised to perform at the championship. As it turns out, swimmers who work hard and tirelessly early on, and who taper appropriately, usually swim considerably faster on race day than they ever have before.

Use Tapering as a Strategy to Get Students Ready to Take the AP Exam in Physics 1

Early in the year, when school is still fresh, the seniors are building their college résumés, and the exam is far in the future, that's when to push the pace. While students may panic about their marking period grades, at the beginning of the class no one panics about the AP exam itself.[7] Time the course such that you finish covering all relevant material by early April.

---

[7] In fact, they usually don't think much about the AP exam itself until at least April. There's a reason that sales of the *5 Steps* book peak in April, not in September or January.

Then in the month or so before the exam, taper. You still must assign work on the same regular schedule that you've been using all year. However, the assignments can be substantially shorter. All you're trying to do in the taper period is to review material you've covered before, to keep it fresh in students' minds. As you review, your students will become confident with topics that previously confused them.

Long or intense assignments are unnecessary and counterproductive during the tapering period. In the spring, everyone, especially seniors, is developing other priorities than school work. Every other AP teacher is likely piling on assignment after assignment, demanding more as the students are willing to do less. Remember the "less is more" principle; what matters is the quality of work that your students do, not the quantity.

Relax the format of the class during the taper. I still give daily quizzes during the taper process, and I still give tests (and do test corrections). But rather than a weekly, structured lab, students do an open-ended laboratory project that extends over several weeks and can be worked on piecemeal. Rather than lecture or "go over" problems, I use class time to foster collaboration. It's quite effective to put on music, hand out an assignment, and expect the students to show you their answers or experimental results as they finish.

Don't cram! With even a slow but reasonable pace, you should be able to cover all the material with a month left for review. In the course of a month, you can slowly and deliberately remind students of the facts and techniques applicable to each topic. It takes that sort of time to absorb physics. But since you've made every test cumulative, "cramming" in the traditional sense will be unnecessary!

I tend to assign one AP-style problem each class period, preferably an authentically released exam question. These questions tend to integrate multiple topics and prepare the students precisely for the style and format of the exam. Then, as often as possible, I have students grade their work to an official rubric. And as often as possible, I have students try setting up AP problems in the laboratory.

In this book, the "Extra Drill" chapter (Chapter 17) provides a targeted review of important topics: inclined planes, graphical analysis, multibody problems, and so on. The problems in this chapter are *not* at the AP Physics 1 level; instead, they're designed to drill these situations until basic calculational approaches are second nature. Assign these to students who are struggling with a particular topic, or give a test that includes a problem on one of these topics, and assign the drill to anyone who performs poorly on that problem.

Become a Better Teacher Every Year

Whether you are teaching AP Physics 1 for the first time or are a veteran teacher who has successfully taught AP Physics 1 for many years, the goal is the same: to become better at physics and constantly improve your teaching skills.

If You Are Teaching AP Physics 1 for the First Time . . .

At a minimum, you must be able to learn the material well enough that you yourself could get a 5 on the AP exam at year's end. If you're not confident that you can get a 5 on the exam right now, that's OK. You haven't failed before you start. You just need to approach your first year of teaching AP Physics 1 a bit differently.

I know you're expecting me to advise you to spend the summer learning the course material well enough so that you can get a 5 before school starts. Um, no. That's great to say, but it doesn't work in practice; just as students need time to process and practice their newly learned physics skills, so do teachers. Sure, read this book before the course begins, take a summer institute or a summer class, and study on your own; but don't expect to be an expert physicist on the first day of school.

Take a long-term approach. This year, be honest with your students that you're learning some of the course material along with them. Seek out a mentor, like an experienced physics teacher at your own school or a college professor. When you have content questions that you can't answer, email your mentor.

And don't get hung up or discouraged when you solve a problem incorrectly and your students tell you so. Handle it in a self-deprecating manner, and move along. Every physics teacher has solved problems incorrectly. The more open and honest you are with your students, the more they'll trust you to guide them to the best of your ability. Teaching AP Physics 1 does require subject-matter expertise; developing that expertise takes a year of teaching.

If You Are a Veteran Physics Teacher. . .

When you combine and follow all five steps to help your students get 5s, your class will do quite well on the exam. But what is "quite well"?

One way to evaluate yourself: How many students got 5s? How many passed? Note that you should never look at the percentage of students who earned a certain score. That's a meaningless statistic open to manipulation. Who do you think is more deserving of a raise: the teacher with 150 AP students, 40 of whom got 5s; or the teacher with only 8 AP students, 7 of whom got 5s? Look at the raw number of your students who earned 5s and the raw number who passed, and see if you can get those numbers to go up in each of the first five years you teach AP.

Nevertheless, I don't think it's productive to say your goal is to have every student get a 5. Sure, every sports team sets out to win a championship. But failure to win a championship isn't really "failure," especially and critically at the high school level, where outcomes beyond wins and losses are so important. Did the players have fun? Did they develop relationships with teammates? Did they win humbly, handle defeat nobly? Are they enthusiastic about playing again next season? Most important, did they improve as individual players and as a team unit?

Some students aren't talented enough to get a 5, no matter how hard they work. Some students will not get their 5 because they have a bad day on the exam. Some are so talented that a 5 should be the minimum expectation; such students might stop working hard once they realize how easily they can meet the goal of earning a 5.